CAREER

OPPORTUNITIES

in the

PUBLISHING INDUSTRY

SECOND EDITION

CAREER OPPORTUNITIES

in the

PUBLISHING INDUSTRY

SECOND EDITION

FRED YAGER

JAN YAGER

Foreword to the Second Edition by
LAUREL TOUBY
Senior Vice President and Cyberhostess, mediabistro.com

Ferguson
An imprint of Infobase Publishing

Career Opportunities in the Publishing Industry, Second Edition

Ferguson
An imprint of Infobase Publishing
132 West 31st Street
New York NY 10001

Library of Congress Cataloging-in-Publication Data

Yager, Fred, 1946–
    Career opportunities in the publishing industry / Fred Yager, Jan Yager. — 2nd ed. / foreword by Laurel Touby.
      p. cm.
    Includes bibliographical references and index.
    ISBN-13: 978-0-8160-7542-3 (acid-free paper)
    ISBN-10: 0-8160-7542-5 (acid-free paper)
  1. Publishers and publishing—Vocational guidance—United States. 2. Newspaper publishing—Vocational guidance—United States. 3. Periodicals—Publishing—Vocational guidance—United States. 4. Book industries and trade—Vocational guidance—United States. 5. Authorship—Vocational guidance—United States. I. Yager, Jan, 1948– II. Title.
  Z471.Y34 2009
  070.5023'73—dc22   2009035347

Ferguson books are available at special discounts when purchased in bulk quantities for businesses, associations, institutions, or sales promotions. Please call our Special Sales Department in New York at (212) 967-8800 or (800) 322-8755.

You can find Ferguson on the World Wide Web at http://fergpubco.com

Series design by Kerry Casey
Composition by Hermitage Publishing Services, Cortlandt Manor, NY
Cover printed by Art Print, Taylor, PA
Book printed and bound by Vail-Ballou, York, PA
Date Printed: December 2009

Printed in the United States of America

10 9 8 7 6 5 4 3 2 1

This book is printed on acid-free paper and contains 30 percent postconsumer recycled content.

Important Note and Disclaimer:
While this book provides general information and opinions on career opportunities in the publishing industry, since every person is unique, it is not intended to be a substitute for individual career counseling or coaching. It is sold with the understanding that the publisher and authors are not engaged in rendering career, book, newspaper or magazine production, legal, literary, or other professional services. Readers are especially advised to consult the appropriate union or association if they have any questions about the most up-to-date minimum rates or salaries as well as qualifications for specific jobs. Throughout this book, especially in the appendixes, you will find contact information for associations, organizations, schools, or companies. Since this information may change at any time, including even the name of an association or company or the existence of a Web site on the Internet, neither the publisher nor the authors take any responsibility for the accuracy of any listings.
    Any corrections to any listings in this book, or suggestions for possible inclusion in the next edition, should be sent to: Fred and Jan Yager, P.O. Box 8038, Stamford, CT 06905-8038 (e-mail: fyager@aol.com or jyager@aol.com).

This book is dedicated, with love, to our family and friends.

———————————

CONTENTS

FOREWORD TO THE SECOND EDITION

by Laurel Touby
Founder and Cyberhostess, mediabistro.com

I was born in Oahu, Hawaii, grew up in Miami, Florida, and graduated from Smith College with a degree in economics. My first job out of college was at Young & Rubicam in New York City. Although I had always dreamed of being a writer, I had no clue how to get started in that kind of career. Instead, I took the first job I could get in a career that seemed relatively creative—advertising. After all, wasn't advertising all about crafting "campaigns" for clients and coming up with cute jingles on television? Well, maybe for the lucky folks who landed in the creative department, but the only position available to me was in the media-planning department for $12,500 a year. I jumped at the chance to get started.

My vague "plan" at the time was to make a lot of money by somehow switching from media planning to advertising sales once I learned the ropes. Then I'd "retire" to a far-off mountaintop and begin my creative lifestyle, writing poetry or novels. But three years later, I was having doubts about whether I could put off a creative career much longer. I also believe you should periodically look five years up the career ladder and ask yourself if you want to be the person one or two rungs above you. Did I really want to become one of those dispirited sales people I dealt with every day as a media planner? They just didn't seem to love what they were doing.

Another factor in my decision to change careers was moving from staid Queens [New York] to the more edgy and artsy East Village. I started meeting people who were leading colorful lives, who had artistic concerns. They were inspired and engaged, even if they weren't earning huge salaries. They were living life the way I had imagined I would one day. Did I really need to make a lot of money to be able to pursue my creative dreams? Not at all, I decided.

So, I started my search. I began by getting a list of the Smith alumnae who were in the business of writing or editing. I called every Smith alumna on the list and asked if she would give me a 15-minute informational interview. I emphasized that I wasn't looking for a job, but, of course, by the end of the interview I would always ask if I could send the person my résumé "in case you hear of an editorial opening." One of these alumna suggested that I accumulate some recent clips, so I started calling local newspapers and offering my services as a volunteer freelance writer. Even the smallest publications in the New York area were highly selective. Luckily, I had written for my college newspaper. The *Brooklyn Phoenix* came through and paid me a whopping $25 to cover a parade; other assignments from them followed.

The informational interviews were paying off too. One conversation I had led to an interview at *Working Woman* magazine. The editors were dubious that anyone in a high-paid job as a senior planner in advertising would want to take such a large step backward, basically becoming an editor's assistant. But having recent clips helped to convince them that I was truly determined to make the move. Plus, I sent a very convincing thank-you letter that stated, "Money is not the important thing. Doing what I am passionate about matters so much more."

I was thrilled when they took a chance and hired me as an editorial assistant. I immediately found that I was happier than I had ever been. My new colleagues were engaged and engaging (they took work home!). The work was intellectually stimulating. I thrilled at writing the smallest things: the captions below photos, a small box to accompany a bigger story, a sidebar. I loved every minute of every workday.

My love affair with media didn't end, even when I was laid off from *Working Woman* three years later. A new editor was at the helm and decided to replace the old employees with a new staff of her choosing. Welcome to the world of magazines!

This turned out to be a blessing in disguise. I soon began writing magazine features as a freelancer, at first for small publications such as *Crain's New York Business* and *Sales & Marketing Management*. Then, I branched out, covering everything from travel to business to breast cancer for such publications as *New York* magazine, *Travel & Leisure, Self, Redbook, McCall's, Family Circle, Good Housekeeping,* and the *New York Daily News.*

After freelancing for a few years, I received an offer to work for *BusinessWeek* magazine. It was so exciting to be hired as a staff editor at one of the most established business publications in America that I didn't think for a moment about what the culture would be like and whether or not I was a fit. I wasn't. While *Working Woman* had felt warm, cuddly, and collegial, *BusinessWeek* was like working in corporate America all over again. So I quit after 14 months.

Before quitting *BusinessWeek,* however, I had done my homework by calling upon my Smith College media network to investigate any other jobs I might apply for. That's how I heard about a semi-freelance position producing *Glamour* magazine's "Getting Ahead Guide to Jobs & Money" column. For the next four years, I was in charge of writing and editing stories about getting ahead in one's career or starting up a company. Perhaps it was

unconscious, but it was while I was working on this column that I came up with a way to boost my own career.

By that time, I had been in the publishing industry for eight years, but I felt as though I barely knew anyone. One day, Russ Baker, a freelance writer I met in a restaurant, suggested we throw a bi-weekly party for like-minded people in media. We wanted the atmosphere to feel like a salon, a place for writers and editors to discuss issues of the day as well as our creative work.

Because we both had small apartments, Russ and I couldn't invite people to our homes. Instead we held the parties at Jules Bistro in the East Village. It was understood that we did the organizing, but guests would pay for their own drinks. At the first party, there were 10 people. That was five more people than I had in my personal Rolodex, so I considered it a great success!

I was by no means a natural social butterfly. At just about every party I'd ever been to in New York City, I'd felt alone and frustrated because of my inability to make small talk. But if our parties were going to work, Russ and I had better get beyond small talk fast. So I decided to go around the room, find out what I could about each guest, what he or she was working on, or some other point of interest, and then force each person to connect with others. I'd say "Rich, you need to meet Fred. You're both doing investigative journalism."

People really responded to that. Someone cared enough to take care of them. We tried to make the events fairly exclusive and there were rules: No networking. No résumé distribution (yes, someone actually tried that!). No uninvited guests.

It didn't take long for attendance to increase. Two weeks after our first mixer, we had twice as many attendees. Two weeks later, there were 50. We soon outgrew the original space and had to move to another bar. We also held the events only once a month because they were becoming a hassle to organize. Russ still attended, but I did the bulk of the work now, inviting people by fax, phone, and mail. I would send out 400 to 600 postcards just to get 100 guests to show up. I would also collect every single business card from each party guest and dutifully type the information into a database. Soon there were thousands of names in the database, all needing constant updating because people change jobs so often in the media business!

It was worth all the effort, as the parties were becoming a very special part of my life and the lives of many others. People felt they had found a home at the events. There was a spirit of camaraderie that bound us together. Soon, I was making friends, dating more, getting invited to people's homes for dinner parties. I noticed this wasn't bad for business. I started to make contacts with senior-level editors in the media business and got assignments from publications that would never have given me the time of day before. Guests made connections and got work too, not by waving around their résumés, but by making friends who later became interested in hiring them. Couples formed and broke up. Marriages resulted—and babies too. All from the parties.

Many attendees of my parties were thankful. Some would say, "You're doing so much for the community. You should find a way to make money from this," but I couldn't think of any way to do that.

Once e-mail became more popular, someone suggested I start an e-mail list to minimize the work I was doing to get attendees to the party each month. It was painstaking to collect all those e-mail addresses on sheets of paper, as no one had them printed on their business cards yet! After that, the invitations to the parties were done exclusively by e-mail, and each one was its own mini-newsletter of relevant media information. After all, I had lots of news to pass along—jobs I was hearing about, apartments for rent, office space, book launches. All of these things made for good reading. By 1996, a young editor named Ann Shoket suggested that I further minimize my work by creating a Web site with all of the same features of my monthly newsletter, plus some.

Ann's suggestion would later take shape as the hottest media Web site around: mediabistro.com! At the time, though, it started as a rinky-dink little site with job listings, event listings, and a bulletin board where people could gossip or discuss issues of interest. The site didn't even have a real name, because it was merely a directory on my programmer's Web site. The URL was www.goldennyc.com/pressclub.

By 1999, I had decided to get more serious about the Web site. It was fast becoming the most popular place to post jobs in the media business. I had even started to make a little money with the job board. In July of that year, I began to ask employers to voluntarily send $100 for each job listing they posted. The first month I asked, I received 22 checks totaling $2,200 and by the end of that year, I was netting over $7,000 per month from the postings.

By 2000, I had received $1 million in funding and renamed the Web site mediabistro.com. The money enabled me to move into a real office, buy equipment, and hire a staff. We were a real company! As the economy took a nosedive, I began adding more services to our popular job listings and bulletin boards. Within a year, mediabistro.com was offering career-related classes, seminars, and other helpful guidance to the hundreds of thousands of media professionals who had found the site. I also began to offer a membership program called AvantGuild, which today offers insights into how to pitch to different media outlets and provides discounts on such services as health care. I also started a freelance marketplace where employers can search for freelancers to work on projects. Over the years, the site has grown and grown, and it now includes news, blogs, and many other offerings. Today, we count more than 7 million page views a month from the million-plus media professionals around the world who have registered on mediabistro.com. In 2007, I sold my company to Jupitermedia for $23 million, and I stayed on as senior vice president and cyberhostess.

What advice would I give to someone who wants to break into the publishing industry? I would say:

- Don't complain that you're "not connected." Make your own connections by getting out in the world.
- Go to trade shows. Go to parties. Go to press events. Meet people, take them for coffee, get to know them, and they will help you make your way in this world.
- Find sources for your stories as well as outlets for your stories.
- Develop a thorough knowledge of your subject area to go narrow and deep. Try to specialize in something. You will find work. There are outlets that need your information.

- Put your all into every assignment and do it to the best of your ability. Don't get a reputation as a hack, someone who just turns in the work with little regard for quality. Strive for excellence in all you do.

The media world has taken me on an amazing journey. Your journey can be amazing too.

Laurel Touby, Founder and Cyberhostess,
mediabistro.com

Laurel Touby has written for various publications including Redbook, New York, Glamour, Salon, Travel & Leisure, Self, *and* Family Circle, *among others. She is widely known for founding mediabistro. com in 1996 and expanding the company over the next decade into a premier international job-hunting and socializing site for media professionals; the company also hosts parties and offers seminars in New York City and at several locations around the world. In 2007, Touby sold her company to Jupitermedia for $23 million.*

FOREWORD TO THE FIRST EDITION

by Pat Schroeder
Former President and CEO, Association of American Publishers (AAP)

When I first took this job, people asked, "Why are you going into publishing? It's passé."

It seems people have been pronouncing the death of the publishing industry as long as I can remember. Yet the business is still looking pretty good.

When publishers focus on having a good story, or if they have good content, people will find out about it, and they will come. Look at the success of *Harry Potter*. It reminded us what publishing is all about.

Publishing is needed now more than ever because, with the Internet, there's so much junk around. High-quality content is something that people really want. If you can produce that and find a way to get it to people, there's a wonderful satisfaction.

What I like about publishing, and why I've always been such an advocate of the written word, is that our society suffers from attention deficit disorder. Books, magazines, and newspapers are the last places in our culture where someone can develop a thought. On television, for example, as a politician, you're given seven seconds to get your point across: "What do you think we should do to reduce world hunger?" Seven seconds and then you're cut off.

I think there's a lot of gratification in publishing, and that's why so many highly qualified people are eager to do it. What is the gratification? It's producing a product you are very excited about. That's one of the vitalizing things for young people going into publishing.

For fiction, the question is, "Is it a good story?" Followed by, "Can we sell it?" For nonfiction, the question is, "Is it new information that needs to be told?" Then it's going out and getting other people excited about what you're publishing. And it's feeling that this is a newspaper article, a magazine story, or a book that people need to read and will want to talk about.

Publishing is a global business. There's no question that New York City is still the capital of book publishing in this country, but it's also very true that there are publishers in every state, including university presses and small presses. Also there's a lot of diversity in publishing. It's one of the few industries where we're not short of females, and there are concerted efforts to recruit new staff from minorities that may have been underrepresented in the past.

Unlike starting so many other businesses, publishing doesn't take much start-up capital to get it going. Obviously a lot of publishing ventures aren't going to make it, because it's still about marketing, and that's very hard without money, but some will. The classic success story is *Chicken Soup for the Soul,* which was published by a smaller press in Florida, Health Communications Inc., and which went on to become a series of books selling millions of copies internationally.

There's a cliché that big publishers are greedy. But compared to other industries, those words don't apply. Publishing is labor intensive, and the profit margin is very slim. What's unique about publishing is that the editor is the person who selects what books or articles will be published. Machines can't do that. Machines can't read. We also need people for marketing, accounting, art, and editing—people actually reading the stuff and deciding what gets published and what doesn't.

Plus, publishing is one industry that caters to a wide variety of interests. For example, if you like cooking, you might want to publish cookbooks or work for a magazine that caters to cooking. The same goes for gardening, poetry, or fiction. There are so many areas where people go into these specialties. There's a huge business in history books and magazines, children's books, and political science. Newspapers have a range of sections to appeal to a variety of their readers' and journalists' interests, from news and sports to features and home furnishings.

The thing that amazes me most about the publishing industry is that people tend to stay in it. They may move from house to house or from magazines to newspapers, but there's not a lot of transfer out. Yet there are an awful lot of skilled people working in publishing who easily could get hired elsewhere if they wanted to leave. I think that, ultimately, this must mean people really do feel a deep satisfaction from working in the publishing industry.

Books also offer a shared reading experience; people can organize reading clubs to talk about something other than the weather. Somehow you feel free to talk about what you're thinking if you can bounce it off of a character in a book. Companies should have reading clubs. It's good to break the vertical hierarchy—to have everyone in the same company reading the same book.

As an author who has been published in all three branches of the publishing industry covered in this book—newspapers, magazines, and books—as well as an advocate of the reader and the written word, I've observed several key similarities and differences among these three divisions within this broad phenomenon known as the publishing industry.

The speed with which information is shared is certainly fastest with newspapers, including their online editions. Often there is a lag of several weeks or months for magazines, except for such weeklies as *Time, Newsweek,* or *Entertainment Weekly.* Of course, books still take, on average, a year from finished manuscript to publication (although some publishers can bring a book out within six months). But you still have to add on at least another year or two for the author to research and write the book, so it could be three or four years for a book to go from an idea or a proposal to seeing the light of print. For a newspaper article, by contrast, the same process is consolidated into just a few hours or days.

Speed, however, does not absolve writers or editors of the need for accuracy and thoroughness in checking spelling, facts, and statements in anything that is published, whether online, in a newspaper column, in a magazine article, or in a book.

Furthermore, all types of writing, whatever format it takes, is an extension of one of the values we hold most dear: the freedom to read. It is a freedom that is very fundamental, a freedom that should not be taken lightly.

Protecting the words of writers, however, is another important concern. It is even more of an issue today with the ability to republish an author's work on the Internet, a form of publishing less common a decade ago. Although a few writers might feel that further exposure of their work on the Internet advances their reputation, most feel that they should be compensated if their work is reused beyond its original place of publication, whether that was in a newspaper, magazine, or book. This is an issue that authors, publishers, Web site owners, webmasters, and even the public will need to scrutinize more carefully if a writer's work is to be paid for, its ownership properly tracked, and its copyright protected.

For that reason, the permissions editor at a newspaper, magazine, or book publishing company needs to be on the lookout for misuses of his or her company's intellectual property; for example, if he or she finds excerpted material on the Internet and permission was not granted for it. He or she needs to have the diligence to track down those uses and ask for proper permission to be obtained, as well as a fee to be offered and obtained (permission without a fee may be granted, but it should be formally requested and given).

Newspapers and magazines share with books those publishing careers that tend to attract men and women who are concerned with making a difference in the world and who desire a career that is fast-paced, exciting, and noteworthy. There are some positions at newspapers and magazines that are highly paid, such as sales director, president/CEO, and executive editor, depending upon the size and revenue of the company, and there are also some writers and even editors who reach celebrity status. Still, average salaries in publishing are not as big as if someone performed a comparable job in another industry. For example, a director of marketing at a magazine tends to earn less than a director of marketing for a corporation outside the publishing industry.

Although salaries are often not huge in publishing, they do seem to be stable. If you're primarily motivated by a need to make a lot of money, the publishing industry may not be the place for you. Of course, those who work in the publishing industry need to be paid for what they do, but most of them know they're not going to make a ton of money.

People who go into publishing and thrive in it are men and women who really care about the culture, the national dialogue, the global dialogue, and making sure voices that need to be heard are published.

Former Democratic representative Pat Schroeder, who retired undefeated after 24 years of congressional service, has a unique perspective on the publishing industry. A former instructor at Princeton University, as well as a lawyer, Pat Schroeder was the president and chief executive officer of the Association of American Publishers, Inc., a trade association made up of more than 300 publishers, from 1997 till 2009. She is also a published author of articles as well as the nonfiction book 24 Years of House Work . . . and the Place Is Still a Mess: My Life in Politics, *published by Andrews McMeel Publishing.*

INDUSTRY OUTLOOK

Whether your dream is to work your way up the corporate ladder to become the CEO of a major publishing company, to run a small press, to start a new magazine, to be a photojournalist, to work as an investigative reporter for a daily newspaper, to write a blog on the Internet, or to be the marketing director for a suburban newspaper, this book will help you explore the variety of career opportunities available to you in the fascinating, complex, and rewarding world of publishing.

In the last few years, there have been some dramatic upheavals in the publishing industry, changes that are definitely affecting careers related to newspapers, magazines, and books. Indeed, careers in electronic publishing are seeing a lot of growth as newspapers and magazines create and maintain content that is distinct from that found in print editions of their publications—if a print version even exists. Just a few years ago, by contrast, newspaper or magazine Web sites made only some of the content from their print versions available to readers. Today, there may even be different writers for the print or online editions of a publication, as well as unique online articles enhanced with video, an option print editions cannot provide.

The positive news about these changes in the publishing industry is that there are still jobs and careers available, but the categories are shifting. Online content editors or producers work with online writers, staff or freelance, who are considered distinct from those writing for print publications, even those published by the same magazine or newspaper. Salaries are also changing; freelance writers for online sites may be offered half or even a quarter of the fee for their articles that they might be offered—or were once offered—by comparable print publications.

Another significant change that has occurred in the last few years is the growth of bloggers or citizen journalists. What does this mean for recent graduates of j-schools if anyone is able to start writing and call himself or herself a blogger or columnist? Is it even necessary to study journalism if anyone is able to self-publish his or her thoughts online or in newsletters? Is there such a thing as a career as a blogger? Is there a way to get paid to blog? These are just some of the questions that journalists have to ask as they contemplate entering the publishing field today.

Niche magazines have continued to proliferate as the more general popular magazines are being reevaluated as a viable way to share information, with print costs rising and readerships shrinking. As these niche publications become more commonplace, those entering publishing as a career need to ask themselves if they should also have a dual major—journalism plus a second major that could become their publishing niche such as science, the social sciences, the arts, or business—or if a graduate degree in a specialized field would be advantageous.

There are younger generations who get their news from the Internet only; they rarely, if ever, read a newspaper; they may read specialty magazines; and their appreciation of printed books is definitely different from that of previous generations.

The book business has been undergoing enormous changes as well. Those younger readers, and even some of their parents, may be reading books on a reading device, like the Kindle, manufactured by amazon.com, or the Sony Reader, or even on their cell or mobile phone. The e-book (electronic book) has definitely had an increase in sales as an alternative way of delivering book content, especially in reference situations, such as for libraries or companies that buy subscriptions. There are also companies that make content from books available online, to be downloaded and read as needed.

Print-on-demand (POD) is finally being recognized as a type of technology and as a way of keeping books in print that are no longer selling in sufficient quantity to justify a traditional short print run of thousands of copies. Today, POD has lost a lot of the stigma that used to be associated with it when it was first introduced in the 1990s. With the expansion of print-on-demand capabilities to all sizes of publishers, there is an increased need for someone whose job it is to keep watch on inventory as well as to determine when or if a book needs to be updated and not just reprinted. In the past, books that were no longer selling well were simply put out of print and, if requested and granted, the rights would revert to the author. It became the author's consideration whether or not he or she would reprint his or her book, and, if it was reprinted, if it was going to be updated or changed in any way. Now that publishers are keeping more and more books in print, someone at the publishing company needs to make the decisions about an ever-increasing backlist of titles.

In the last few years, reading books electronically has become more common, just as reading newspapers or magazines online instead of in print versions is also gaining in popularity. Physical copies of newspapers, magazines, or books, however, are not going to disappear. The publishing industry may be morphing into something different, but it is still an industry that needs more than a million workers in a wide range of jobs.

Yes, the publishing industry, like so many other industries, was hard hit in the United States and internationally during the economic downturn of 2008, when book publishers had to trim their staffs and even cut back on acquisitions, and some newspapers or magazines folded or became available only as online publications. As traditional advertising declined in print publications because of the economic slowdown, some publications shrank in size or ceased publication. Others moved to the Web and exploited digital methods of generating revenue.

Despite the recent economic challenges, publishing is an industry that will survive and, in time, reinvent itself in a more efficient way, whether that is on the Web or through bookstores becoming publishers by adding print-on-demand machines that print one copy of a book housed in the store's digital library.

You can be a pessimist and look at how the industry used to be and bemoan that there are fewer jobs than before, or you can be an optimist who sees myriad opportunities as the Internet continues to strengthen publishing as a way to provide information. Readers want to read words, whether on paper or on a screen. The changes in the industry, however, have necessitated rethinking what kinds of skills you need to enter the industry or to climb the ladder, with more and more jobs requiring a combination of writing and editing skills, as well as an understanding of computer software and even Web graphics or digital photocopying.

In the rest of this introduction and industry outlook, we look back at the history of publishing in the three categories of newspapers, magazines, and books. We discuss where each of those facets of the publishing industry is today, then forecast where it may be headed.

Newspaper Publishing

Some could argue that early cave drawings, which told stories in pictures, were probably the first attempts by humans to make public information that could be shared by others. The first newspaper, *Tsing Pao*, began in China in the early 500s, according to Leonard Mogel's "A Short History of Newspapers," which begins his book, *The Newspaper*. *Tsing Pao*, which was basically a court journal made from carved blocks, was published until 1935.

The genesis of newspapers can be traced to 1,000 B.C., when scribes handwrote newsletters about what was going on in ancient Rome that were then dispatched to other cities.

But it was not until Johannes Gutenberg of Frankfurt, Germany invented printing from movable type that newspaper publishing was truly born. In 1609 the *Strasburg Relation* became the first regularly printed newspaper. But it took nearly another hundred years before the first daily newspaper, the *London Daily Courant,* was published in England in 1702.

The first newspaper in America was the *Publick Occurances Both Foreign and Domestick,* published in 1690. Unfortunately there was only one issue, and 14 years passed before another newspaper appeared in 1704, the *Boston News-Letter,* published by John Campbell. Benjamin Franklin and his brother James started a newspaper in 1721 called the *New England Courant.*

The oldest newspaper still in existence today is the *Hartford Courant,* published in Hartford, Connecticut. Founded in 1764, it is now owned by the Tribune Company, and it has a daily circulation of more than 200,000 and a Sunday circulation of almost 300,000.

Newspapers flourished during the 1800s as the price dropped from six cents to a penny a copy. Many of today's newspapers started during this period. The *St. Louis Dispatch* was founded by Joseph Pulitzer in 1819. (Pulitzer willed $2 million upon his death, one quarter of which was to be used to set up an award for excellence in journalism, the inception of the prestigious Pulitzer Prize, administered through the Columbia University School of Journalism.)

In 1841 Horace Greeley, who had been an apprenticed printer and became a writer, founded the *New York Tribune.* Joseph Medill (after whom the world famous Medill School of Journalism at Northwestern University in Evanston, Illinois, is named) first published the *Chicago Daily Tribune* in 1847, and the *Washington Post* was founded in 1877. In 1889 Charles Dow and Edward Jones began publishing the *Wall Street Journal.*

The 1900s saw the birth of the tabloids, which were smaller in size and tended to sensationalize the news. The *Daily News* was founded in 1919 by Joseph Patterson and was quickly followed by the *Mirror.* Both were launched during a period in which the term *yellow journalism* was coined to describe newspapers that seemed to exploit crime, disasters, and scandals to generate sales.

Newspapers were plentiful and powerful in the early 1900s. By 1930 New York City had eight daily newspapers, including the *New York Times, Daily News, Mirror, World, Telegram, Sun,* and the *Journal,* which was published by the legendary William Randolph Hearst. In addition, there were two dailies published in the borough of Brooklyn, as well as numerous ethnic newspapers, including four Yiddish and two Italian-language papers.

By the end of World War II, the newspaper expansion began to ease. During the second half of the 20th century, people began to turn to radio and television as their primary sources for news. Instead of numerous competing newspapers, each city began to have just one. Smaller towns went from dailies to weeklies. Although the number of newspapers dwindled, newspaper employment in the last three decades of the 20th century increased 60 percent. This growth in editorial, sales, and business employees ended in 2000, and for the following two years, newspaper employment in those categories declined by 7 percent.

Since 1940 the number of papers has declined more from almost 1,900. Today there are around 1,450 newspapers in the United States, representing a $56 billion industry. Two daily newspapers in the United States have a circulation of more than 2 million: *USA Today* and the *Wall Street Journal.* The *New York Times* has a daily circulation of more than 1 million.

Although there is always the worry that the newspaper industry is "dying" and that readership and advertising is diminishing, the newspaper industry, especially with the addition of online editions, is still a prestigious and exciting career for reporters and editors as well as those involved in the production, sale, and marketing of a newspaper.

Most newspapers in the United States are owned by chains. In fact, 600 daily newspapers are owned by just 25 companies. Eight of those companies have newspaper revenues totalling more than a billion dollars a year. Newspaper advertising totals $40 billion a year. Advertisers spend more money on newspaper ads than they do on television ads, and they spend twice as much as they allocate to radio and magazine ads.

Another trend affecting newspapers is the growth of alternative news weeklies, a substitute for the traditional daily newspaper for a rural, suburban, or urban community. Although the number of alternative news weeklies has leveled off since reaching its circulation height in 1999–2000, according to the Association of News Weeklies (ANW), circulation for these unique news weeklies reached more than 7 million in 2006.

Daily newspapers, as well as newspaper syndicates, such as Knight-Ridder and United Media, have a constant need for stories. For some, working at a local or national newspaper is a stepping stone to a career in another area of publishing, such as magazines, where the pace may be somewhat slower than on a daily or weekly newspaper and the pay somewhat higher. But for others, working at or for a newspaper is a lifetime calling that they would not trade for anything.

The excitement of working at a newspaper, immortalized in such classic works as the play *Front Page* and the movies *Absence of Malice* and *The Paper,* is legendary for the daily pressure of meeting deadlines and working in a fish bowl of an office with dozens or hundreds of others. There is also the excitement and gratification of breaking a story that has political, national, and historical consequences, such as Carl Bernstein and Bob Woodward of the *Washington Post,* who broke the Watergate scandal that was a catalyst to the resignation of former president Richard Nixon.

However, as the kidnapping and tragic death of the *Wall Street Journal* reporter Daniel Pearl in Pakistan and the death of hundreds of other foreign correspondents has shown, some newspaper jobs, especially that of war correspondent or freelancer in a perilous area, are more dangerous than others.

For the most part, online publishing is supplementing, not replacing, print publishing, as seen in the thriving sites created and maintained by the *Wall Street Journal,* including www.careerjournal.com, www.collegejournal.com, and www.startupjournal.com. Although there is original content written just for those sites, the *Wall Street Journal* is an example of an online site that offers a way to archive previously published articles from the print edition. Those published articles, before the online editions, would have had just one chance to be read. Now the online version is available indefinitely at the paper's companion online site. In May 2009, the online edition of the *Wall Street Journal* announced that it would try a new payment and subscription model: charging for individual articles as well as a premium online annual subscription. It will be interesting to watch how this approach fares, as well as how many other online newspapers follow suit, and what its impact, if any, is on the evolving newspaper part of the publishing industry.

Some daily general newspapers, such as the *Las Vegas Sun* (www.lasvegassun.com), also use their Web sites for daily news, in addition to archived articles easily retrieved using the "search" button on the homepage.

Certainly numerous Pulitzer Prize winners have been staff writers at newspapers. Some staff journalists also write books, nonfiction or fiction, on a freelance basis in their spare time. Herman Melville, author of the American classic novel *Moby-Dick,* was a newspaper reporter, as was Theodore Dreiser, whose novel *An American Tragedy* is another revered work of fiction, as well as Margaret Mitchell, author of the much-beloved novel *Gone with the Wind,* who began her career as a staff writer for four years for the *Atlanta Journal.* Contemporary examples abound: Steven Hunter, who writes film criticism as well as novels, and *Miami Herald* reporter Carl Hiaasen, who writes adult thrillers, young adult novels, and a regular Sunday column for the newspaper since 1985. Newspaper journalists who also write nonfiction books include Ralph Blumenthal of the *New York Times,* who wrote *The Stork Club,* among other titles, and Jeffrey Zaslow, senior writer and columnist for the *Wall Street Journal,* who is coauthor of the blockbuster book *The Last Lecture* (2008) with the late Randy Pausch and author of *The Girls from Ames* (2009). Others leave full-time newspaper jobs to teach journalism or write books as a second career. But whether you're writing, editing, or working in the marketing department as a stepping stone to a career in other fields, working at a newspaper is a fast-paced, exciting, and stimulating place for part or all of your career.

Magazine Publishing

With a total of 19,532 magazines published in the United States in 2007, according to the American Society of Magazine Editors, magazines offer an abundance of job opportunities at general or specialized publications.

The word *magazine* comes from the French word *magasin,* which means "general storehouse." In the beginning, that is what magazines covered:

storehouses. The first magazines were published in France and were basically catalogs that highlighted books being offered by publishers. Eventually magazines evolved away from book catalogs to contain articles, criticism, and essays about a variety of subjects.

Benjamin Franklin is credited with starting one of the first American magazines in 1741, a monthly entitled the *General Magazine and Historical Chronicle, For All the British Plantations in America.*

During the mid-19th century, such magazines as *Atlantic Monthly* and *Harper's Monthly* appeared, to be followed in the late 19th and early 20th centuries by *National Geographic, Time,* and *Life.*

During the 20th century, the American magazine industry thrived as publications, such as *Playboy, Rolling Stone, Cosmopolitan,* and *Ms.,* reflected changes in culture and social mores. While such favorite magazines as *McCall's, George,* and *Mademoiselle* may have disappeared from the magazine horizon, along with big launches such as *Talk* and *Rosie,* several new magazines have emerged in the same period. *Lucky,* a magazine about shopping, became an overnight success and now looks like it is here to stay. However, *Lifetime,* inspired by the cable television station, was launched in March 2003 but ceased publication in October 2004. Television talk-show host and media mogul Oprah Winfrey's magazine *O,* launched in 2000, became one of the biggest magazine success stories in recent memory, but a spin-off, *O at Home,* was cancelled in 2008.

At most magazines the majority of jobs, except writing and some editing, are still done "in house," as staff positions, although this is changing as more employees in a range of positions work off-site some or all of the time. As with other publishing careers, flexibility and creativity are as necessary to succeed in magazine publishing, as is the ability to meet deadlines, work hard, and survive and even thrive under daily, weekly, and monthly pressure.

Job opportunities in the magazine industry range from weekly news magazines, including *Time* and *Newsweek,* and twice-monthly *U.S. News & World Report,* to monthly women's magazines, such as *O, Good Housekeeping,* and *Redbook,* as well as specialized magazines in travel, business, music, computers, the environment, hair styling, and ecology, among other subjects. As with newspapers,

online versions of popular magazines, such as www.lhj.com, the online version of *Ladies' Home Journal,* as well as magazines only published online, offer additional job opportunities for writers, editors, webmasters, and graphic designers. Magazines may have monthly or, sometimes, weekly deadlines, so the pace is somewhat slower than if you work on a daily newspaper, but there is still the pressure to meet deadlines, work hard, and to produce a consistently excellent publication issue after issue, year after year.

There are numerous options today for training for a career in magazine publishing. Courses in magazine publishing are offered at colleges and universities throughout the United States as part of a journalism major, as well as at graduate school in a nondegree or degree program with a magazine publishing focus. For example, the Emerson College master of arts in publishing and writing offers three focuses, including magazine publishing, and Stanford University offers a nine-day, post graduate, nondegree book/magazine course each summer for publishing professionals. Paid and unpaid internships are available at magazines throughout the school year and over the summer, providing valuable on-the-job training as well as potential job opportunities after graduation. Internships at magazines are also available as part of New York University's certificate or master's degree programs in publishing.

A magazine is certainly an exciting, fast-paced, and interesting place to work. The teamwork that is necessary to get out a magazine, each and every week, two weeks, or month, helps every member of that team to feel part of that informative and entertaining monthly product. Getting in the door at major magazines is as hard as it has always been, but some of that difficulty, like finding out about job possibilities in the first place, is diminished today by the job banks available on the Internet. One such site, www.mediabistro.com, provides job postings for openings at magazines. The Magazine Publishers of America (MPA) provides an up-to-date and easy-to-navigate job bank at its Web site (www.magazine.org) for those seeking a job in any area of the magazine industry. Social networking sites, such as LinkedIn (www.linkedin.com), also provide an opportunity to connect with current or former coworkers or classmates who are working in the magazine industry and who might provide a referral to a job opening at their publication.

Book Publishing

Book publishing and distribution is a significant industry in the United States, with book sales totaling $24.3 billion in 2008, a 2.8 percent decrease from the $25 billion of 2007, bucking the industry trend over the previous six years of 1.6 percent growth, according to the AAP (American Association of Publishers). (This downturn coincides with the national and international economic challenges in a multiplicity of industries during 2008.)

It is a vast and diverse industry representing literally tens of thousands of completely new products each year, including popular adult books (known as trade publishing), juvenile or children's books, young adult fiction and nonfiction (known as YA titles), higher education materials (known as textbook publishing), and, finally, the professional/scholarly/scientific publishing (often referred to as professional publishing). Book publishing also tries to keep available to its customers as many of its previous products, known as backlist titles, as feasible. When you compare the relatively few products in other retail industries, such as clothing, and consider that last year's fashions are rarely kept in inventory, let alone kept viable and readily available, you can see what a challenge it is for book publishers to keep up with the current, future, and previously published titles that number in the millions.

Looking at a history of the number of books that are published in the United States confirms that this is a growth industry: In 1948 the annual *Books in Print* index listed 85,000 titles from 357 publishers; in 1992, 135,000 new titles were listed from more than 40,000 publishing houses. In the year 2003, R.R. Bowker reported more than 175,000 new books published from approximately 70,000 publishers. In 2007, according to Bowker, new title output in the United States was 284,370 from more than 72,000 publishers. The year 2008 was historic for the book publishing industry, not because title output was down by 3.2 percent to 275,232 new titles, according to Bowker, but because there were more POD titles than books produced by traditional printing

methods, bringing the total output of books published in the United States up by 38 percent to an astounding 560,626 new titles.

The history of book publishing predates the printing press by a few thousand years. In Egypt, around 3,000 B.C., books were scribed on rolls of papyrus. This was followed by the Roman codex, which actually looked more like a book because sheets of papyrus were folded into leaves resembling pages.

In the 6th century A.D., the Chinese invented a form of printing that used wooden blocks. A hundred years later, another Chinese invention, paper, made its way to the Middle East and Europe. Still, it was not until Gutenberg invented the printing press in Germany in 1439 that modern-day book publishing was born.

The first book published in America was *The Whole Book of Psalme* in 1640 by printer Stephen Day and his sons. It took them two years to print and distribute it.

The first best seller, a romance novel entitled *Charlotte Temple* by Hannah Rawson published in 1797, was reported to go into 200 printings.

America experienced a book publishing revolution in the 19th century. During that period, an estimated 8 million titles were published. An early, famous best-seller was Harriet Beecher Stowe's *Uncle Tom's Cabin*, which is considered by some to have been one of the catalysts leading to the Civil War.

In the early 20th century, many of today's top book publishers began to emerge. McGraw-Hill started in 1909, followed by Alfred A. Knopf in 1915, and Simon & Schuster in 1924. Random House and Viking came on the scene a year later in 1925.

Despite the number of books that are currently being published, there are only about a dozen major publishing companies in existence today, mostly based in New York City, that publish a lion's share of the popular, or "trade," books. Outside of New York City, there are still significant publishing houses, including imprints or subsidiaries of New York–based houses, such as Prima Publishing in California, which is now part of Random House of New York, and Contemporary Books in Chicago, which is now part of McGraw-Hill, also based in New York. In 2001 Storey Books, in rural Vermont, became part of New York–based Workman Publishing, but independent houses keep popping up, such as the enormously successful Sourcebooks of Naperville, Illinois, founded in 1987 by Dominique Raccah, which now publishes more than 300 titles each year with a backlist that includes numerous *New York Times* best sellers. Some new publishing houses remain independent despite their expansion and growth, but others consolidate with the larger houses.

Traditionally the majority of women entered the publishing industry by working their way up from secretarial or editorial assistant positions; men got their start in the sales department. But today there is no longer as clear a gender split as to who enters book publishing or in what capacity, with male assistants to editors and literary agents as common today as women starting out in the sales department.

Book publishing offers someone who cares about books the chance to be involved in the writing, editing, design, printing, selling, publicizing, advertising, marketing, or distribution of books through a wide range of job opportunities, from the artist who designs book jackets, the publicist who helps book a new author on a morning talk show, and the editor who acquires the book to the nonfiction, fiction, children's book, or specialized book author who writes the book in the first place. There are copy editors whose expertise is dealing with the consistencies in the manuscript, as well as spelling and grammar, and there is the literary lawyer who works for a publishing company or has his or her own firm. There are sales representatives who presell new titles to bookstores as well as other markets, such as libraries or gift stores and personnel managers or human resource professionals who work in the book publishing industry. Other job opportunities in the book industry include the wholesalers, distributors, and booksellers who get the books from the publishers to the customers, as well as those who teach book publishing at colleges or universities. Salaries in book publishing, especially for entry-level jobs, may seem low, especially in editorial, with $25,000 to $30,000 on average for college graduates—which is still a lot higher than the $5,200 a year that Jan started out at as an editorial assistant at Macmillan Publishing Company in the 1970s—but the upside of earnings has also improved, with some executives earning six figures or more. Still, for most publishing has never been primarily about the money. It is a career that offers stimulation, satisfaction, and a range of working situations, from self-employment to working as part of a team at companies with just a few employees or tens of thousands and a global reach. Most of all, it is a career that allows those who have a passion for the written word and for books to be part of the creation of the newest titles, as well as keeping previously published works available.

*****

These three parts of the publishing industry—newspapers, magazines, and books—interact in so many ways. First, some of those involved in the writing, editing, marketing, and production process move back and forth among all three types of publishing. Second, books directly depend on newspapers and magazines, as well as online publications, in numerous ways. It is through book reviews published in magazines for the book trade, such as *Publishers Weekly* or *Kirkus Reviews,* as well as for librarians who also buy books, including *Library Journal, School Library Journal, Booklist,* and *Foreword,* that new titles are presold to booksellers, wholesalers, and librarians several months before publication. Reviews in newspapers, popular magazines, or online publications or blogs may make the difference between a book that finds an audience and one that is ignored and doomed to obscurity. Prestigious awards for children's books, such as the Caldecott, and the Newbery, and the National Book Awards for adult titles help to highlight excellence in book publishing for the industry and for librarians, authors, and the public. Third, advertising revenues in newspapers and magazines for books provides income, which can be used for the feature or cultural parts of the publications that write about authors or books or that review books. Finally, articles in newspapers or magazines may lead to a book, such as *Time* magazine columnist Margaret Carlson's book, *Anyone Can Grow Up: How George Bush and I Made It to the White House* published by Simon & Schuster, which includes selected published columns by Carlson.

While the term *new media* has existed for more than 20 years, it should probably be considered the fourth category within the publishing industry, in addition to the traditional three of newspapers, magazines, or books. The increase in online publications, as well as in the number of those who write online content exclusively, such as bloggers, include some of the largest growth areas for the publishing industry, now and in the foreseeable future. As Laurel Touby, who wrote the foreword to this second edition, points out, you can move from traditional journalism to having only an online presence, like the Web site Laurel Touby launched, mediabistro.com. But it still involves the same skills and offers the creative rewards and financial potential of traditional print journalism.

ACKNOWLEDGMENTS

Thanks to our editor Sarah Fogarty, and to James Chambers, editor in chief, Arts & Humanities, at Facts On File, Inc., headquartered in New York City, as well as, to Matthew Anderson, editorial assistant. We also want to express our gratitude to Laurie Katz, director of publicity at Facts On File, and Emily Sprague, publicity associate.

Next we want to thank Pat Schroeder, a friend to all in the publishing industry, for her insightful foreword to the first edition of this book, and to Laurel Touby, a role model of success in the publishing industry, for her foreword to the second edition of this book.

Special thanks to Harlan Coben, Margaret Chittenden, Katie Davis, Katie Blough, Andrea Rotondo, Leslie Banks, Michael O. Laddin, Priscilla Treadwell, Sonya Giacobbe, Bill Contardi, Bob Diforio, Peggy Stautberg, Kristin Reidlinger, Betty Yarmon, Adriana Navarro, Ib and Bebbe Lauritzen, Brenda Marsh, Jeffrey Zaslow, Lily Garcia, Judy Mandel, Jim Hood, Joan Lisante, Jessica Jonas, Tory Glerum, Arlynn Greenbaum, Howard Siner, Susannah Greenberg, Adina Kahn, Jim Randel, Katie Rose Hope, Donna Hardy, Robin Trum, Mike Cassidy, Deb Hollis, Karen Strauss, Jeannette Zolan, Jenny Dunne, Chris Denman, Brian Beirne, Lindy Nass, DJ Smith, the Women's Media Group, the Authors Guild, the Publishers Publicity Association, Publishers Marketing Association, Women's National Book Association (New York chapter and national association), the Association of American Publishers, and the American Society of Journalists and Authors.

In addition to those named or quoted in this book, there are scores of men and women we interviewed at newspapers, magazines, online publications, book publishers, literary agencies, distributors, wholesalers, booksellers, libraries, public relations agencies, unions, and associations who are not named or quoted in the book but whose contributions were still pivotal to the background research for this reference work. Thank you for taking the time to share your educational and work experiences with us.

Over the years, Fred and I have learned on the job, in freelance capacities, as well as from running our own companies, and we want to thank those who have been our mentors, our coworkers, and our friends—at the Associated Press, Fox News, CBS, Macmillan Publishing Company, Grove Press, Hannacroix Creek Books, Simon & Schuster, Prentice Hall, Scribner's, Wiley, RAND Publishing, and Sterling Publishing—as well as foreign agents, foreign publishers, U.S. publishers, editors, staff or freelance writers, illustrators, and others at newspapers, magazines, book publishing companies, and online publications too numerous to name here. But you know who you are, and we thank you for your guidance and your friendship.

HOW TO USE THIS BOOK

This book is really three books in one, since it provides information about career opportunities in three separate divisions of the publishing industry: newspapers, magazines, and books. Ninety jobs are covered, ranging from writing and editing to art, photography, publicity, and sales.

For each job you will find a brief definition of the duties for that job, alternate titles (if any), and a concise overview of the job, including the salary range to expect, employment or advancement prospects, the best geographical location, and such prerequisites as education and training, experience, special skills, and personality traits. A career ladder shows typical routes to and from the position.

After the career ladder, these synopses are expanded, beginning with a longer description of the position with all the key areas listed above expanded upon as well: salaries; employment and advancement prospects, including ways to increase the likelihood that you may accomplish both employment and advancement; education and training; experience, skills, and personality traits; any unions or associations that are required or recommended for employment and advancement; and, finally, specific "Tips for Entry" for this job.

Although some may choose just one of the three types of publishing in which to work for an entire career, others may move back and forth among newspapers, magazines, and books, sequentially or even simultaneously, depending on what jobs are available or for personal or professional concerns. For example, it is not uncommon for a journalist working at a newspaper to get a magazine assignment and, in time, to write a book, perhaps one that even developed out of the initial research for an assigned newspaper or magazine article. Photojournalists work for newspapers, magazines, and book publishers.

There are, of course, many differences among these three categories of publishing. For example, newspapers are generally published daily, while a few magazines are published weekly, but most are published monthly or bimonthly. Newspaper articles may be published within hours of completion; except for the occasional weekly magazine, most magazine articles will not appear for three to six months after completion. Books, by contrast, typically take at least one to two years from contract to completion and at least another nine months to 18 months (or a year, on average) from final manuscript to publication (although some books have been written and published within months, and others have taken 10 or more years to write and publish).

The publishing industry covered in this guide is the print industry; online publications are covered as extensions of print. In most cases, the online publications support and even archive what is first available in print. Each newspaper or magazine has a formula: The entire paper is archived online at least a day or more after it is released in its print version. Others only post selected articles at their Web site rather than the entire publication. Still others, such as the *Wall Street Journal's* online publications, career journal.com, startupjournal.com, and college journal.com, are unique in that these online publications completely replaced the previous weekly print publication, the *National Business Employment Weekly. Ladies' Home Journal* archives selected articles from the monthly magazine at their Web site in addition to original materials written and published for the online site only.

Sources of Information

To research *Career Opportunities in the Publishing Industry,* we relied on a range of experiences and sources to gather the information, including

- Fred's training at the United States Defense Information School of Journalism while in the navy, which included reporting on the Vietnam War for the newspaper *Stars and Stripes* and sending stories back to the Associated Press, when he served for 18 months in Vietnam. After the navy Fred was hired by the Associated Press wire service, where he worked for 13 years as a reporter, founding managing editor of AP-TV, entertainment writer, and film critic. Fred was awarded the prestigious Associated Press Writer of the Year award. He also has firsthand experiences as a freelance writer for magazines, syndicates, newspapers, and online publications and is the author of six nonfiction and fiction books.
- Jan's firsthand experiences working at book publishing companies (Macmillan Publishing Company, Grove Press, and RAND Publishing), running her own small press since 1996 (Hannacroix Creek Books, Inc.), and writing more than 26 nonfiction and fiction titles published by Facts On File, Simon & Schuster, Doubleday, Sterling Publishing Co. Inc., Wiley, Prentice Hall, Hannacroix Creek Books, and Scribner, among others. Jan was a freelance theater critic for *Back Stage* newspaper for seven years and has authored scores of newspaper and magazine articles for such publications as the *New York Times, Parade, Newsday, Family Circle, Redbook, Seventeen, Executive Update, Opera News,* online publications of the *Wall Street Journal, Ladies Home Journal,* and other online publications.
- In-person and phone interviews with professionals working in the various job categories at newspapers, magazines, and book publishing companies, or as freelancers.
- Attending publishing industry lectures and educational seminars, such as panels sponsored by the Women's National Book Association, New York City branch; the annual conference for Smaller and Independent Presses, organized by the Association of American Publishers (AAP); and educational sessions at regional bookseller trade shows, such as New England Bookseller Association (NEBA), and at the national BookExpo and the London Book Fair and Frankfurt Book Fair.
- Surfing the Internet and examining Web sites of agencies, colleges and universities offering journalism programs, professional associations, and others.
- Reading magazine articles and books about the publishing industry and career books in general, including the latest edition of the U.S. government's *Occupational Outlook Handbook.*
- Studying newspaper, magazine, and online articles in such publishing industry publications as *Publishers Weekly, Library Journal,* the *New York Times, Editor & Publisher, Writer's Digest,* and the daily free Internet publication with book publishing news, www.publisherslunch.com.
- Belonging to associations that provide an ongoing discussion of the publishing industry through association newsletters, corresponding online with members, and networking by phone and in person, at conferences and holiday gatherings, such as Jan's memberships in the American Society of Journalists and Authors (ASJA), the Association of American Publishers (AAP), the Connecticut Press Club, the National Association of Science Writers (NASW), the National Federation of Press Women, Women's Media Group, and New York Women in Film and Television, as well as Fred's membership in the Writers Guild of America, East and the Connecticut Press Club.
- Regularly reading industry newsletters, such as Jennie L. Phipps's weekly *Freelance Success* (www.freelancesuccess.com), Mimi Backhausen's monthly *Travelwriter Marketletter* (www.travelwriterml.com), *Publishing Trends* (www.publishingtrends.com), and *Publishers Marketplace* (www.publishersmarketplace.com).

How This Book Is Organized

The 90 job profiles in *Career Opportunities in the Publishing Industry* are organized within the three types of publishing covered in this book:

Within each section, a range of jobs is covered, such as writer, editor, artist, sales manager, publicist, or distributor, with each job explained according to the type of publishing that is being discussed—newspapers, magazines, or books. Certain occupations, such as writer, even have a different name depending upon what industry it is in, such as *reporter* and *columnist* for the newspaper, *writer* for the magazine, and *author* for books. Just as terms are different, so too are key considerations, such as how much money one is paid, how it is paid (by the word, by the assignment, or as an advance against royalties), as well as how much time is given for an assignment, the style of the writing, and even how much control the writer has over the final copy.

The Job Profile

Each job profile gives you basic information about that position's contribution to the publication of a newspaper, magazine, or book. Each profile starts with a Career Profile, a brief description of the position's major duties, salary range, job outlook, and opportunities for promotion. We also describe educational requirements, skills, and personality traits best suited for each position. A career ladder section addresses a typical career path, showing where different positions can lead. The remainder of the profile is in an extended narrative with further discussion that contains the following:

- Position description along with key duties
- Salary ranges from entry-level to top earnings
- Employment expectations or job forecast
- The possibility for advancement and suggestions for facilitating moving up
- Licensing or certification requirements (if any)

- Union requirements (if any)
- What education or special training is expected
- Necessary or useful experience, skills, and personality traits
- Suggestions for garnering that initial job in this job category

The Appendixes

Seven appendixes offer further resources for the 90 positions profiled in the book. A list of the colleges that are accredited journalism schools is included, as well as a sampling of other college programs offering communication majors; nondegree intensive summer programs in book and magazine publishing, such as the Columbia Publishing Course; and graduate nondegree or master's degree programs in book or magazine publishing.

Professional unions and associations are listed, as are sources for finding internship opportunities that offer pivotal on-the-job training in the publishing industry. Selected fellowships and competitions, publishing industry conferences, and trade shows are also listed. The bibliography includes books, industry publications, and Web site resources, with separate sections for newspapers, magazines, and books. The glossary is also divided into newspapers, magazines, and books; although there is some overlap, in general, there are very distinct terms for each part of the publishing industry, so three unique glossaries are required. Basic proofreading symbols used throughout the industry as well as a sample proofread paragraph complete the appendixes.

An extensive index follows to help you find what you are looking for in this book. About the Authors concludes this book, providing further biographical information about its coauthors, such as information on the book publishing and promotion seminars and consulting that Jan offers, as well as the Yagers' contact information.

PART I
NEWSPAPER PUBLISHING

EDITORIAL

EDITOR

CAREER PROFILE

Duties: Manages the newsroom and is in charge of the entire editorial staff; trains journalists; makes policy decisions; fills vacancies, and fires staff

Alternate Title(s): Executive Editor; Editor in Chief

Salary Range: $36,000 to $110,000+

Employment Prospects: Fair

Advancement Prospects: Poor

Best Geographical Location(s): Any rural, suburban, or urban area where there is a newspaper

Prerequisites:

Education and Training—A bachelor's degree is required, preferably with a major in journalism or communications, although other majors, such as history or political science, combined with a minor in journalism or communications, are acceptable; a graduate degree in journalism or additional related noncredit courses may be helpful

Experience—Previous jobs as a managing editor or overseeing daily operations of the newsroom,

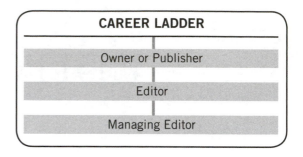

CAREER LADDER

Owner or Publisher

Editor

Managing Editor

as well as on-the-job experience as a reporter or copy editor; previous part-time, summer, or college internships in as many other editorial positions as possible

Special Skills and Personality Traits—Excellent management skills; leadership; intelligent; broad knowledge of current events; strong writer; visionary; ethical; detail oriented, yet able to see the big picture; objective; having a nose, or sixth sense, for the news

Position Description

The Editor is in charge of the newsroom, which means the entire editorial staff, from managing editor and copy editors to reporters and news assistants. The Editor, who is sometimes referred to as the executive editor or editor in chief, is ultimately responsible for all editorial content.

The Editor sets policy and makes policy decisions. A good example of this is found in the book *All the President's Men.* Authors Bob Woodward and Carl Bernstein often refer to former *Washington Post* Editor Ben Bradlee's "two source" policy, which meant that they could only run their investigative Watergate stories if two sources corroborated their information.

Sometimes the Editor will hand out key assignments, although this is often left to the managing editor. The Editor sometimes trains new reporters, in addition to hiring and firing editorial employees. On some papers, the Editor writes the editorials, which will reflect the paper's opinion on a variety of issues. In this regard, the Editor will have to take a stand, such as backing a political candidate or a referendum. What this means is that the position of Editor has a

distinct political element to it. Since most papers have a particular political slant—be it conservative, liberal, or moderate—the Editor will also probably hold those values in order to complement the publisher's or owner's views.

The size of the newspaper will play a key role in determining what the Editor's job entails. On smaller papers, the Editor will wear many hats, while on large metropolitan newspapers, he or she may have hundreds of people reporting to him or her. On newspapers in smaller markets, the Editor may even write headlines and lay out pages. In nearly every case, Editors are managers and are responsible for the editorial budget of a newspaper.

An Editor's typical day is filled with making a series of decisions that will ultimately determine what goes into the paper that day, especially about what goes on the front page, above the fold.

Whether an Editor does certain tasks or delegates those tasks to others to carry out, the Editor still makes the final decision over what stories and photographs will go into the paper that day. He or she will determine, in consultation with a staff of editors or alone, where the stories will appear, their length, and what photographs or color graphics will accompany them.

On smaller papers, such as weeklies, the Editor might also be the paper's only reporter, which is why you might see one byline on all the stories of a small town's weekly.

Deciding what story goes above the fold on the front page is one of the Editor's key responsibilities. Many people decide whether to buy a paper based on what they see on the upper half of the front page. This means that deciding what goes above the fold has a direct impact on sales.

Besides daily decisions regarding content, an Editor will also be called upon to decide how the paper will look on an ongoing basis. This includes whether the paper will use more color, run longer stories, add or drop columnists and features, insert special sections, develop investigative pieces, espouse politics, and experience budget cutbacks.

During the day, the Editor will hold at least one and sometimes two "page one" meetings. At the *New York Times,* these meetings are at noon and at 4:30 P.M. The first meeting will include the team of editors that head each desk to present the important stories of the day that could possibly be page-one stories. At the second meeting, top editors meet with section editors for specific recommendations. Only the most important news of the past 24 hours will make a spot above the fold. Below the fold, there may be one or two features—trend or human interest stories—as well as promotional copy of interesting stories inside the paper. By 6 P.M., the page-one list is decided and distributed. Pages are designed, photos are selected, stories are edited. By 6:10, the lock up begins. Early sections are printed by 10 P.M., and the rest by 4 A.M. Home delivery begins at 6 A.M.

It is a daily race against the clock, and as soon as one paper is delivered, preparations begin to do it all over again, each and every day. Obviously being an Editor at a newspaper is a job filled with constant pressure, decisions, and ever-changing news—a demanding but rewarding job.

Salaries

The salary for the Editor of a small-town weekly could be $36,000 and lower; salaries for Editors range from below $80,000 for daily newspapers in small cities to more than $110,000 in larger metropolitan areas. An Editor for one of the top four newspapers, which have the largest daily circulation and are national in scope (*New York Times, USA Today, Wall Street Journal,* and *Los Angeles Times*), earns even more.

Employment Prospects

This is a position where there is not a lot of turnover, so prospects for employment are only fair. It is one of the top positions on the newspaper, and each paper has only one Editor in charge. Competition for this position is tough in any market, but even greater in larger cities.

Advancement Prospects

Editors of smaller, local newspapers can advance by becoming Editor at a larger, regional paper. Prospects for advancement to the next level of owner or publisher are poor, since those positions tend to be filled for long periods of time. Besides, being a great Editor does not necessarily mean you would be a good publisher, which is the top management position. An Editor has to have an ability to fill the paper with interesting, provocative editorial content, whereas the publisher or owner is focused on total content, including editorial and advertising, and whether the paper is making any money from advertisers and subscribers.

Education and Training

A bachelor's degree in journalism, communications, or another major such as history, political science, or English (with a minor in journalism or communications), is required. A graduate degree in journalism or communications is recommended but not a requirement to be a good Editor. On-the-job training and an overall knowledge of the world and current events are as important as education. Working as an editor for a college newspaper and for a weekly or small-market, daily newspaper would be excellent training.

Experience, Skills, and Personality Traits

As an Editor, you should have had experience as a reporter covering a variety of beats. Most Editors have also been copy editors, city editors, feature editors, and Sunday editors. They have worked their way up the ranks at the newspaper or have worked their way up from smaller markets to larger ones.

Skills include strong communication and a "nose for news." An Editor has to be able to lead and manage people and be able to train novice reporters. An exemplary Editor has a strong visual sense, an eye for detail, excellent grammar skills, and a knowledge of current events as well as history. He or she should have high ethical standards and a sense of fairness.

The cliché of the "gruff editor" probably stems from the fact that by the time someone is able to assume the position of Editor, he or she has seen it all and is fazed by nothing. Actually an Editor's personality, while showing off a gruff exterior, should have a keen sense of the human condition and be able to deal with a wide range of emotions. While there is an unwritten rule that "no tears are shed in the newsroom," it is almost impossible to work in the newspaper business without being emotionally battered by the best and worst humanity has to offer. A noteworthy Editor must be able to withstand these emotional storms and put out a paper each and every day, no matter how painful some of the content contained within it happens to be.

Unions and Associations

The Editor is usually a member of management and not in a union. There are a number of associations to which an Editor may belong, such as the American Society of Newspaper Editors (www.asne.org).

Tips for Entry

1. Get assigned as an Editor for a smaller paper owned by a newspaper chain and work your way up to larger papers in the chain.
2. Read *Editor and Publisher* (www.editorand publisher.com) on a regular basis, as well as other journalism publications.
3. Speak at or attend journalism conferences such as the annual meeting of SPJ (Society of Professional Journalists) (www.spj.org).
4. Network with other Editors and publishers informally and through the American Society of Newspaper Editors (www.asne.org) and networking sites such as LinkedIn (www.linkedin.com).
5. Check out listings at online job sites, such as www.journalismjobs.com or www.mediabistro.com.

MANAGING EDITOR

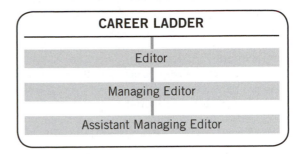

CAREER LADDER

Editor

Managing Editor

Assistant Managing Editor

Position Description

The Managing Editor is the person who supervises all editorial operations, making sure deadlines are met, editorial policy and guidelines are adhered to, and everyone on the editorial staff is doing his or her job to put out the paper each day.

On a typical day, the Managing Editor will read over all copy, checking for accuracy, fairness, any libel concerns, and taste. He or she will make sure the writing follows the newspaper's style and will appeal to its readership.

A Managing Editor's role varies greatly depending on the size of the newspaper. On larger newspapers, there will be an assistant managing editor to share the workload. The assistant Managing Editor typically hands out local assignments to reporters and photographers. This position is seen as a stepping stone to, as well as preparation for, the position of Managing Editor.

On smaller papers, the Managing Editor may be called upon to edit copy, direct the layout, and assign stories. For these smaller-market papers, the Managing Editor may also write headlines, lay out pages, select photographs and graphics, and determine the length of copy.

On some papers, the Managing Editor and editor are the same person, which means he or she will be in charge of hiring, firing, promoting, and demoting, as well as handling the front page and handing out assignments to reporters.

The Managing Editor or assistant managing editor, depending on the size of the paper, also takes requests over the phone and via fax, e-mail, and mail for coverage of certain events, such as press conferences. He or she will determine whether it merits coverage; if it does, he or she will then assign a reporter and photographer to cover it.

The Managing Editor will review all additional editorial resources, such as wire-service copy, graphics, and syndicated material that arrive at the paper every day.

Overall, whereas it is the editor's job to set editorial policy, it is the Managing Editor's job to make sure this policy is carried out among the editorial staff.

Once the editor decides what stories are going into the paper that day, it is the Managing Editor who makes sure this happens. He or she will hand out the assignments to specific reporters, then monitor their progress.

Salaries

Salaries for Managing Editors range from below $41,000 for papers in smaller cities to more than $110,000 on national papers. The average salary at newspapers with a circulation of 75,000 is about $73,000.

Employment Prospects

Since most newspapers have a Managing Editor, employment prospects should be good. However, since it is one of the most coveted and powerful positions on the newspaper, competition is tough because Managing Editor is seen as a stepping stone to the top spot of editor.

Advancement Prospects

Prospects for advancing to the position of editor are only fair, since editors tend to hold their positions for long periods of time. A Managing Editor may have to go to another paper in order to move up to editor, as is common in the newspaper business.

Education and Training

A bachelor's degree, preferably with a major or a concentration in journalism or communications, is required. A graduate degree in journalism or communications or additional noncredit courses are recommended but not required. On-the-job training and an overall knowledge of both local and global events are important. Working as an editor for a college, weekly, or small-market daily newspaper would be excellent training.

Experience, Skills, and Personality Traits

A Managing Editor usually has at least five to eight years of broad newspaper experience as a reporter and editor. Like editors, Managing Editors work their way up the ranks at the newspaper or have worked their way up from smaller markets to larger ones.

A Managing Editor has strong communication skills and "a nose for news," excellent management skills, a solid visual sense, an eye for detail, exemplary grammar, and a knowledge of current events, globally and locally. The Managing Editor must also be a taskmaster, driving reporters and editors to meet the day's deadline.

Unions and Associations

The Managing Editor is usually a member of the management team in the editorial department and is not in a union. There are a number of associations to which a Managing Editor may belong, such as the American Society of Newspaper Editors (www.asne.org).

Tips for Entry

1. Get assigned as an assistant Managing Editor, city editor, or Managing Editor for a smaller paper owned by a newspaper chain and work your way up to larger papers in the chain.
2. Read *Editor and Publisher* (www.editorandpublisher.com) on a regular basis, as well as other journalism publications.
3. Attend local, regional, or national journalism conferences.
4. Network with other editors and Managing Editors informally and through the American Society of Newspaper Editors (www.asne.org).
5. Check out listings at online job sites, such as www.journalismjobs.com or www.mediabistro.com.
6. Network with your college or graduate school alumni as well as with previous coworkers or employers and discreetly ask to be kept in mind if this position opens up.
7. Check the Web sites of such major wire services and newspaper chains as the Associated Press, Gannett, Hearst, and Cox. (See Appendix V for listings.) Job openings for this category may be posted there.

EDITORIAL PAGE EDITOR

Duties: Manages the editorial page to reflect the newspaper's policy, opinion, and politics

Alternate Title(s): None

Salary Range: $38,000 to $100,000+

Employment Prospects: Fair to Good

Advancement Prospects: Fair

Best Geographical Location(s): Wherever there is a newspaper large enough to employ this position

Prerequisites:

    Education and Training—A bachelor's degree in journalism, communications, or a related field is required; a graduate degree in journalism or writing is recommended

    Experience—At least several years of overall journalism experience in such positions as news editor, copy editor, or reporter; have a working knowledge of as many editorial positions as possible

    Special Skills and Personality Traits—Able to write persuasively; ethical; intelligent; able to manage a small staff; broad knowledge of current events; able to express strong opinions and make judgments

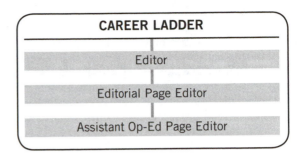

CAREER LADDER

Editor

Editorial Page Editor

Assistant Op-Ed Page Editor

Position Description

The Editorial Page Editor is one of the most powerful and prestigious positions on a newspaper. Reporting directly to the publisher, the Editorial Page Editor is on an equal level with the managing editor and news editor.

The primary duty of the Editorial Page Editor is to oversee the editorial pages of the newspaper. This is the page that reflects the policies and opinions of the newspaper and its owner. It is here that the paper will take sides on any given issue or come out for or against specific political candidates.

Depending on the size of the paper, the Editorial Page Editor will have a staff of editorial writers to which he or she will assign that day's editorials. In this capacity, the Editorial Page Editor will study a variety of situations and form an opinion that would reflect the paper's policy. These situations can be government actions, political campaigns, or actions by individuals that spark controversy. This staff is usually separate from other editing and newsgathering functions.

On larger newspapers, the Editorial Page Editor is responsible for as many as 30 or more editorial writers—columnists who write material for the editorials and, in some cases, the opposing side, or for the op-ed page. This page is filled with a combination of regular columnists and guest op-ed pieces dealing with important issues of the day.

Small papers often lack an Editorial Page Editor; it is then usually up to the publisher or editor to write the editorials.

Larger newspapers will have an assistant op-ed page editor who supervises the daily content for the op-ed page. He or she works with a number of regular columnists and guest contributors. This editor is inundated with thousands of potential op-ed pieces by politicians, business leaders, community members, and others seeking to have their views printed on the op-ed pages. Out of all the submissions, just one or two articles will make it into the paper each day.

Salaries

Salaries for Editorial Page Editors are similar to those of a managing editor, ranging from $38,000 for papers in smaller cities to more than $100,000 at top national papers.

Employment Prospects

Since most large newspapers have an Editorial Page Editor, employment prospects are fair to good. It is one of the most prestigious and powerful positions on the newspaper, second only to editor. Competition is as tough for Editorial Page Editor as it is for managing editor. It is seen as a stepping stone to the top spot.

Advancement Prospects

Advancing to the next level of editor is challenging, since the Editorial Page Editor will also be competing with the managing editor and, in some cases, the news editor for the job of editor. An Editorial Page Editor on larger newspapers, however, seems to have a competitive edge, since, in many cases, they have already been managing editor and since the Editorial Page Editor wields so much power.

Education and Training

A bachelor's degree in journalism, communications, or a related field is required; a master's degree in journalism is recommended for aspiring Editorial Page Editors. On-the-job training and an overall knowledge of national, local, and global issues are also important.

Experience, Skills, and Personality Traits

An Editorial Page Editor usually has at least several years of broad newspaper experience as a reporter and editor. Editorial Page Editors work their way up the ranks at the newspaper, filling a number of journalistic and editorial positions.

These editors have strong writing and editing skills and a broad knowledge of issues, be they national, global, or local. They must be able to form judgments and express and support their opinions clearly and provocatively.

Unions and Associations

The Editorial Page Editor is a member of management and not in a union. There are a number of associations to which an Editorial Page Editor may belong, such as the American Society of Newspaper Editors (www.asne.org).

Tips for Entry

1. Accept a variety of news assignments, from reporting to editing.
2. Have strong political connections within your community.
3. Network with other editors and publishers.
4. Have your own op-ed pieces published so that your skill at writing editorials will be noted.
5. Check the online job sites, such as www.journalismjobs.com and www.mediabistro.com, as well as the Web sites for the largest newspapers or newspaper chains, such as the *New York Times*, Hearst, Tribune, or Gannett, for job postings.
6. Keep in communication with classmates from undergraduate or graduate school, as well as with coworkers or bosses from previous jobs. Let them know that you are interested in the position of Editorial Page Editor if it opens up.

NEWS EDITOR

CAREER PROFILE

Duties: Coordinates all aspects of editorial production, including selection and placement of stories, layout and design, and assignment of stories and photographs; edits copy for style and accuracy; writes headlines

Alternate Title(s): None

Salary Range: $40,000 to $100,000+

Employment Prospects: Good

Advancement Prospects: Fair

Best Geographical Location(s): Anywhere there is a newspaper that has this position, especially major urban centers, such as New York, Los Angeles, Chicago, Boston, San Francisco, and Washington, D.C.

Prerequisites:

Education and Training—A bachelor's degree in journalism, communications, or a related field is required; a graduate degree in journalism is recommended

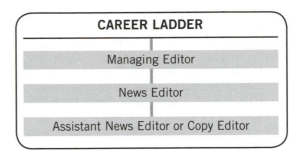

CAREER LADDER

Managing Editor

News Editor

Assistant News Editor or Copy Editor

Experience—At least five years of experience working as a reporter and copy editor

Special Skills and Personality Traits—Strong editing and writing skills; detail oriented; a "nose for news"; excellent management and leadership skills; intelligent; broad knowledge of current events and libel laws; able to meet deadlines; sense of graphic design

Position Description

A front page is normally a combination of local, national, and international stories, and it also contains features designed to attract readers not interested in general news. The News Editor chooses what stories go where within the newspaper. He or she coordinates the selection and placement of all major stories to give the paper a certain balance so that readers can easily find articles of interest to them. Inside pages often have a cohesive theme. International stories will usually be in one place, while political or Washington stories will be in another.

It is the News Editor's job to supervise all aspects of editorial production, which includes laying out and designing the paper's pages, assigning stories to reporters and photographers, determining if graphics are needed to help support a story, and overseeing the copy desk. The News Editor also edits copy for accuracy and style to catch any typos the copy editor missed. The News Editor may also write headlines and design pages. He or she sometimes has the responsibility of training and evaluating copy editors, although this job is often left to the assistant managing editor. On those papers where there is no assistant managing editor, it may by up to the News Editor to perform this function.

On larger papers, the News Editor will have an assistant to coordinate the flow of news copy to make sure deadlines are met. On other papers, this is the responsibility of the News Editor.

Salaries

Salaries for News Editors start at $40,000 or below at papers in smaller cities; the average salary at newspapers with a circulation of 50,000 is $40,000 to $48,000. At larger papers, the average salary is more than $90,000; on the top four national papers, the salary could be more than $100,000.

Employment Prospects

Employment prospects for News Editor are good, since nearly every paper has one. On smaller papers, this position may also include performing the tasks of managing editor and editor. On larger papers, prospects are good as well, since it is one of the key positions on the paper. There is, however, a lot of competition for this demanding job.

Advancement Prospects

Advancing to the next level of managing editor or editorial page editor will depend on turnover at the paper.

Managing editors and editorial page editors tend to hold those positions for long periods of time. A News Editor may have to move to another paper to advance.

Education and Training

A bachelor's degree in journalism, communications, history, political science, English, or a related field is required. A graduate degree in journalism or communications or noncredit graduate courses in journalism are recommended. On-the-job training and an overall knowledge of both local and global events are also important. Working as an editor for a college, weekly, or small-market daily newspaper is excellent training, as is an internship during the academic year or over the summer.

Experience, Skills, and Personality Traits

A News Editor needs at least five years of experience as a reporter and copy editor. News Editors work their way up the ranks at the newspaper or work their way up from smaller to larger markets.

Skills include strong writing and editing talents, as well as a nose for news. A News Editor has a solid visual sense, an eye for detail, excellent grammar, and a knowledge of current events, globally and locally. The News Editor should be a good teacher and a taskmaster, motivating reporters and editors to meet the day's deadline.

Unions and Associations

The News Editor is usually a member of management and not in a union. There are a number of associations to which a News Editor may belong, such as the American Society of Newspaper Editors (www.asne.org).

Tips for Entry

1. Get assigned as a copy editor, city editor, or news editor for a smaller paper owned by a newspaper chain and work your way up to larger papers in the chain.
2. Read *Editor and Publisher* (www.editorand publisher.com) on a regular basis, as well as other journalism publications, such as the *American Journalism Review (AJR)* and the *Columbia Journalism Review (CJR)*.
3. Attend journalism conferences.
4. Network with other editors as well as coworkers at former jobs and classmates from your undergraduate or graduate school.

CITY EDITOR

CAREER PROFILE

Duties: Supervises all local and area news coverage; determines assignments; edits the news section

Alternate Title(s): Metro Editor

Salary Range: $35,000 to $80,000+

Employment Prospects: Good

Advancement Prospects: Fair

Best Geographical Location(s): Major urban centers, such as New York City, Los Angeles, Chicago, Boston, San Francisco, and Washington, D.C.

Prerequisites:

Education and Training—A bachelor's degree in journalism, communications, history, or English is required; a graduate degree or additional training is recommended

Experience—At least five years as a reporter and copy editor

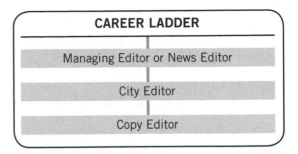

Special Skills and Personality Traits—Strong editing and writing skills; detail oriented; a "nose for news"; excellent management and leadership skills; intelligent; broad knowledge of local current events; able to work hard for long hours and, if necessary, take the night shift (midnight to 8 A.M.)

Position Description

The City Editor reports directly to the managing editor and supervises all local and area news coverage. This is one of the most powerful positions on the paper, because a newspaper's success or failure is often dependent on its solid coverage of local or regional news. The City Editor also makes up the assignments for reporters and the rewrite staff.

Stories may come from anywhere, such as the police scanner, calls from citizens, or what are called "leg reporters" and "stringers," people who are not on staff but get paid when their stories or tips are used in the paper. The City Editor will get a call from a leg reporter and turn it over to a rewrite person, who will quickly turn the information into readable copy. A rewrite person is often a former reporter who is a fast and accurate writer capable of turning out colorful and readable prose under deadline pressure.

On larger papers, a City Editor will have an assistant city editor who edits copy for accuracy, assigns reporters and photographers, and acts as a teacher or mentor to young reporters. On smaller papers, the City Editor performs all of these functions.

Howard Siner is an editor at the *Staten Island Advance* in Staten Island, New York. Since he works the night shift, his official title is Night City Editor. Siner is a veteran journalist whose first newspaper job

dates back to his college years. He explains, "In college, I worked during the school year and the summer for newspapers, the *Home News,* in central New Jersey and at the *Perth Amboy News,* often covering college football and basketball."

After two years in the army, Siner got a job at the major news service, the Associated Press (AP), in New York City: "I walked into the AP off the street and got a job." Siner worked there for the next five years. When he left to go to Costa Rica to take a break, the AP rehired him to cover Costa Rica part time for the next year.

When Siner returned from Costa Rica, he got a job at Newspaper Enterprise Association, which soon merged with United Feature Syndicate to form United Media, a larger feature syndicate. He worked there for 17 years, returned to the Associated Press for a few years, and took the job at the *Staten Island Advance* a few years ago. Siner, who directs three editors and up to 12 reporters, is an excellent example of how working during the college years at newspapers could help to land that first job after graduation. "There's still an old school in journalism that prefers work experience to academic credentials," says Siner.

Salaries

Salaries for City Editors depend on the size of the city in which they work, where the paper is based, and the paper's circulation. The salaries range from $35,000 for papers in smaller cities to $80,000 and higher for larger papers.

Employment Prospects

Employment prospects for City Editor are good, since nearly every paper has one.

Advancement Prospects

Advancement to the next level of managing editor depends on turnover at the paper. Competition is stiff, since news editors and others also vie for this position. Developing a reputation for being an excellent manager, getting the paper out on time each day, and handling the reporters and other staff members that report to you will get you far. Being reliable and working hard, as well as having excellent editing skills, will also help speed your advancement.

Education and Training

A bachelor's degree in journalism, communications, or another major supplemented by journalism courses is required. A graduate degree in journalism or specialized seminars (such as the week-long seminars offered through the Poynter Institute [www.poynter.org]) are recommended. On-the-job training and an overall knowledge of local and world events are key.

Experience, Skills, and Personality Traits

A City Editor needs at least five years of experience as a reporter and copy editor. Solid writing and editing talents, as well as a "nose for news," are necessary skills. A City Editor has to be plugged into the community and know what is going on in the area at all times. He or she will have developed a team of eyes and ears within the community to receive tips about possible stories not apparent from police scanners or daybooks, a collection of events being held that day that the public should know about.

He or she must have an eye for detail, be a strong grammarian, and have a knowledge of current events. The City Editor should be a good teacher and a taskmaster, driving news reporters and assistant editors to meet the day's deadline.

Unions and Associations

The City Editor is usually a member of management and not in a union. There are several associations a News Editor might join, such as the American Society of Newspaper Editors (www.asne.org).

Tips for Entry

1. Get assigned as a reporter, copy editor, or City Editor for a smaller paper owned by a newspaper chain and work your way up to larger papers in the chain.
2. Read *Editor and Publisher* (www.editorand publisher.com) regularly, as well as other journalism publications, such as the *American Journalism Review (AJR)* and the *Columbia Journalism Review (CJR)*.
3. Attend journalism conferences, such as the annual conference of the American Society of Newspaper Editors (www.asne.org).
4. Check the Web sites for such major newspapers or chains as the *Oregonian,* the *New York Times,* the *Detroit News,* the Gannett Company, and Hearst and see if there are job openings posted. Follow up by e-mail, fax, phone, or mail for any listed job opportunities. Also contact the human resources department and get your résumé into their files.
5. Network with other editors, including those you worked with at previous jobs, or former classmates at undergraduate or graduate school. Use social networking sites such as LinkedIn (www. linkedin.com) to find out about job openings.

COPY EDITOR

Duties: Responsible for getting the news and photographs into the newspaper while they are still new; edits copy and writes headlines; designs and produces pages

Alternate Title(s): Copy Chief

Salary Range: $32,000 to $60,000+

Employment Prospects: Good

Advancement Prospects: Fair

Best Geographical Location(s): Major urban centers, such as New York, Los Angeles, Chicago, Boston, San Francisco, and Washington, D.C.

Prerequisites:

    Education and Training—A bachelor's degree with a major in journalism, communications, or English; a graduate degree in journalism is recommended

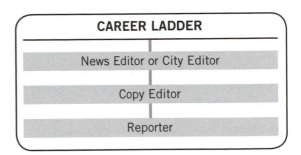

CAREER LADDER

News Editor or City Editor

Copy Editor

Reporter

    Experience—At least two years of experience working as a reporter

    Special Skills and Personality Traits—Strong editing and writing skills; detail oriented; excellent grammar; knowledge of computerized editing systems; graphics; design; team player; easy to work with; outgoing; ethical; intelligent; nonjudgmental

Position Description

The Copy Editor reports to the news editor or assistant news editor, depending on the size of the newspaper. On smaller papers, the Copy Editor may report directly to the managing editor or editor.

It is the job of the Copy Editor to make sure the news and photographs are ready to go into the paper. Each story and photo must be edited and cropped in order to provide the most compelling, complete, timely, and accurate news content possible for the next day's paper.

On larger newspapers, there are usually Copy Editors for each section. For example, the paper's lifestyle section will have its own Copy Editor, who edits stories and writes provocative headlines for the features and lifestyle stories.

Some papers will have their own business section, which will also have its own Copy Editor. In that case, the business section Copy Editor will need to have some financial reporting experience and an understanding of financial terms and concepts.

A typical day for a Copy Editor involves an assortment of responsibilities, from creating exciting and provocative headlines to correcting spelling, grammar, and style.

As copy comes in from reporters and correspondents, the Copy Editor goes through each story to make sure it is as accurate and as readable as possible. This might entail rewriting to correct incomplete or run-on sentences, fixing errors in fact, or polishing the prose to tighten some of the copy to make it fit within the area assigned in the paper. For example, if the editor wanted eight column inches, and the story came in at 10, the Copy Editor might rework some sentences to keep as many salient facts as possible while trimming the story by two column inches.

Copy Editors are often the last readers to see the copy before it goes to press, so they are under enormous pressure to meet strict deadlines as well as to make sure all copy is as accurate and up-to-date as possible.

Salaries

Salaries for Copy Editors vary widely and depend on the size and circulation of the paper. They range from $35,000 for papers in smaller cities to more than $60,000 for larger papers.

Employment Prospects

Employment prospects for Copy Editors are good, since nearly every paper has at least one and, in most cases, more than one, depending on the number of special sections.

Advancement Prospects

Advancing to the next level of news editor or city editor will depend on turnover at the paper. Competition is stiff, since you will be competing with Copy Editors and others for this position. To help your advancement prospects, get known as someone who does the job well and as a reliable team player who is accurate, hard-working, and able to meet deadlines and work under constant pressure.

Education and Training

A bachelor's degree is required, preferably in journalism, communications, or English; a graduate degree in journalism is recommended.

Experience, Skills, and Personality Traits

A Copy Editor needs at least two and, in some cases, several years of experience as a reporter. Skills include strong writing and editing, as well as a mastery of grammar and style. A Copy Editor must perform well under deadline pressure. He or she should be knowledgeable about local and national events, as well as culture, if working on the lifestyle section. A Copy Editor must be skilled at using various editing systems, such as InDesign or QuarkXPress, and other software systems.

A Copy Editor must have an eye for detail, be a team player, be able to edit fairly, be ethical, honest, and have a high degree of integrity.

Unions and Associations

The Copy Editor may be a member of the Newspaper Guild (www.newsguild.org), but on some papers this is a management position. There are a number of associations to which a Copy Editor can belong, such as the American Society of Newspaper Editors (www.asne.org).

Tips for Entry

1. Get assigned as a reporter or Copy Editor for a smaller paper owned by a newspaper chain and work your way up to larger papers in the chain.
2. Read *Editor and Publisher* (www.editorand publisher.com) on a regular basis, as well as other journalism publications.
3. Attend journalism conferences.
4. Network with other editors, as well as with alumni of your undergraduate or graduate school.
5. Check the job listings at www.journalismjobs. com, www.mediabistro.com, and www.monster. com.

BUSINESS EDITOR

Duties: Supervises all content (such as articles and columns) for business, financial, and real estate sections, including up-to-date market data; maintains contact with business associations and companies; reads press releases about new products or business ventures and decides if the information should be covered in the newspaper or if a reporter should be assigned to write a story about it

Alternate Title(s): Financial Editor

Salary Range: $37,000 to $85,000+

Employment Prospects: Fair

Advancement Prospects: Fair

Best Geographical Location(s): Major urban centers, such as New York, Los Angeles, Chicago, Boston, San Francisco, and Washington, D.C.

Prerequisites:

Education and Training—A bachelor's degree with a major or minor in journalism, communications, business, finance, or economics is required; a master's degree in journalism or an MBA is recommended

Experience—At least five years as a business or financial reporter

Special Skills and Personality Traits—Excellent editing and writing skills; detail oriented; expertise in grammar; knowledge of financial terms and concepts; management skills; contacts in business community; easy to work with; outgoing; ethical; intelligent

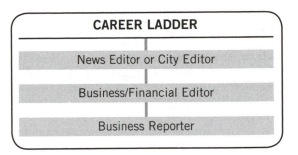

CAREER LADDER

News Editor or City Editor

Business/Financial Editor

Business Reporter

Position Description

The Business Editor oversees all editorial content for the business pages or section of a newspaper. The extent of business coverage usually depends on the paper's circulation and reach. On some large newspapers, this can mean a section with several pages a day; for smaller newspapers, it might mean two to five pages a week. For some newspapers, such as the *Wall Street Journal* (second in circulation to only *USA Today*) or *Investor's Business Daily,* business is the focus of the entire paper.

Overall, the Business Editor oversees the writing and editing of all business articles and columns and the posting of all market data, such as daily stock listings from major markets.

It is up to the Business Editor to make and maintain contacts with key members of the business community and to edit copy from wire services covering financial news, such as Reuters, Dow Jones, Bloomberg, and the Associated Press. At many papers the Business Editor will also write a column or articles for the business section.

A typical day in the life of a Business Editor would begin with scanning the financial and public relations wire services for stories involving local businesses or for those that would have an economic impact on the community, such as rising oil prices or the stock market. He or she would then meet with the paper's business reporters and assign stories for that day or longer pieces for the weekend business section. The Business Editor might also delegate to a business reporter or an assistant business editor the assignment of gathering information for a daily or Sunday business calendar that lists upcoming seminars or presentations, especially those offered for free or a low fee by local business or professional associations.

A typical business section will be a mix of local, national, and international business news, a personal finance column or two, and consumer news, such as product reviews. The Business Editor is in charge of keeping this section fresh and interesting, especially for advertisers.

Salaries

Salaries for Business Editors vary widely and depend on the size and circulation of the paper. They range from $37,000 for papers in smaller cities to more than $70,000 for larger papers.

Employment Prospects

Employment prospects for Business Editor are only fair, since not every paper has one.

Advancement Prospects

Advancing to the next level of news editor or city editor is tough since Business Editors tend to remain in their positions until retirement, unless they move to a larger paper.

Education and Training

A bachelor's degree with a major, minor, or courses in journalism, communications, finance, business administration, and economics is required. An MBA or a graduate degree in journalism is recommended.

Experience, Skills, and Personality Traits

A Business Editor needs at least five years of experience as a business reporter.

Skills include solid writing and editing talents, as well as a mastery of grammar and style. In addition, a Business Editor must have an excellent knowledge of financial terms and concepts. He or she must be able to take complex stories about the financial markets and write them in language anyone can understand.

A Business Editor should have an outgoing personality, feel comfortable around wealthy, powerful people, and not be intimidated by high stakes or prominence. He or she must have a nose for business news, be a team player, be able to edit fairly, be ethical, honest, and have a high degree of integrity.

Unions and Associations

The Business Editor may be a member of management on larger newspapers. If not, he or she may be a member of the Newspaper Guild (www.newsguild.org). There are a number of associations to which a Business Editor may belong, including the New York Financial Writers Association (www.nyfwa.org), the American Society of Newspaper Editors (www.asne.org), and the Society of American Business Editors and Writers (www.sabew.org).

Tips for Entry

1. Get assigned as a business reporter or Business Editor for a smaller paper owned by a newspaper chain and work your way up to larger papers in the chain.
2. Read *Editor and Publisher* (www.editorand publisher.com) on a regular basis, as well as other journalism and business publications, such as the *Wall Street Journal* and *Investor's Business Daily.*
3. Attend journalism and business conferences, such as the annual meeting of the Society of American Business Editors and Writers (www. sabew.org).
4. Network with other Business Editors through annual meetings of associations and through social networking sites such as www.linkedin. com. Attend business conferences, and maintaining relationships with previous coworkers or employers, as well as classmates at undergraduate or graduate programs.
5. Check out the available job listings for registered members posted online at the Web site for the Society of American Business Editors and Writers (www.sabew.org).

ARTS AND ENTERTAINMENT EDITOR

CAREER PROFILE

Duties: Supervises all the editorial content for the daily and Sunday arts and entertainment section, including staff-written articles, columns, and freelance assignments and stories

Alternate Title(s): Lifestyle Editor, Features Editor

Salary Range: $30,000 to $60,000+

Employment Prospects: Poor

Advancement Prospects: Poor

Best Geographical Location(s): Major urban centers, such as New York, Los Angeles, Chicago, Boston, San Francisco, and Washington, D.C.

Prerequisites:

Education and Training—A bachelor's degree is required with a major or minor in journalism, communications, or related fields such as English, writing, theater, film, and other liberal arts areas; a graduate degree in journalism, communications, writing, or one particular aspect of the arts (such as art history, theater, or film) is recommended

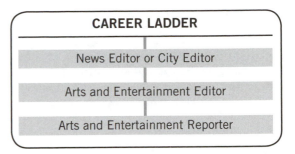

CAREER LADDER

News Editor or City Editor

Arts and Entertainment Editor

Arts and Entertainment Reporter

Experience—At least five years as a feature and entertainment reporter

Special Skills and Personality Traits—Strong editing and writing skills; detail oriented; knowledge of arts, entertainment, and culture; contacts among various art, entertainment, and cultural organizations; outgoing; intelligent; love of the visual and performing arts, movies, theater, music, books, and culture

Position Description

The Arts and Entertainment Editor supervises all arts and entertainment editorial content for the daily, Sunday, and any special weekend sections. He or she decides what art and entertainment events to cover; what books, plays, movies, concerts, art exhibitions, and music to review; and what photos or graphics will accompany these articles.

At smaller papers, this position will likely be handled by a lifestyles or features editor, who also handles leisure and travel, food, and other feature sections, such as science and technology or home design and health. Arts and Entertainment Editors are also the smaller paper's chief film or theater critics and entertainment reporters.

Larger papers will even have an assistant Entertainment Editor along with a separate staff of entertainment writers, columnists, and critics.

The Arts and Entertainment Editor will coordinate the design and look of the arts and entertainment section, working closely with the paper's photo and graphics department.

A day in the life of an Arts and Entertainment Editor might include scanning the Celebrity Service Bulletin to see who is in town promoting his or her latest movie, DVD, CD, or book, then assigning a reporter and photographer to get an interview for that day's paper or an upcoming issue. The Arts and Entertainment Editor would also attend the daily editors' meeting to present that section's stories for the day.

Although this is considered one of the "softer" sections, Arts and Entertainment is also one of the most popular. It is up to the Arts and Entertainment Editor to keep the readers satisfied with news and information about upcoming events, what movies or plays to see, and what new restaurants have just opened. Get on the screening lists and get galleys or early review copies of books in order to assign reviewers and reviews early enough to publish your interviews or reviews in a timely way. Invitations to art gallery openings as well as press conferences or parties for the media will also help you become known in the arts community so that you get a jump on the competition for news or stories for your section. Attract the best staff and freelance talent to research and write trend stories, which provide an overview of the arts and entertainment and inform your readers in-depth and exclusively. If your newspaper permits it, have your section's columns or articles syndicated so that your newspaper and writers get added national exposure.

Salaries

Salaries for Arts and Entertainment Editors vary widely and depend on the size and circulation of the paper. They range from $30,000 for papers with a circulation of 50,000 to $60,000 and higher for larger papers.

Employment Prospects

Employment prospects for Arts and Entertainment Editor are poor, since many smaller newspapers do not have one.

Advancement Prospects

Advancing to the next level of news editor or city editor is tough, since the Arts and Entertainment Editors will be competing with other editors for the same spot. Most Arts and Entertainment Editors stay at that position and also write features and reviews. To help advance in this job, without compromising your objectivity, develop relationships with publicists, book publishing companies, and the marketing departments of the major music, television, and movie companies so that you are offered exclusives or at least original interviews with their top talent in connection with the release of new products.

Education and Training

A bachelor's degree is required, preferably with a major or minor in journalism, communications, or a related field, such as English, writing, theater, film, or another liberal arts discipline. A graduate degree in journalism or communications, writing, or one particular aspect of the arts (such as art history, theater, or film) is recommended. A broad liberal arts education is also helpful. Attending seminars in the arts is recommended, including the series of interviews with actors, producers, and directors conducted by James Lipton, dean of the graduate program in drama, at the Actor's Studio graduate program affiliated with Pace University in New York City.

Experience, Skills, and Personality Traits

An Arts and Entertainment Editor needs at least five years' experience as an arts and entertainment reporter. Skills include strong writing and editing, as well as a mastery of grammar and style. Beyond that, an Arts and Entertainment Editor must have a thorough knowledge of arts, entertainment, and cultural events. An Arts and Entertainment Editor should have a love of all arts, both visual and performing, and all forms of entertainment from theater to movies and concerts.

Unions and Associations

The Arts and Entertainment Editor may be a member of management at larger newspapers. If not, he or she may be a member of the Newspaper Guild (www.newsguild.org). There are a number of associations to which an Arts and Entertainment Editor may belong, such as the American Society of Newspaper Editors (www.asne.org) and the American Association of Sunday and Feature Writers (www.aasfe.org), based at the College of Journalism at the University of Maryland in College Park.

Tips for Entry

1. Get assigned as an arts and entertainment reporter or features and lifestyle editor for a smaller paper owned by a newspaper chain and work your way up to larger papers in the chain.

2. Read *Editor and Publisher* (www.editorandpublisher.com) regularly, as well as other journalism publications such as the *Quill,* published nine times a year by the Society of Professional Journalists (SPJ).

3. Attend journalism conferences, including the annual convention of the American Association of Sunday and Feature Editors (www.aasfe.org) or the National Federation of Press Women (www.nfpw.org).

4. Network with other Arts and Entertainment Editors.

5. Go to the "Links to Member Papers" page at the Web site of the American Association of Sunday and Feature Editors (www.aasfe.org/links.htm), where you will find links in alphabetical order, according to state, from Alabama to Wisconsin. You can use that information to visit the Web site of those newspapers and become more familiar with those newspapers and their arts and entertainment sections, as well as see if there are any jobs for Arts and Entertainment Editor listed.

6. Be willing to relocate if a job opportunity arises. Find out about possible openings by visiting the Web sites of the major newspaper chains, such as Hearst, Gannett, and Cox, as well as such job sites as www.journalismjobs.com, www.mediabistro.com, and journalistusa.com (a fee-based résumé posting/job search site).

SPORTS EDITOR

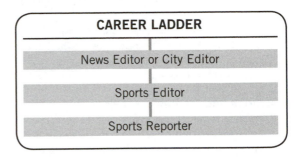
Position Description

The Sports Editor supervises all editorial content for the sports pages. He or she reports directly to the managing editor or assistant managing editor and generally hires and fires his or her staff. The Sports Editor often writes columns and articles, as well as edits copy from a team of sportswriters.

The sports section is one of the most popular sections of the paper, usually among male readers, although there has been an effort made to cover women's sports whenever possible, especially among women's college and professional basketball teams.

Local sports coverage is also important. Besides the obvious national professional sports teams, the Sports Editor has to have direct relationships with local high school, college, and community sports teams and their coaches and to make sure their games are covered as well.

The Sports Editor coordinates all copy with photographs, which are an important element of any sports section. Finding the best photo to run is a key responsibility of the Sports Editor. He or she also writes the headlines that grab the reader's attention.

Sports writing has its own specialized style, designed to make the reader feel as if he or she was reliving exciting moments of the game. It is active, emotional, and dramatic. A good Sports Editor has a responsibility to train up-and-coming sports reporters in this highly competitive and exciting field. If there is a hard news story related to sports—such as the injury or death of a player during training or practice—or the involvement of a player in a newsworthy situation—including being a crime victim, being accused of a crime, winning an award, or making a philanthropic donation—it is the job of the Sports Editor to assign those stories to sports reporters who can rise to the occasion of those news/sports stories.

Designing pages and statistics is also a responsibility of the Sports Editor, who works with the paper's design and graphics department.

Salaries

Salaries for Sports Editors vary widely and depend on the size and circulation of the paper. They range from $35,000 for papers with a circulation of 50,000 to $65,000 and higher for larger papers.

Employment Prospects

Employment prospects for Sports Editor are fair, since most newspapers have one; however, competition for these positions is high.

Advancement Prospects

Advancing to the next level of news editor or city editor is tough, since the Sports Editor will be competing with editors of other sections for the same spot. Most Sports Editors, however, seem to stay at that position and advance by moving to larger papers, where there will be more staff reporting to them, as well as a bigger circulation and more readers.

Education and Training

A bachelor's degree is required; recommended majors or minors include journalism, communications, English, social science of sports and leisure, sports science, or liberal arts. A graduate degree or noncredit courses in journalism are recommended. On-the-job training throughout the school years, at a high school or college newspaper, as well as at local or regional newspapers during the school year or over the summer, will provide excellent preparation.

Experience, Skills, and Personality Traits

A Sports Editor needs at least five years' experience as a sports writer before taking on the responsibilities of Editor. Skills include strong writing and editing, as well as a mastery of grammar and style. Beyond that, a Sports Editor must have a strong knowledge of all sports. A Sports Editor should have a love of sports, enjoy competition, be a team player, and have an outgoing personality. Prior experience during high school or college actually playing one or more sports will also help the Sports Editor to relate to the unique demands and pressures on the sports participants, umpires, managers, and coaches that he or she is writing about (or that their staff reporters are covering).

Unions and Associations

The Sports Editor may be a member of management on larger newspapers. If not, he or she may be a member of the Newspaper Guild (www.newsguild.org). There are a number of associations to which a Sports Editor may belong, such as the American Society of Newspaper Editors (www.asne.org).

Tips for Entry

1. Get assigned as a sports reporter or Sports Editor for a smaller paper owned by a newspaper chain and work your way up to larger papers in the chain.
2. Read *Editor and Publisher* (www.editorandpublisher.com), as well as other journalism publications, such as the *Quill,* the *American Journalism Review (AJR),* and the *Columbia Journalism Review (CJR).* Read leading sports publications, such as *Sports Illustrated,* and the sports sections of the *New York Times,* the *New York Daily News,* and the *Detroit Free Press,* for excellent examples of sportswriting.
3. Attend journalism conferences, such as the annual convention of the American Society of Newspaper Editors (www.asne.org).
4. Network with other Sports Editors at conferences and sports events, as well as with alumni from your college or graduate school who are in journalism.
5. Check out the listings at online job search sites, such as www.mediabistro.com, www.journalismjobs.com, www.hotjobs.com, and www.monster.com.

SUNDAY EDITOR

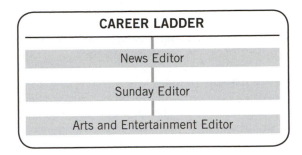

CAREER LADDER

News Editor

Sunday Editor

Arts and Entertainment Editor

Position Description

It usually takes all week to create the editorial content for the thick Sunday newspaper, with its special sections and magazine covering arts and entertainment, travel, business, home, book reviews, and television. The Sunday Editor is responsible for all of this content. (At larger papers, there may even be a Sunday Editor for each of these Sunday special sections.) He or she assigns stories and photo essays, then works with the writers and photographers to make these longer pieces ready for that book-size pile of newsprint that arrives every weekend. Some newspapers sell as many advertisements for this one paper as they do for all the other papers in the week, so it is up to the Sunday Editor to make sure there is enough editorial content to justify so many pages of additional advertising.

The Sunday Editor has to fill several special sections of this paper, which may include a special travel section, sports section, a Sunday magazine, an expanded arts and leisure section, a lifestyle section, book reviews, business section, and even special local sections for those papers covering a large geographical area. It is almost like editing a weekly magazine, since articles tend to be longer and in-depth. There are more feature stories than hard news; some are investigative pieces or celebrity interviews.

The Sunday Paper is intended to be experienced at a leisurely pace, so stories may be written to be read that way as well. The Sunday Editor manages many different types of specialty reporters and columnists covering everything from food, health, and science to travel and religion. Many stories are assigned months in advance, and it is up to the Sunday Editor to keep track of various deadlines for these long-term assignments.

Salaries

The salary for Sunday Editor ranges from $37,000 to $75,000 and higher for larger market papers. The average salary at a paper with a circulation of 75,000 to 100,000 is $55,000.

Employment Prospects

Employment prospects for Sunday Editors are fair, since not all newspapers employ one. Larger papers may have a Sunday Editor covering each major unique section of the Sunday paper, such as book review, television, or travel.

Advancement Prospects

Prospects for advancement to the next level of news editor are fair. Competition is stiff, since the Sunday Editor will be competing with other key editors, such as the editorial page editor, who are also vying for this top editorial position. One of the best ways to advance is by gaining a reputation for producing such a terrific Sunday section that readership soars on Sunday and readers write in or send e-mails to the newspaper praising the Sunday edition and naming it as the reason they have decided to subscribe to the newspaper.

Education and Training

A bachelor's degree is required, with a major or minor in journalism, communications, or a related field, such as writing or English literature. A graduate degree in journalism, additional noncredit courses, or journalism seminars are recommended.

Experience, Skills, and Personality Traits

As a Sunday Editor, you need to have experience in editing and coming up with story ideas, and you must be well organized. Since you may have a staff reporting to you, you should have management and leadership skills.

Since many sections deal with the arts and entertainment, the Sunday Editor should have a diverse cultural background that includes being well read and knowledge of trends in television and cable, upcoming feature films ready for release, and travel destinations that the newspaper's readership would be especially interested in.

Unions and Associations

The Sunday Editor is usually a member of management, but where it is a union position, the Editor may be a member of the Newspaper Guild (www.newsguild. org.). There are a number of associations to which a Sunday Editor may belong, such as the American Society of Newspaper Editors (www.asne.org) and the American Association of Sunday and Feature Writers (www.aasfe.org).

Tips for Entry

1. Take a job as a feature reporter or Sunday Editor at a small newspaper and work on building a reputation for being able to write excellent Sunday features, as well as to assign, edit, and produce some or all of the Sunday edition. Build on that experience to move to a position of more responsibility at a medium-sized or larger newspaper with a wider readership and greater revenue.

2. Read *Editor and Publisher* (www.editorand publisher.com) regularly, as well as other journalism publications such as the *Columbia Journalism Review (CJR)* and the *Quill.* Also keep up on your reading in the arts, literature, entertainment, and travel fields, key areas that are highlighted in a newspaper's Sunday sections. Reading *Publishers Weekly* and *Travel & Leisure* can keep one informed of current developments in the publishing and travel industries.

3. Attend journalism conferences, such as the annual convention of the American Society of Newspaper Editors (www.asne.org), as well as seminars and conferences related to the content areas of the Sunday newspaper. For example, the annual BookExpo, organized by Reed Exhibition and cosponsored by the American Booksellers Association, takes place in May or June each year in Chicago, New York City, or another major city. The books to be published next fall are highlighted, so the Sunday Editor can find out what will be newsworthy in a few months and start lining up the interviews, book reviews, and feature stories that his or her newspaper will want to cover. Travel conferences as well as press conferences about the upcoming fall season for television and films should also be attended by the Sunday Editor or a staff reporter.

4. Network with other Sunday Editors through professional associations as well as at press conferences sponsored by arts and entertainment travel companies, or public relations agencies.

5. Check out job listings at such online sites as www. journalismjobs.com, www.hotjobs.com, www. mediabistro.com, www.journalistusa.com (a fee-based job posting site), and www.asne.org (there is a job section at this professional association's site).

WRITER

COLUMNIST

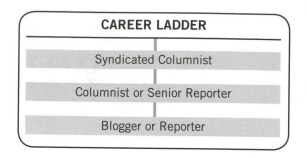

CAREER LADDER

Syndicated Columnist

Columnist or Senior Reporter

Blogger or Reporter

Position Description

For a reporter who prefers to stay a reporter and not advance to editor, being a Columnist is considered one of the best jobs on a newspaper. It means the newspaper values what he or she has to say as a writer, rather than just reporting on the news or the words of others. Columnists no longer report stories; instead, they express their opinions and thoughts on world or local events. They are considered stars, and their photographs often accompany their columns as their reputations grow with the consistency of exposure that their weekly or biweekly columns bring.

A Columnist may work under the supervision of an editor but usually has free reign on what to write. While subjects tend to be timely and topical, Columnists get to choose what they write independent of all other reporters. There are all kinds of Columnists. Some write about sports; others about politics. The one thing they have in common is that their columns are analytical or interpretive. There are such beloved newspaper columnists as the late Erma Bombeck, who also wrote books, commenting on her suburban life as a wife and parent in a humorous and distinct way, as well as the columns about movies by Roger Ebert, syndicated columnist, cohost of a television

movie review show, and a staff writer for the *Chicago Tribune*.

A Columnist could work for a newspaper, for a syndication, or for a wire service. Syndicated Columnists may make more money if they are picked up by hundreds of newspapers, because they are paid based on the number of papers in which their columns appear.

Many Columnists write what are called commentaries. These may be on a variety of subjects, from parenthood to problems in the Middle East. Often a columnist will write a series of columns on related subjects. Although it is tough to get started and to make it profitable, another option is to self-syndicate a column, starting locally and building up the number of papers that buy a column, one paper at a time. If a self-syndicated column becomes successful enough, it may get picked up by one of the syndicates for distribution.

Salaries

The salary for Columnists varies widely, depending on the status of the columnist and whether it is a local or syndicated column. The salary for a local columnist at a paper with a circulation under 50,000 would be around $37,000. Well-known, popular nationally syndicated columnists in thousands of newspapers may earn more than $300,000 a year.

Employment Prospects

Employment prospects for Columnists are poor, since this is a very elite club among reporters. Only a few achieve Columnist status. This is a very competitive field. It is even more difficult for a Columnist at a daily or weekly newspaper to be picked up by a syndicate or wire service and distributed nationally or internationally.

Advancement Prospects

Advancing from local Columnist to syndicated Columnist is extremely difficult but not impossible. Chances for advancement are poor, but since the stakes are high in terms of visibility, income, and international branding as a Columnist expert, it is definitely a worthwhile goal to pursue. Ways to increase the likelihood of advancement as a Columnist include having a unique voice; gaining a reputation for provocative, thoughtful, and memorable columns; and choosing a topic that is underserved but not so obscure that it fails to produce the large readership that a Columnist needs to survive and thrive.

Education and Training

A Columnist should have a bachelor's degree, with a major or minor in journalism or communications, as well as course work in any other field that is important to the Columnist's credentials, since many columnists specialize in their fields. For example, a political columnist would be expected to have a political science degree or at least a minor or ample course work in that field. A financial Columnist would be expected to have a degree or courses in economics, finance, or even an MBA (master's of business administration). General Columnists, who just write their opinion on national or world events or local issues, would do fine with a degree or courses in writing, sociology, psychology, political science, history, journalism, or communications.

Experience, Skills, and Personality Traits

Columnists are usually expected to have at least five years' experience as a reporter. In order to get your own column, you probably broke a powerful story or won an award. To succeed as a Columnist, you have to have something to say, as well as the writing skills to say it in a distinct, memorable, and reader-friendly way.

Personality-wise, you should be opinionated, judgmental, outspoken, and well read, with a keen understanding of your area of expertise or unique point of view and the ability to express yourself with compelling writing. You want to be able to write columns that are clipped and saved by readers—insightful perspectives that help readers see an old topic or issue in a new and eye-opening way.

Unions and Associations

The Columnist is often an independent writer, a freelancer, who may have worked his or her way up the ranks from staff reporter to become an independent contractor. He or she may not necessarily be a member of a union. However, this varies from position to position, and some Columnists belong to the Newspaper Guild (www.newsguild.org).

There are a number of associations to which a Columnist may belong, such as the National Press Club (npc.press.org), Overseas Press Club of America (www.opcofamerica.org), New York Financial Writers Association (www.nyfwa.org), and the American Society of Journalists and Authors (www.asja.org) among others. (See Appendix III for contact information for these and related associations.)

Tips for Entry

1. Take a job at a major newspaper as a reporter or as a Columnist at a small newspaper or weekly.
2. Read *Editor and Publisher* (www.editorandpublisher.com) for available job openings on a regular basis, as well as other journalism publications.
3. Attend journalism conferences.
4. Network with columnists and editors through social networking sites such as www.linkedin.com and seminars and courses in writing offered at local universities or colleges through their continuing education programs or as nondegree options sponsored by their graduate programs in journalism.
5. Ask your editor if you could try out a column in addition to your reporting duties and see if there is a positive response to the topic or your style.
6. Contact the available syndicates and pitch your column idea. Most ask for several actual samples as well as an overview of other topics you would cover and who your target audience would be. Make sure you check out the competition to rule out any other columns currently running that are too similar. (See Appendix V for a list of key companies that syndicate Columnists.)
7. Try self-syndicating a column for little or no money and see if enough newspapers pick it up to justify continuing. You might also become an online blogger and see if that leads to a print column opportunity.

REPORTER

CAREER PROFILE

Duties: Writes the news that he or she is assigned to cover, whether general, investigative, or specialized, including sports, lifestyle, business, or the arts; gathers information by conducting interviews over the phone or in person, visiting the scene of the crime, attending a press conference or a speaking engagement, and by checking statistics associated with a story

Alternate Title(s): Writer, Journalist, Newspaper Reporter

Salary Range: $15,000 to $75,000+

Employment Prospects: Good

Advancement Prospects: Fair

Best Geographical Location(s): Wherever there is a newspaper, from small towns or suburban areas to major cities, such as New York, Los Angeles, Chicago, Boston, San Francisco, Detroit, Dallas, Seattle, Denver, and Washington, D.C.

Prerequisites:

    Education and Training—A bachelor's degree, preferably in journalism, required at major newspapers and recommended at smaller papers; a graduate degree in journalism, communications, or an area of expertise for specialty reporters (such as science,

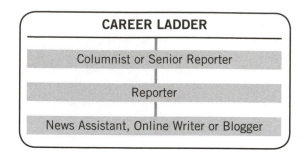

CAREER LADDER

Columnist or Senior Reporter

Reporter

News Assistant, Online Writer or Blogger

health, nutrition, food, the arts, business, or lifestyle) is recommended

Experience—Experience as a reporter on a college paper or a paid or unpaid internship at a local newspaper during college or over the summers is expected

Special Skills and Personality Traits—Strong writing ability; able to write under deadline pressure; able to think on your feet; good listener; observant; detail oriented; fair-minded, nonjudgmental; courageous; thick-skinned; persistent; hardworking; energetic; able to work long hours without a break; able to recognize a news story when you see one

Position Description

Reporters are responsible for generating most of the editorial content that appears on the pages of our daily newspapers. They tell us what's new in the world and what will have an impact on our lives. They provide the who, what, where, when, and why of history in the making. Reporters are our eyes and ears around the world and in the streets of our cities, providing a daily dose of data and observations to keep us knowledgeable and informed about the current state of the world in which we live.

Basically, there are four categories of reporters— general assignment, investigative, specialty, and feature. These categories apply whether you are considering a job at a newspaper or one of five major news-gathering operations, the Associated Press, United Press International, Reuters, Dow Jones, and Bloomberg.

General Assignment Reporter

A General Assignment Reporter covers assignments on anything the city editor or news editor wants cov-

ered, such as accidents, police reports, political events, strikes, and bond hearings. After breaking in, they are assigned beats, such as city hall, the police department, or the governor's office.

A daily routine would include covering press conferences, following up on news tips, interviewing politicians, covering a fire, taking notes, and working with a photographer or taking pictures if a photographer is not assigned.

If a story is breaking fast, a Reporter may have to write a first draft on a laptop or notebook computer and send it in over the Internet. In the past, the Reporter would call in the facts to an editor or rewrite person. This still occurs, but technology is making it easier to send information in over handheld personal data appliances (PDAs).

There is a certain amount of pressure in being a Reporter: the deadline pressure of having to research, and write, within a limited period of time, even if more time is needed or wanted; the strain to get sources, who may be reluctant to talk about what they know, to open up; and the necessity of fact-checking a story to make sure names and places are spelled correctly and facts are accurate. Especially in the beginning, Reporters are not able to choose their assignments; they may be asked to cover yet another school board meeting or a holiday celebration at the local elementary school.

Investigative Reporters

Once you have proven your worth as a General Assignment Reporter, you may be assigned to a team covering a story that could take weeks or months to develop. These are called investigative pieces and tend to result in a series of articles that probe newsworthy and usually controversial events or issues.

Since investigative reports tend to be expensive, most papers only handle one or two a year. Reporters on these assignments usually spend weeks and months gathering information. These reports may spur a lawsuit, since they are designed to bring to light a major injustice and effect change. To do this, feathers are often ruffled, careers put under scrutiny, and reputations reevaluated. This is reporting at its most aggressive, and there are huge risks but also amazing rewards, such as being the catalyst for change.

Investigative Reporters have had their lives threatened and their families terrorized; some have even been killed while trying to uncover something someone else wanted left unexposed.

Watergate made heroes of Bob Woodward and Carl Bernstein and gave birth to a generation of would-be investigative journalists. The title may seem glamorous, but this is serious, dangerous journalism and should not be entered lightly.

Specialty Reporters

The third category is Specialty Reporters. These are Reporters who cover news within a particular specialty, such as medicine, health or science, business or financial news, sports, food, nutrition, or entertainment.

Usually, Specialty Reporters will have proven themselves as General Assignment Reporters before getting assigned to cover a particular category. Working in these categories demands knowledge or experience beyond traditional journalism. For example, a Financial Reporter has to understand complex economic terms, while a Medical Reporter has to have a working knowledge of health and medicine.

Sports Reporters are a category unto themselves. Sports-page writing is of a particular style, full of energy and wit, enthusiasm and color. Many fans think

the sports section is the only section in the paper worth reading and will always read it first.

One of the most difficult assignments for a Sports Reporter is getting the locker room interview of a major sports figure after his or her team has just lost or won. Sports Reporters often have to work under noisy, rambunctious conditions, composing their prose on the sidelines, rushing to get their copy in before deadline just as the game ends.

Feature Reporter

Another category, the Feature Reporter, is often the unsung hero of journalism. Rarely do they make the front page, although sometimes they do, and usually they take us to places we would never go without their stories. Feature Reporters tend to write longer stories or articles and to deal with emotions as they are involved with issues that spark debate. Feature Reporters are similar to columnists in that they tend to cover whatever interests them, but they differ in one major area— they keep themselves out of the story.

Salaries

Salaries for Reporters vary widely, depending on whether someone is a beginner or a veteran, whether he or she covers a specialty, such as sports or business, and what the paper's market is in terms of circulation and geographical location or region. The salary for an entry-level Reporter at a small paper will be around $15,000, while an experienced Reporter on a paper with a circulation of 100,000 will earn an average of $45,000. Reporters in larger markets earn between $47,000 and $75,000. However, some bylined star Sports Reporters have been known to make between $350,000 and $500,000 a year.

Employment Prospects

Employment prospects for Reporters are good, since they make up the bulk of editorial positions on any newspaper, daily or weekly, rural, suburban, or major urban paper.

Advancement Prospects

Advancing from General Assignment Reporter to Investigative Reporter or Specialty Reporter depends on turnover at the paper and the needs of the editors. Competition increases in various areas. There are only a limited number of positions for an Entertainment Reporter; however, there may be a number of slots in sports or business. Advancement possibilities increase by gaining a reputation for balanced and accurate writing as well as by developing a distinct style (but one that fits in with the tone and overall style of the newspaper). Being able to get along with other Reporters as well as the editors and management will also get you far.

Education and Training

A Reporter should have a bachelor's degree, preferably in journalism or communications, but other fields are important as well, since many Reporters want to specialize in a particular field. For example, a political or Washington, D.C. Reporter might be expected to have a political science degree, and a Financial Reporter expected to have a degree in economics or business. There are a number of internship programs for novice journalists. A graduate degree in journalism or in a specialized field (such as nutrition, finance, or film) is recommended, especially if you wish to become a Specialty Reporter or columnist.

Experience, Skills, and Personality Traits

Reporters should get as much experience as possible working on a high school or college newspaper or in an internship program for a local newspaper or wire service. Working at a small town weekly is also useful experience, since you will probably get to do more than just reporting, which is all you will be able to do in a larger newspaper (the other tasks there will be handled by other staff members).

Skills include having a strong writing ability and being observant, able to recognize news, a good listener, able to write fast and accurately under pressure, and tenacious and persistent.

It also helps to have an outgoing and nonjudgmental personality. If your image of a Reporter is Clark Kent, the mild-mannered reporter of Superman fame, then you are in for a wake-up call. Typically, Reporters are not mild-mannered. While it does not help to be abrasive, most good Reporters are aggressive and rarely let manners get in the way of getting a good story.

Unions and Associations

The Reporter is usually a member of the Newspaper Guild (www.newsguild.org). There are also a number of associations to which a Reporter may belong, such as the National Press Club, Overseas Press Club, New York Financial Writers Association, Society of Professional Journalists, Investigative Reporters and Editors, Asian American Journalists Association, New York Association of Black Journalists, National Association of Science Writers, National Association of Black Journalists, National Association of Hispanic Journalists, and American Society of Journalists and Authors. (See Appendix III for listings.)

Tips for Entry

1. Take a job as a paid or unpaid intern at your local paper while you are in school or over the summer.
2. Work on your college or graduate school paper.
3. Read *Editor and Publisher* (www.editorand publisher.com) on a regular basis, as well as other journalism publications, such as the *Quill*.
4. Take noncredit courses in journalism or writing, especially those that include lots of actual writing assignments as part of the course requirements.
5. Attend journalism conferences and press conferences.
6. Offer to write articles for local community publications to gain experience.
7. Network with Reporters and editors through conferences and by frequenting restaurants located near the newspaper that are known to attract the staff members.
8. Join the Society of Professional Journalists (www.spj.org) as a student and continue to attend their regional or national conferences and network after graduation.
9. Ask your journalism department or alumni association to help you find a job. Network with other alumni who are working for newspapers. Visit Web sites posting job openings for Reporters, such as www.journalismjobs.com, www. mediabistro.com, www.hotjobs.com, and www. monster.com.
10. Visit the Web sites for the major newspapers or chains and see if they include a job search component that tries to match potential Reporters with openings.
11. Keep developing a portfolio of clips of your work, even if you have to cover events and write articles on speculation (without an assignment) or for free, so that you have sample clips to show potential employers.
12. Another way to get into reporting is to be an online writer or blogger, whether paid or unpaid. Do the best reporting possible, gather your credits, and use those works published on the Internet to land a job with a traditional newspaper. Some of the online writing communities that offer opportunities to new or seasoned writers—each has its own way of compensating authors—include www.suite101.com, www. ehow.com, www.helium.com, www.associated content.com, and www.howtodothings.com.

NEWS ASSISTANT

Duties: Assists reporters and editors around the office with clerical tasks; researches statistics and facts to help reporters and editors get their jobs done

Alternate Title(s): Copy Boy, Copy Person

Salary Range: $16,000 to $34,000+

Employment Prospects: Good

Advancement Prospects: Good

Best Geographical Location(s): Wherever there is a newspaper, from the smallest town to the largest major urban centers where there may be numerous newspapers with job possibilities, such as New York, Los Angeles, Chicago, Boston, San Francisco, and Washington, D.C.

Prerequisites:

Education and Training—A high school diploma is required; some newspapers may require some college, especially if this job is considered an internship for credit; at larger newspapers, a bachelor's degree

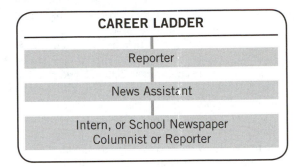

CAREER LADDER

Reporter

News Assistant

Intern, or School Newspaper Columnist or Reporter

in journalism is recommended for advancement but not required for employment

Experience—As an intern at a variety of school, local daily, or weekly papers

Special Skills and Personality Traits—Able to take orders and follow directions; punctual; computer literate; strong research and organizational skills; excellent written and verbal communication skills; able to get along with strong-willed people; a team player; easygoing; hardworking and energetic

Position Description

The News Assistant is the "go-fer" of the newsroom. If an editor or reporter needs something done, it is likely the News Assistant will be asked to do it. Other than the paid or unpaid intern, this position is the lowest rung on the ladder. Still, it is an entry-level position that many of the country's top reporters once held.

Years ago News Assistants were called "copy boys" and then "copy persons." Today, a News Assistant is likely to be called upon to assist an editor or reporter in actually gathering information and preparing news for publication. Most of the time, he or she will be answering the phone, delivering the mail, or sending and retrieving faxes and e-mails.

There will be times when a News Assistant will help research a story or transcribe an interview. On sports or business desks, he or she will be collating statistics.

This is the equivalent to working in a mailroom for a talent agency or movie company, and it is considered a job at the beginning of a career in newspapers.

Salaries

The salary for a News Assistant can range from nothing—if this position is being filled by an intern using it to earn college credit—to $34,000 at larger newspapers. It is an entry-level position, so the salary will depend on the circulation and location of the newspaper.

Employment Prospects

Employment prospects for News Assistants are good, because newspapers hire a lot of them as inexpensive or free labor.

Advancement Prospects

Advancing to the next level of Reporter is going to be harder, because the newspaper will have to decide if the News Assistant has enough writing talent to deserve a chance to become a Reporter. Since the News Assistant job probably does not require any reporting, it is up to the News Assistant to cleverly show his or her bosses that he or she can do a reporter's job without being too pushy or too conceited.

Education and Training

A News Assistant should be studying journalism or a related field in college or have a bachelor's degree in journalism.

Experience, Skills, and Personality Traits

A News Assistant does not really need much experience. This is an entry-level position, but working on a school paper in high school or college would be helpful in preparing the individual for what to expect.

As for skills, being able to type on a computer is a necessity today. The individual should have strong writing, communication, organizational, and research skills. A News Assistant should be able to gather information and conduct the occasional interview.

A News Assistant should have an easygoing personality; he or she should also be hardworking, punctual, able to work under pressure, able to take directions, and be humble enough to work at this low level.

Unions and Associations

The News Assistant may or may not be a member of the Newspaper Guild (www.newsguild.org). There are a number of associations to which a News Assistant may belong, such as the National Press Club (npc.press.org), or the National Federation of Press Women (www.nfpw.org).

Tips for Entry

1. Take a job as an intern or News Assistant at a small town newspaper.
2. Read *Editor and Publisher* (www.editorandpublisher.com) on a regular basis, and check out their job listings. Also read other journalism publications, such as the *Quill,* to keep up on trends in the field.
3. Attend regional or national journalism conferences through the Society of Professional Journalists (www.spj.org).
4. Attend the local job fairs sponsored by the American Society of Newspaper Editors (www.asne.org). A list of upcoming local job fairs is posted at their Web site.
5. Search the Web for internships or entry-level jobs at newspapers. Go to such sites as www.monster.com, www.mediabistro.com, and www.journalismjobs.com.
6. Network with reporters and other News Assistants at conferences and conventions as well as through your college journalism department or alumni association.

BLOGGER

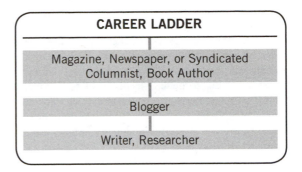

Position Description

The position of professional Blogger is relatively new. In fact, the term didn't even exist a decade ago. But as more and more companies are using blogs as marketing tools, and as stories about Bloggers who become rich and famous become better known, positions for Bloggers have grown considerably, as has the popularity of the job of Blogger.

Blogging began as way for anyone to voice his or her opinions on a variety of subjects. The first Bloggers were called "citizen journalists" because anyone with access to a computer and the Internet could create a "blog," the name of which comes from the term *Web log*. Most of them were not considered in the same serious vein as traditional journalists; they were considered to be more like vanity publishing than serious journalism. A few, however, like Matt Drudge and his Drudge Report, broke major news stories and have since become a mainstay of mainstream media.

For those who may still be unfamiliar with the term, blogs are basically columns on the Internet or an entire Web site that address a particular subject. Usually a

blog invites readers to respond to content that the Blogger posts. It is this interactive element that sets blogs apart from more traditional and static print or online publications. The Pew Institute, which conducts periodic surveys on Internet use, says approximately one out of every six Americans read blogs.

Three to five posts a week is the normal blog post production requested, although some Web sites may ask a guest Blogger to post just weekly. Typically, blog posts are 200–500 words each, though some request more in-depth coverage. The average posts per month are 20, generating approximately 10,000 words per month of content.

In general, the more controversial or useful the content, the greater the blog's readership. The number of blogs online grows daily. The Web site Technorati tracks more than 113 million blogs, but only a small percentage have significant readership numbers.

Veteran newspaper columnist Bill Tammeus of the *Kansas City Star* says that for a Blogger to be effective, he or she must give readers something useful they cannot get elsewhere and do so consistently. He says a blog is more than just another column full of words. It should offer links to related Web sites, contain helpful graphics, provide an opportunity to correspond with the Blogger, and provide a chance to enter into discussion with other readers.

A Blogger should set up a schedule and post consistently at the same time each day, each week, or each month, depending on what schedule is followed. A Blogger needs to include plenty of links; Tammeus notes that blogging is all about links. If the blogging system allows a Blogger to have the linked sites open in a new window, that should be done so readers do not leave the Blogger's site. If the site to which readers are being linked contains potentially objectionable material or requires plug-ins or other software, the Blogger should say so.

Another tip from Tammeus is to develop a consistent voice. The Blogger needs to decide how formal or informal he or she plans to be and then stick close to that. Don't be William Faulkner one day and 50 Cent the next.

Bloggers should let readers have their say in the comments section.

As blogs have become more popular, some have drawn negative attention and are being targeted with lawsuits claiming defamation, infringement of intellectual property rights, disclosure of trade secrets, or online harassment. In these suits, both employers and employee Bloggers may be held liable. In 2008, the FBI even arrested one Blogger who was suspected of streaming songs from an unreleased Guns N' Roses album, claiming this could result in a "significant" financial loss for the band.

Among the more popular blogs and sites are the Huffington Post, Women on the Web, Mashable, TMZ, Seth Godin, Daily Dish by Andrew Sullivan, Wonkette, RedState, and Hot Air. Over 300 Bloggers received credentials to cover the 2008 Republican and Democratic presidential campaigns. By contrast, fewer than 50 Bloggers were given press credentials for the 2004 campaign. Both Hot Air and RedState offer video as well as text on their blogs. Hot Air gets about 600,000 visitors a day, while RedState gets about 50,000. Both have a mostly conservative audience. Wonkette, which is liberal in its leanings, takes a more irreverent and humorous approach to politics, posting about 20 items a day, many of them gossip oriented.

Salaries

According to Indeed.com, as of September 1, 2008, the average salary for a Blogger ranged from $24,000 to $54,000 a year. That said, there are a handful of bloggers

who have made a small fortune from their blogs, primarily through advertising and other revenue sources. There are also Bloggers who are asked to blog for free, in exchange for exposure at the major site where they are blogging or for compensation based on a sharing of the revenue generated by any ads that are associated with the blog or the Web site. Bloggers may use their blogging as the stepping-stone to a more lucrative business. For example, Markus Frind started out as a Blogger, but then he developed a dating Web site called www.plentyoffish.com, which reportedly gives him an annual salary of more than $3.65 million. Steve Pavlina reportedly makes an estimated $1,000 a day from his personal development blog.

Employment Prospects

As the "blogosphere" grows, so does the number of jobs for Bloggers. Here is a partial list of online resources featuring paid blogging jobs: www.problogger.com is one of the best sites for blogging jobs, followed by www.craigslist.org, www.indeed.com, www.authorityblogger.com, www.bloggerjobs.biz, www.writersweekly.com, www.mediabistro.com, and www.freelanceblogging-jobs.com.

Advancement Prospects

Prospects for advancement for Bloggers will depend on the popularity of a specific blog and a Blogger's reputation and ability to generate readers as well as publicity, media attention, and breaking news. A Blogger paid by the number of visitors he or she has will earn more money as the blog becomes more popular. On the other hand, a work-for-hire Blogger may advance from Blogger to online staff writer, or to blog editor or administrator. But there are many more Bloggers than there are positions open for advancement, so advancement prospects are poor.

Education and Training

A four-year college degree is preferable, along with experience in blogging, community building, social networking, blog technology, Web design, and Web development. Three to five years experience in Web technology and blogging is a typical requirement.

Training in WordPress for content management systems (CMS) and blogging programs, theme design, and coding experience is helpful. A Blogger focused on a specialized topic—science, ecology, business, the arts, politics, or the media—may find that taking undergraduate or graduate courses, or having an advanced degree, in that field will be helpful.

Experience, Skills, and Personality Traits

Blog administrators are looking for experienced and skilled writers who know punctuation, spelling, and grammar and have an innate creative writing ability. They should also have a clear understanding of language comprehension, proofing, and editing. Since blogs tend to specialize, Bloggers must be fluent in that specialty.

Bloggers must be self-motivated and have strong self-discipline. They will be working with very little direction and often no editorial control. Deadlines will be set and need to be met consistently, without fail. The Blogger must stay on top of industry news and trends and report on them accordingly.

Bloggers must be able to take direction yet be able to work independently and in line with the company's needs, finding story ideas the company wants published. The Blogger must be able to translate the needs of the company into the needs of the blog.

A Blogger does not have to be best writer in the world, but does have to have passion and a vested interest in the blog's subject. A Blogger also must be able to write with experience and authority. For example, a Blogger with no children should avoid writing a blog about being a work-at-home parent. A Blogger who cannot speak about the automobile industry should not apply for a position at a blog about motor trends. The Blogger needs to know what he or she is writing about, and experience blogging about the subject for one to five years is even better.

Experience in search engine optimization (SEO) as well as public relations and marketing is a plus, as is familiarity with social networking. It is also important for Bloggers to keep up on the latest technological changes and trends.

A Blogger must be able to generate energized content consistently, which means coming up with new ideas, new perspectives, and fresh content on the same subject week after week. Interview skills are also helpful. Most companies need a variety of writing skills, from technical to editorial. Since many blogs today contain more than just text, experience with audio and video creation will be extremely useful.

As for personality, Bloggers should be spirited, enthusiastic, hardworking, able to meet deadlines, passionate, creative, and innovative. Companies want original thinkers and original writers.

Some companies want a Blogger to attend public events, conferences, conventions, and media affairs, which means he or she should be sociable, able to interact in social settings, be able to read a crowd, and possess excellent verbal communication skills.

There is a growing demand for translators to translate blog content from one language to another. The majority of these are for translating from English to another language, often Chinese, Japanese, and Spanish. Familiarity with blogging is required, in addition to having a knowledge of the second language thorough enough to provide translation services that will meet a professional standard.

Unions and Associations

Bloggers might want to join associations that put them in contact with experts and researchers in the area in which they are blogging, such as associations for scientists or science writers for blogs about science, or business associations for blogs about business. A Blogger might also want to consider joining any of the writers' associations, such as the National Federation of Press Women (www.nfpw.org) or the National Association of Science Writers (www.nasw.org), if they accept the blogs he or she writes as meeting their criteria for membership.

Tips for Entry

1. Apply only for blog positions in industries and markets in which you are an expert and about which you feel passionate. Do not waste people's time unless you really know the subject matter well.

2. Research the company. Find out who they are, what they do, what they have done online—or not done—and what they need. The more you know about the company, the more you can direct your application to their specific needs.

3. Have your CV/résumé up to date and ready to e-mail. Have it in the following forms: text, HTML, Word document (older versions), and PDF. All versions except text should have easy-to-read clickable links to your blog(s), work samples, guest blog posts, and other linkable sources.

4. Put together a minimum of five published samples of your work. Many think they can just send links, but the companies want these printable. Put the examples in a Word document and PDF for easy e-mailing as an attachment. It can be a single file or five separate files. Keep file sizes to a minimum.

5. Be easy to find. Provide at least two e-mail addresses (in case the first one doesn't work), at least one phone number, and as many online communication methods as you can, such as Skype, Google Talk, Yahoo, Jabber, Twitter, etc. Put this information on every file and

communication to link you with the sample work and correspondence.

6. Write at least five different versions of a one-paragraph introduction to your blogging job skills. Go through each version carefully to make sure it represents your very best writing skills and presents you in the best light, spelling out the reasons you are worth hiring. Use action verbs and descriptions and get right to the point. Make these of varying lengths from 50 to 150 words. Use these as a base reference for responding to initial job correspondence. These are the make-or-break sales pitches to convince someone to take the next step toward hiring you.

7. Look for job postings for Bloggers. If you go to the job search site www.indeed.com, you will find job postings for bloggers from a variety of sites such as www.careerbuilder.com or www.back-page.com. Other sites to visit that may have job openings for Bloggers include www.problogger.com, www.craigslist.org, www.authorityblogger.com, www.bloggerjobs.biz, www.writersweekly.com, www.mediabistro.com, and www.freelance bloggingjobs.com.

PHOTOGRAPHY
AND DESIGN

PHOTO EDITOR

CAREER PROFILE

Duties: Supervises press photographers; coordinates schedules with city editors and special section editors; helps select and edit photos for the newspaper; assists in designing news and special sections

Alternate Title(s): Director of Photography, Photo Director, Picture Editor

Salary Range: $34,000 to $75,000+

Employment Prospects: Good

Advancement Prospects: Fair

Best Geographical Location(s): Major urban centers, such as New York, Los Angeles, Chicago, Boston, San Francisco, and Washington, D.C.

Prerequisites:

Education and Training—A bachelor's degree in photo journalism and photography or equivalent on-the-job training

Experience—At least five years' experience as a press photographer

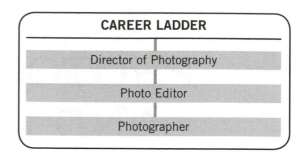

Special Skills and Personality Traits—Should have a thorough knowledge of photography, strong design and photo editing skills, and be able to tell a story in pictures; must be able to work well with others; enthusiastic; creative; eye for detail; strong news judgment; a leader, a mentor, and a team player

Position Description

The Photo Editor is responsible for all photographs used in the newspaper. He or she may also be asked to assist in the paper's overall design, but the Photo Editor's main job is to make sure all key stories have a photo to accompany them, whether the photo is used or not. To do this, the Photo Editor coordinates the schedule of available press photographers and freelancers with those of reporters covering breaking stories.

When the photographer turns in his or her roll or digital camera, the Photo Editor will select and crop the final photograph to be used in the story. He or she then gives the photo to a copy editor, who will write a caption.

A good Photo Editor has an eye for news and works as part of the editorial team. He or she will work with editors of various sections on overall page design and the look of various sections.

A typical newspaper with a circulation of about 100,000 will have a Photo Editor and several photographers on staff to cover everything from breaking news to sports and political rallies.

Salaries

The salary for a Photo Editor varies widely, depending on the newspaper's circulation. A Photo Editor at a small newspaper of 50,000 circulation might earn $34,000 a year, while Photo Editors on larger papers in major markets receive $75,000 and up.

Employment Prospects

Employment prospects for Photo Editors are good, because most newspapers have at least one.

Advancement Prospects

Advancing to the next level may be difficult, because only the largest papers have a Photo Editor with a staff of photographers under him or her.

Education and Training

Today a Photo Editor should have a bachelor's degree in photojournalism, but many famous news photographers had no academic training at all.

Experience, Skills, and Personality Traits

A Photo Editor should have at least five years' experience as a news photographer. He or she should have a strong photographic and design sense, the ability to tell stories in pictures, an eye for detail, a sense of good taste, management skills, and mentoring ability.

Personality-wise, a Photo Editor must be a team player, nonjudgmental, and able to console and commiserate when a photographer's best photo gets cropped or killed.

Unions and Associations

The Photo Editor may or may not be a member of the Newspaper Guild (www.newsguild.org). There are a number of associations to which a Photo Editor may belong, such as the National Press Photographers Association (www.nppa.org).

Tips for Entry

1. Work as a photographer on a newspaper or wire service.
2. Read *Editor and Publisher* (www.editorand publisher.com) regularly, as well as other journalism publications.
3. Attend local or national journalism conferences.
4. Network with editors and other Photo Editors.
5. Search Web sites such as JournalismJobs.com and mediabistro.com.

PHOTOGRAPHER

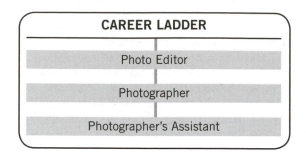

Position Description

Like the reporter or the columnist, being a Photographer is one of the most glamorous and exciting jobs in newspapers for those who are creative and want to make a name for themselves and for their work. Photographers take the pictures that are used in the newspaper. Called "shooters" by fellow journalists, the Photographer has to do with photographs what a reporter does with words. He or she takes the picture that helps explain the story a reporter will use a few hundred or a thousand words to tell. One picture has to say it all. Even if a Photographer's name is unknown, several photographs have become defining images—of the Kent State shootings, of Vietnam, of the September 11th, 2001, terrorist attacks—and are known internationally and become part of history.

Some aspects of photojournalism can be taught, but great news photography is an art. A news Photographer has the creative gift to know exactly when to snap the shutter to freeze forever a timeless portrait that will provide a visual record of events or human emotion and achievement.

Pictures in a newspaper play a variety of roles. They show images that project social, economic, or political issues. They share with the world horrifying disasters as well as inspiring moments. Portraits can expose a private personal moment in the life of a world leader, showing that even the strongest among us have moments of doubt and fear.

Today's news Photographers usually shoot with digital cameras that produce images that can be fed over the phone lines or through high speed modems or cables to computers manned by photo editors, who then select the best shot for the story it will be accompanying. On breaking news stories, speed is the key, and today's technology allows instant reproduction of photos from the scene of the event.

Salaries

The salary for a Photographer varies widely, depending on the newspaper's circulation. A Photographer at a small newspaper of 50,000 circulation might earn $600 a week (approximately $31,000 a year), while Photographers on larger papers in major markets receive $65,000 a year and up.

Employment Prospects

Employment prospects for Photographers are good, because most midsize to large newspapers have at least one on staff as well as others on call as freelancers. Small weekly newspapers may have a camera, which the editor or reporter uses to take pictures that will accompany any copy.

Advancement Prospects

Advancing to the next level of photo editor may be difficult, because newspapers usually only have one photo editor and many Photographers, so competition is stiff. Photographers are also expected to have at least five years' experience. Many Photographers prefer to remain Photographers, because they find it more exciting than working at a computer as a photo editor. Advancement will be aided by having excellent working relationships with the reporters and editors as well as by getting a reputation for producing compelling photographs in a timely fashion.

Education and Training

It is recommended that a Photographer have an undergraduate degree in photojournalism, but this is optional. Many accomplished news Photographers are self-taught. Today, however, majoring in photojournalism at an accredited journalism school is generally expected. In addition, Photographers should keep up with trends and technology changes in the field in terms of the newest and best digital camera equipment, zoom lenses, or any other tools that could improve their ability to get the portrait or action photograph that makes a story memorable.

Experience, Skills, and Personality Traits

A Photographer should have some experience as a news photographer for a school paper or as a freelance photographer. He or she should have a strong photographic sense, a gift for telling stories in pictures, and a photographer's eye, which is a natural talent for knowing when he or she has the shot.

Personality-wise, a Photographer must be brave, a team player, nonjudgmental, and able to do whatever it takes to get the shot.

Unions and Associations

The Photographer may be a member of the Newspaper Guild (www.newsguild.org). There are a number of associations to which a Photographer may belong, such as the National Press Photographers Association (www. nppa.org).

Tips for Entry

1. Work as a Photographer on a high school or college newspaper or as a freelancer for local or community newspapers.

2. Read *News Photographer,* published by the National Press Photographers Association (www.nppa.org), as well as *Editor and Publisher* (www.editorand publisher.com), regularly to keep up in the field and to review job postings.

3. Attend journalism conferences and go to seminars on photojournalism.

4. Network with photo editors and other Photographers at conferences and training programs offered by the National Press Photographers Association (www.nppa.org).

5. Check out the job fairs sponsored by the American Society of Newspaper Editors (www.asne. org).

6. Periodically check the help wanted ads in the local newspaper as well as such Internet sites as www.journalismjobs.com.

7. Carry your camera with you at all times so you are able to take pictures. If you happen to capture an image with news value, offer it to a newspaper for sale or as an example of your photojournalism abilities.

8. If you have friends or fellow students who have assignments for newspapers, ask if you could accompany them and take pictures for the story. Even if the photographs are not used, you could show a potential employer how you would have illustrated the story had you gotten the assignment.

9. Contact the photojournalism editor or the human resources department at specific newspapers and ask if they have any openings. Have a portfolio of sample photographs available to send electronically or through the mail if you are asked for work samples. (For a list of major companies, see Appendix V. You could also do an Internet search using search engines such as google.com for any newspaper daily or weekly by name to find the Web site and contact information.)

PAGE DESIGNER

CAREER PROFILE

Duties: Designs pages; creates the overall look of a newspaper by combining words and visuals (photographs, cartoons, artwork, and other graphics) in a compelling and appealing way that makes for easy and clear reading

Alternate Title(s): Art Director; News Designer; Page Editor

Salary Range: $35,000 to $75,000+

Employment Prospects: Fair

Advancement Prospects: Fair

Best Geographical Location(s): Major urban centers, such as New York, Los Angeles, Chicago, Boston, San Francisco, and Washington, D.C.

Prerequisites:

Education and Training—A bachelor's degree in journalism, with a specialization (major or minor) in design and graphic arts

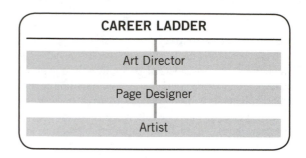

CAREER LADDER

Art Director

Page Designer

Artist

Experience—Several years of experience as a layout person, graphic designer, or photojournalist

Special Skills and Personality Traits—Should have a thorough knowledge of art direction, photography, photo editing, and design; strong design and photo editing skills; able to combine words and pictures in a visually captivating way; team player; enthusiastic; creative; knowledgeable; hardworking; able to perform under deadline pressure

Position Description

The Page Designer combines words and visuals to create the overall look of the newspaper. He or she works with photo editors and news editors to lay out the pages and special sections of the newspaper.

This is a relatively new position, coming into being in the late 1970s and flourishing in the 1980s as computers took over the newsroom and color began to appear on the front page of daily newspapers.

In order to compete with magazines and the growing popularity of the Internet, newspapers had to become easier to read and more colorful to look at. While it continues to be true that content is still more important, how that content is presented visually is becoming more and more significant.

The Page Designer tries to make each page and section compelling to look at. He or she combines skills as a designer with news judgment. On some newspapers, this position is actually called news designer, since that is what a Page Designer does: He or she designs the way the news is displayed.

Under the Page Designer heading, there are a number of related jobs, such as graphic artist, newsroom artist, and infographics specialist.

While Page Designers work on every page, the most important page is the front page. Like a magazine or

book cover, it is the front page that attempts to attract the readers' attention and makes this issue a "must read."

Page Designers not only deal with such obvious design choices as color or black white but also with more subtle graphic elements, such as styles of type faces, fonts, and strategically placed cut-lines.

Salaries

The salary for a Page Designer varies widely, depending on the newspaper's circulation and design needs. A Page Designer on a newspaper of 100,000 circulation might earn $35,000 a year, while Page Designers and art directors on larger papers in major markets receive $85,000 a year and up.

Employment Prospects

Employment prospects for Page Designers are fair, but they are improving as more and more newspapers are hiring them to redesign their pages. Still, only larger newspapers usually hire Page Designers.

Advancement Prospects

Advancing to the next level of art director may be difficult, because these positions are usually found on the largest newspapers and competition is tough. Page

Designers should have at least five years' experience before applying for a position as art director.

Education and Training

A Page Designer should have a bachelor's degree in photojournalism or newspaper design. A degree in graphic design is also helpful. Additional courses related to this area, including on the cutting-edge technology impacting the way the job is done, will also be useful.

Experience, Skills, and Personality Traits

A Page Designer should have pagination experience—he or she should have assembled or laid out pages of a newspaper, including copy, photographs, and ads. A Page Designer should have copyediting skills, have a strong sense of design, have strong news judgment, and be a team player. He or she will have worked as a news pagination editor, a graphics coordinator, or a graphic artist. A Page Designer will have working knowledge of software, such as Adobe Photoshop, Adobe Pagemaker, and FreeHand.

Unions and Associations

Page Designers may be members of the Graphic Artists Guild (www.gag.org). There are also several associations to which a Page Designer may belong, such as the Society for News Design (www.snd.org).

Tips for Entry

1. Join the Graphic Artists Guild (www.gag.org) and become active in a local chapter, if one is nearby.
2. Access the job line, updated regularly, at the Web site of the Graphic Artists Guild (www.gag.org), available to members.
3. Read *Editor and Publisher* (www.editorand publisher.com) regularly, and look for job openings; read other journalism publications, such as the *Quill,* to stay informed about the field.
4. Attend journalism conferences.
5. Network with other Page Designers through the Society for News Design (www.snd.org), which offers workshops and training.

PRODUCTION AND CIRCULATION

PRODUCTION DIRECTOR

CAREER PROFILE

Duties: Directs all production operations at the newspaper, including prepress, pressroom, maintenance, and transportation

Alternate Title(s): Director of Operations

Salary Range: $75,000 to $200,000+

Employment Prospects: Good

Advancement Prospects: Fair

Best Geographical Location(s): Major urban centers, such as New York, Los Angeles, Chicago, Boston, San Francisco, and Washington, D.C.

Prerequisites:

Education and Training—A bachelor's degree in newspaper production; training in printing management and technology

Experience—Several years of experience as a production manager and production coordinator

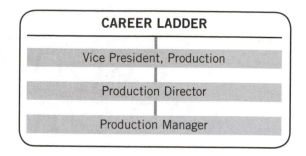

CAREER LADDER

Vice President, Production

Production Director

Production Manager

Special Skills and Personality Traits—Should have a thorough knowledge of newspaper production, printing systems, telecommunications, and information systems; be able to manage large groups of people performing factorylike functions to produce a daily newspaper out of newsprint, ink, and information; strong leader; technology oriented; team player; able to perform under deadline pressure

Position Description

The Production Director oversees all operations related to producing the newspaper. This includes all prepress activities, pressroom operations, and transportation of the newspaper to distribution points.

The prepress stage includes gathering all of the copy, visuals, design elements, and page designs and putting them through a process known as pagination, or the assemblage of all the elements on the page. Once this is done, a copy editor and page designer print a proof on a plain paper printer. Corrections are made and then digitized for sending over the Internet to the pressroom, which usually is miles away from the building housing the reporters, editors, and photographers.

Once corrected copies of the page proofs are made, they are released in digital files to production. This digital package is plated and put on a giant offset digital press, which means the paper does not even touch the plate.

On a typical day, the Production Director has an enormous responsibility, overseeing a large team of line managers, quality control professionals, process engineers, and a newsprint traffic control manager, among others.

The production staff and operation for a newspaper is a major part of the paper's overall expense. The Production Director's primary job is to make sure this

operation is as cost-effective as possible. He or she must keep up on the latest technology and innovations that could help keep costs down.

Salaries

The salary for a Production Director varies widely, depending on the newspaper's circulation and design needs. A Production Director on a newspaper of 100,000 circulation might earn $125,000 a year, while a Production Director on larger papers in major markets receives $200,000 a year and up. Small papers pay less.

Employment Prospects

Employment prospects for Production Directors are good, since most newspapers have one. However, a Production Director needs to have several years' experience in a variety of production jobs before rising to the position of Director.

Advancement Prospects

Advancement prospects are fair, as competition is stiff for this position and because it is usually found only on larger newspapers. Years of experience as Production Director are usually required before being promoted to vice president, and promotion often requires leaving to join a newspaper with a larger circulation or a newspaper group.

Education and Training

A Production Director should have a bachelor's degree in printing management and technology. Years of on-the-job training are also required in as many areas of production as possible.

Experience, Skills, and Personality Traits

A Production Director should have at least five years' experience in all phases of production. He or she should have once been a production manager or information systems manager.

He or she should have strong management skills and be able to run a factory that physically produces a daily newspaper under intense deadline pressure.

Unions and Associations

The Production Director is a member of management. There are a number of associations to which a Production Director may belong, such as the Newspaper Association of America (www.naa.org).

Tips for Entry

1. Read *Presstime* on a regular basis, as well as other printing trade publications.
2. Attend printing conferences.
3. Network with other Production Directors through local and national associations, such as the Newspaper Association of America (www.naa.org).

CIRCULATION DIRECTOR

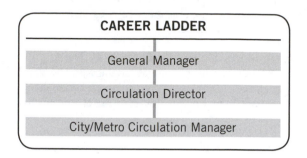

Special Skills and Personality Traits—Strong interpersonal and problem-solving skills; excellent written and oral communication skills; organizational and leadership skills; ability to work hard without the glory or public visibility usually associated with the reporter, editor, or photographer jobs at a newspaper; able to multitask and work with a wide array of distribution situations and individuals

Position Description

The Circulation Director reports to either the general manager or publisher and is responsible for all sales and distribution of the newspaper. On larger newspapers, the Circulation Director supervises a staff of circulation managers or carrier advisers, as well as the marketing, telemarketing, and promotion groups.

This staff includes a city/metro circulation manager, who supervises carriers, agency distributors, and wholesalers, as well as zone and district managers. Some papers, such as nationally distributed newspapers, even have regional marketing managers.

The Circulation Director works with a circulation marketing manager on sales strategies designed to increase circulation. The circulation market manager will know the demographic makeup of the newspaper's readers and design marketing campaigns aimed at that demographic. There may also be a circulation promotion manager, who is responsible for creating carrier incentives and recognition.

Another key member of the Circulation Director's staff is the circulation sales representative. He or she is responsible for circulation sales and customer service. The circulation sales manager solves customer service problems and assists independent distributors in ways to increase sales.

Circulation is very labor intensive and is a direct revenue-producing department. Indirectly, it also affects the newspaper's advertising revenue in that the larger a newspaper's circulation, the more it can charge for advertising space.

On a day-to-day basis, the Circulation Director not only oversees a department that is responsible for distributing the newspaper to subscribers and newsstands but also oversees promotion, marketing, transportation, and administration. This means the Circulation Director will interact with every other department in the newspaper.

The Circulation Director's management team works closely with the editorial, production, research, and marketing departments to determine who is reading the paper and how to best position it to attract new readers.

Salaries

Salaries for Circulation Directors vary widely, depending on the size and market of the newspaper. A newspaper with a circulation of 75,000 would pay its

Circulation Director between $53,000 and $95,000. On larger papers, a Circulation Director earns well into the six figures.

Employment Prospects

Circulation Director is a primary position at most newspapers, so employment prospects are good. As technology impacts a growing competition for readers, the role of Circulation Director has become even more important.

Advancement Prospects

Prospects for advancement to general manager are fair, since many people from several positions will by vying for that one job. The way to advance as a Circulation Director is to get a reputation for being a quick and pleasant problem solver, as well as for working effectively with those who report to you and for working hard to expand circulation.

Education and Training

Circulation Directors usually have a bachelor's degree in business, sales, or marketing. A graduate degree in business (MBA), although not a requirement, would be useful, especially for advancement.

This is definitely an on-the-job training position; actual experience at a small daily or weekly newspaper, whether as an intern or part-time during college, will help you to gain the basic skills in circulation that this senior position relies upon.

Experience, Skills, and Personality Traits

A Circulation Director will have at least five years' experience in circulation sales and marketing, as well as experience as a district manager supervising carriers.

Personality-wise, a Circulation Director should have good interpersonal and problem-solving skills, be able to write well and to speak clearly. He or she should be a leader, well organized, and willing to be available for problem solving 24 hours a day, seven days a week. Being able to delegate is important, as is being friendly and aggressive in generating new accounts and business to increase circulation.

Unions and Associations

The Circulation Director is part of management and is not usually in a union. Membership in newspaper publishing associations, such as the National Newspaper Association (www.naa.org), may be useful for networking and keeping up with trends in the industry through seminars and annual meetings.

Tips for Entry

1. Take a carrier or loading job or an entry-level job as a district manager and work your way up to circulation manager.
2. Network among Circulation Directors. Find out who might be moving to another newspaper and apply for his or her current job.
3. Check classified ads in newspapers as well as Internet sites, such as www.journalismjobs.com.

ADVERTISING AND MARKETING

ADVERTISING DIRECTOR

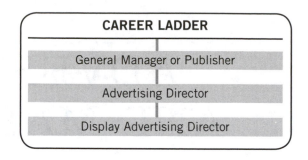

Position Description

The Advertising Director runs the advertising department, which includes all display and classified advertising, as well as national sales, where relevant. Editors and reporters may get all the glory and byline recognition, but it is the advertising department that brings in the money to pay everyone's salary. Advertising represents 70 to 85 percent of the newspaper's total revenues.

At a typical large paper, the Advertising Director has a staff of seven to 10 managers and account executives, each handling a different piece of the advertising pie. There is a display advertising manager, who handles all local and national display advertising, and supervises a group of outside sales representatives. Another manager handles classified ads, which can account for one-third to one-half of the newspaper's advertising revenues. Then there are the account executives, who actually sell advertising space to advertisers.

Traditionally, there is a wall between advertising and the editorial staff. This is to ensure that reporters covering a story will not be influenced if the story is about a company that spends millions of dollars in advertising every year. Because of this barrier, a negative story about a firm or local advertiser may cost the newspaper money if the company pulls its advertising over the

article. When this happens, it is up to the Advertising Director to muster his or her troops to find another source for those lost ad revenues.

On a daily basis, the Advertising Director will meet with various sales departments. He or she may start the morning working with the display advertising manager to come up with a way to keep a company from pulling its ads (because another paper or the local cable television service is offering a more competitive price). In the afternoon, he or she might meet with the classified advertising manager about developing new business strategies to boost the classified section.

Salaries

Salaries for Advertising Director vary widely, depending on a newspaper's circulation. However, even on small newspapers, the Advertising Director is one of the highest paid employees on the paper. For example, on a paper with just 20,000 circulation, the Advertising Director earns about $75,000 in salary plus bonus. On larger newspapers, Advertising Directors earn well into six figures.

Employment Prospects

Employment prospects for Advertising Directors are good, since nearly every newspaper in the country has one. Prospects for future employment should remain good, since newspapers depend on advertising for most of their revenue, and a good Advertising Director is a valuable asset.

Advancement Prospects

Prospects for advancement to general manager are poor, since many people from several positions will by vying for that one job. By developing a positive reputation for being able to manage employees well, to meet deadlines, and for hard work, you improve your advancement prospects. Generating new sources of advertising revenue, especially if it is a major account with repeat business, also helps you stand out in your position and increase the likelihood of promotions.

Education and Training

Advertising Directors tend to have a bachelor's degree in marketing, advertising, communications, or journalism. A master's degree in journalism or an MBA, with an emphasis on advertising, is recommended.

Experience, Skills, and Personality Traits

An Advertising Director will have several years of experience in all phases of advertising management and sales. He or she will be a skilled salesperson and marketer, be a creative leader and visionary, and possess strong writing and speaking talents.

Personality-wise, an Advertising Director will be an outgoing team player, friendly and gregarious, hardworking, and easy to get along with.

Unions and Associations

The Advertising Director is part of management and not in a union. Membership in associations such as the National Newspaper Association (www.naa.org) is useful for networking or keeping up with trends in the industry.

Tips for Entry

1. Work as a display or classified advertising manager.
2. Work in advertising or public relations at an advertising or public relations agency.
3. Network with Advertising Directors at the annual meeting of the National Newspaper Association (www.naa.org), as well as through local or regional associations.
4. Search job Web sites such as www.mediabistro.com or http://marketing=jobs.theladders.com.

MARKETING DIRECTOR

Position Description

The Marketing Director works with the advertising and public relations departments to create and manage marketing strategies that will increase circulation, strengthen the paper's market, and attract potential advertisers. To do this, the Marketing Director is responsible for a variety of types of promotion, from radio and television commercials to special events. For example, the newspaper might improve its visibility and image by sponsoring a fund drive or a concert to raise money for victims of a disaster, such as flooding or fire.

Another popular method aimed at reaching younger readers is to take part in education programs in which free copies of the newspaper are given out to schools, who then distribute the papers to their students. The strategy here is to generate interest among potential future readers. Having guest speakers from the newspaper's reporting or editorial staffs address classes in public or private schools, as well as at colleges, also helps to highlight the educational, business, and career benefits of reading a newspaper.

At larger newspapers, the Marketing Director will have a staff that might include a marketing specialist who writes press releases and handles event promo-

tions. He or she may also have a creative director who supervises a staff of copywriters, designers, and photographers whose sole function is to develop advertising campaigns for the newspaper.

There may also be a marketing data analyst who analyzes the newspaper's marketing efforts. Then there may be a promotion manager responsible for in-house advertising, circulation, promotion, and advertising in other mediums such as radio, television, or the Internet.

At smaller papers, the Marketing Director will handle all of these tasks. Depending on the size of the newspaper, an average day for a Marketing Director would include meeting with the advertising and public relations departments to coordinate the latest marketing strategy, reviewing ad copy and press releases, overseeing any event promotions coming up, going over the most recent market data from the research department to see how the paper is performing alongside its major competitors, and possibly even negotiating with vendors who supply marketing and promotional material to get a price break on brochures or printing.

Salaries

The salary for a Marketing Director varies widely, depending on the newspaper's size. The average salary is somewhere between $80,000 and $120,000 (higher for the largest newspapers).

Employment Prospects

Employment prospects for Marketing Directors are fair, since most newspapers need to market themselves. However there is intense competition for this position among marketing specialists, promotion managers, and creative directors.

Advancement Prospects

Advancing to the next level of vice president of marketing could require moving to a larger newspaper. Many smaller papers do not even have this title, in which case the Marketing Director, advertising director, and circulation director would all be vying for the job of general manager. Building the regional and national reputation of the paper during the years you serve as Marketing Director will help increase your chances of being hired for the next spot. Winning awards in all departments and letting the newspaper's management and the community know about those awards will also enhance your advancement prospects.

Education and Training

A Marketing Director should have a bachelor's degree in marketing, communications, or journalism. It is also recommended that he or she have a graduate degree in business (MBA).

Experience, Skills, and Personality Traits

A Marketing Director should have four to six years of marketing management experience. He or she should have strong creative, management, and communica-tions skills and be able to manage a sizable marketing and promotions staff.

Personality-wise, he or she should be friendly, outgoing, and have a positive attitude, since the Marketing Director is the newspaper's representative to potential advertisers and readers.

Unions and Associations

The Marketing Director is a member of management and not usually in a union. There are a number of associations to which a Marketing Director may belong, such as the International Newspaper Marketing Association (www.inma.org).

Tips for Entry

1. Work as a marketing specialist or promotion manager.
2. Get marketing experience in other industries.
3. Attend newspaper marketing conferences.
4. Network with other Marketing Directors through the International Newspaper Marketing Association (www.inma.org) and its annual World Congress, as well as through regional seminars throughout the year.
5. Keep up on trends in the industry by reading online and print publications about the newspaper business, such as *Editor and Publisher* (www.editorandpublisher.com), as well as articles posted at the International Newspaper Marketing Association Web site (www.inma.org).
6. Check the Web sites of associations and publications as well as job search sites for possible openings, such as www.hotjobs.com, www.journalismjobs.com, www.careerbuilder.com, www.mediabistro.com, www.monster.com, and http://marketing=jobs.theladders.com.

NEW MEDIA
DEPARTMENTS

NEW MEDIA DIRECTOR

CAREER PROFILE

Duties: Directs the newspaper's entire online operation, including supervising the online editor (who manages the reporters and online producer)

Alternate Title(s): New Media Manager

Salary Range: $46,000 to $120,000+

Employment Prospects: Fair

Advancement Prospects: Fair

Best Geographical Location(s): Major urban centers, such as New York, Los Angeles, Chicago, Boston, San Francisco, and Washington, D.C.

Prerequisites:

Education and Training—A bachelor's degree in communications, journalism, or marketing, with specialization in digital or new media, is required; graduate work in journalism and new media is recommended

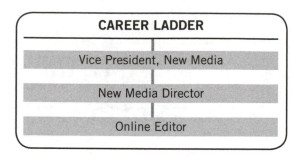

CAREER LADDER

Vice President, New Media

New Media Director

Online Editor

Experience—Experience as a general manager, executive editor, or online editor

Special Skills and Personality Traits—Creative; strong communication skills; innovative; strategic planning and leadership skills; flexible about scheduling; hardworking; able to meet multiple deadlines

Position Description

The New Media Director supervises all areas of the newspaper's online operations, including all editorial, advertising, marketing, technical, and design decisions. At larger newspapers, the New Media Director will have a staff that includes an online editor, a newsroom liaison, an online producer, a staff of editors and writers, and a webmaster. There will also be online advertising directors, an online sales representative, an online marketing director, and online designers and artists.

Unlike the print version of newspapers, which has one or possibly two deadlines a day, the online operation has what is called a 24-hour deadline. That means a breaking news story can appear on the newspaper's Web site at any time, day or night, whenever it is ready to run. It is not unusual for a newspaper's Web site to break a story, which enables it to compete with radio and television, rather than waiting until the newspaper is ready to run it. If a newspaper's Web site breaks a story, the newspaper gets credit for it.

For the New Media Director, one key challenge is to help the newspaper to expand into markets that the print version of the paper cannot reach. This has a major impact on advertising, since some local advertisers, seeking to reach a wider market, might be influenced by a newspaper's Web site to buy ad space online, even if they were reluctant to purchase ads in the print version.

Some publications might also offer the online version as an added benefit of advertising in the print version; the ad runs in the print version for that day, but it is archived for a certain period of time, or even indefinitely, as part of that initial fee or for an additional cost.

One of the New Media Director's key responsibilities is to cultivate these advertisers. Online classified ads are another important source of revenue, since they are now available to a much larger audience. This allows newspapers with Web sites to charge more for a classified ad.

At smaller papers, one person may be responsible for every role, from online editor to webmaster.

Salaries

The salary for a New Media Director varies widely, depending on the newspaper's size. The average salary is somewhere between $46,000 and $120,000 and higher for the largest newspapers.

Employment Prospects

Employment prospects for New Media Directors are only fair, since only large newspapers usually employ them.

Advancement Prospects

New Media Directors can advance to the position of vice president of new media, though competition is stiff. Advancement generally requires moving to a larger newspaper. Bringing in lots of new advertisers, winning awards for your online efforts, and increasing print circulation or online subscribers will help your ability to advance.

Education and Training

A New Media Director should have a bachelor's degree in communications, journalism, or marketing, with a specialization or at least courses in digital media. A graduate degree in journalism, communications, or a related field is recommended.

Experience, Skills, and Personality Traits

A New Media Director should have experience running an online operation or as an online editor or as a webmaster.

He or she should have strong management and communications skills, be able to handle a variety of tasks from editorial to technical, and be proficient in advanced HTML, CGI, and other programs needed to maintain Web servers.

A New Media Director will be a team player, have excellent people skills, and be intelligent, well organized, creative, detail oriented, and a hard worker.

Unions and Associations

The New Media Director is usually a member of management. There are a number of associations to which a New Media Director might belong, such as the Online News Association (www.onlinenewsassociation.org).

Tips for Entry

1. Work at online journalism sites as a webmaster, online editor, or online producer.
2. Check out the job listings posted at journalism and job sites on the Internet, such as www.journalism jobs.com and www.mediabistro.com. Check in the newspaper classified ads as well.
3. Enter competitions for online journalism organized by the Online News Association, such as the Online Journalism Awards in the categories of independent or affiliated Web sites. (See www. journalists.org/awards/enter/index.html for further details.)
4. Attend online conferences, such as the annual meeting of the Online News Association (www. journalists.org).
5. Network with other New Media Directors at meetings, seminars, and conferences organized by other journalism associations, such as the National Newspaper Association (www.nna.org) or the American Society of Newspaper Editors (www.asne.org).

ONLINE EDITOR

CAREER PROFILE

Duties: Responsible for a newspaper Web site's editorial content, including deciding what content will be put on the daily online version, coordinating the acquisition of any additional text (including statistics, links to other articles, sources, or Web sites; and photographs or graphics), and making sure that all content is posted on time

Alternate Title(s): Online Producer; Online Manager; Online Director

Salary Range: $45,000 to $120,000+

Employment Prospects: Fair

Advancement Prospects: Fair

Best Geographical Location(s): Major urban centers, such as New York, Los Angeles, Chicago, Boston, San Francisco, and Washington, D.C.

Prerequisites:

Education and Training—A bachelor's degree with a major or minor in communications, journalism, or information technology is required, with additional courses in Web design, writing for the Inter-

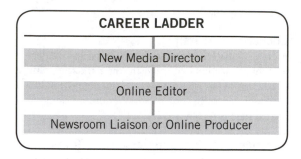

CAREER LADDER

New Media Director

Online Editor

Newsroom Liaison or Online Producer

net, or Web page management; a graduate degree in journalism, publishing, or information technology is recommended

Experience—Several years of experience as an editor or online producer or writer are required, especially for larger newspapers

Special Skills and Personality Traits—Strong journalism skills, including writing and editing; some technical skills; strong leadership and management skills; detail oriented; able to perform under constant deadline pressure; ethical; honest

Position Description

The Online Editor is the editor in chief of the newspaper's Web site. He or she is responsible for all editorial content as well as any other electronic publishing efforts. To do this job, the Online Editor works with two editorial staffs—the writers, editors, content producers, and freelancers assigned to the new media department and the editorial staff of the newspaper's print unit.

An Online Editor tends to be more concerned with the Web site's overall content than with the words or photos in any given story. (The online producer will probably be working directly on specific assignments or stories with the staff or freelance reporters, especially at larger newspapers.) This means the Online Editor will be interested in additional content that does not appear with articles in the printed paper but which will support those articles online. This additional content can be in the form of a searchable database of statistics, audio and video clips pertaining to a story's subject, or a poll the Web site is conducting regarding views and opinions on a subject or person.

Sometimes the Web site will include original content, and it is the Online Editor's responsibility to make sure this is accurate and up-to-date. This becomes especially important when the Web site "breaks" a story, or runs a story before it appears in the next printed version of the newspaper. When this happens, the Online Editor takes on the same function as the executive or managing editor of the print edition. He or she must make sure the story is accurate, its sources are credible, and it follows the newspaper's journalistic style and policy. He or she will also manage the freelance reporters who might write original articles or gather additional material for the online edition. The Online Editor will work with an online producer to create this additional content, including its design and function.

Salaries

The salary for Online Editors will vary, depending on the newspaper's size and market. The average salary is between $45,000 and $120,000. It can be higher for the largest newspapers.

Employment Prospects

Employment prospects for Online Editors are fair. Not all newspapers have this position, although most large newspapers do.

Advancement Prospects

Online Editors face stiff competition when seeking to advance to new media director, a position limited to larger papers. At many papers the Online Editor is the top position when it comes to the online version of the newspaper. In this case, advancement requires moving into another job category that is higher in terms of job responsibilities or salary or relocating to another paper, probably with a larger circulation.

Education and Training

An Online Editor will probably be expected to have a bachelor's degree in journalism, communications, or information technology, with training in Web site design, development, and maintenence as well as writing or editing for the Internet. A related graduate degree, or additional courses to keep up with online journalism trends and technology, is also recommended. On-the-job training, beginning in middle school, high school, or college, developing and maintaining a Web site, including the editorial content and the related graphics or photographs, will be a useful background.

It is also important for the Online Editor to have an instinct and knowledge about the differences in layout design, and even length between original articles posted to the Internet and those of traditional print newspapers. The Online Editor should know how to break up text with additional headings, the size of the font, and how to code the content to facilitate searching for an article by the name of the reporter or by keyword search, title, or the name of those mentioned in the story.

Experience, Skills, and Personality Traits

Online Editors should have broad journalism experience as editors, reporters, and online producers, as well as strong editorial, reporting, and leadership skills. He or she should be a creative problem solver, ethical, honest, and able to work hard under constant deadline pressure. Since at many newspapers the online edition takes the daily content and reformats or archives it, rather than breaking stories and providing original articles, the Online Editor needs to be someone who is comfortable with being out of the limelight. He or she needs to be at ease with the accolades garnered by the print version, reporters, and editors, as they are usually considered the online version's key content providers. Among those who edit online versions, however, there will be an appreciation of how unique and specialized the Online Editor's skills are in creating an effective, distinctive, accurate, and easily searchable online version of the paper.

Unions and Associations

The Online Editor could be a member of management. If not, he or she may be a member of the Newspaper Guild (www.newsguild.org). There are a number of associations to which an Online Editor might belong, such as the Online News Association (www.online-newsassociation.org).

Tips for Entry

1. Work at online journalism sites as a reporter or online producer.
2. Attend seminars and take courses in online production and editing.
3. Network with other Online Editors at the conferences offered by the Online News Association (www.onlinenewsassociation.org).
4. Check out the job openings listed in the print and online versions of *Editor and Publisher* (www.editorandpublisher.com) available to subscribers; www.journalistusa.com (fee-based job search site); and such free job sites as www.journalismjobs.com, www.mediabistro.com, www.hotjobs.com, and www.monster.com.
5. Network with the faculty and alumni at your college or graduate school. Attend reunions or participate in a career day, if they offer one for alumni and new students. Keep the school informed on your activities, especially if they also sponsor a job bank for new and former students.

RESEARCH
AND EDUCATION

NEWS LIBRARIAN

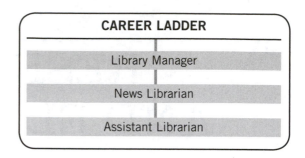

Position Description

The News Librarian runs the newspaper's vast library, which was once called the "morgue." This is a massive job in that a News Librarian is responsible for collecting, filing, and cross-referencing an enormous amount of information that pours in daily.

Beside filing articles into a cross-reference subject file, the News Librarian is responsible for clipping articles from other publications, retrieving stories and photographs from other newspapers, and then preparing them for review by the editorial staff or the general public who has access via the Internet.

Larger newspapers will have a library manager, who will have a staff and several assistants, while smaller papers will often rely on one News Librarian and an assistant, often an intern.

News Librarians are a valuable resource to reporters, columnists, and editors. They are the keeper of a vast storehouse of knowledge and can often point a lost reporter in the right direction when researching stories.

Technology has affected the News Librarian's job as much as any other on the newspaper. With the Internet providing instant access to information it once took hours or even days to collect, News Librarians have to keep up to date on the latest online search engines and research resources available.

Unfortunately, the Internet has also had a negative impact on this position: As newspapers seek ways to trim costs, the News Librarian position is often seen as vulnerable when reporters and editors can access some of the same information directly by going online. But the News Librarian should have such a superior, seasoned knowledge of information and research that he or she can show reporters or editors how to find resources and information that they cannot easily find on their own.

Salaries

The average salary for a News Librarian will depend on the size of the newspaper. At a newspaper with a circulation of 50,000, a News Librarian could earn between $25,000 and $30,000. At larger newspapers, a veteran News Librarian could earn as much as $75,000.

Employment Prospects

Employment prospects for News Librarian are poor, since many smaller papers are eliminating this position, due to the Internet making the search for information, once the News Librarian's job, easier for reporters and editors to accomplish themselves.

Advancement Prospects

Advancing to the next level of library manager is difficult, since there are fewer and fewer openings in this category.

Education and Training

A News Librarian should have a bachelor's degree in library science; a graduate degree is recommended. It is also beneficial to take courses in news research and journalism.

Experience, Skills, and Personality Traits

A News Librarian should have experience as a librarian for either a school newspaper or a local library or as an assistant News Librarian.

Skills include being able to quickly file and cross-reference material under a variety of subjects and being detail oriented, well organized, a skilled researcher, able to think under deadline pressure, able to take directions, and able to deal with others who are under pressure.

Unions and Associations

The News Librarian may or may not be a member of the Newspaper Guild (www.newsguild.org), depending on the newspaper.

Tips for Entry

1. Read *Editor and Publisher* (www.editorand publisher.com) on a regular basis for job postings, as well as other journalism publications and *Library Journal,* which may also list available jobs.
2. Attend journalism conferences.
3. Network with other News Librarians.

JOURNALISM PROFESSOR

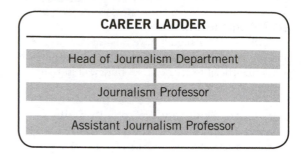

Position Description

The Journalism, or J School, Professor, unlike many college professors in other subjects, such as English or sociology, will spend much of his or her time supervising journalism students in on-the-job activities. The theory here is that the best training for a would-be reporter or editor is to do the actual work.

Some professors even arrange their classes to resemble newsrooms, while others get students assignments at local newspapers or on the college newspaper. Most, if not all, Journalism Professors are either former veteran or current journalists who teach to supplement their income or because they like the interaction between teacher and student.

As Leonard Mogel points out in his excellent book, *The Newspaper,* at one of the nation's top journalism schools, the University of Missouri's School of Journalism in Columbia, students and Journalism Professors work together writing, editing, and designing a daily community newspaper called the *Columbian Missiourian,* which has been published since 1908.

Mogel notes that a similar situation occurs at Syracuse University's S. I. Newhouse School of Public Communications. A visiting Journalism Professor who taught "News Reporting" in spring 1999 required that his class read two textbooks plus the *AP Stylebook and Libel Manual;* the local daily newspaper, *Syracuse Post Standard;* the school's paper, *Daily Orange;* and the Sunday *New York Times.* Students also had to read an online newspaper and begin writing stories during the very first week of class. "By week 15, they will have written 10 beat stories, a profile, and even an obit," Mogel notes.

At other journalism schools, such as the University of Minnesota's School of Journalism and Mass Communications, students are required to study general college courses for most of their first or second years. At that point, they apply for the J School, and, if accepted, they also pick a specialization in journalism, advertising/public relations, or mass communication.

Some Journalism School Professors will specialize in particular areas of journalism or communications, such as public relations or advertising.

Like other college professors, Journalism Professors will teach a varying number of courses; for each they must prepare a detailed syllabus outlining what they intend to teach during the semester, an overview for the course usually with a week-by-week list of topics to be covered, and required reading assignments or written work due, as well as information about required readings and the final grade breakdown (with the weight for class participation, attendance, midterm exam, final, and any papers or writing assignments). Many Journalism Professors are required to work with students on the school paper or local community paper. Typically, they are required to hold regularly scheduled office hours for meetings with students or department heads.

Salaries

Salaries for Journalism Professors depend on a variety of factors. These include the Journalism Professor's rank, the school in which he or she teaches, and the part of the country in which the school is located. One of the major factors in salary is whether or not a Journalism Professor works full time or part time, whether or not he or she has a master's degree or a doctorate, and his or her number of years teaching in general or at a specific school. Average salaries for Journalism Professors range from $31,000 to $120,000 and higher for top-ranked professors in one of the top 10 journalism schools.

Employment Prospects

Employment prospects for Journalism Professors are fair, since so many schools and universities have either journalism schools or departments or offer journalism courses. As with all college teaching today, it is harder to get a full-time appointment with salary and benefits than it is to get a position as an adjunct, teaching just one or more courses on a per-course basis. At the high school level, teaching journalism is often done in addition to teaching English or creative writing courses as well as supervising the students who run the monthly high school newspaper. This is a very competitive field as well, and in the larger communities and at the more prestigious high schools, having educational credentials in journalism and on-the-job newspaper journalism experiences will be required. In smaller or rural communities, as well as in high schools with fewer faculty competing to get a job there, educational or work-related requirements may be less stringent. As long as you are willing to learn on the job, they might be open to your application if they are desperate for a journalism teacher and newspaper adviser.

Advancement Prospects

Advancement prospects are poor, since competition for the position of journalism department head is extremely intense. You can increase your desirability as a candidate for this position if, under your tutelage, the college newspaper gains awards and your former students tout you and their education as the reason they have landed the top spots in the most prestigious newspapers throughout the country and world. If, in addition to teaching and advising, you are able to continue working full time or part time at a top newspaper or syndicate, advancing your own reputation as a journalist as well, you may also help your prospects of moving up the ladder.

Education and Training

A full-time Journalism Professor should have a graduate degree in journalism as well as on-the-job training as a journalist or in newspaper management, especially if he or she hopes to achieve tenure. For part-time (adjunct) teaching positions, especially at the undergraduate level, some schools may wave the academic requirements in favor of 10 or more years of on-the-job experience as a journalist at a major newspaper. Other schools may still require an undergraduate or graduate degree, plus related work experiences.

At the high school level, journalism teachers may also teach English or creative writing. A bachelor's degree in journalism and experience working for a school or professional newspaper are recommended and required in those communities with a surplus of qualified applicants to draw upon. In smaller or rural areas, however, those credentials and related experiences may not be required but are highly recommended.

If necessary, take courses or attend seminars on effective presentation skills and teaching techniques to enhance your teaching skills.

Special Requirements

The Journalism Education Association (www.jea.org) has educational and test procedures for becoming a certified journalism educator for those with a bachelor's as well as master's degree. To teach journalism in a high school, there may be state teaching licensing and certification requirements that have to be considered and met.

Experience, Skills, and Personality Traits

Journalism Professors have broad journalistic experience as editors, reporters, and communications professionals. The more firsthand experience the Journalism Professor has had, the more he or she may enliven the lectures with real-life examples.

He or she should have strong communication, presentation, and leadership skills. Journalism Professors should be inspirational and motivational, as well as taskmasters to prepare students for the often grueling work of a reporter or editor.

Journalism Professors should be outgoing, social, ethical, and honest. Being able to give feedback to students so they are motivated to work harder and better is another skill that a Journalism Professor needs to master and excel at teaching. Bringing in occasional guest speakers, which usually depends on having a wide network of associates and friends who are willing to share with your students for no financial gain, will also help you enrich your classes.

Unions and Associations

Journalism Professors may belong to a number of associations, such as the Society of Professional Journalists (www.spj.org), the Journalism Education Association (www.jea.org), and the National Press Club (npc.press.org).

Tips for Entry

1. Work as an assistant Journalism Professor or gain experience as a part-time or adjunct Journalism Professor so you have college-level teaching experience.
2. Work as a guest lecturer at a journalism school.
3. Attend journalism educational conferences.
4. Network with other Journalism Professors at local or national meetings of journalism associations, such as the American Society of Newspaper Editors, the American Society of Journalists and Authors, the Journalism Education Association, the Society of Professional Journalists, and the National Newspaper Association. (See Appendix III for complete listings.)
5. If you attended a journalism school, network with fellow alumni.
6. Visit your alma mater and let them know that you're interested in a teaching position. Check want ads that might be posted on the bulletin board or on the Internet at the Web site for the journalism school you attended. You could also consider posting a notice that you are looking for a teaching position or contact the department chair at the journalism schools where you would like to teach.
7. Read the major journalism print and online publications and check the classified ads for possible teaching positions, including www.editorand publisher.com, www.mediabistro.com, www.journalismjobs.com, www.hotjobs.com, www.monster.com, and www.careerbuilder.com, as well as the Web sites of the leading newspaper associations that have job listings or career sections available to members.
8. For public high school journalism teacher positions, check with the local school district and see if there are any openings in the upcoming months or year. Find out if there are private schools lacking a school newspaper who might hire someone who could teach journalism as well as work with students to run the school paper.
9. Develop an internationally renowned reputation as a newspaper journalist or editor so that colleges invite you to be a visiting or full-time Journalism Professor.

MANAGEMENT

PUBLISHER

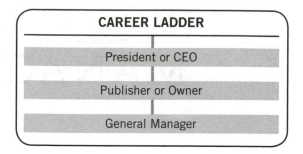

Position Description

Publisher is one of the top positions at a newspaper. He or she is responsible for the newspaper's bottom line, either as an owner or to a president (CEO) and board of directors, as well as for the publication's editorial performance. As boss, the Publisher runs the newspaper, overseeing every phase of its operation, from editorial and advertising to production and circulation. It is the Publisher's responsibility to produce a profitable and well-regarded newspaper.

Depending on the size of the paper, some Publishers take a more hands-on approach to the day-to-day management of the paper. They get actively involved in editorial, advertising, and production decisions.

The Publisher also sets the policy, style, and tone of the newspaper. Basically, he or she determines its editorial slant, such as whether it is politically conservative, liberal, or moderate. The Publisher is supposed to embody and personify what the newspaper stands for. For example, Rupert Murdoch, who is the publisher of the *New York Post,* among other newspapers, is seen as someone who publishes conservative newspapers. The late Katharine Graham, longtime publisher of the *Washington Post,* had a more liberal or moderate reputation.

At larger newspapers the Publisher will have a management staff that includes a general manager and business manager. At smaller papers the Publisher will usually assume those roles and responsibilities along with many others, sometimes including the positions of editor, senior reporter, and copy editor.

At a large newspaper, one of the Publisher's most important responsibilities is to hire the paper's editor; it is the editor who will, in turn, direct the Publisher's editorial policies. The relationship between Publisher and editor thus becomes the key to the success or failure of the newspaper.

A Publisher's day is a made up of a variety of tasks, from budget reviews to meetings with top advertisers. He or she will also keep up on what is happening in the newsroom, such as what big or controversial stories are coming up and what legal entanglements might be encountered down the road.

There will be times when the Publisher and editor disagree, such as whether to run a special edition that would cost more money but possibly attract more readers and attention. Other times they might clash over running a controversial story that could lose advertisers. Hopefully, the Publisher's decision will be whatever is in the best interest of the newspaper.

Salaries

Salaries for Publishers for small papers with a circulation of less than 15,000 would be around $50,000. For papers with a circulation of 50,000 to 75,000, the Publisher's salary jumps to more than $140,000. For the nation's top newspapers with a circulation of more than 1 million, Publishers can earn more than $350,000.

Employment Prospects

This is the top position at any newspaper. There is not a lot of turnover, so prospects for employment are poor.

Advancement Prospects

Advancing to the next level of president of a newspaper is extremely difficult, since competition is so stiff, especially at a larger daily or a newspaper that is part of a major chain. Publisher is usually as high as you can go in the newspaper industry. Developing an excellent reputation for helping a newspaper to achieve excellence in reporting, generating revenue, and staying within budget will help your advancement possibilities.

Education and Training

A bachelor's or master's degree in journalism or communications is recommended but not a requirement. Having an MBA (master's in business administration) or training as a certified public accountant may be just as important.

Experience, Skills, and Personality Traits

As a Publisher, you will need experience in as many functions of a newspaper as possible, from editorial and advertising to production and circulation. Many Publishers have never been editors, but they must all be good businesspeople. They probably have experience running a company and now want to own their own newspaper, or they have worked on the business side of newspaper publishing, perhaps in circulation or advertising.

Skills include being strongly business- and management-minded and being a leader and a visionary. Publishers have a strong desire to make a difference and to effect change. They take pride in keeping the public informed and have a commitment to keep freedom of speech alive.

Unions and Associations

The Publisher is a member of management and not in a union. There are a number of associations to which a Publisher might belong, such as the Newspaper Association of America (www.naa.org).

Tips for Entry

1. On your own or with the help of other investors, purchase a newspaper that is for sale. Document how you are the best person to run the newspaper and to grow their investment, because you have newspaper publishing experience, you have journalism or business credentials, you are a quick study, or you will surround yourself with competent administrative, advertising, circulation, and editorial staff.
2. Start a newspaper from scratch.
3. Take on as many jobs at a newspaper as possible to gain experience in all aspects of newspaper publishing, from editorial and advertising to circulation and production.
4. Read *Editor and Publisher* (www.editorandpublisher.com) regularly, as well as other journalism publications, to keep up on trends in newspaper publishing.
5. Attend regional and national newspaper conferences.
6. Network with other newspaper Publishers and publishing groups.

GENERAL MANAGER

CAREER PROFILE

Duties: Reporting directly to the publisher, the General Manager oversees the advertising, circulation, and production departments and the business office; responsible for profit and loss

Alternate Title(s): Editor/General Manager

Salary Range: $75,000 to $200,000+

Employment Prospects: Poor

Advancement Prospects: Poor

Best Geographical Location(s): In any city that is large enough to have a major newspaper

Prerequisites:

Education and Training—A bachelor's degree in business is required; an MBA and training as a certified public accountant are recommended; journalism courses are helpful

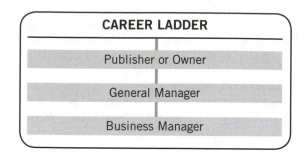

CAREER LADDER

Publisher or Owner

General Manager

Business Manager

Experience—Newspaper advertising, circulation, and production; budget management

Special Skills and Personality Traits—Excellent management and leadership skills; superb business sense; ethical; bottom-line oriented; team player

Position Description

The General Manager is just under the publisher on the business side of the management hierarchy at a newspaper. He or she is the top executive responsible for advertising, circulation, and production. The General Manager is equal to the editor in power and prestige. He or she is also responsible for whether the paper makes or loses money.

Working closely with the business manager, the General Manager makes such business decisions as whether the paper should expand its circulation area or whether to increase the price of subscriptions or single copies. A General Manager also keeps a close eye on advertising sales and production. He or she will decide when a printing press or system needs to be upgraded and replaced.

It is up to the General Manager to balance the various needs of the newspaper's sectors (advertising, circulation, production, and editorial). He or she has to keep up on the latest printing technologies as well on strategies to improve circulation.

The General Manager will often be involved in contract negotiations with the newspaper's various unions.

Typically, the position of General Manager is found only at larger newspapers. At smaller publications, either the publisher or business manager would handle tasks assigned to a General Manager.

Salaries

The average salary for General Managers at a newspaper with a circulation of 50,000 is approximately $116,000. At a paper with a circulation of 100,000 to 150,000, the average salary for General Manager is $174,000. At larger papers, a General Manager may earn well over $200,000.

Employment Prospects

This is a position with little turnover at any newspaper, so prospects for employment are poor.

Advancement Prospects

Advancement to the next level of owner or publisher is extremely difficult, since competition for the top job is stiff. Not only is the General Manager after this position, but so are other publishers of smaller newspapers, some editors, and other owners or publishers who are seeking to expand their newspaper empire.

Education and Training

A General Manager should have a bachelor's degree in business. A graduate degree in business, such as an MBA, or training as a certified public accountant is also useful.

Experience, Skills, and Personality Traits

As a General Manager, you will need experience in advertising, circulation, and production. Many General

Managers will have been business managers, directors of production, and heads of advertising.

A General Manager should be business- and management-minded, be detail oriented, and have a very clear sense of bottom line. He or she should also be able to manage and work with creative people.

Unions and Associations

The General Manager is a member of management and is not in a union. There are a number of associations to which a General Manager may belong, such as the Newspaper Association of America (www.naa.org).

Tips for Entry

1. Intern or work part time or full time during college or graduate school in a newspaper's business office.
2. Read *Editor and Publisher* (www.editorandpublisher.com) regularly, as well as other journalism publications.
3. Attend newspaper conferences.
4. Network with publishers and other General Managers.

BUSINESS MANAGER

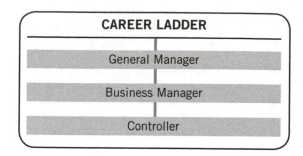

Position Description

The Business Manager reports to the general manager or publisher and is responsible for all financial information needed to manage the business side of the newspaper, such as advertising sales, circulation, and accounting. For example, the Business Manager would be able to advise the general manager or publisher as to whether it made financial sense to update the paper's printing process as a way to lower production costs.

The Business Manager also keeps track of financial data relating to circulation, such as whether current circulation regions are meeting profit margins or need to be expanded or reduced.

Other areas the Business Manager oversees include newsroom operations and promotion. An example of financial decisions he or she might be involved in would be whether to add or delete a special section or to eliminate redundant news services. As for promotion, the Business Manager oversees marketing budgets.

The Business Manager schedules daily or regular meetings with the heads of the departments he or she oversees and helps them make strategic financial decisions for their departments. The editor may need to add a reporter to the city desk to cover expanded coverage of city hall. It would be up to the Business Manager to review this head-count addition and issue a recommendation for or against it to the general manager or publisher.

In advertising, the sales director might want permission to take his or her biggest advertisers on a weekend to reward them for their loyalty. The Business Manager would be involved in reviewing whether such a trip would be a sound financial decision.

Salaries

The average salary for Business Managers at a paper with 50,000 circulation is $50,000. At larger papers, a Business Manager may earn well over $100,000. At a paper with more than a million circulation, the salary for Business Manager is more than $125,000.

Employment Prospects

This is a top position at any newspaper, on par with an editor or production manager. Therefore, competition is stiff and employment prospects only fair. At some newspapers, individual managers for the advertising sales, promotion, circulation, and accounting departments report directly to the publisher. At these papers the Business Manager position may not exist.

Advancement Prospects

Advancement to the next level of general manager is difficult, since competition is so fierce. Heads of circulation, production, and advertising are also trying to climb the ladder to general manager. As Business Manager, one way to advance is to get hired by a larger newspaper or a chain.

Education and Training
A Business Manager is required to have a bachelor's degree in business and should have passed the CPA exam. An MBA is recommended.

Experience, Skills, and Personality Traits
As a Business Manager, you will be expected to have at least three to five years of experience in advertising, circulation, and promotion. You will need strong business and management skills. Business Managers are detail oriented and have a strong sense of the bottom line.

Unions and Associations
The Business Manager is a member of management and is not in a union. There are number of associations to which a Business Manager might belong, such as the Newspaper Association of America (www.naa.org).

Tips for Entry
1. Read *Editor and Publisher* (www.editorandpublisher.com) regularly, as well as other journalism publications.
2. Take a lower-level job, such as assistant controller, and work your way up.
3. Attend journalism conferences.
4. Network with general managers and other Business Managers.

CONTROLLER

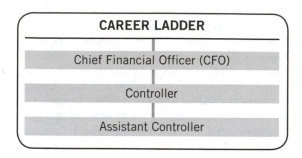

Position Description

A Controller makes sure that all of the newspaper's accounting and financial records are kept properly. The Controller prepares all financial and operational statements, supervises accountants, and prepares an annual corporate budget for the newspaper company. The Controller reports either to the chief financial officer or to the president of the parent company.

At a large newspaper, the Controller could be in charge of a staff of 25 people. At smaller papers, the Controller may be the only person assigned to keep financial records.

Unlike the business manager, who is involved in financial strategies, such as pricing, promotion, and new product development, the Controller's task is to ensure the proper accounting of all expenses and revenues to internal and external auditors.

The need for accurate accounting plays a key role in short-term and long-term financial planning, billing, credit and collection operations, computing taxes, general accounting, and financial control functions.

Controllers do more than just present figures in a quarterly or monthly income statement. They must also be able to explain those figures, so they have to understand the newspaper business.

Salaries

The average salary for a Controller is from $35,000 to $58,000 at newspapers with under 100,000 in circulation. At larger papers, a Controller may earn well over $75,000.

Employment Prospects

Employment prospects for Controllers are fair in that most newspapers need at least one. These days with proper financial accounting coming under closer public scrutiny, the need to have accurate financial statements is even greater.

Advancement Prospects

Prospects for advancement to the next level of chief financial officer are fair; competition is stiff.

Education and Training

In addition to a bachelor's degree in finance or business, a Controller is required to have at least passed the CPA exam and, in many cases, have an MBA as well.

Experience, Skills, and Personality Traits

As a Controller, you will need experience in accounting and bookkeeping. Controllers have to be honest, ethical, and experienced in all areas of accounting as well as informed about all new accounting rules and regulations.

You will need strong business skills, be detail oriented, and have a keen sense of the bottom line.

Unions and Associations

The Controller is a member of management and is not in a union. There are number of associations to which a Controller may belong, such as the American Institute of Certified Public Accountants (www.aicpa.org).

Tips for Entry

1. Read *Editor and Publisher* (www.editorand publisher.com) regularly, as well as other journalism publications.
2. Attend business and journalism conferences.
3. Network with financial executives of newspapers and other Controllers.

PART II
MAGAZINE PUBLISHING

EDITORIAL

EDITOR IN CHIEF

CAREER PROFILE

Duties: Responsible for the magazine's content, style, vision, and editorial philosophy; involved in all editorial decisions as well as in budget planning and marketing

Alternate Title(s): Editor; Editorial Director

Salary Range: $25,000 to $275,000+

Employment Prospects: Good

Advancement Prospects: Poor

Best Geographical Location(s): Anywhere magazines are published, which today is practically anywhere

Prerequisites:

Education and Training—A bachelor's degree is expected and a master's degree is recommended; on-the-job training for several years at one or more magazines

Experience—Seven to 10 years' experience in various magazine writing and editing jobs; some experience in marketing and management

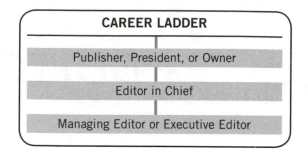

CAREER LADDER

Publisher, President, or Owner

Editor in Chief

Managing Editor or Executive Editor

Special Skills and Personality Traits—Creative; intelligent; artistic; strong leadership skills; able to delegate; able to spot and nurture writing talent; able to provide for an atmosphere of teamwork; outgoing; personable; able to communicate the magazine's vision and philosophy; knowledgeable about what readers want

Position Description

As the magazine's top creative person, the Editor in Chief is mainly responsible for guiding the publication's vision, content, and philosophy to the satisfaction of its audience. To do this, he or she makes all final decisions on articles and artwork, including photographs, cartoons, and graphic elements.

Although he or she reports to the publisher or owner, the Editor in Chief is in charge of the editorial or creative staff as well as concerned with the overall design and look of the magazine. Not only does the Editor in Chief guide the editorial and creative aspect of the magazine, but he or she works closely with the publisher on budget planning and with the advertising and public relations departments on sales and marketing.

The Editor in Chief needs to be a visionary in order to anticipate what content the magazine's audience will respond to in several months or a year or two in the future. Whereas newspapers report on the day's events, a magazine's content is often planned months ahead of publication, while appearing timely and important when it appears in print. In this regard, the Editor in Chief will often be working on several issues of the magazine at the same time. For example, he or she may be putting the finishing touches on next month's issue,

along with working on what stories to promote, changing the cover story on the following month's magazine, and editing articles for future issues.

The Editor in Chief is also responsible for hiring the best editors, writers, photographers, and other key staff members, along with creating an environment that inspires teamwork, cooperation, and innovation.

Perhaps the greatest responsibility for any Editor in Chief is to know better than anyone what the magazine's readers want from every issue. To do this, he or she must get out into the world to meet with the readers by offering to be a guest speaker at lunches, dinners, or conferences or to give talks at community groups. (Today, most Editors in Chief also have an e-mail address that they list in the magazine or in the masthead, inviting readers to share their concerns.)

For the Editor in Chief, one of the most important decisions that plays a large factor in the success or failure of any given issue is what to put on the cover. While many staff members, such as the art director, publisher, and managing editor, will contribute their opinions, it is usually left to the Editor in Chief to make the final decision about who or what will be on the cover, as well as what subject will be the cover story. In some cases, the publisher may have final say on the cover.

Salaries

There is a wide salary range for Editors in Chief, depending upon the size and scope of the magazine and whether it is local, national, or international. Average salaries range from $45,000 to $110,000. Some celebrity magazine editors or editors of major national magazines will earn more. According to *Folio* magazine's 2006 salary survey, the lowest-paid Editor in Chief at consumer magazines made $25,000, while the highest-paid earned $275,000 a year.

Employment Prospects

With more and more magazines springing up all the time, the job of Editor in Chief has good employment prospects, since every magazine needs an editorial leader.

Advancement Prospects

Editor in Chief is the highest creative position in a magazine, so for many this is the apex of a career. Advancement prospects for Editors in Chief moving up to become publishers or owners (or CEOs) are poor. Plus, not all good Editors make excellent publishers, which is a more business-oriented position responsible for the magazine's profit and loss statement.

Education and Training

An Editor in Chief is expected to have a bachelor's and a master's degree is recommended in communications, journalism, or marketing. Most who have the Editor in Chief position get on-the-job training, first as a magazine writer, then as a managing or executive editor.

Experience, Skills, and Personality Traits

A magazine Editor in Chief has to be in touch with the world around him or her. He or she should be a visionary with a keen eye toward future trends and an excellent judge of good writing. As the boss of the magazine's editorial staff, the Editor in Chief should be a good manager, able to delegate work according to staff size while also offering guidance to developing talent, such as writers, editors, and photographers.

Personality-wise, an Editor in Chief should be outgoing, personable, and able to personify the magazine's philosophy and outlook, while also being a mentor, leader, and salesperson.

Unions and Associations

There are no unions for magazine Editors in Chief, but there are a number of related associations to consider joining, such as the American Society of Magazine Editors (www.magazine.org/Editorial/ASME).

Tips for Entry

1. Work your way up from managing editor or executive editor. Position yourself to be next in line should the current Editor in Chief be retiring, leaving for a bigger magazine, or needing to be replaced.
2. Attend conferences sponsored by the American Society of Magazine Editors (www.magazine.org/Editorial/ASME).
3. Network with other Editors in Chief and publishers.
4. Develop a reputation for being able to attract top writing talent and for heading a magazine that gets critical writing and design awards and is profitable and internationally acclaimed.
5. Think up a concept that could, in time, define your magazine, such as the list of the 100 best companies to work for that is published annually by *Working Mother*. Your vision, creativity, and ability to direct and expand may lead to offers from other magazines to head up their publication.
6. Search the online job sites that specialize in editor jobs such as www.journalismjobs.com, www.mediabistro.com, and the job bank of Magazine Publishers of America (www.jobs.magazine.org).

MANAGING EDITOR

CAREER PROFILE

Duties: Manages the editorial staff, making sure that articles are finished on schedule; maintains deadlines; hires and fires staff as well as freelance writers and photographers; responsible for getting all editorial content to the art department on time for layout

Alternate Title(s): Executive Editor

Salary Range: $40,000 to $75,000+

Employment Prospects: Good

Advancement Prospects: Good

Best Geographical Location(s): Anywhere magazines are published, but more often in major urban centers, such as New York, Los Angeles, Chicago, Boston, San Francisco, and Washington, D.C.

Prerequisites:

Education and Training—A bachelor's degree is required; on-the-job training at one or more magazines is expected

Experience—Five to seven years' experience in various writing and editing jobs at a magazine, prefera-

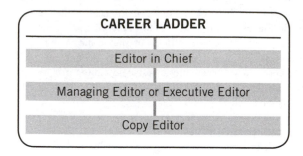

bly in the same type of magazine—such as consumer or specialized—and in the same or a related genre, such as health, parenting, or news

Special Skills and Personality Traits—Detail and deadline oriented; creative; intelligent; artistic; strong leadership skills; able to recognize writing and photographic talent; strong editing and writing skills

Position Description

Reporting directly to the editor in chief, the magazine's Managing Editor is in charge of the day-to-day editorial operation, keeping all article, photography, and art assignments on track, setting and maintaining deadlines, conceptualizing and handing out assignments, and cultivating and keeping a strong stable of freelance writers. Some Managing Editors may even write some of the articles in the magazine on a steady or occasional basis.

The Managing Editor works in hand-in-hand with the editor in chief to keep the editorial content moving steadily through to completion and on time. He or she is often the last person to see an article before it goes to the art department for production, so the Managing Editor is responsible for catching any errors that were not caught before.

Many Managing Editors work with a tracking chart to follow the detailed progress that an article is making, checking that the writer and photographer (if one is assigned) are going to make their deadlines. Since different assignments will have distinct lead times, there are often a variety of deadlines that the Managing Editor has to track.

On some magazines, the Managing Editor may also be the editor in chief, especially if that title is given to the person in charge of a group of magazines. Other magazines have an executive editor instead of a Managing Editor, while some even have both an executive editor and a Managing Editor. This may be the result of having an editor in chief who is primarily a writer and may lack necessary administrative or management skills. In these cases, you might see the title executive editor for someone who focuses more on schedules, budgets, and administrative responsibilities.

Salaries

There is a wide salary range for Managing Editors, depending on the size and scope of the magazine. Salaries range from $55,000 a year at smaller magazines to $75,000 or more at top national publications. According to *Folio* magazine's 2006 survey of salaries, the lowest-paid Managing Editor earned $35,000 and the highest-paid made $200,000 a year.

Employment Prospects

Most magazines have a Managing Editor; therefore, employment prospects are good. This is also a highly competitive position, and while positions are available, there will be many copy editors and writers seeking to fill them.

Advancement Prospects

Prospects for Managing Editors advancing up the ladder to editor in chief are good, since this is the normal career track. However, reaching the top spot in the magazine editorial hierarchy takes a lot of work and experience. There is also stiff competition for this coveted and often glamorous position. Increase your chances for advancement by getting a reputation as a Managing Editor who has control over the editorial content in her or his magazine, with writers and photographers meeting their deadlines and issues staying on schedule.

Education and Training

A Managing Editor will probably be expected to have an undergraduate degree in communications or journalism; a graduate degree is recommended. Years of on-the-job training in magazine writing and copyediting or as a senior editor of a particular section is also expected.

Experience, Skills, and Personality Traits

A magazine's Managing Editor is an experienced supervisor, line editor, proofreader, and writer. He or she is knowledgeable about all areas covered by the magazine. As a taskmaster, the Managing Editor may seem to have a demanding personality. He or she must be detail oriented, deadline focused, and have strong leadership skills and experience in most magazine editorial positions. The Managing Editor has to have an eye for recognizing talent among writers, photographers, and artists.

Unions and Associations

There are no unions for magazine Managing Editors, but there are a number of associations to which it may be helpful to belong. These include the American Society of Magazine Editors (www.magazine.org/Editorial/ASME) and the American Society of Journalists and Authors (www.asja.org).

Tips for Entry

1. Work your way up from senior writer or copy editor.
2. Attend conferences sponsored by the American Society of Magazine Editors (www.magazine.org/Editorial/ASME).
3. Network among other Managing Editors or editors in chief.
4. Develop a reputation for being able to meet deadlines in copy editor, staff writer, or freelance writer positions.
5. Attend dinners and conferences organized and staffed by those in the magazine field, such as the annual American Society of Journalists and Authors Writers Conference. If asked to be a guest speaker, accept as a way of increasing your visibility in the magazine and writing field. Network with other editors and writers.
6. Check the online or print job openings posted in *Editor and Publisher* magazine (www.editorand publisher.com) and at www.mediabistro.com, www.journalismjobs.com, www.hotjobs.com, www.career builder.com, and www.monster.com.

SENIOR EDITOR

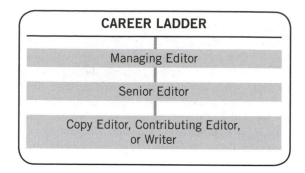

Position Description

The role of Senior Editor varies from magazine to magazine. At some magazines, the Senior Editor is the editorial head of a department, such as fashion or finance. At other publications, a Senior Editor may be a feature editor or a staff writer responsible for major articles.

In many cases, a Senior Editor will generate story ideas, create writing assignments for staff writers or freelancers, and work with writers to make sure the articles fit the style and tone of that particular magazine. For example, an article on dating for *Seventeen* will read differently from one written for *Newsweek*.

In those situations where Senior Editors are section editors or department editors, they are expected to have a solid working knowledge of whatever area they are covering. Fashion editors should be plugged into the fashion industry, while entertainment editors should have contacts and sources in Hollywood and New York.

Reporting to either the editor in chief or the managing editor, Senior Editors play a key role in keeping content fresh and provocative by being part of the creative collaboration that goes into producing each issue.

On some magazines, a Senior Editor will not only be a wordsmith, but he or she may also be asked to come up with ideas for photographs to accompany a particular article.

Salaries

There is a wide salary range for Senior Editors, depending on the size and scope of the magazine. Salaries range from $40,000 a year at smaller magazines to $80,000 or more at top national publications.

Employment Prospects

Most magazines have one or more Senior Editors, so employment prospects are good. But since this is a much sought-after editorial position, there will be lots of competition from writers and junior editors seeking to fill any job openings.

Advancement Prospects

Prospects for Senior Editors who wish to advance up the ladder to managing editor or editor in chief are good, since this is the normal career track. However, it may mean switching to another magazine. To increase your chances of advancement, develop a stable of excellent and award-winning freelance writers that you can call on to fill any assignment with excellent articles delivered on time. Be pleasant to work with and get along with those you report to. Develop a reputation as a valued and exceptional editor as well as a strong writer.

Education and Training

Today, a bachelor's degree is usually required for most editorial positions on a magazine, and Senior Editor is no exception. He or she will most likely have a bachelor's degree in communications or journalism, with a major or at least courses in magazine writing or creative writing, and a graduate degree is recommended. At least three years of on-the-job training in magazine writing and editing will also be expected.

Experience, Skills, and Personality Traits

A Senior Editor should be highly organized, a skilled wordsmith, and both detail and deadline oriented. As part of a collaborative process, he or she should be a team player, energetic and hardworking, creative, and inquisitive. Strong editing and proofreading skills are a must, and versatility is a plus. Since Senior Editors have to work with freelancers, they should have some management ability, along with necessary proficiency on both Macintosh and PC-based computers. Many magazines use Quark or Adobe software, so a knowledge of that is useful.

Unions and Associations

Since some magazines are unionized, check with the Newspaper Guild (www.newsguild.org) to find out if a particular magazine and this position are unionized.

There are a number of associations to which it may be helpful to belong. These include the American Society of Magazine Editors (ASME) (www.magazine.org/Editorial/ASME) and the American Society of Journalists and Authors (ASJA) (www.asja.org). ASME offers member lunches and roundtables monthly in New York City. Beginning in 1996, a two-day magazine workshop for junior editors was initiated for additional training for those pursuing a magazine career. ASJA offers monthly educational dinners and programs as well as an annual all-day conference in the spring with dozens of guest speakers from magazine and book publishing and several hundred attendees.

Tips for Entry

1. Work your way up from senior writer, contributing editor, or copy editor.
2. Attend conferences, including the fall job fair sponsored in New York by the American Society of Magazine Editors (www.magazine.org/Editorial/ASME) and the annual spring conference offered by the American Society of Journalists and Authors (www.asja.org).
3. Network with other Senior Editors.
4. Edit school papers and newsletters; write for those publications as well.
5. Check the job listings in the print and online version of newspapers, at journalism job sites, and at general job search sites, such as the Sunday *New York Times*, www.mediabistro.com, www.careerbuilder.com, www.hotjobs.com, and www.monster.com.
6. Develop a track record writing for a magazine. Once you have an excellent relationship with the section editor or Senior Editor that you report to, let him or her know that you are open to a full-time staff job if one becomes available.

CUSTOM PUBLISHING EDITOR

Position Description

The custom publishing division of a magazine or publishing organization produces content for corporate magazines or newsletters. Typically, a custom publishing editor will work with a company's marketing department to develop editorial content that provides information for a target audience that can be internal (such as the company's sales force) or external (such as clients and prospects).

The editor in custom publishing is responsible for interpreting client creative briefs as well as conceiving, developing, and executing a high quality of editorial content across multiple platforms to exceed clients' marketing objectives and their aspirations for the work.

Successful custom publications are primarily based on a client's marketing objectives. For example, a financial services company has targeted high–net worth investors and commissioned a quarterly publication aimed at that market. It will be up to the editor to make sure the content will be compelling, interesting, and informative as well as appealing to that particular audience segment.

Custom Publishing Editors work on both ongoing as well as solo magazine projects. He or she monitors and maintains deadlines, develops story ideas, manages freelance writers, updates the editorial lineup, plans, attends, and runs interdepartmental meetings, handles proofs, and oversees all copy and research. The editor may also act as a project manager who coordinates writers, designers, and photographers. At some companies the job may entail travel; some jobs require writing the article as well as editing, but other positions have the editor assigning articles to freelance writers and then working in more of a supervisory and editing capacity rather than primarily as a writer.

Salaries

Salaries for Custom Publishing Editors range from $70,000 to $110,000 a year.

Employment Prospects

Since custom publishing is still considered one of the more profitable divisions in publishing, employment prospects are good.

Advancement Prospects

Advancement prospects from editor to managing editor or executive editor are fair.

Education and Training

A four-year college degree is preferable, in English, journalism, or communications, along with experience in editing a magazine or newspaper. Three to five years experience in magazine editing and Web technology is a typical requirement.

Experience, Skills and Personality Traits

This person must have a strong copyediting background, be extremely detail-oriented and organized, have a tremendous ability to follow through on assignments and with individuals, and have the ability to manage a variety of responsibilities at one time. Since most custom publishing content is specialized to a particular industry, such as financial service, air travel, or high tech, an editor should have educational or practical experience in that sector as well.

Unions and Associations

It may be helpful for the Custom Publishing Editor to be a member of associations that include the target industry in which the editor is publishing, such as the National Association of Realtors if you are publishing a newsletter or magazine for real estate agents. There is an organization for custom publishers, Custom Publishing Council (www.custompublishingcouncil.com), which offers networking and educational opportunities as well as a listing of job openings in the industry.

Tips for Entry

1. Learn about how custom publishing is different from or similar to traditional publishing, and how custom-published magazine and newsletter products compare to these products for consumers.

2. Find out what companies have the most jobs in custom publishing and the kinds of industries that they service.

3. Have your CV/résumé up to date and ready to e-mail. Have it in the following forms: text, HTML, Word document (older versions), and PDF. All versions, except for the text version, should have easy-to-read clickable links to your editing or writing work samples.

4. Put together a minimum of five published samples of your work. Many think they can just send links, but the companies want these printable. Put the examples in a Word document and PDF for easy e-mailing as an attachment. It can be a single file or five separate files. Keep file sizes to a minimum. To demonstrate editorial skills, you might want to show how an article read and looked in its original format and how you edited and formatted it for publication. Since many editor positions require writing as well as editing copy, be prepared to show articles you have written, preferably for a custom publication, as well as those you have edited.

5. Check out the job listings at the Web site for Custom Publishing Council (www.custompublishingcouncil.com) as well as at the major job hunting Web sites, including www.monster.com, www.mediabistro.com (for media-related jobs), www.hotjobs.com, and www.careerbuilder.com.

COPY EDITOR

CAREER PROFILE

Duties: Checks all editorial copy, including each article, title, or pull-quote; corrects any errors in grammar, style, punctuation, and spelling; reads copy for any errors in fact or potentially libelous statements; corrects syntax; fixes awkward or poor writing

Alternate Title(s): Copy Chief

Salary Range: $20,000 to $73,000+

Employment Prospects: Good

Advancement Prospects: Good

Best Geographical Location(s): Anywhere magazines are published, but more often in major urban centers, such as New York, Los Angeles, Chicago, Boston, San Francisco, and Washington, D.C.; for some magazines this job could also be handled out of the office on a freelance basis

Prerequisites:

Education and Training—A bachelor's degree is required, in most cases, with a major or minor in journalism, specializing in magazines, or writing; on-the-job training at one or more magazines

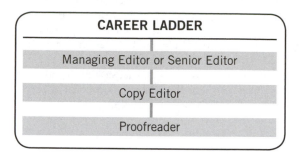

CAREER LADDER

Managing Editor or Senior Editor

Copy Editor

Proofreader

Experience—Three to five years' experience in proofreading and fact checking

Special Skills and Personality Traits—Detail-oriented; excellent grammar and spelling; strong writing skills; able to handle intense deadline pressure; proficiency in Adobe InDesign or Quark CopyDesk and QuarkXPress; strong knowledge of style manuals, especially *Associated Press Style Book* or the *Chicago Manual of Style*

Position Description

Copy Editors read and check the magazine's editorial content before it goes into production, including every article, title, subtitle, caption, cutline, and pull-quote. The Copy Editor's job is to correct errors in grammar, spelling, usage, punctuation, and style. Each magazine has its own style of how words are used, and it is up to the Copy Editor to know and follow this style. Sometimes it is up to the Copy Editor to even create some stylistic guidelines whenever unusual or special situations arise.

The Copy Editor reports to the managing editor. He or she works closely with senior and associate editors when getting articles in shape for publication. For example, if the Copy Editor feels some writing is unclear or awkward, he or she may either fix the problem or return the article to a senior or associate editor, who will then decide whether to rewrite it themselves or send it back to the writer for alterations.

One common misconception regarding Copy Editors is that they are merely proofreaders. Proofreaders only look for typographical, punctuation, or spelling errors; Copy Editors deal with that and much more,

including whether or not an article is well organized and the writing style fits the magazine's distinctive form.

An important part of a Copy Editor's job is watching out for libel. Every now and then, damaging information makes its way into an article that might cause harm to someone's reputation or ability to earn a living. Often it is because the information is false, and someone failed to find that out before the information was included in the article. Most magazines have fact checkers to check information before it goes to the printer, but it is the Copy Editor who then has the responsibility to make sure all facts have been checked when he or she reads the copy. It is often the Copy Editor who is the last to see the copy before it goes to print.

Salaries

Like most editorial positions on a magazine, there is a wide salary range for Copy Editors, depending on the size and scope of the publication. Salaries range from $25,000 a year on smaller magazines to $73,000 or more on top national publications.

Employment Prospects

Most magazines have one or more Copy Editors, so employment prospects are good. Turnover is fairly rapid as well, since this job is very demanding and also seen as a stepping-stone to higher-paying editing or management jobs; there are usually openings for this position in most metropolitan areas.

Advancement Prospects

Advancement prospects for Copy Editors are improving. At one time Copy Editor was considered a dead-end job, relegated to burned-out writers nearing the end of their careers. This is not the case anymore, as more up-and-coming writers seeking experience in editing take on this job on their way to managing editor or editor in chief.

Education and Training

A Copy Editor usually has a bachelor's or master's degree in communications or journalism, with a major, or at least courses, in magazines. There are courses in copyediting for magazines in college, even for those who do not major in journalism. Postgraduate educational opportunities are also available, such as taking the magazine-related courses offered at the intensive summer publishing institutes organized each year at New York University, Columbia University, and other colleges. (See Appendix II for a list.) On-the-job training to learn a magazine's style is also very important.

Experience, Skills, and Personality Traits

A Copy Editor is an experienced proofreader and writer, and he or she should be computer literate, a strong grammarian, a great speller, and wordsmith. Personality-wise, a Copy Editor should be detail-oriented, inquisitive, intelligent, and able to work under the stress of deadline pressure. It is also important that the Copy Editor's ego be strong enough that he or she can edit a story and still maintain the writer's "voice" and style, as well as the magazine's style, without having to impose his or her own style on the material.

Special skills include a working knowledge of Quark CopyDesk and XPress or Adobe InDesign and an intimate knowledge of style manuals, such as the *Chicago Manual of Style* or the *Associated Press Stylebook*.

Unions and Associations

Since some magazines are unionized, check with the Newspaper Guild (www.newsguild.org) to see if a specific magazine and the job of Copy Editor are covered by a contract or minimum salary requirements. Most positions, however, are not unionized.

There are a number of associations to which it may be helpful to belong. These include the American Society of Magazine Editors (www.magazine.org/Editorial/ASME), the American Society of Journalists and Authors (www.asja.org), and the Editorial Freelancers Association (www.the-efa.org).

Tips for Entry

1. Work your way up by showing your skills as a good writer, editor, and proofreader.
2. Attend conferences and network with other Copy Editors through the American Society of Magazine Editors (www.magazine.org/Editorial/ASME), including their annual fall job fair held in New York City.
3. Copyedit smaller magazines or newsletters to get practice, and keep samples of the "before" and "after" of your work.
4. Work as a paid or unpaid intern at a magazine while in college, whether it is a school-sponsored publication or a local magazine.
5. If you are an editorial assistant or a fact checker at a magazine, offer to copyedit an article in addition to your regular job duties to show that you can do it.
6. Check out the online and print job openings available through www.mediabistro.com, www.hotjobs.com, www.journalismjobs.com, www.monster.com, the Sunday *New York Times* classified ads, and others.
7. Go to the Web sites for the major magazine companies, such as Hearst, Primedia, Condé Nast, and Time. (See Appendix V for contact information.) Job openings at the various magazines are often listed at the corporate headquarters Web site or at the sites for the individual magazines. Apply for specific job openings; get your résumé and a work sample to the human resources department to keep on file if a Copy Editor job opens up.

ASSOCIATE EDITOR

Duties: Assists senior editors and managing editor in assigning shorter articles; writes and edits front-of-the-book or back-of-the-book content; writes the table of contents; creates the titles and subtitles for the articles

Alternate Title(s): Assistant Editor

Salary Range: $25,000 to $60,000+

Employment Prospects: Good

Advancement Prospects: Fair

Best Geographical Location(s): Anywhere magazines are published, but more often in major urban centers, such as New York, Los Angeles, Chicago, Boston, San Francisco, and Washington, D.C.

Prerequisites:

Education and Training—A bachelor's degree is required; graduate degree in journalism or communications is recommended; on-the-job training at one or more magazines

CAREER LADDER

Senior Editor

Associate Editor or Assistant Editor

Staff Writer

Experience—Two to three years of experience in writing, fact-checking, and editing magazine articles

Special Skills and Personality Traits—Able to work under deadline pressure; strong writing skills; organized; detail-oriented; creative; intelligent; proficiency in a variety of publishing software, such as Quark CopyDesk and XPress; able to use either a Macintosh or PC computer; motivated; a team player

Position Description

The Associate Editor position varies from magazine to magazine, but, in most cases, this position assists senior editors or the managing editor in preparing the magazine's content for publication.

Some magazines have both Associate Editor and assistant editor positions. Both titles are about equal in stature, although the assistant editor title tends to imply more administrative-type responsibilities, such as filing, research, and answering the phone.

Associate Editors may be called upon to write and edit full-length articles, but most often they are assigned front of the book (such as brief articles) or back of the book material (such as brief first-person essays). These are usually special departments, in which articles tend to be shorter and fall within specific categories.

On some magazines, the Associate Editor writes the table of contents and what is called the contributor's page. This may include succinct biographies of the freelance writers who have articles in the magazine or summaries of those articles.

Since the Associate Editor reports to either a senior editor or the managing editor, duties are determined by the needs of his or her supervisor. Some senior editors want their assistants to help come up with titles for articles, while others do not.

Salaries

The average salary for Associate Editors ranges from about $25,000 to $60,000 a year. Some Associate Editors may earn more, but this is still considered a junior position, one step up from fact checker and editorial assistant. Many Associate Editors earn less than writers, even though they appear to be at a higher rank on the masthead.

Employment Prospects

Most magazines have one or more Associate (or assistant) Editors, so employment prospects are good.

Advancement Prospects

Advancement prospects are fair for Associate Editors, who will have to compete with other Associate Editors and staff writers for the senior editor position. To increase your chances of advancement, get a reputation for working well with others as well as for being detail oriented and hardworking. If writing articles is also part of your job, do your assignments well and within your deadline, but make sure your administrative duties are also handled effectively and efficiently.

Education and Training

A bachelor's degree is usually required for most editorial positions on a magazine. An Associate Editor probably will have a bachelor's or master's degree in communications or journalism, as well as at least two years of on-the-job training in magazine writing and editing.

Experience, Skills, and Personality Traits

An Associate Editor should be highly motivated, a team player, organized, and a skilled writer and editor. He or she must be willing to take mundane assignments; senior editors will usually reward hard workers with better assignments.

Like most editors, Associate Editors need to be proficient in magazine software, such as Quark and Adobe programs.

Unions and Associations

Most magazines are not unionized, but since some magazines are, check with the Newspaper Guild (www. newsguild.org) for information about a specific publication. (They maintain a list of magazines that are unionized.)

There are associations to which it may be helpful to belong such as the American Society of Magazine Editors (www.magazine.org/Editorial/ASME).

Tips for Entry

1. Work your way up from senior writer, contributing editor, or copy editor.
2. Attend conferences sponsored by the American Society of Magazine Editors.
3. Network with other Associate Editors at seminars and at annual writing workshops, such as the American Society of Journalists and Authors Writers Conference held each spring.
4. Write for and edit school or college papers and community newsletters to gain a range of experiences.
5. Check out print and online job listings at *Editor and Publisher* (www.editorandpublisher.com) and the Sunday *New York Times,* as well as such sites as www.mediabistro.com or www.hotjobs.com.
6. Visit the Web sites of companies that publish a variety of magazines, such as Condé Nast (www. condenast.com), Time (www.timeinc.com); Primedia (www.primedia.com), and Hearst (www. hearst.com). Check their job listings for current openings at the various magazines, or visit the individual Web sites for each publication.

ONLINE EDITOR

CAREER PROFILE

Duties: Edits and oversees the magazine's Web site, which may be a sample of the magazine's current issue or contain separate original content

Alternate Title(s): Content Editor; Content Manager

Salary Range: $25,000 to $90,000+

Employment Prospects: Good

Advancement Prospects: Fair

Best Geographical Location(s): Anywhere magazines are published, but more often in major urban centers, such as New York, Los Angeles, Chicago, Boston, San Francisco, and Washington, D.C.

Prerequisites:

Education and Training—A bachelor's degree is expected

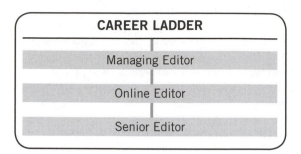

Experience—Three to five years' experience in magazine editing and online production

Special Skills and Personality Traits—Creative; intelligent; artistic; strong writing and editing ability; able to recognize good story ideas; inquisitive; energetic; motivated

Position Description

An Online Editor is in charge of a magazine's Web site. This position is becoming more and more important, as most magazines now have an Internet presence in some form, from offering entire electronic versions of the magazine by subscription to teaser sites that encourage people to either buy or subscribe to the printed version.

The Online Editor oversees the creation and production of all content on the magazine's Web site. At larger magazines, he or she will have an editorial and production staff to handle the content. At smaller publications, the Online Editor might be responsible for doing everything. The Online Editor is also in charge of editing online articles, archiving the current issue on the site, and creating additional original content.

Normally the Online Editor reports directly to the magazine's editor in chief. While acting as a liaison between the print magazine staff and the online staff, the Online Editor is responsible for all online content. Sometimes, content is created solely for the Web site. Some Online Editors write some of the content themselves, alongside a staff of writers (who may also work for the print version of the magazine) and a stable of freelance writers. Experts may write online columns that also need to be edited and posted to the site.

If a development dates an article that appeared in the print version, the Online Editor can update the online version with that new information. Online Editors can link articles to related stories, create "search" features

for previous content, and offer video versions of some stories. Selecting photographs or art to accompany an online article is another job for the Online Editor.

Salaries

Since this is a relatively new position, the income range for Online Editors tends to mimic that of print editors. At smaller publications, salaries are low, starting at $25,000 but averaging as much as $90,000 at larger national publications.

Employment Prospects

More and more magazines are using Online Editors, so employment prospects are good.

Advancement Prospects

Prospects for advancement from Online Editor to managing editor are fair at best, since there are so many editors competing for the top slots. Obtaining a reputation for producing an excellent online version that gets picked up in the major search engines, as well as attracting additional subscribers to the online or print magazine, will help your advancement options.

Education and Training

An Online Editor is expected to have a bachelor's degree and perhaps a graduate degree in magazine editing or communications and will have established himself or herself in magazine publishing.

Experience, Skills, and Personality Traits

An Online Editor is creative, inquisitive, and an innovative wordsmith. He or she is energetic and willing to explore different angles on the same story, prolific, dependable, and hardworking. Online publishing has different demands and concerns than print publishing. The Online Editor knows what those differences are and how to make those variations work to the advantage of the content and the look of his or her online magazine. Although this is changing, there is still more status to the print version of most magazines; the Online Editor has to be secure enough that he or she is not discouraged or disappointed by that perception.

Unions and Associations

There are no unions for magazine Online Editors, but there are a number of associations to which you may belong, such as the Online News Association (www.journalists.org).

Tips for Entry

1. Develop a reputation as a solid editor and innovative online writer and editor.
2. Attend conferences sponsored by the American Society of Journalists and Authors.
3. Network with other Online Editors and editors in general.
4. Develop a reputation for being able to produce provocative Web sites.
5. Get awards for your publication from associations, such as the Online News Association.

EDITORIAL ASSISTANT

Duties: Performs administrative and clerical work; conducts research; makes photocopies; files; opens and sorts mail; answers e-mails and the phone; assists editors or a specific editor at the magazine

Alternate Title(s): Administrative Assistant; Fact Checker/Editorial Assistant

Salary Range: $20,000 to $36,000+

Employment Prospects: Good

Advancement Prospects: Good

Best Geographical Location(s): Anywhere magazines are published, but more often in major urban centers, such as New York, Los Angeles, Chicago, Boston, San Francisco, and Washington, D.C.

Prerequisites:

Education and Training—A bachelor's degree is expected; a degree in journalism with a concentration in magazines from one of the top journalism programs (see Appendix I) will be helpful

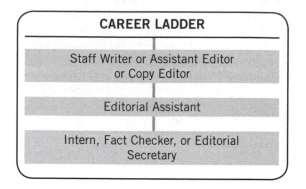

CAREER LADDER

Staff Writer or Assistant Editor or Copy Editor

Editorial Assistant

Intern, Fact Checker, or Editorial Secretary

Experience—One to two years' experience in magazine writing or editing; any administrative jobs during school, college, or summers will help

Special Skills and Personality Traits—Creative; intelligent; artistic; strong writing ability; able to recognize good story ideas; inquisitive; energetic; motivated; able to meet deadlines and take orders

Position Description

Editorial Assistant is an entry-level position at most magazines that may or may not include fact-checking duties. In the position of Editorial Assistant, someone will usually work for one, two, or sometimes three senior editors, providing administrative support, such as filing, answering phones, opening mail, making copies, and doing research.

In some cases, Editorial Assistants are given writing assignments, such as short, back-of-the-issue or front-of-the-issue pieces. This position and that of fact checker are the two primary ways of breaking into the editorial side of magazine writing.

An Editorial Assistant is the equivalent of the individual working in the mail room of a literary agency. They often work in these low-level positions for a couple of years, then move up to staff writer.

Salaries

As an entry-level administrative job, this position is underpaid and is basically just a way to get your foot in the door. In time, it may lead to a more prestigious and lucrative career. For starters, however, even at the larger magazines, an Editorial Assistant may earn between $20,000

and $36,000 a year. Some Editorial Assistants supplement that income with freelance writing assignments for other publications, freelance editing, or research projects.

Employment Prospects

Employment prospects for Editorial Assistants are good, because there is a lot of turnover for this entry-level job, with most only lasting one to three years in the position before moving up or on to a different career.

Advancement Prospects

Prospects for advancement are usually good if Editorial Assistants have gotten along with their bosses and done their work efficiently and effectively. If you feel thwarted at one magazine, you may have to go to another one, but at least you will have gained experience to advance to the next level. The next level could involve editing, writing, or copyediting. It may be necessary to take another Editorial Assistant position in a different department or area of magazine publishing if you decide to pursue that path. The additional training, however, will serve you well as you move up from that career path with the all-important entry-level experience that you need.

Education and Training

It is expected that an Editorial Assistant has a bachelor's degree. Since this is an entry-level position, Editorial Assistants aren't expected to have had much training, except in school working on a school magazine or having one or more summer or year-round internships. For long-term career goals, a degree from a prestigious journalism program with a concentration in magazines is recommended.

Experience, Skills, and Personality Traits

Editorial Assistants are hardworking, organized, creative, inquisitive, and energetic. They are willing to do mundane work and work long hours. They are easy to get along with, take orders well, and are dependable.

Unions and Associations

Since some magazines are unionized, check with the Newspaper Guild (www.newsguild.org) to see if the company you are looking into or interviewing for has union guidelines.

There are a number of associations to which it may be helpful to belong, such as the American Society of Magazine Editors (www.magazine.org/ASME) and the Online News Association (www.journalists.org), or any other associations that will help you network and learn more about the aspect of magazine publishing that you wish to pursue.

Tips for Entry

1. Intern at a magazine. One way to try to find an internship is through the Magazine Internship Program, sponsored by the American Society of Magazine Editors (www.magazine.org/ASME), which has placed more than 1,500 students at 200 magazines since the intern program was started. Internships are also listed at www.mediabistro.com, www.hotjobs.com, and www.monster.com.

2. Attend the monthly educational evening get togethers held in New York City or the annual conferences held each spring by the American Society of Journalists and Authors (www.asja.org).

3. Network with other Editorial Assistants and senior editors through the American Society of Magazine Editors (www.magazine.org/ASME) and at the annual job fair that it sponsors each fall.

4. Go to writer conferences or take courses in magazine editing and writing. Instructors often also work at a major magazine. Find out if their magazine has positions for interns or is hiring Editorial Assistants and ask how to apply.

5. Go to the Web site for the magazine where you would like to work and see if it lists available jobs, or visit the site for the parent company if it is part of a major corporation that publishes multiple magazines. Follow the guidelines for applying for any available jobs.

6. Read the Sunday classified job listings in the *New York Times* or any other major newspaper, including the online edition. This entry-level job is often listed.

7. After graduation, go to a summer intensive publishing program that also includes training in magazine writing and editing. (See Appendix IV for a list of possible programs.) These programs usually emphasize finding a job as the second most important reason for being there, after learning more about the business and upgrading basic or advanced skills.

FACT CHECKER

CAREER PROFILE

Duties: Checks all information in articles by calling up the named sources as well as verifies any statistics or other facts, including the correct spelling for any named companies or other entity

Alternate Title(s): Researcher

Salary Range: $20,000 to $37,000+

Employment Prospects: Good

Advancement Prospects: Good

Best Geographical Location(s): Anywhere magazines are published, but more often in major urban centers, such as New York, Los Angeles, Chicago, Boston, San Francisco, and Washington, D.C., since this is usually a staff job; if the Fact Checker is a freelancer, however, this job could be done from anywhere, since the article could be sent via e-mail, fax, or through the mail, and the fact checking could be done by phone

Prerequisites:

Education and Training—A bachelor's degree is required, with a major or minor in journalism (spe-

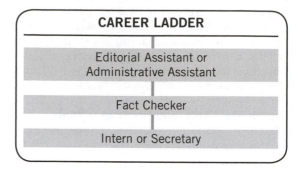

CAREER LADDER

Editorial Assistant or
Administrative Assistant

Fact Checker

Intern or Secretary

cializing in magazines) or any field that relies on learning research techniques, such as sociology, psychology, or marketing

Experience—One to two years' experience in magazine writing or research

Special Skills and Personality Traits—Intelligent; inquisitive; well-read; knowledgeable; accurate speller; strong writing ability; persistent

Position Description

Like editorial assistants, a Fact Checker, instead of working for one or two editors, will often work for the managing editor or associate editor in this entry-level position. His or her job is to make sure all the information in all of the articles is correct. It is a challenging job that requires persistence and patience, since sources may be hard to locate and facts difficult to verify.

The Fact Checker cannot assume anything in the article is true just because the writer submitted the article with those quotes or statistics. It is the job of the Fact Checker to check everything that is written, ranging from quotes to the spelling of names and places. Often, when a Fact Checker contacts a source, the source may question if he or she ever said what is being quoted and may want to change or eliminate what the writer has written. If the change is not that significant, the editor and writer may agree to the changes. But if it is necessary to have a confrontation so the original quote can be verified for the article, the writer may be asked to confirm the quote through either an audio recording or explicit notes from the interview.

Sometimes the Fact Checker may be asked to rewrite some of the article if errors are extensive. This is only done after consulting with the managing editor or senior editor handling the article, and if the writer consents to someone else doing the rewrite.

Salaries

Salaries for Fact Checkers are similar to those of editorial assistants. They average between $20,000 and $37,000 a year.

Employment Prospects

Employment prospects for Fact Checkers are good, because most magazines require them.

Advancement Prospects

Prospects for Fact Checkers' advancement are encouraging. After one or two years in this position, with excellent references and a strong reputation for accuracy and the ability to meet deadlines, you may be able to move up to the next level of editorial assistant (if the Fact Checker did not already have that job as part of his or her job description) or other more advanced positions, such as assistant editor, assistant staff writer, or assistant copy editor.

Education and Training

A Fact Checker is required to have a bachelor's degree. Individuals are not expected to have had much training for this entry-level position, but any experience as an intern over the summer or during college may help demonstrate a work ethic and commitment to magazine publishing.

Experience, Skills, and Personality Traits

Fact Checkers are intelligent, well read, inquisitive, and persistent. They are not afraid to challenge information and question facts. They will be hardworking, motivated, and seekers of truth. They should be able to remain calm and pleasant, even if those sources they are checking quotes with become upset or defensive and imply that the quotes seem to be distorted, especially out of the context of the initial interview. Therefore, being a diplomat is important to mediate among the sources, the writer, and the editor. A dedication to finding out facts, no matter how much digging it might take, is another important trait of the Fact Checker.

This is a pivotal job at a magazine, but since it is entry level and considered the lowest job—only higher than an intern and on the same level as the editorial assistant—having one's ego in check and being able to take instructions is essential.

Unions and Associations

There are no unions for magazine Fact Checkers, but there are a number of associations to which it may be helpful to belong for networking and educational purposes such as the American Society of Journalists and Authors (www.asja.org) and the Authors Guild (www.authorsguild.org).

Tips for Entry

1. Intern at a magazine to learn firsthand what goes into putting an issue out each month.
2. Network with other Fact Checkers and senior editors through associations, such as the American Society of Magazine Editors (www.magazine.org/ASME), which sponsors a yearly magazine job fair in late fall in New York City.
3. Check for jobs at such sites as www.mediabistro.com, www.hotjobs.com, and www.monster.com.

WRITER

STAFF WRITER

CAREER PROFILE

Duties: Conducts research and writes articles for the magazine; sometimes helps to write titles, pull-quotes, and photo captions

Alternate Title(s): Feature Writer

Salary Range: $20,000 to $65,000+

Employment Prospects: Poor

Advancement Prospects: Good

Best Geographical Location(s): Anywhere magazines are published, but more often in major urban centers, such as New York, Los Angeles, Chicago, Boston, San Francisco, and Washington, D.C.

Prerequisites:

Education and Training—A bachelor's degree is expected; on-the-job training at one or more magazines

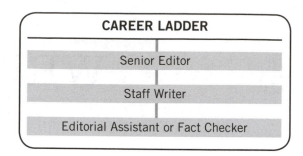

CAREER LADDER

Senior Editor

Staff Writer

Editorial Assistant or Fact Checker

Experience—Two to five years' experience in magazine writing

Special Skills and Personality Traits—Creative; intelligent; artistic; strong writing ability; able to recognize good story ideas; inquisitive; energetic; motivated

Position Description

As more and more magazines have come to rely on freelance writers and contributing editors, the number of available positions for Staff Writers appears to be shrinking. Large, well-established magazines, such as *Time* and *Newsweek,* still employ a healthy stable of Staff Writers, who usually specialize in a particular field, such as finance or entertainment. However, other major magazines are beginning to use mostly freelance writers and contributing editors for a large portion of their articles.

Staff Writers are usually given the most difficult and complicated assignments, since they have experience with the magazine and should know what works and what does not. They often work in the office full or part time and receive a steady salary as well as medical and dental benefits.

Besides coming up with article ideas and writing them, Staff Writers may also be called upon by their editors to help write titles for other articles or captions for photographs and artwork, which are called cutlines in magazines.

Staff Writers might also be assigned to write front-of-the-issue material, such as article promos, authors bios, or short features. For example, in the front of *Entertainment Weekly,* there are pages of pithy, paragraph-long pieces about "what's hot, and what's not"

and a page of trends that need short descriptive paragraphs to give them relevance.

Basically, a Staff Writer works for senior editors or the managing editor. He or she produces most of the written content not being assigned to freelance writers or contributing editors.

Salaries

There is a wide salary range for Staff Writers, depending on the size and scope of the magazine. Salaries range from $20,000 a year at smaller magazines to $65,000 or more at top national publications.

Employment Prospects

More and more magazines are turning to freelance writers, reducing the need for Staff Writers. Employment prospects are poor.

Advancement Prospects

Prospects for Staff Writers to advance up the ladder to senior editor are good, since this is the normal career track. However, they are competing with freelance writers and contributing editors for this spot. Increase your advancement prospects by getting a reputation for writing excellent, even award-winning articles, as well as for being a team player who meets his or her deadlines. In addition to completing assigned stories, you might think up new article ideas to be assigned to you or other Staff Writers.

Education and Training

A Staff Writer probably will have a bachelor's or master's degree in communications or journalism, with a major or minor in magazine writing. On-the-job training writing and editing magazine articles, at school or in college, as well as internships during the school year or summers will also be helpful training.

Experience, Skills, and Personality Traits

A magazine's Staff Writer is creative, inquisitive, a wordsmith, energetic, willing to handle tough assignments, a hard worker, and not afraid of intense deadline pressure. Excellent research skills, including how to conduct secondary research and how to conduct effective interviews, and writing talent are also required to succeed at this job. Being well-organized as well as attending to details and checking facts are other traits that serve the Staff Writer well.

Unions and Associations

Some jobs at magazines are unionized, such as *Time* magazine and Consumers Union, so check with the Newspaper Guild (www.newsguild.org) to see if Staff Writer at a particular magazine is a unionized position.

There are a number of associations to consider joining for such membership benefits as networking, information on possible job openings, monthly dinners and educational seminars, or annual meetings, including the American Society for Journalists and Authors (www.asja. org) and the National Writers Union (www.nwu.org).

Tips for Entry

1. Get a paid or unpaid internship at a magazine. Check with specific magazines by phone, by writing and sending your resume, or through their company Web site. You could also check the listings at the Web site of the American Society of Magazine Editors (www.magazine.org/ASME).

2. Attend the annual conference sponsored by the American Society for Journalists and Authors.

3. Network with other Staff Writers and editors through the American Society of Magazine Editors (www.magazine.org/ASME), which sponsors an annual job fair in late fall.

4. Develop a reputation for being able to write good articles and work effectively with the editorial staff.

CONTRIBUTING EDITOR

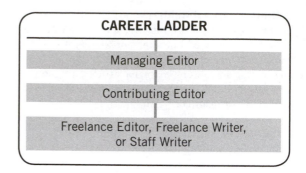

Position Description

The Contributing Editor is a freelance writer who normally writes exclusively for a specific magazine. His or her name usually appears in the masthead. Contributing Editors are paid regularly, either on retainer or by contract.

Unlike freelance writers, Contributing Editors usually write about a particular subject or in a specialized genre. Often they will have a weekly, biweekly, or monthly column, and, in many cases, their names are recognizable, since they have achieved a certain reputation from writing.

Contributing Editors will usually choose the subjects for their articles or columns, whereas freelance writers are often given assignments by senior editors. Often a Contributing Editor will be an expert in a particular field, such as business or entertainment.

Contributing Editors may be former freelance writers who have written extensively for the magazine and are becoming associated with the publication.

Some may have been staff writers or even editors; one reason they make the plunge into the world of freelance writing is that they have the best of both worlds—no longer having to go to the office everyday but having a steady commitment for a certain number of articles each month or year, as well as a steady paycheck.

This position reports either to senior editors or the managing editor. As freelancers, Contributing Editors either work from home or their own office outside the magazine. They also set their own hours, although they have to generate a certain amount of copy for each magazine. They may choose to hand-deliver their assignments, even if their editors ask them to be sent as an e-mail, since they want to keep up their connection with the assignment editors. If they do send their assignments electronically or through the mail, they may still want to come into the office to reconnect with the staff or try to arrange a luncheon where ideas for additional assignments may also be discussed.

Salaries

There is a wide income range for Contributing Editors, although they tend to earn more than freelance writers, because they have a regular column or assignment for nearly every issue of the magazine. They are usually on retainer whereby they receive a monthly fee or are paid for each assignment and have a contract. Average salaries range from $25,000 a year for small-circulation magazines to $90,000 and more for top national publications.

Employment Prospects

More and more magazines are using Contributing Editors as a compromise between the completely freelance writer, who works from assignment to assignment and may be busy if an editor asks for an article with a quick turnaround, and the staff writer, who is always available, in theory, but also commands a full-time salary and benefits. As the demand for Contributing Editors increases, employment prospects look good.

Advancement Prospects

Prospects for advancement from Contributing Editor to senior editor or managing editor are fair at best, since there are so many writers competing for the senior editor slots. On the other hand, Contributing Editors are often content to keep that position, because it gives them a regular income without having to actually be on staff. Most Contributing Editors try to advance their reputations and reach by getting increased media attention for their articles. They may also try to advance by putting articles together into a book or—with permission of the magazine that they work for—syndicate the column (referred to as second serial rights) in other noncompeting magazines, online publications, or print newspapers.

Education and Training

A Contributing Editor will probably have a bachelor's or master's degree, but this is not a requirement. They will have established themselves in the magazine writing field and as experts in whatever area in which they write.

Experience, Skills, and Personality Traits

A Contributing Editor is creative, inquisitive, a wordsmith, energetic, and willing to handle tough assignments, no matter how difficult. They are prolific, dependable, and hardworking. Since their picture may appear with their column or article, just like the contributing writer or columnist for a newspaper, he or she has to be careful to keep his or her ego in check and not get too conceited or difficult for the magazine staff to work with.

Unions and Associations

There are no unions for magazine Contributing Editors, but there are a number of associations to which it may be helpful to belong, such as the American Society of Journalists and Authors (www.asja.org) and the Authors Guild (www.authorsguild.org).

Tips for Entry

1. Develop a reputation as a solid writer, able to write good articles and columns.
2. Attend the annual conferences held each spring by the American Society of Journalists and Authors (www.asja.org) as well as the annual meeting of the American Society of Magazine Editors (www.magazine.org/ASME).
3. Network with other Contributing Editors and senior editors.
4. Try specializing in a topic you have studied at college or graduate school or have on-the-job training so that your writing and articles set you apart from the competition.
5. Become thoroughly familiar with the magazines that you might want to be a Contributing Editor for. Obtain magazine assignments and, through hard work, prove yourself invaluable to your magazine. After enough successful assignments, the position of Contributing Editor may be offered to you.

FREELANCE WRITER

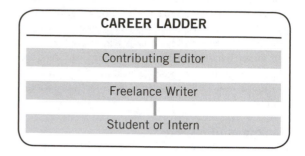
Position Description

The Freelance Writer is the workhorse of magazine publishing. More and more magazines have come to rely on Freelance Writers to provide content, rather than staff writers, because it keeps their overhead low (since they pay only for an accepted article and avoid the cost of a full-time salary and benefits).

Most managing editors will have a stable of Freelance Writers they can call on consistently to either cover stories the editorial staff has come up with or to consult for story ideas worth pursuing.

Most Freelance Writers work for more than one magazine, unless they are listed on the masthead as a contributing editor, in which case they may be prohibited by contract from writing for a competing periodical.

In many cases, a Freelancer has had some staff writing or editing experience on a magazine. Others have to develop reputations by submitting query letters, getting assignments, and completing them successfully before they can begin receiving assignments from editors on a regular basis.

In the beginning, there is little or no financial security in being a Freelance Writer, a deterrent to many would-be freelance magazine writers. But once you have earned an editor's trust, he or she can be a steady source of income. Once a Freelance Writer has established him or herself as a magazine's regular, being a

Freelancer has many other rewards beyond the financial. Typically, Freelancers work from home, set their own hours, and feel as if they are their own bosses, even though they eventually have to answer to a senior editor or a managing editor at the magazine. It is a great life if you can sustain it financially.

There are Freelance Writers for magazines who are generalists; they tend to get assignments to interview celebrities or cover articles that would be written by the general reporter at a newspaper. As a Freelance Writer writes more articles, however, he or she may start to specialize in a certain type of article or topic, such as writing investigative stories or health articles. As the Freelance Writer specializes in terms of topic and style, his or her magazine contacts and assignments may also begin to get more specialized. It is important to find out if a particular magazine has a non-compete clause or tradition. If this is the case, the Freelance Writer can write for other magazines as long as they are not that magazine's main competition.

Salaries

There is a wide income range for Freelance Writers. Since they are not on salary, they are usually paid per article or by the word. They do not receive medical or retirement benefits, and once one assignment is done, they have to find another one to keep money coming in. Freelancers can earn from less than $10,000 a year to more than $70,000. Some well-known Freelancers can make six figures, though they are few in number. The top magazines today pay $1 to $2 per word. Some magazines may ask Freelance Writers to take on the assignment for free just for the experience or the credit line. Others may pay as little as 15 cents a word. In addition to the fee for an article, it is important for the Freelance Writer to try to sell only what is known as FNASR (First North American Serial Rights), which means that after the article is published, the magazine usually has a six-month exclusive on the material, but after that time all rights are controlled by the Freelance Writer. He or she may resell the article or publish it on his or her own Web site without any compensation to the original magazine; it is expected that where the article originally was published will be noted. By selling only FNASR (rather than all rights), there may be additional revenue from multiple publications for the same freelance article.

Employment Prospects

More and more magazines are turning to Freelance Writers, so employment prospects are improving.

Advancement Prospects

Prospects for Freelance Writers advancing to contributing editor are fair, but this may take a long time, since you have to establish yourself as a good writer within a particular field, such as financial writing or entertainment. It is also important to take the time to cement each working relationship with every magazine editor with whom you are working. If those editors move to a new job, it is worthwhile to put time and effort into strengthening those new relationships. There are thousands upon thousands of Freelance Writers all competing for the same plum assignments from the major magazines. Gaining a reputation for writing excellent articles and making your deadlines, as well as for being easy to get along with, will help you to stand out from the competition. Consistent assignments from the same editor or publication may lead to the coveted contributing editorship, the next step up the ladder, since it often is accompanied by a commitment to a certain number of magazine assignments each year, as well as a monthly stipend and one's name on the magazine's masthead.

Education and Training

Freelance Writers will probably have at least a bachelor's degree and possibly a master's degree in communications or journalism (or an area they are specializing in for their article assignments). They will have gone through some kind of training in magazine writing, usually acquired on the job as a staff writer.

Experience, Skills, and Personality Traits

A Freelance Writer is creative, inquisitive, a wordsmith, energetic, and willing to handle tough assignments, no matter how difficult. He or she is a hard worker, is able to handle intense deadline pressure, and can cope with the uncertainty of not knowing where the next assignment will come from.

Unions and Associations

There are no unions for magazine Freelance Writers, but there are a number of associations to which it may be helpful to belong, such as the American Society of Journalists and Authors (www.asja.org).

Tips for Entry

1. Become a paid or unpaid intern at a magazine or work part time or full time at a magazine during college or over the summers.
2. Attend conferences sponsored by the American Society of Journalists and Authors (www.asja.org).
3. Network with other Freelance Writers and editors through writer and editor associations, such as the American Society of Magazine Editors (www.magazine.org/ASME), which sponsors seminars and conferences in New York City, or the conferences sponsored by colleges offering an undergraduate or graduate degree in magazine writing.
4. Develop a reputation for being able to write outstanding articles.
5. Enter competitions and get awards for writing excellent magazine articles.
6. Once you have enough credits, apply to be listed in Bacon's print media contacts, updated annually. There is a volume for magazines and newspapers as well as a comprehensive volume about New York's media called *Bacon's New York Media Directory*, with a section on Freelance Writers.
7. Hire a webmaster or create a Web site on your own. Include samples of your freelance articles as well as contact information. If possible, buy the domain name for your name or create a title for your Web site that has some relationship to you or what you write about. List your Web site on your own or hire someone to list it for you so your site, sample articles, and contact

information will come up in search engines on the Internet.

8. Subscribe to *Freelance Success* (www.freelance success.com) a weekly newsletter that explores potential markets with contact information.

9. Read or subscribe to *Writer's Digest* or the *Writer* and check out their listings for markets that you could query for assignments.

10. Join online social networking sites such as www. linkedin.com and develop a network of other writers as well as editors. Join groups related to your freelance writing and participate in dialogues with other subscribing group members.

ONLINE WRITER

Duties: Writes articles for the online version of a print magazine or a site that is purely Internet-based

Salary range: $0 to $.50 a word, on average, for free-lancers; full-time staff salaries range from $35,000 for news writers to $70,000 for marketing writers

Employment Prospects: Good

Advancement Prospects: Fair

Best Geographical Location(s): Although technically an Online Writer can work anywhere as long as there is Internet access, some publications may prefer their Online Writers (if it's a staff job) to work from their headquarters, wherever that is based, if the online magazine is an extension of a major publication that might be in an urban publishing center such as New York City, Los Angeles, Chicago, Boston, Washington, D.C., or San Francisco

Prerequisites:

Education and Training—A bachelor's degree is expected; on-the-job training as a writer at print or online publications is useful; taking courses in writing, especially magazine writing or writing for the Internet, should be helpful

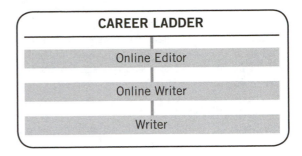

CAREER LADDER

Online Editor

Online Writer

Writer

Experience—Any kind of magazine writing experience will be useful, especially writing for online publications

Special Skills and Personality Traits—Excellent research and interviewing skills are expected; attention to detail; able to work under pressure and meet deadlines; able to multitask; ability to write in short blocks and to use subheads to divide the text for easier reading on the Internet; interested in current events and keeping up with what is new at the online magazine as well as in the writer's subject area

Position Description

Online Writers could be on staff for the online publication or could be a freelancer writing for an Internet publication. The online magazine could be a completely separate publication from the major magazine with which it is associated, and it could have its own staff of Online Writers, or it could share content and staff or freelancers with its print publication. Although it is still a magazine writing position, there are certain differences in writing for an online publication versus a print publication. For example, in general, articles for an online magazine tend to be shorter (600–800 words) than the typical 1,000 to 3,000 length of a print magazine article. Being able to insert subheads to break up the text is also a skill that helps the readability of online magazine articles. For some publications, however, creating and inserting subheads to break up the article is the role of the online editor. For other online magazines, the Online Writer may be expected to create and insert those subheads. Furthermore, some online magazines expect their Online Writers to also supply photographs to run with the articles, either their own pictures or links to photographs that may be used for free or purchased. Other publications will expect only text from their Online Writers. The short turnaround time for Online Writers is another way in which writing for an online publication can differ dramatically from writing for a print publication. Most print magazines, except for those that are weekly or biweekly, have longer deadlines.

Salaries

Earnings range from zero to 50 cents a word, on average, for freelancers. Full-time staff salaries range from $35,000 for online news writers to $70,000 for online marketing writers.

Employment Prospects

More and more magazines are becoming entirely based on the Internet, and more print publications look to archive their content online as well as to supplement it with original online articles, so the possibilities for

Online Writers are good. However, Online Writers for magazines tend to get paid at a lower rate than those who write for print publications or print plus online publications, so it might not be a niche that is as lucrative as other options. Since there may be more job openings for Online Writers than for print writers, this could be a stepping-stone to getting some published credits that could lead to a staff or freelance job as a print publication magazine writer.

Advancement Prospects

There are fewer positions for online magazine editors than there are for Online Writers, so advancement prospects are only fair. Another advancement possibility for an Online Writer is for a freelance writer to become a staff writer, or for a freelance or staff writer to become a regular contributing writer or even a columnist. There will be a lot of competition, but assignments and pay are steadier when the arrangement with the online publication is more regular.

Education and Training

A bachelor's degree is expected; on-the-job training as a writer at print or online publications is useful; taking courses in writing, especially magazine writing or writing for the Internet, should be helpful. If writing on a specialized topic, rather than just general interest, having an educational background in that field—such as business, psychology, physical sciences, or technology—would be helpful.

Experience, Skills, and Personality Traits

Any kind of magazine writing experience will be useful, especially writing for online publications. Excellent research and interviewing skills are expected, as is attention to detail; the ability to work under pressure and to meet deadlines; the ability to multitask; the ability to write in short blocks and to use subheads to divide the text for easier reading on the Internet; interest in current events and staying current with the online magazine as well as one's "beat" topic.

Unions and Associations

The National Writers Union (NWU) (www.nwu.org) is a trade union for writers, including freelancers or contract writers, those who write for the Web as well as journalists, book authors, and poets. The union provides staff and freelance job listings for members at its Web site. (Membership dues are on a sliding scale based on how much income a writer earns, from $120 a year for those earning less than $5,000 to $340 for

those earning $45,001 and above. Belonging to writing associations may be helpful to networking for jobs as well as learning about new trends in the industry. The American Society of Journalists and Authors (ASJA) (www.asja.org) is a professional association of more than 1,000 writers who meet the society's criteria for membership. Other specialized writer associations, such as the National Association of Science Writers (NASW), could be helpful, especially since they offer as part of membership a free job e-mail alert for staff and freelance writing opportunities.

Tips for Entry

1. Write articles throughout your school years and assemble a portfolio of excellent work so you have samples of your writing when asked to provide "clips."
2. Get an internship, unpaid or for credit, during your school years so you graduate with as much varied writing work experience as possible.
3. Go to writing conferences and especially attend panel workshops with presentations by editors at online publications. Introduce yourself to those editors and let them know that you are interested in getting a position as a staff or freelance Online Writer.
4. Subscribe to *Freelance Success* (www.freelance success.com), a $99 per year weekly newsletter that features at least one or more markets actively buying from freelance writers.
5. The ASJA (American Society of Journalists and Authors) has a one-day conference for nonfiction each spring in Manhattan, usually in April. Check if they have a panel of buying editors and a seasoned writing pro about writing for the Internet that you could attend.
6. Go to writers' conferences with buying magazine editors on panels. Print magazines usually have online versions, often with a separate staff, but this could provide an entrée to getting an assignment.
7. Master the art of writing the query letter and send out queries to online magazine editors who might give you an assignment. Find their names by visiting the Web site's "About Us" page; also read *Writer's Digest* magazine as well as the annual *Writer's Market*, which is updated annually with names and thumbnail sketches of buying editors. Be prepared to send one or more sample clips of your writing, especially your online magazine publication credits.

8. Join writers' associations that offer job referrals for freelance or staff jobs as well as associations geared to your areas of specialization. The latter may include the National Association of Science Writers (NASW) (www.nasw.org) or the American Medical Writers Association (AMWA) (www.amwa.org), which offers a job listing for members and has 20 local chapters nationwide. The American Society of Journalists and Authors (ASJA) (www.asja.org) has a writer referral service for members only.

PHOTOGRAPHY

PHOTO EDITOR

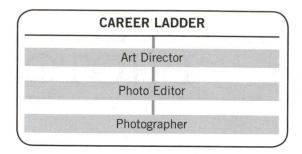

Position Description

At a magazine, the Photo Editor is in charge of all editorial photographic content. These are primarily photos that will accompany the articles or photojournalistic pieces that actually drive the content, with captions or cutlines being the supporting material.

Not all magazines have Photo Editors. At many magazines this job is managed by the art director. But on those magazines that use a lot of new photographs, such as news and entertainment weeklies or *National Geographic,* a Photo Editor is necessary to manage the large number of pictures and photographers providing them.

Photo Editors will work closely with writers and senior editors to determine not only who should be assigned to a particular story but also what pictures will be needed. Once the pictures are available, the Photo Editor then works with the art director to select which shots will be used and in what shape or size they will appear.

Since only a few magazines have staff photographers, Photo Editors tend to work with a number of freelance photographers. It is up to the Photo Editor to know their strengths and weaknesses when matching a photographer to an article.

When the magazine cannot afford to hire a photographer for an article, the Photo Editor is responsible for acquiring a suitable replacement, either from the magazine's own archives or a stock photo house.

Choosing which photo to use is extremely subjective, as is how to crop or shape the photograph into the magazine's layout. Most Photo Editors should have a strong sense of design to help in these decisions.

Salaries

The salary range for Photo Editors, like most positions on magazines, depends on the publication's stature and circulation. At smaller publications, starting salaries for Photo Editors are $25,000. They can average $90,000 at larger national publications.

Employment Prospects

Since not all magazines have this position, employment prospects for Photo Editors are only fair. Many magazines have art directors handle this responsibility.

Advancement Prospects

Prospects for advancement from Photo Editor to art director are good, since there are potentially more openings for art directors than for Photo Editors. Increase your advancement prospects by developing an excellent reputation for working effectively with staff editors, writers, and photographers, as well as with freelancers. If the photographs you select to appear with articles win awards, so much the better; enter those images in contests or encourage your staff or freelance photographers to participate.

Education and Training

A Photo Editor will probably have a bachelor's or master's degree in photojournalism or a related field, but this is not a requirement. They will have had extensive training in the fundamentals of photography, including internships in a variety of photography studios or situations, as well as additional training as magazine photographers.

Special Requirements

The Professional Photographers of America has developed the PPA Certified program with the categories of CPP (certified professional photographer), CPPS (specialist or artist), or CEI (certified electronic imager); details about these categories are available at their Web site (www.ppa.com).

Experience, Skills, and Personality Traits

A Photo Editor is creative and artistic, with an eye for design and a strong photographic sense. He or she will know how to tell a story in pictures and how to assign a story to the right photographer for that particular article. In addition to ability as a photographer, the Photo Editor knows how to delegate as well as how to be part of the creative team at the magazine that gets out each issue.

Unions and Associations

There are no unions for magazine Photo Editors, but there are a number of associations to which it may be helpful to belong, such as the Professional Photographers of America (www.ppa.com), International Freelance Photographers Organization (www.ifpo.net), American Society of Media Photographers (www.asmp.org), and the Photographic Society of America (www.psa-photo.org).

Tips for Entry

1. Develop a reputation as a solid magazine photographer and innovative Photo Editor.
2. Attend conferences sponsored by photography associations, including the one week–long annual meeting held by the Photographic Society of America (www.psa-photo.org).
3. Network with other Photo Editors and editors in general through monthly or annual meetings, such as at the annual job fair in New York City sponsored by the American Society of Magazine Editors (www.magazine.org/ASME).
4. Develop a reputation for being able to produce provocative photographs and photographic layouts. Enter your magazine's photographs in competitions; winning will provide you with greater visibility for your photographic accomplishments.
5. Search the available job listings in print magazines, such as *Today's Photographer* (published by the International Freelance Photographers Organization), as well as job sites, such as www.mediabistro.com, www.journalismjobs.com, www.hotjobs.com, and www.careerbuilder.com. Check the jobs page of the American Society of Magazine Editors Web site: www.magazine.org/ASME.

PHOTOGRAPHER

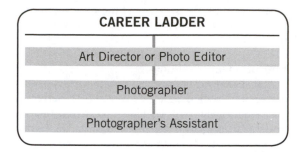

Position Description

These days, most magazine Photographers are freelancers. There are a few publications, such as *Time, Newsweek, People,* and *National Geographic,* that have Photographers on staff, but those numbers are shrinking.

Whether they are staff or freelance, Photographers will work for either the magazine's photo editor or art director. Once given an assignment, it is up to the Photographer to schedule the shoot, decide what equipment is needed, obtain any necessary photo releases from people being photographed, hire any models if necessary, and then process the film or turn in the digital photos on computer discs or send it electronically over the Internet.

Getting the right photograph for a particular article is an art form that sometimes takes as long as it does to write the article. A Photographer has to visualize how the photograph will appear in the article. If one of the photos has the chance of making the cover, even more time will be taken to get just the right shot.

Salaries

The salary range for Photographers varies greatly. It usually depends on how much the Photographer wants to work, since they are normally paid per assignment. Staff Photographers, depending on the size of the magazine, earn between $20,000 and $75,000 and more at larger national publications. Freelance Photographers may earn from as little as $5,000 a year to more than $100,000.

Employment Prospects

Since most magazines use Photographers, employment prospects are good, primarily for freelancers.

Advancement Prospects

Prospects for advancement from Photographer to photo editor or art director are only fair, since there are many Photographers and designers vying for these positions. To increase the likelihood of advancing, gain a reputation for capturing unique and memorable photos. Carry your camera with you, and keep shooting till you get the right shot. With digital equipment today, it is easier to shoot dozens or even hundreds of pictures to get the right one and deliver the pictures quickly and before the deadline. Being easy to work with and gaining a reputation for working well with your subjects, as well as with the editors and writers, will help your career.

Education and Training

A Photographer will probably have a bachelor's degree, although this is not a requirement. They will have had extensive training as Photographers, taking photography courses and working for/being mentored by esteemed photographers.

Experience, Skills, and Personality Traits

A Photographer is creative and artistic, with an eye for design and a strong photographic sense. He or she will know how to tell a story in pictures.

Unions and Associations

There are no unions for magazine Photographers, but there are a number of associations to which it may be helpful to belong, such as the American Society of Media Photographers (www.asmp.org), American Society of Picture Professionals (www.aspp.com), National Press Photographers Association (www.nppa.

org), and the Professional Photographers of America (www.ppa.com).

Tips for Entry

1. Develop a reputation as a solid newspaper or magazine Photographer.
2. Network with other Photographers and photo editors.
3. Develop a reputation for being able to produce provocative photographs.
4. Check the classified ads for Photographer jobs in the magazine *News Photographer* or online at www.mediabistro, www.journalismjobs.com, or www.hotjobs.com.

PRODUCTION, DESIGN, AND ART

ART DIRECTOR

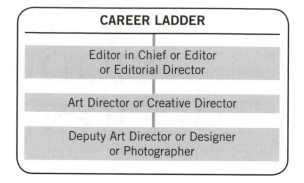
Position Description

The Art Director is responsible for the overall look of the magazine. He or she is in charge of all visual elements, including design, photography, art, and graphics. Reporting to the editor in chief, the Art Director must make sure that all visuals relate to and complement editorial content.

He or she is responsible for assigning the best photographers and designers for each article or cover. The Art Director ensures that all pictures and designs enhance and improve whatever article or column they accompany.

Working closely with the production director, the Art Director plans the layout and design of each issue. He or she will also set deadlines for all photo and design assignments.

A few magazines will have a creative director, who is basically an Art Director with the added responsibility of acting as a go-between for the design and editorial departments. Like the Art Director, the creative director supervises the overall look of the magazine and makes sure the design elements work with the editorial content.

An Art Director may also be responsible for type fonts, size of headlines, and how an article looks on the page. Therefore the Art Director should have a good working relationship with the editor, to avoid conflicts between design and editorial content. Sometimes this cannot be avoided, and whenever this happens, it is up to the Art Director and editor to work out any differences. Usually the editor in chief has the final say.

One of the most important visuals the Art Director has to deal with is the magazine's cover. Working closely with the editor in chief and publisher, the Art director will often provide a variety of potential covers. While it is usually the editor in chief who makes the final decision on what or who goes on the cover, it is the Art Director who brings that decision into print by overseeing the design of that cover.

Other responsibilities for the Art Director include planning design budgets and layout and working with the production director on production deadlines.

Salaries

There is a wide salary range for Art Directors, depending on the size and scope of the magazine. Salaries range from $20,000 a year on smaller magazines to $100,000 or more at top national publications.

Employment Prospects

Most magazines have an Art Director or creative director; therefore employment prospects are good. This is also a highly competitive position, and while positions are available, there will be many assistant Art Directors or photo editors trying to fill them.

Advancement Prospects

Prospects for Art Directors to advance up the ladder to editor in chief are poor, since the editor in chief usually comes from the editorial side of the magazine. An Art Director for a small magazine can advance to artistic or creative director for a larger magazine or group of magazines.

Education and Training

An Art Director will probably have a bachelor's or master's degree in magazine design, communications, or photography. Years of on-the-job training in magazine design and photography are also helpful.

Experience, Skills, and Personality Traits

A magazine's Art Director has the skill to visualize a magazine's character. He or she is a skilled artist and designer who knows how to create excitement out of every visual element.

Personality-wise, the Art Director will be a team player, opinionated, visually creative, energetic, and able to work under severe deadline pressure.

Unions and Associations

There are no unions for magazine Art Directors. Associations include the Association for Women in Communications (www.womcom.org) and the New York–based Partnership in Print Production (www.wip.org).

Tips for Entry

1. Work your way up from deputy Art Director.
2. Attend conferences organized by the American Society of Magazine Editors (www.magazine.org/ASME) as well as art and communications associations.
3. Network with other Art Directors.
4. Develop a reputation for being able to create exciting-looking magazines and to meet or beat every deadline.
5. Let your college or art school alumni or career placement office know that you are interested in becoming an Art Director at a magazine. Develop a portfolio of samples to show at a job interview.
6. Visit the print or online job listings of magazines or Web sites, such as www.mediabistro.com and www.journalismjobs.com.

PRODUCTION DIRECTOR

CAREER PROFILE

Duties: Responsible for overseeing final production of the magazine and ensuring that all advertising and editorial pages are ready for printing; supervises print run; may also be in charge of distribution

Alternate Title(s): Production Manager; Production Editor

Salary Range: $45,000 to $100,000+

Employment Prospects: Good

Advancement Prospects: Poor

Best Geographical Location(s): Anywhere magazines are published, but more often in major urban centers, such as New York, Los Angeles, Chicago, Boston, San Francisco, and Washington, D.C.

Prerequisites:

    Education and Training—A bachelor's degree is usually required; graduate degree in magazine production is recommended, but is not required; on-the-job training at one or more magazines

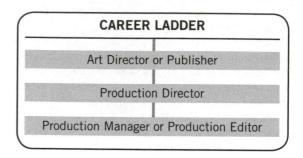

CAREER LADDER

Art Director or Publisher

Production Director

Production Manager or Production Editor

Experience—Five to seven years' experience in various magazine production departments

Special Skills and Personality Traits—Strong design and layout skills; knowledge of Quark required; detail-oriented; able to work under deadline pressure; able to multitask; strong knowledge of Macintosh software programs

Position Description

The Production Director is responsible for making sure that all advertising and editorial pages are ready for printing, for getting these pages to the printer on time, and then for overseeing the final print run. At some magazines, the Production Director is also responsible for distributing the magazine to newsstands and subscribers.

Reporting to the publisher, the editor in chief, or, in some cases, the art director, the Production Director heads the magazine's production department.

He or she coordinates the content coming from the editorial, advertising, art and photo, promotion, circulation, and sales departments to make sure everything is running on time and printing deadlines are being met.

Production Directors may have a production manager or production editor to help them prepare the pages for printing. A lot of work goes into the production of a magazine, and the Production Director is responsible for making sure everything works efficiently.

He or she will oversee content flow, select paper and color, prepare art for reproduction, and supervise the final print run and binding.

Today computers are used for almost all of the production work, from layout to cost estimates. In fact, production department computers are now used for many prepress jobs, such as color correction and four-color digital proofing.

On some magazines, the Production Director is responsible for deciding which article or advertisement goes on a particular page. This responsibility is known as "break of the book." On other magazines, these decisions are made by the editor in chief or art director and then given to the Production Director as a pencil layout.

A magazine's production department is affected most by technology, so a Production Director has to keep up on the latest state-of-the-art advances in production and printing technology.

Salaries

There is a wide salary range for Production Directors, depending on the size and scope of the magazine. Salaries range from $45,000 a year at smaller magazines to $100,000 or more at top national publications.

Employment Prospects

Most magazines have a Production Director or production manager; therefore employment prospects are good. This is also a highly competitive position, and while new magazines are starting all the time, there will only be one Production Director per magazine.

Advancement Prospects

Prospects for Production Directors to advance up the ladder to publisher or editor in chief are poor, since most editors in chief come from the editorial side of the magazine and most publishers seem to come from the circulation department.

Education and Training

A Production Director will probably have a bachelor's and possibly a master's degree in magazine production or design. They will also have years of on-the-job training in magazine production.

Experience, Skills, and Personality Traits

A magazine's Production Director has the skill to coordinate a magazine's advertising and editorial departments' deadline schedules. He or she is able to negotiate printing prices, manage large production staffs, and handle multiple tasks.

Personality-wise, the Production Director will be a leader, a team player, technologically proficient, and able to work under intense deadline pressure.

Unions and Associations

Production Directors might belong to associations for networking and educational reasons; two such associations are Partnership in Print Production (www.wip.org) and the American Society of Magazine Editors (www.magazine.org/ASME).

Tips for Entry

1. Work your way up from production manager.
2. Attend conferences.
3. Network with other Production Directors.
4. Develop a reputation for being able to produce exciting-looking magazines.
5. Check out the posted jobs at the Web site of the American Society of Magazine Editors (www.magazine.org/ASME).

DESIGNER

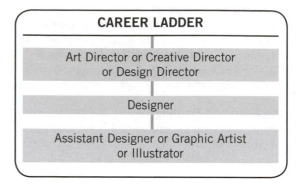
Position Description

These days, most Designers working on magazines are freelancers rather than staff. Some art directors will have a staff of assistants and designers, but only at the largest magazines. For the most part, Designers, like writers, now may work on a variety of publications from their home or outside office.

The Designer reports to the art director, who assigns whatever design elements are necessary. This can range from the all-important cover design to the table of contents or a redesign of the magazine's logo.

Designers are also hired to create a look for a new magazine or to update the look of an old one to make it look fresh. In these cases, Designers will come up with an original vision and turn this over to the art director, who then makes it happen. Some magazines are redesigned every five or six years just to stay current.

A magazine's design is one of the key elements that sets it apart from all other magazines—as much a part of its personality as its editorial content. Designers collaborate with the art director and editors to conceptualize, plan, and design feature articles, back-of-the-issue and front-of-the-issue sections, as well as special design projects for special issues.

Today most Designers work on computers using QuarkXPress, Adobe Illustrator, Adobe InDesign, and Adobe Photoshop. This allows Designers to produce integrated layouts using text, photos, and design elements in one digital file.

Salaries

There is a wide salary range for Designers, depending on the size and scope of the magazine. Salaries range from $20,000 a year at smaller magazines to $100,000 or more at top national publications.

Employment Prospects

Most magazines employ Designers either on staff or as freelancers, so employment prospects are good. Some small magazines may just have an art director who also handles all design functions.

Advancement Prospects

Prospects for advancement from Designer to art director are only fair, since there are so many more Designers than there are art directors. To increase the likelihood of your advancement and promotion, commit yourself to helping your magazine become one that wins awards for its design. Develop a reputation for being a hard worker with creative and innovative design ideas who always meets deadlines.

Education and Training

A Designer will probably have a bachelor's degree in art and design or magazine design; a master's degree is recommended; he or she will also have on-the-job training in magazine design.

Experience, Skills, and Personality Traits

A Designer will usually have between two and five years of experience in magazine design. He or she will be well organized and detail-oriented. A magazine Designer is an artist with a strong sense of conceptualization. He or she must also be proficient in design software, including QuarkXPress, Adobe Illustrator, and Adobe Photoshop.

Personality-wise, he or she will be a team player, opinionated, visually creative, energetic, and able to work under intense deadline pressure.

Unions and Associations

There are no unions for magazine Designers. Associations that might be useful to join include the Graphic Artists Guild (www.gag.org).

Tips for Entry

1. Work your way up from illustrator and layout artist.
2. Attend conferences.
3. Network with other Designers and art directors.
4. Develop a reputation for being able to create exciting-looking magazines.
5. Check out postings for magazine Designer jobs at sites including www.mediabistro.com and http://jobs.myspace.com.

MARKETING AND PUBLIC RELATIONS

MARKETING DIRECTOR

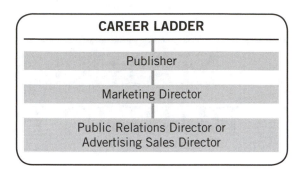

Position Description

The Marketing Director is responsible for creating awareness of the magazine through promotion and publicity in order to sell as many copies of the publication as possible. Reporting directly to the publisher, the head of marketing develops advertising sales support and promotional materials and manages budgets relating to promotional activities and publicity. He or she also supervises the compilation, evaluation, and analysis of market data to support advertising strategies.

Marketing Directors oversee all event marketing, trade and consumer advertising, sponsorships, and affinity groups. It is up to the Marketing Director to build and manage the magazine's brand in the marketplace.

The magazine may be the best magazine in the world, full of exciting, provocative articles packed with life-enriching information, but if no one knows it exists, no one is going to buy it. So it is up to the Marketing Director to get the word out about this "must-have" publication.

Marketing Directors have two primary goals associated with promotion: increase the magazine's circulation and increase advertising sales. To boost advertising, the Marketing Director might have his or her staff send copies of the magazine to potential advertisers. To increase circulation and reader interest, a press release might be sent to print and broadcast media highlighting a particular newsworthy article.

A recent marketing trend involves cross-merchandising or cross-branding. Examples of this are *O, the Oprah Winfrey Magazine,* and *People,* which now has a *People* television program on CNN.

Salaries

There is a wide salary range for Marketing Directors, depending on the size and scope of the magazine. Salaries range from $55,000 a year at smaller magazines to $125,000 or more at top national publications.

Employment Prospects

Most magazines have a Marketing Director; therefore employment prospects are good. This is also a highly competitive position, and while positions are available, there will be many assistant Marketing Directors and publicity directors vying for this job.

Advancement Prospects

Prospects for advancement from Marketing Director to publisher are poor, since most publishers now come from the circulation or advertising side of the magazine.

Education and Training

A Marketing Director is expected to have a bachelor's or master's degree in marketing or advertising. Years of on-the-job training in magazine marketing are also helpful.

Experience, Skills, and Personality Traits

A Marketing Director should have at least five years' marketing experience, with some direct mail experience; have strong project management, communication, and analytical skills; and be good at problem-solving. He or she is expected to have strong creative abilities.

Personality-wise, a Marketing Director should be a team player, outgoing, competitive, goal-oriented, energetic, and likeable.

Unions and Associations

There are a number of associations to which it may be helpful to belong. These include the American Business Media (www.americanbusinessmedia.com), the Direct Marketing Association (www.the-dma.org), and the International Association of Business Communicators (www.iabc.com).

Tips for Entry

1. Work your way up from publicity or advertising sales support.
2. Attend conferences sponsored by the American Business Media (www.americanbusinessmedia.com).
3. Network with other Marketing Directors.
4. Develop a reputation for being able to create exciting promotional campaigns that generate a lot of attention from the press (print, broadcast, and online), especially campaigns that generate more revenue than expenditures.
5. Check out postings for Marketing Director at www.marketinghire.com, a division of www.marketingtoday.com or check out the postings at www.linkedin.com.

PUBLIC RELATIONS DIRECTOR

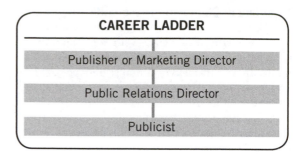

Position Description

The Public Relations Director is in charge of generating publicity and promotion for the magazine in any way that does not involve advertising. Reporting to either the publisher or marketing director, the Public Relations Director runs what is called the publicity and promotions department. Since most magazines have a relatively small advertising budget, they rely more and more on the publicity department for promotion.

At larger magazines, he or she will have a staff of publicists or media relations specialists who spend their time creating press and media kits, writing press releases, holding press conferences, and coming up with innovative ways to get the magazine noticed. The Public Relations Director will oversee and manage his or her staff. But at smaller publications, the Public Relations Director may have to do it all.

Magazine publicists spend their day trying to get other media outlets, such as newspapers, other magazines, or television, to mention the magazine in a favorable manner. An example is tipping off a daily gossip columnist about an upcoming comment or unknown fact about a celebrity from the magazine's next issue. Another way is to go on television to talk about special stories or issues. *People* magazine is well-known in the magazine business for having its spokespeople appear on entertainment talk shows to promote celebrity interviews or newsworthy stories.

Salaries

There is a wide salary range for Public Relations Directors, depending on the size and scope of the magazine. Salaries range from $39,000 a year at smaller magazines to $100,000 or more at top national publications.

Employment Prospects

Many, but not all, magazines have a Public Relations Director; therefore employment prospects are fair.

Advancement Prospects

Prospects for advancement from Public Relations Director to marketing director are fair.

Education and Training

A Public Relations Director will have a bachelor's degree in communications, journalism, marketing, or public relations. A master's degree in one of those fields is recommended. They will also have at least seven to 10 years of on-the-job training in magazine promotion and publicity.

Experience, Skills, and Personality Traits

A magazine's Public Relations Director has the skills to organize and manage a magazine's publicity department. He or she will have a proven track record in generating media awareness. Skills include strong communication abilities. Personality-wise, the Public Relations Director will be a leader as well as a team player. He or she will be highly motivated, persuasive, persistent, creative, intelligent, and innovative.

Unions and Associations

There are several associations that are useful for networking and keeping up with trends in the industry, including the Public Relations Society of America (www.prsa.org), which has local chapters, and the International Association of Business Communicators (www.iabc.com).

Tips for Entry

1. Work your way up from publicist.
2. Attend conferences.
3. Network with other Public Relations Directors.
4. Develop a reputation for being able to generate positive publicity for a magazine.
5. Check out postings for Public Relations Director at O'Dwyer's Public Relations News (www.jobs.odwyerpr.com), the job listings for Public Relations Society of America (www.prsa.org), media sites including www.mediabistro.com and http://jobs.myspace.com, and check out job postings at www.linkedin.com, www.theladders.com, and www.simplyhired.com.

RESEARCH DIRECTOR

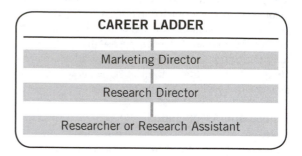

Position Description

A Research Director oversees the magazine's various research needs, which primarily pertain to gaining an in-depth understanding of readers—their behavior, buying habits, attitudes, and likes and dislikes. Once gathered, this information is broken down and analyzed to help determine what sort of advertisers will most likely be attracted to buying ad space in the magazine. It is also used to help circulation directors go about selling the magazine to potential readers and subscribers. This information can also tell the editorial department how it should cover its stories and which topics are of the most interest to its readership.

Reporting to either the publisher or editor in chief, the Research Director spends a great deal of time analyzing readership data and pulling out pertinent information. Some of this data will be used to compare the magazine to its competitors, which will later be used by advertising sales representatives when they call on advertisers and prospective advertisers. Ad sales reps are aware of the fact that advertisers are actually buying access to the magazine's audience. So when advertisers and their agencies are deciding on where to spend their ad dollars, they take a close look at what the Research Director has found in terms of reader demographics and psychological profiles.

The key information this research will cover is age, income, education, geographic location, hobbies, likes, dislikes, behavior, work or leisure and reading and other magazine-related habits.

Research Directors help circulation directors by tracking where most people buy single-issue magazines, as well as what magazines are selling at particular location.

As for helping the editor in selecting what stories to cover, research on readership interest, attitudes, and behavior is extremely helpful. For instance, if a survey showed that enough readers had a desire to travel to a specific location or take a cruise, an article might be assigned to address that interest.

Salaries

There is a wide salary range for Research Directors, depending on the size and scope of the magazine. Salaries range from $25,000 a year at smaller magazines to $100,000 or more at top national publications.

Employment Prospects

These days, most magazines outsource the position of Research Director to market research companies. A few larger publications still have their own Research Director, but more and more marketing and advertising directors or editors are taking over this responsibility. Most magazines do not have a Research Director; therefore employment prospects are poor. However, market research firms that specialize in magazine research may have openings.

Advancement Prospects

Prospects for advancement from Research Director are poor, since many magazines are outsourcing this position. However, some Research Directors advance to marketing or advertising sales directors. Make yourself indispensable to a magazine by getting to know who their readers are and what kinds of articles they will most likely want to read.

Education and Training

A Research Director will have a bachelor's degree, preferably in marketing or market research. He or she will have either worked for a magazine as a researcher or for a market research company specializing in magazine research.

Experience, Skills, and Personality Traits

A magazine's Research Director has at least three years' experience in magazine market research. He or she has strong mathematical and statistical skills and is able to analyze large quantities of readership data.

The Research Director has to be detail oriented and able to spot trends in attitudes and behavior. He or she has to be able to extract information from large numbers of strangers and should be personable and trustworthy.

Unions and Associations

Research Directors can join the Direct Marketing Association (www.the-dma.org) and the International Association of Business Communicators (www.iabc.com) to network and to keep up with trends in the magazine, marketing, and research fields.

Tips for Entry

1. Work your way up from researcher in a marketing research company.
2. Attend conferences sponsored by the Direct Marketing Association (www.the-dma.org) as well as the International Association of Business Communicators (www.iabc.com).
3. Network with other Research Directors and marketing directors.
4. Develop a reputation for being able to analyze data that helps sell advertising.

ADVERTISING AND SALES

ADVERTISING SALES DIRECTOR

CAREER PROFILE

Duties: Heads the advertising sales department; responsible for bringing in revenues by selling ads in the magazine; creates ad rates; develops advertising support material; approves contracts with advertisers

Alternate Title(s): Advertising Director; Advertising Sales Manager

Salary Range: $35,000 to $150,000+

Employment Prospects: Good

Advancement Prospects: Fair

Best Geographical Location(s): Anywhere magazines are published, but more often in major urban centers, such as New York, Los Angeles, Chicago, Boston, San Francisco, and Washington, D.C.

Prerequisites:

Education and Training—A bachelor's degree is expected; graduate degree in advertising is recommended; on-the-job training at one or more magazines

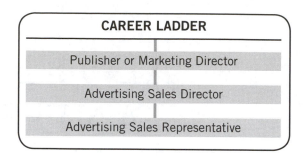

CAREER LADDER

Publisher or Marketing Director

Advertising Sales Director

Advertising Sales Representative

Experience—Seven to 10 years' experience in magazine advertising sales; experience in meeting or exceeding sales goals

Special Skills and Personality Traits—Outgoing personality; able to motivate sales staff; strong sales and leadership skills; willing to travel; able to analyze sales and marketing data

Position Description

There are basically two ways a magazine makes money—by selling copies of the magazine to readers and by selling advertising to companies wanting to advertise in the magazine. The Advertising Sales Director is responsible for generating income through the sale of advertising that appears in the magazine.

At large magazines, he or she will have a staff of advertising sales representatives and support. At small publications, the Advertising Sales Director may be the only person selling ads.

Among other responsibilities, the Advertising Sales Director is expected to research and analyze audience data, oversee the creation of advertising support material, such as brochures and media kits, approve final contracts with advertisers, and sometimes schedule ad placement.

At most magazines, the Advertising Sales Director reports to the publisher, but sometimes this position reports to the marketing director. At other magazines, the head of advertising sales is also the publisher.

It is up to the Advertising Sales Director to hire and train a top sales force in order to compete in one of the most difficult advertising arenas. Not only are advertising sales representatives competing against representatives from other magazines, but they are also competing against ad reps for television and newspapers. The Advertising Sales Director makes sure the sales staff is motivated and has the necessary support to carry out the magazine's advertising strategy.

The Advertising Sales Director is also responsible for establishing an advertising budget that includes audience research, advertising and promotion, direct mail, travel, and entertainment.

Salaries

There is a wide salary range for Advertising Sales Directors, depending on the size and scope of the magazine. Salaries range from $35,000 a year at smaller magazines to $150,000 or more at top national publications.

Employment Prospects

Most magazines have an Advertising Sales Director, so employment prospects are good. This is a highly competitive position and while new magazines are starting all the time, there will only be one Advertising Sales Director per magazine.

Advancement Prospects

Prospects for advancement from Advertising Sales Director to publisher are fair; the main competition for this position will come from the circulation department.

Education and Training

An Advertising Sales Director will have a bachelor's degree in magazine sales and marketing; a master's degree in those fields is recommended. He or she will also have at least seven to 10 years of on-the-job training in magazine production.

Experience, Skills, and Personality Traits

A magazine's Advertising Sales Director has the skills to organize and manage a magazine's advertising department. He or she will have a proven track record in generating advertising sales and motivating a sales force.

Personality-wise, the Advertising Sales Director will be a leader as well as a team player. He or she will be highly motivated, persuasive, persistent, and innovative.

Unions and Associations

Networking with others in the magazine business as well as in advertising will be useful for developing rela-tionships and keeping up on trends in the industry. Consider joining the American Advertising Federation (www.aaf.org).

Tips for Entry

1. Work your way up from a position as an advertising sales representative.
2. Attend conferences and take courses in advertising sales taught by seasoned magazine and advertising professionals.
3. Network with other Advertising Sales Directors.
4. Develop a reputation for being able to sell advertising.
5. Visit the American Advertising Federation's online job bank (www.aaf.org) for available jobs.
6. Check out online job postings at AdAge.com: TalentWorks (http://adage.com/talentworks), and general job sites such as www.CareerJournal.com (from the Wall Street Journal) and www.monster.com.

ADVERTISING SALES REPRESENTATIVE

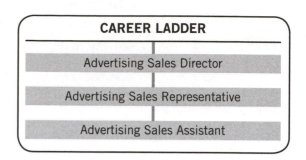

CAREER LADDER

Advertising Sales Director

Advertising Sales Representative

Advertising Sales Assistant

Position Description

Advertising Sales Representatives are the foot soldiers in an ongoing and demanding battle for a piece of the billions of dollars spent each year by advertisers on television, radio, newspaper, and magazine ads. Competition is brutal, and Advertising Sales Representatives have a key and stressful job at the magazine. They are responsible for bringing in much of the revenue necessary to keep the magazine in business.

Advertising Sales Representatives are divided either by geographical territories or categories. Larger national magazines will sometimes have both, with special sales reps that have a particular expertise in a business sector, such as airlines, beverages, automotive, or apparel.

Advertising Sales Representatives spend a great deal of time calling on advertisers and advertising prospects in their region or specialty. Their primary duties are to service advertisers so that they continue buying space in the magazine, while also looking for new business by either getting current clients to buy more space or finding new advertisers.

They have to convince advertisers that the magazine they represent will be read by the kind of customers potential advertisers are trying to reach. To do this, each sales rep is armed with two key tools: the media kit and research. The media kit contains promotional material about the magazine, such as articles, videos, surveys, an ad rate card, and testimonials from other advertisers. The research contains statistics on readers that include buying habits, education, income, age, and even how long they spend reading the magazine and how many other people might also read it. Advertising Sales Representatives use this information to show potential advertisers how their magazine stacks up against others that might also be trying to get the advertiser's money.

Reporting to the director of advertising sales, the Advertising Sales Representative is usually given a quota to keep him or her motivated. These quotas usually go up each year. But the more ad space they sell, the more they earn. A top Advertising Sales Representative could be a magazine's highest paid employee if he or she brings in the advertising sales to warrant it.

An Advertising Sales Representative will also develop relationships with media planners who work for advertising agencies used by advertisers. They do this to keep up on any new advertising campaigns the agency is working on for the advertiser and its brands. A good sales rep will also talk with media buyers to make sure their magazine gets a piece of this business by being put on the schedule for the advertising campaign. The Advertising Sales Representative negotiates ad rates and placement of the ads in the magazine.

Salaries

Advertising Sales Representatives are usually paid on commission, with some getting a base salary plus commission. Depending on the size and scope of the magazine, an Advertising Sales Representative earns from a low of $25,000 a year at smaller magazines to $125,000 or more at top national publications. A few Advertising Sales Representatives can earn even more with commissions and bonuses.

Employment Prospects

Most magazines need Advertising Sales Representatives to survive, so employment prospects are good. Still, this is a competitive area in which survival is dependent on performance.

Advancement Prospects

Prospects for advancement from Advertising Sales Representative to advertising director are good. Individuals may have to move to another magazine to advance, but this is the traditional route to becoming a director. Some Advertising Sales Representatives prefer to remain as sales reps, since they have the potential of earning more than a director. Advancement means getting a reputation for generating advertising revenue and beating whatever quotas are set for you.

Education and Training

An Advertising Sales Representative will have a bachelor's degree in magazine sales and marketing; a master's degree in these fields is recommended.

Experience, Skills, and Personality Traits

A magazine's Advertising Sales Representative has to be able to sell. He or she must know the magazine inside and out and know what the advertisers need. The Advertising Sales Representative must be a skilled communicator, creative, and energetic.

Personality-wise, the Advertising Sales Representative will be highly motivated, persuasive, persistent, and innovative. Being a people person and developing solid relationships with current customers, as well as always generating new business, are traits that will take someone far as an Advertising Sales Representative.

Unions and Associations

For networking and keeping up with trends in the advertising field, join magazine and advertising associations, such as the American Society of Magazine Editors (www.magazine.org/ASME), and the American Advertising Federation (www.aaf.org).

Tips for Entry

1. Work your way up from advertising sales assistant.
2. Take any job at the magazine to learn how the magazine business works. Ask to be kept in mind if there is an opening in the advertising or sales departments.
3. Attend conferences.
4. Network with other Advertising Sales Representatives.
5. Develop a reputation for being able to sell advertising.
6. Check out the available job listings at the American Advertising Federation online job bank (www.aaf.org) and also search www.hotjobs.com and www.careerbuilder.com.

CIRCULATION DIRECTOR

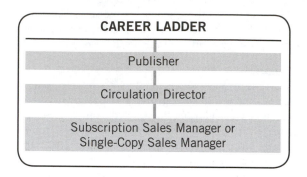

Position Description

The Circulation Director is in charge of getting the magazine to the reader, either through a subscription or single-copy sales at the newsstand or supermarket. It is up to the Circulation Director to not only service and maintain existing readers but to also increase readership circulation.

Reporting to the publisher, the Circulation Director is in charge of one of the magazine's two key revenue-producing units (the other is advertising sales).

One of the Circulation Director's most important tasks is to keep a balance between subscription sales and single-copy sales. Advertisers prefer a high rate of single-copy newsstand sales compared to subscription sales, because single-copy buyers tend to read the issue, where as subscribers are apt to let their magazines pile up unread.

Also single copies bring in more revenue per issue than subscription magazines. So an overly large subscription size could actually cost the magazine money, even though subscriptions bring in money in advance.

Besides keeping the balance between newsstand sales and subscriptions, the Circulation Director has to maintain sales records, schedule mailings, negotiate terms with distributors and newsstand proprietors, and analyze circulation statistics for the advertising department.

It is the Circulation Director who schedules direct-mail campaigns to increase readership. The direct-mail campaign usually makes an attractive offer to first-time subscribers. This could even be a "first issue free" trial, in which a prospective reader can cancel a subscription when he or she receives an invoice or a giveaway as a way of encouraging new subscribers, such as a radio, telephone, or tote bag.

Salaries

There is a wide salary range for a Circulation Director depending on the size and scope of the magazine. Average salaries range from $40,000 a year at small to medium magazines to $140,000 or more at top national publications.

Employment Prospects

Almost all magazines have a Circulation Director; therefore employment prospects are good. This is also a highly competitive position, since it has become one of the prime spots on the way to becoming a publisher.

Advancement Prospects

Prospects for advancement from Circulation Director to publisher are good, since most publishers now come from the circulation side of the magazine.

Education and Training

A Circulation Director is expected to have a bachelor's degree in sales, marketing, or business; a master's degree in one of these fields is recommended. Years of on-the-job training in magazine circulation are also required.

Experience, Skills, and Personality Traits

A Circulation Director should have at least five years' experience in magazine circulation. He or she will have experience in the subscription department as well as newsstand sales.

Circulation Directors possess strong leadership, communication, analytical, and problem-solving skills. They should be team players, outgoing, competitive, goal oriented, energetic, creative, and likeable.

Unions and Associations

There are a number of associations to which it may be helpful to belong, such as the Fulfillment Management Association (www.fmanational.org).

Tips for Entry

1. Work your way up from subscription and newsstand sales management.
2. Attend conferences sponsored by the Fulfillment Management Association (www.fmanational.org).
3. Network with other Circulation Directors.
4. Develop a reputation for being able to grow readership at a magazine.

MANAGEMENT

PRESIDENT

CAREER PROFILE

Duties: One of the top positions at a magazine (usually a larger magazine with a corporate structure) who oversees the company that owns the magazine or magazines

Alternate Title(s): CEO; President/CEO

Salary Range: $50,000 to $200,000+

Employment Prospects: Poor

Advancement Prospects: Poor

Best Geographical Location(s): Anywhere magazines are published, but more often in major urban centers, such as New York, Los Angeles, Chicago, Boston, San Francisco, and Washington, D.C.

Prerequisites:

Education and Training—A bachelor's degree is expected; an MBA is recommended; on-the-job training in senior management at a magazine or media company is expected

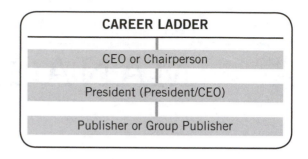

CAREER LADDER

CEO or Chairperson

President (President/CEO)

Publisher or Group Publisher

Experience—Seven to 10 years of experience in various senior management positions at media companies, especially those that publish magazines

Special Skills and Personality Traits—Strong leadership, management, and communication skills; outgoing; intelligent; a visionary; able to lead and motivate a company toward growth and profitability; excellent decision maker

Position Description

The President is often the top management position in any company or corporation, reporting only to the chairperson or board of directors. (At some companies, however, the President might report to the CEO, with the latter job a rung higher on the corporate ladder.) In the magazine business, the position of President (or President/CEO) usually only exists at those companies that own and publish magazines, such as large media companies.

While the President is generally not involved in the day-to-day operations of the magazine and is removed from editorial content decisions, he or she may be responsible to a board of directors regarding how the magazine impacts the company's or corporation's profit and loss. A President may be involved in acquiring a particular magazine or may oversee its development within the media company.

An example of one of the most successful President and CEOs is Rupert Murdoch, a former Australian newspaperman and publisher, who is now chairman of the News Corporation, a corporation that he has built into one of the world's largest media companies, owning magazines, newspapers, television stations, a television network, a publishing company, and a movie studio.

In the publishing group organizational chart of the Meredith Corporation of Des Moines, Iowa, reprinted in Sammye Johnson and Patricia Prijatel's informative book, *The Magazine from Cover to Cover,* the President is at the top of the magazine group, with eight group vice presidents, publishing directors, or senior vice presidents/editors in chief reporting to her or him. Each of the President's direct reports is responsible for one to three magazines, or functions, such as *Ladies' Home Journal, More,* or *Successful Farming,* or strategic marketing.

Salaries

Salaries for President (or President/CEO) will range according to the size and profitability of the company he or she runs, from $50,000 to the mid to high six figures to well into seven and eight figures.

Employment Prospects

Employment prospects for President are poor, since there are so few positions available for this coveted and extremely competitive spot.

Advancement Prospects

Prospects for advancement from President to CEO or chairperson are even tougher than prospects of becoming President. Getting to be President is often as high as you can go.

Education and Training

In general, a President is expected to have a bachelor's degree. A master's degree in management, business administration, or publishing or a law degree is recommended. Most Presidents get their management training as publishers or senior executives within the company. There are also executive management training programs offered throughout the United States—such as the prestigious programs at the Kellogg School of Management, Northwestern University, and Harvard Business School's management training program—that could be useful for additional credentials and knowledge to help garner this high-level and key position at a magazine.

Experience, Skills, and Personality Traits

Presidents must have excellent leadership skills. They are able to lead and motivate a team of senior executives to grow revenues and build companies by increasing market share through internal growth or acquisitions. Their written and verbal communication skills are superb, as is their ability to network within the company and with other company presidents, service providers, and industry leaders. They also usually have admirable speaking skills as well as an ability to be interviewed by the print and broadcast media on behalf of their company as well as by reporters about their industry news, such as financial gains or losses, in addition to commenting on key new products, or current events that impact on their company's performance.

Presidents usually have powerful personalities but are also likable, gaining the respect of colleagues and peers.

Spend time getting to understand each and every editorial, design, marketing, and sales function that makes for a successful magazine. Whether you work in paid or unpaid part-time or full-time positions, the firsthand experience you gain through your related work experiences will eventually take you far in becoming a successful President.

Unions and Associations

There are no unions for Presidents, but they may belong to an association in the magazine industry, such as Magazine Publishers of America (www.magazine.org) or the Periodical and Book Association of America (www.pbaa.net).

Tips for Entry

1. Work your way up the corporate ladder from the position of publisher or group publisher.
2. Be a successful publisher or President of a smaller company that publishes one or more magazines.
3. Network with other Presidents through associations as well as by attending educational seminars and annual association meetings.
4. Develop a reputation for being able to grow a magazine's business, profits, and reputation, with the magazine you direct earning awards for editorial content and graphic design.

PUBLISHER

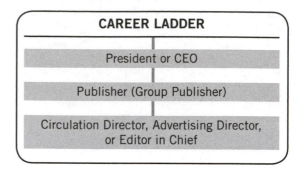

Position Description

The Publisher is the boss of the business side of the magazine. He or she is either ranked on an equal level with the editor in chief or slightly above (especially if the publisher is also the magazine's owner). It is the Publisher's responsibility to make sure the magazine turns a profit.

A typical day for the Publisher may involve budget planning, meeting with top administrative staff to plan strategies for growing circulation, working with his or her advertising director on developing ways to increase ad sales, or even debating with the editor in chief over a controversial cover. He or she may be visiting a top advertiser or meeting the production director to discuss cost overruns. The Publisher might even get involved in negotiating better terms with distributors.

At companies that publish numerous magazines, a Publisher may have financial responsibility over several of those publications; in those cases, the position is called Group Publisher. When there are several titles involved, the Group Publisher would be able to offer advertisers multiple marketing opportunities by placing just one ad in each of the magazines, if the publications are similar enough and suitable for that advertising campaign.

Indeed, the role of Publisher varies from company to company. At smaller magazines, the Publisher may be the publication's top salesperson, as well as getting involved in promotion and circulation.

The Publisher is ultimately responsible for the financial health of the magazine. If the publication is not making money, he or she will be held accountable. On the other hand, if the magazine is doing well and growing in advertising sales as well as circulation, the Publisher will share the credit and financial rewards.

Salaries

For Publishers, like all top magazine positions, there is a wide salary range, depending on the size and scope of the magazine, whether it is local, national, or international. Publishers may earn from $50,000 a year to well into the six and seven figures, if they have a share of the magazine's profits.

Employment Prospects

Employment prospects for Publishers are good, since every magazine needs a business leader. Keeping the job may be harder, since a publisher's success depends on how well the magazine performs financially.

Advancement Prospects

Prospects for advancement from Publisher to president and/or CEO are not good, with so few openings. A large publishing company may have dozens of Publishers or Group Publishers, but it will have only one CEO. Therefore, competition for the top job is fierce, and only the most successful Publishers manage to make it to the top. Turning a huge profit at your magazine or the group of magazines under your watch as Publisher and getting your publication(s) recognized through awards and positive media attention will definitely help your advancement prospects.

Education and Training

A Publisher will probably have a bachelor's degree in marketing, communications, business administration, or journalism, with a concentration in magazines, marketing, public relations, or advertising; a master's degree in one of these fields is recommended. Most Publishers get their training in sales, circulation, or advertising. Occasionally they come up the corporate ladder from the editorial side.

Experience, Skills, and Personality Traits

A magazine Publisher is experienced in sales and business administration; his or her focus is on the magazine's bottom line. A Publisher has to have strong accounting and management skills. He or she should be a great sales person, amiable, and able to personify the magazine he or she represents. In that regard, the Publisher should have an extensive knowledge of the area or subject his or her magazine covers, whether it is fashion, news, or entertainment.

Unions and Associations

There are no unions for magazine Publishers, but there are a number of associations to which it may be helpful to belong. These include the Magazine Publishers of America (www.magazine.org), Periodical and Book Association of America (www.pbaa.net), and Western Publications Association (www.wpa-online.org), for those magazine Publishers west of the Mississippi.

Tips for Entry

1. Work your way up from circulation or advertising director.
2. Start a magazine or newsletter, or buy an existing one, and become its Publisher. Develop a reputation for publishing an excellent and profitable magazine.
3. Network with other Publishers through associations, such as the Magazine Publishers of America (www.magazine.org) or the Women's Media Group (www.womensmediagroup.org).
4. Develop a reputation for being able to grow advertising and circulation for a magazine.
5. Send your résumé to the human resources department, or check out the job openings listed at the corporate Web sites for Publishers of a specific title or dozens of magazines, such as Time Inc., Primedia, Hearst, Rodale Press, and Condé Nast. (See Appendix V for contact information.)
6. Check the job listings at online job banks available through associations, such as the American Society of Magazine Editors (www.magazine.org/ASME) or the American Business Media (www.americanbusinessmedia.com), as well as www.mediabistro.com, www.journalismjobs.com, www.hotjobs.com, and www.careerbuilder.com.

BUSINESS MANAGER

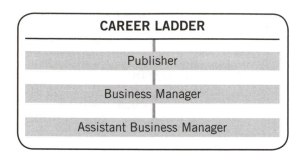

Position Description

The Business Manager reports to the publisher and is in charge of keeping track of the magazine's budget. He or she oversees the publication's revenue streams and all expenses that are paid out in order to bring revenue in. Simply put, the magazine has to bring in more than it pays out in to stay in business, and it is up to the Business Manager to see that it does. Therefore, a good deal of a Business Manager's work involves balancing cost controls with the need to spend some money to make money. He or she does this by working with the publisher on developing not only a business plan but a budget and overall business policy as well. The Business Manager spends a good deal of time on financial planning, reviewing profit and loss statements, making salary proposals, and overseeing bill payment as well as bill collection from advertisers and subscribers.

One of the key tasks involved in balancing costs to revenue involves projection of expenses. The Business Manager has to perform detailed analyses of both future economic trends and past performance in order to come up with a sound financial plan.

On some magazines, the Business Manager is also in charge of managing the office as well as day-to-day operations of advertising sales, circulation, editorial, and promotion. At smaller magazines, the Business Manager might also manage the circulation, advertising sales and promotion, or public relations departments.

Salaries

There is a wide salary range for Business Managers, depending on the size and scope of the magazine. Salaries range from $40,000 a year at smaller magazines to $160,000 or more on top national publications.

Employment Prospects

Most magazines have a Business Manager; therefore employment prospects are good. This is also a highly competitive position.

Advancement Prospects

Prospects for Business Managers to advance to publisher are fair, since more and more publishers are coming from circulation departments. By gaining a reputation for running an efficient department as well as for making your magazine profitable, your advancement prospects should be increased.

Education and Training

A Business Manager will have a bachelor's degree in business administration; an MBA is recommended. He or she will also have years of on-the-job training in magazine accounting and financial analysis. Stay up on trends in the magazine industry by taking educational seminars, especially those on new technology that might result in savings and increased profitability.

Experience, Skills, and Personality Traits

A magazine's Business Manager has the skill to visualize a magazine's financial future. He or she is a skilled accountant, financial planner, or analyst with experience in managing a magazine's financial responsibilities.

Personality-wise, he or she will be a team player, a hard worker, bottom-line oriented, and able to say "no" to expenses that will cause cost overruns.

Unions and Associations

For networking and staying up on industry trends and technological advances, belonging to an association might be useful. Associations include the Magazine Publishers of America (www.magazine.org) and the American Society of Magazine Editors (www.magazine.org/ASME). The Business Manager might also want to be a member of the local chamber of commerce.

Tips for Entry

1. Work your way up from assistant business manager or accountant.
2. Attend conferences offered through national magazine associations, such as the Magazine Publishers of America (www.magazine.org), as well as local breakfasts, lunches, dinners, or educational seminars sponsored by the local chamber of commerce.
3. Network with other Business Managers and publishers.
4. Develop a reputation for being able to handle a magazine's finances, and be associated with a magazine that is turning a profit, increasing circulation, and gaining positive critical acclaim.

PART III
BOOK PUBLISHING

EDITORIAL

EDITOR IN CHIEF

CAREER PROFILE

Duties: Supervises the entire editorial staff; has the last word on acquisitions and the first word on the allocation of funding to the marketing of the finished book; some may continue acquiring and editing books, even though the bulk of their day is consumed in administrative duties

Alternate Title(s): Managing Editor; Acquisitions Editor; Editorial Director; Executive Director

Salary Range: $70,000 to $200,000

Employment Prospects: Fair

Advancement Prospects: Fair

Best Geographical Location(s): New York City and other hubs of book publishing activity, such as Boston, Chicago, and Los Angeles

Prerequisites:

Education and Training—A bachelor's degree is expected; graduate degree in English literature or business is recommended; on-the-job training working up the ranks of a publishing company through editorial positions; courses in editing, marketing, and acquisitions on a nondegree or degree basis

Experience—Although some Editors in Chief work their way up from editorial assistant at the same

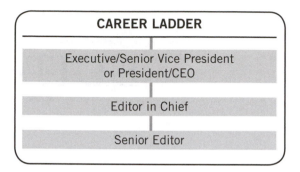

CAREER LADDER

Executive/Senior Vice President or President/CEO

Editor in Chief

Senior Editor

company for their entire career, others prefer to work at a range of publishing companies, from smaller independent companies to large commercial publishers; acquisitions and line-editing experience; in general, this position requires 10 to 15 years of experience

Special Skills and Personality Traits—Excellent editor as well as a people person; superior business skills; competitive personality; intelligent; hardworking; able to handle multiple projects in various stages of completion; able to meet deadlines; superb communication skills; skillful negotiator and marketer

Position Description

Editor in Chief is the top position in the editorial department at a major publishing company; although the job title may be different, such as editor or publisher, at smaller or medium-sized houses, the duties are the same. The Editor in Chief supervises all the editors and editorial activities at his or her company. This is a powerful position at a publishing company, and the Editor in Chief is often interviewed by the media as a representative of the company. The Editor in Chief job is often the stepping-stone to getting a job in management, as either an executive or senior vice president or president/CEO of a major publishing conglomerate; at a small or medium-sized house, the Editor in Chief may also be the president or publisher and CEO.

The Editor in Chief job is more administrative and strategic than editorial, but the Editor in Chief may also choose to edit the manuscripts of high-profile authors, such as politicians, Hollywood celebrities, or controversial sports or literary figures. This position

has a lot of prestige and clout; the Editor in Chief will be invited to literary parties and events, and he or she will be the one whose picture is sought after for a photograph in a trade journal, such as *Publishers Weekly,* in relation to attendance at the annual national book publishing trade show, BookExpo, or at international book fairs, such as the Frankfurt Book Fair or the London Book Fair. The Editor in Chief may also set the goals for the publishing company, in consultation with other editors as well as the CFO (chief financial officer) of the publishing company and/or the publisher or CEO.

There can be confusion at different houses, and throughout the industry, about the title and duties of an Editor in Chief. Some companies may use the term *executive editor* or *executive director,* but each is really the same position. Other companies may have a president who is also Editor in Chief. More important than the title are what a specific company considers to be the duties of their Editor in Chief, as well as the status of the position at that house and what, if any, advancement prospects are available.

Salaries

Salaries range from $70,000 to $200,000, depending on the company's size, revenues, and location, with companies in major urban areas, such as New York City, usually offering higher salaries than those based in small towns or suburbs.

Employment Prospects

Editor in Chief tends to be a position associated with major houses, and since the universe of large publishing companies is relatively small compared to other industries, with only seven major houses, the employment prospects for Editor in Chief are fair. Larger publishing companies with multiple divisions may also have an Editor in Chief for each division, such as the Editor in Chief for the Arts, the Editor in Chief for the Sciences, and so forth.

An Editor in Chief may be employed by a trade or popular publishing company, but there are also scholarly or professional publishing companies and university presses that have this position, such as John Wiley and Sons, Harvard University Press, Oxford University Press, and Wadworth Publishing.

Advancement Prospects

It is quite difficult to advance from Editor in Chief, because the next level is publisher, CEO, or owner of a major company. Once an Editor in Chief becomes associated with a particular house, it is also very difficult to move laterally to another company at the same level, since loyalty is seen as an important job credential in book publishing. Jumping from house to house is frowned upon, so advancement for the Editor in Chief lies mainly in enhancing one's reputation in the field, obtaining raises based on improved performance of one's company, increased profits, including publishing the most number of best-sellers, and garnering more awards, such as the prestigious National Book Award.

Education and Training

A bachelor's degree is expected in order to become an Editor in Chief. A master's or doctoral degree is recommended, especially for those pursuing this position at a scholarly or university press.

Experience, Skills, and Personality Traits

Most Editors in Chief have worked their way up the ranks of publishing, either through editorial, sales, or marketing. A minimum of 10 to 15 years of work in publishing is expected, as are excellent editing, business, sales, marketing, and communication skills. The Editor in Chief must be able to say "no" even more easily than "yes" in terms of acquisitions and budget issues. He or she must stay organized and focused in the midst of full-time editorial and other staff members, who might number in the hundreds or thousands, not to mention the dozens or hundreds of authors, booksellers, sales representatives, wholesalers, and distributors that are essential to the publishing company's survival. The Editor in Chief needs to stay informed on copyright issues and legal concerns as well as on trends in the culture and in the industry. He or she should able and willing to travel and have a genuine enthusiasm about the book publishing industry and books.

Unions and Associations

Membership through one's company in publishing associations such as the Association of American Publishers is recommended (www.publishers.org).

Tips for Entry

1. Develop a reputation as an editor for acquiring excellent books that perform well and/or win prestigious awards.
2. Keep informed about job openings at your own company or other companies through networking with other editors and internal job searches posted by the human resources department.
3. Find out who the key executive search companies are for the book publishing industry and take the time to form a relationship with specific recruiters, letting them know about your background, salary requirements, and whether or not you are willing to relocate.
4. Read *Publishers Weekly* and the daily e-mail newsletter Publishers Lunch (www.publisherslunch.com), so you know what is happening in the industry and where job opportunities are opening up.
5. Go to the annual meeting of the Association of American Publishers (www.publishers.org), and network with other editors so more people know about you in case a job becomes available.
6. Write articles about the publishing industry for *Publishers Weekly.*
7. Get quoted as an industry insider in the *New York Times* or *Wall Street Journal* as an editor or senior editor with wisdom and a proven track record.

8. Let your best-selling authors tell management that you were one of the reasons they are with that particular house and that you were key in their book publishing career's advancement.

9. Check the job openings in the *New York Times* as well as at www.mediabistro.com, the job zone of www.publishersweekly.com, www.mediajobmarket.com, www.indeed.com, or www.linkedin.com/jobs.

10. Let publishing industry executive recruiters, such as Lynne Palmer, and the human resource department at your company know that you are interested in the Editor in Chief position, when one opens up.

11. Write a blog at your own Web site or at a Web site for a publishing industry association or even for a major online publication, like www.huffingtonpost.com. Become known in the industry as a book publishing opinion leader and industry guru and you may find Editor in Chief job opportunities start to seek you out.

SENIOR EDITOR

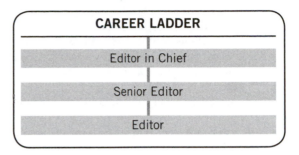

Position Description

The Senior Editor, or executive editor, at a major publishing company is a high-level editor who acquires titles and works on the manuscripts by editing content, although grammar and spelling may be edited by a copy editor. The Senior Editor is the advocate for the book and the author from the initial acquisition meeting until publication and even afterward.

The Senior Editor has his or her own list of authors. Depending on the size of the house, the Senior Editor may have been promoted from the position of editor or associate or assistant editor. The Senior Editor has an associate or assistant editor who reports to him or her as well as an editorial assistant (or administrative assistant).

In addition to working with authors on specific manuscripts, the Senior Editor meets with literary agents to find out what projects and authors are available. If a project sounds as if it would fit the publishing program of the company, the Senior Editor will request a formal book proposal. For a nonfiction book, this will consist of an overview of the project, an annotated table of contents, a discussion of competing and comparative titles, a marketing plan, and, for unpublished authors unknown to the editor, or if requested, a sample chapter. For a novel, quite often the entire novel is required, since it is usually difficult to judge a novel based on just a sample chapter and outline.

The Senior Editor will present the new project at an editorial meeting. If the committee decides to make an offer for the new book—upon consultation with the sales, marketing, and publicity departments—they will make a financial offer for a new book to the literary agent (or if the author is not represented, directly to the author) or to the author's lawyer. The deadline for the book, the amount of money to be offered as an advance, and the royalties offered on each book that is sold will be stipulated, among other terms.

It is the job of the Senior Editor to make sure when a manuscript is submitted that it conforms to the expectations for the project, based on the book's proposal, as well as the publishing program or style of her or his particular imprint or company. Each department or company has its own distinctive style; a nonfiction book published by Free Press, an imprint of Simon & Schuster, may have a very different style and approach than a book on the same topic that is published by Workman Publishing or Wiley. It is the Senior Editor's job to make sure the publishing company's unique style remains consistent in all new books and that the author's material conforms to that style.

The Senior Editor will let the author know what the publication date is for his or her book and will present the book at the sales conference, which usually occurs six months before the book is published. The Senior Editor will take more of a back seat once the book is actually published, as the publicity department takes over at that point. However, the Senior Editor has to keep track of how well a book is selling so he or she can put in for a second printing if the inventory falls below a specific level.

Salaries
There is a wide salary range for Senior Editors, depending upon the size of the publishing company and how high up the position is at that company. Salaries range from $50,000 to $110,000 or more.

Employment Prospects
A Senior Editor plays a very valuable role at a publishing company and has good employment prospects. However, finding that exact job title at all but the largest publishing company may be difficult, since at medium-sized or smaller houses, the functions of the Senior Editor may be performed by the editor or the editor in chief. A key consideration is how much authority the position offers, as well as whether the Senior Editor is developing his or her own list of authors, meeting regularly with literary agents, and having the authority to take at least one project from an idea or proposal to a committee and, once it is accepted, to follow that project through to a finished book.

Advancement Prospects
Advancement prospects are fair, because the next step up in most larger publishing companies is to an administrative position that requires less hands-on editing and acquisitions. To move laterally to another company is also controversial, because loyalty is very important in publishing and traditionally the career path is to move up within the same company rather than jump around from company to company, especially at the higher levels. Advancement will be tied to how well regarded the list of the Senior Editor is, and whether his or her books generate excellent reviews and impressive sales records.

Education and Training
A bachelor's degree is expected for a Senior Editor. Unless a Senior Editor works for a specialized publisher or subject area, such as chemistry or mathematics, a graduate degree in any subject is useful but not required. An educational background in the classics and being well-read in contemporary literature is also useful, especially for those working with fiction. Working one's way up the ladder in publishing companies, from editorial assistant to assistant or associate editor to acquisitions editor, is excellent training for a Senior Editor. Editing term papers while at college or graduate school or, after graduation, taking courses in copyediting and criticism and other aspects of publishing, such as advertising, promotion, and sales, may also be useful.

Experience, Skills, and Personality Traits
Senior Editors need to have patience, excellent judgment about writing, and the ability to read and critique the subject matter of a wide range of projects. What experience is required will differ based on whether a Senior Editor is at a professional or scholarly house or a trade or popular house, since the audience for the books that are acquired and published will be vastly different.

Knowing when to delegate and when to interact directly is another important skill. For instance, a Senior Editor's editorial assistant or administrative assistant could certainly make or confirm appointments for lunch, but only the Senior Editor should talk directly with the literary agent or author about what a manuscript needs or why a book is being published during one season over another.

Unions and Associations
Through their publishing company, Senior Editors can be members of the Association of American Publishers (www.publishers.org). Other associations to consider joining are the Women's National Book Association, founded in 1917, which has chapters throughout the United States (www.wnba-books.org), as well as the Women's Media Group, based in New York City (WMG).

Tips for Entry
1. Work your way up by working at a publishing company in the editorial department and gain valuable on-the-job experience first as an editorial assistant, then as an assistant or associate editor, followed by the job of editor.

2. Attend the annual trade show for book publishing, the BookExpo, held in late spring each year, and network with the executives at publishing companies and editors.
3. Take nondegree or degree courses in editing and publishing at a local university and network with students and faculty to learn about available jobs. (See Appendix II for a list of programs and courses.)
4. Bring well-regarded authors to your publishing company and ask to work directly with them.
5. Join the Association of American Publishers (www.publishers.org) and network with other members. Consider joining other networking associations, such as the Women's Media Group (www.womensmediagroup.com), based in Manhattan, which has monthly educational luncheons with keynote speakers from the publishing and film industries (as well as from politics and government).
6. Become known for acquiring and editing excellent books that get rave reviews, garner lots of foreign sales and book club deals, and sell well; your reputation may lead to job offers from rival publishing companies.
7. Search or place a classified ad in the print or online *Publishers Weekly* or at www.mediabistro.com, www.monster.com, or www.hotjobs.com.
8. Get your résumé to the book publishing industry recruiting companies, such as Bert Davis or Lynne Palmer, and let them know that you are interested in a Senior Editor position.

EDITOR

CAREER PROFILE

Duties: Acquires manuscripts; works with authors and the production department or freelance editors and designers, depending on the size of the publishing company and how it is structured, to produce the book; reports to either a senior editor/executive editor or editor in chief/editorial director

Alternate Title(s): Acquisitions Editor; Production Development Editor

Salary Range: $41,000 to $80,000

Employment Prospects: Good

Advancement Prospects: Fair

Best Geographical Location(s): New York City, where much of the book industry is headquartered, and other urban areas with major book publishers, such as Boston and Chicago; medium or smaller-sized publishers may be located in any town, suburb, or city

Prerequisites:

Education and Training—A bachelor's degree is expected, with a major, minor, or course work in English literature, communications, or publishing; course work or an advanced degree in the particular area that a publishing company specializes in, such as education, science, art history, or the social sciences; a graduate degree in English literature or publishing is recommended; on-the-job training as an unpaid intern or assistant at a book publishing company or literary agency as well as working part time or over the summer at a bookstore, publishing company, or literary agency is also helpful

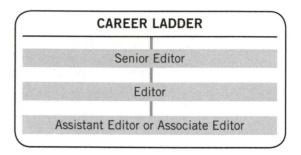

CAREER LADDER

Senior Editor

Editor

Assistant Editor or Associate Editor

Experience—One to three years of experience as an editorial assistant followed by two to four years as an assistant editor or associate editor; experience in the editorial department of a publishing company, especially working with both the authors and one's boss (the senior/executive editor or editor in chief/editorial director) coordinating the many tasks that are necessary to take a manuscript from idea or proposal to finished book

Special Skills and Personality Traits—Excellent writing and editing skills, including a superior vocabulary, excellent grammar, and spelling ability; attention to detail; able to sustain interest for months or years on complicated projects that are taken from idea to finished book; a team player; able to work with people; able to take orders; a creative thinker with a business sense; able to interface with a wide range of departments, from the marketing and sales departments to the production department.

Position Description

Depending on the size of the publishing company and the titles that are used, the Editor could be the position right between editorial assistant and senior editor, or there may be additional steps before or after Editor, such as assistant editor or associate editor. The Editor has more responsibility than either the assistant or associate editor and certainly more than the editorial assistant, who reports directly to the Editor.

The Editor takes on more responsibility for specific projects, often working with the author and literary agent from the idea-stage of a book through its proposal, presenting the proposal at the editorial committee meeting where new books are considered, making

the offer to the author or agent, participating in contract negotiations, and coordinating the delivery of the manuscript, as well as scheduling and supervising the production stages of the manuscript. Depending upon the way the book publishing company has divided up the tasks, the Editor may or may not present a book at the sales conference; this may be relegated to the senior editor. At a small press, the Editor may also be the president of the company.

The responsibilities for an Editor depends on the size of the publishing company, how acquired books are divided among the Editors, and how far up the food chain the Editor is at a specific house. For example, some publishing companies allow Editors to acquire fiction or nonfiction; at other houses, an editor specializes as either the fiction Editor or the nonfiction Editor. (Within non-fiction, positions may be as specialized as cookbook Editor, business book Editor, travel book Editor, and so on.)

At some very small publishing companies, the Editor will work with the sales force and coordinate with foreign rights agents internationally. By contrast, at medium-sized to larger publishing companies, there may be someone, such as the foreign rights manager, whose sole job is foreign rights.

Salaries

Depending upon how large the house is and what the job entails, salaries for the job of Editor can range from $41,000 to $80,000 or more, if the Editor is also the publisher or president and CEO of the company.

Employment Prospects

Although it is hard to break into book publishing, the job of Editor is one that is necessary for the evolution of a book, so book publishers need Editors. Since there are so many titles and functions in the editorial department of a publishing company, it is important for an Editor to be clear about what his or her job responsibilities are, whom he or she reports to, how large a staff he or she will manage, if any, and to know if the particular Editor position being considered is a step up, a step down, or a lateral move in an Editor's career.

Advancement Prospects

Advancing as an Editor is difficult; in the hierarchy of any publishing company, there are fewer and fewer positions the higher up one goes in terms of responsibility and salary. Getting a positive reputation as an excellent Editor and competent administrator who gets along well with authors, literary agents, staff people, and those in the sales, marketing, and publicity departments helps advancement prospects. In trade book publishing, getting known for best-selling and/or award-winning books certainly helps advancement as well.

Education and Training

A bachelor's degree is expected. If you plan to edit fiction, you might want to major or minor in English literature. If you plan to edit nonfiction, you might want to major or minor in the subject area that you will be editing, such as business, cooking, travel, biology, history, or education. Would-be Editors can take editing courses or enroll in a postgraduate degree or nonde-gree program in book publishing, such as the Columbia Publishing Course or the master's program in book publishing at New York University. A graduate degree

in English literature or in an area you plan to specialize in for your publishing career, such as music, art history, or science, is recommended.

Editing is a skill that is honed through on-the-job training, which can be obtained through part-time jobs at a variety of publishing companies. You could work during the school year or over the summers. Paid or unpaid internships at a publishing company are also excellent ways to get training.

Experience, Skills, and Personality Traits

The typical way to become an Editor is by working your way up from editorial assistant to assistant or associate editor. Work hard and learn from those you work for as well as co-workers so that you become indispensable to your employer.

Editors should be well-read, so read as much as you can and also work on your editing, proofreading, and writing skills. You may be the one who has to write up a book for the catalog or present it at a sales meeting, so work on your presentation skills as well. At larger houses, there may be copywriters who create the sales copy for catalogs or back covers, but at smaller houses the Editor may have to do a wide range of editing and writing projects related to each book. You may also be asked to acquire new books, so you will want to stay in tune with what is happening in the literary world as well as in your area of specialization, if you edit a particular kind of nonfiction book.

Editors have to be hardworking and dedicated as well as detail oriented. They often get a great deal of satisfaction out of helping authors complete their manuscripts. An Editor must be able to deal with the wide range of personalities that will be encountered at the publishing company and among authors, illustrators, and literary agents.

Unions and Associations

Though publishing companies are often the members of the Association of American Publishers (www.publishers.org), Editors may attend their annual conference or network with other members on various committees. The Women's National Book Association (www.wnba-books.org), with several regional chapters, including a major one in Manhattan, offers monthly educational programs as well as a membership directory useful for networking.

Tips for Entry

1. Get a job as an editorial assistant and work your way up at that company by getting promoted to assistant editor or associate editor.

2. After working as an editorial assistant for one to three years at one company, if a promotion to Editor is unlikely, look for a job at another company. Contact the publishing search firms, such as Bert Davis or Lynne Palmer, or network at publishing associations' annual conferences.

3. Work for a literary agent and move from that aspect of book publishing into editing at a publishing company.

4. Get a paid or unpaid internship at a publishing company working in the editorial department.

5. Attend the annual BookExpo, and walk from booth to booth talking to the sales or publicity staff and finding out the name of the person to contact for a possible job at the company's headquarters. By going from booth to booth, you could see which companies seem to be a good fit between your interests and abilities and their products.

6. Check the job listings available in the print or online *Publishers Weekly,* as well as at www.mediabistro.com, www.monster.com, and www.hotjobs.com, and www.bookjobs.com

7. Use the most recent *Literary Market Place* to find contact information for the human resource department at publishing companies for whom you would like to work. Also visit those companies online to see if they list available openings for an Editor. These are just a few of the publishing companies that have a careers section at their Web site: Simon & Schuster (www.simonsays.com), Random House (www.randomhouse.com), Sourcebooks (www.sourcebooks.com), and Wiley (www.wiley.com).

ASSISTANT EDITOR

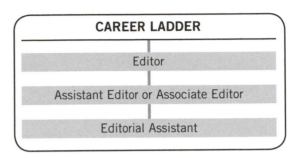

CAREER LADDER

Editor

Assistant Editor or Associate Editor

Editorial Assistant

Position Description

The Assistant Editor job is the step between the entry-level editorial assistant and job of editor, which has more responsibility and authority. Depending upon the publishing company, an Assistant (or Associate) Editor may be allowed to begin selectively to acquire titles under the editor's supervision. At some companies, however, this job is still very much of a right-hand-to-the-editor position with many of the labor intensive tasks, such as entering changes on various stages of the manuscript, from final manuscript and galleys to corrected galleys, completed by the Assistant Editor. Some smaller companies may eliminate this level completely, with individuals rising from editorial assistant directly to editor or acquisitions editor.

Other job duties may include keeping track of a manuscript through all the various editing, proofreading, design, and production stages; making sure the author has cleared any necessary permissions; writing copy for the cover or catalog; preparing a title information sheet; maintaining author and agent relationships; working with authors and their agents on concepts and outlines for new projects as well as revisions of manuscripts under contract; reading and evaluating new proposals or manuscripts; keeping authors aware of changes in style, content, or format of their manuscripts; and gathering the illustrations and art-work for a book and making sure any necessary permissions are cleared.

Salaries

Depending upon the size of a publishing company, its revenue, and its location, salaries range from $25,000 to $45,000. Companies in large metropolitan areas such as New York City, Chicago, or Los Angeles, tend to pay more than in small towns.

Employment Prospects

Excellent editorial assistants who learn enough to be able to handle an Assistant Editor (or Associate Editor) position have good employment prospects, since there is a lot of turnover in these positions. However, if a company is having financial challenges, it could try to absorb the functions of this job into either the higher or the lower job categories. Getting superb recommendations from employers for working as an editorial assistant or getting promoted from within will help your job opportunities as you work your way up the traditional editorial ladder.

Advancement Prospects

Advancement prospects for Assistant Editors (or Associate Editors) are only fair, because as salaries increase and someone outgrows a more subordinate position, there are fewer and fewer higher-paid positions of authority to move into in most publishing companies. Those working at smaller companies, where the next slot up is publisher or the owner of the company, may have to move to another company to advance or even into another aspect of publishing, such as management or sales. Working hard, getting along with your boss and coworkers, the authors and agents you deal with, and being respected and liked by other departments in the company will help you to advance.

Education and Training

A college degree is expected. A graduate degree is recommended. If you plan to specialize in trade books— especially editing novels—a graduate degree in English literature, preferably from a prestigious college or university, is suggested. If your goal is to edit nonfiction, a graduate degree with a specialization in the area that you plan to edit, such as business, cooking, travel, biology, history, or education, will give you an advantage. Noncredit or credit courses in publishing will also be useful; the Columbia Publishing Course or master's program in publishing at New York University might be educational options to consider. Take courses in aspects of book publishing beyond your editing responsibilities, such as marketing, publicity, online sales, or foreign rights.

Experience, Skills, and Personality Traits

Since a career in editing will benefit from as much editing experience as possible, work as an unpaid or paid intern in a variety of editing situations—at a law firm, at a newspaper or magazine publishing company, or at a book publisher.

Read a lot and learn how to critique what you read. Master proofreading, spelling, and grammar. Other skills that you need include the business skills of being able to keep track of your various editing projects, set and meet deadlines, and communicate to your boss how a manuscript is moving along.

Assistant Editors need to be detail-oriented as well as articulate and efficient. They have to be patient,

because there are tasks that need to be mastered and on-the-job knowledge that needs to be gained before achieving the confidence and experience to move to the next, more autonomous step on the ladder in the book-publishing hierarchy.

An Assistant Editor has to control his or her tongue and temper when dealing with others who may be very demanding, including some authors or literary agents, and he or she is expected to be calm and professional at all times. Giving feedback in a gentle and delicate way is another skill that needs to be acquired, since criticism, if handled improperly, can sabotage editor-author relations.

Unions and Associations

Networking and educational opportunities are available through membership in the Women's National Book Association (www.wnba-books.org), with several regional chapters, including a major one in Manhattan. Although it is the publishing company, rather than the individual editors, who belongs to the major trade association for the publishing industry, the Association of American Publishers (www.publishers.org), editors may attend their annual conference or network with other members on various committees.

Tips for Entry

1. Work as an editorial assistant for one to three years, and get promoted from within to the Assistant Editor (or associate editor) slot.
2. After working as an editorial assistant for one to three years at one company, if a promotion to Assistant (or associate) Editor is unlikely, look to another company for your promotion. Contact publishing search firms, such as Bert Davis or Lynne Palmer, or network at publishing association annual conferences.
3. Work for a literary agent, and use that experience to move into an editing position at a publishing company.
4. Bring an amazing property to your boss. If she or he publishes it and it becomes a mega–best-seller, you may get a promotion and even a bonus.
5. Attend the annual BookExpo, and network with exhibitors and at the industry-wide parties that invite all attendees.
6. Check out www.bookjobs.com, a site for publishing jobs in all categories.
7. Use online resources for job hunting, such as www.mediabistro.com, as well as groups related to publishing that are organized through social media sites such as www.linkedin.com.

EDITORIAL ASSISTANT

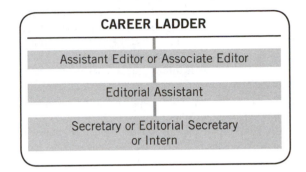

Position Description

Editorial Assistant is the traditional entry-level job into the editorial side of book publishing. The job consists of a combination of secretarial tasks and some editing functions. The Editorial Assistant is indispensable to the specific editor that she or he works for, such as a senior editor or an editor in chief. Unlike the assistant for a specific editor or department who plans to be a career administrative assistant, the Editorial Assistant is expected to move up the ladder, after one to three years, to assistant editor (or associate editor, depending upon the size of the company and its hierarchical structure).

The clerical or secretarial tasks required of an Editorial Assistant may depend on what type of publishing someone works in, such as school or educational publishing versus reference or trade (popular) books. Whether or not an Editorial Assistant works for a small, medium, or large house may also impact on what the job entails. At a smaller publishing company, the Editorial Assistant may have to photocopy a manuscript; at a large house, there may be an entire photocopy department to do the copying for him or her.

Some of the secretarial tasks that are part of the Editorial Assistant's job include answering the phone, confirming or arranging lunch appointments or meetings, and following up on the myriad of secretarial duties, such as filing, that are related to taking a manuscript from an idea to a finished book.

The second component of the Editorial Assistant's job is editing. It is expected that an Editorial Assistant will perform basic editing tasks; how simple or complex those tasks are will be up to the boss as well as the way the job has been defined and structured at a particular company.

For most Editorial Assistants right out of college, even if they have gone to a postcollege training program in book publishing, landing a job as an Editorial Assistant may be their first paid position at a publishing company. There is a lot of glamour and excitement in working with authors and facilitating the successful development of a book from idea to publication, but there is also an enormous amount of paperwork, clerical and secretarial details to be attended to, and deadline pressure. Taking on the job of Editorial Assistant, although a window into the world of book publishing, is usually a necessary step on the road to more editing responsibility, a bigger salary, and, someday, even having one's own Editorial Assistant.

This entry-level job helps reveal whether someone's personality is suited to book publishing, whether the particular type of publishing that they are now working in is where they want to stay, and how well they take orders and work with authors, literary agents, the other departments in the company, such as production, publicity, sales and marketing, and foreign or subsidiary rights.

In addition to moving up the ladder to assistant or associate editor, it might be advantageous to consider taking a job at the same level in a different aspect of book publishing if you are still deciding what part of the publishing process you want to specialize in. Although working as an editorial assistant for an editor may seem like the most obvious first job for someone wishing to enter book publishing, there may be opportunities within book publishing that are more suited to your specific skills or interests, such as publicity or sales, rather than being involved in the development of a book manuscript from start to finish.

As more and more publishing companies eliminate the "slush" pile, the popular term for those manuscripts that come into the company unsolicited, for a whole host of legal and administrative reasons, the Editorial Assistant has to work harder to find ways to distinguish himself or herself as someone able to pick out a winning new author before anyone else discovers him or her. More and more publishing companies rely on submissions only through literary agents or attorneys or by referrals from others in the industry whose opinion they respect. Reading solicited manuscripts from agents and writing a reader report may be one of the job functions for some Editorial Assistants.

The hardest part of being an Editorial Assistant, especially at a larger company, may be knowing when you have learned enough to move up to the next step, assistant editor, or, if there are no openings at the next level at the company you are currently working for, when to start looking for a new job at another company.

In addition to proving yourself an invaluable aid to your editor/boss with the day-to-day demands of scheduling and paperwork, you also want to be learning as much as possible about how book publishing works. Ask to have editing tasks assigned to you if your boss does not volunteer such responsibilities. Whatever editing tasks you are asked to do or volunteer to complete, do an excellent job, and make sure you do it on time or beat your deadline. Reread and carefully check everything you do for your boss or others in the company. Being careful, conscientious, and pleasant to be around as well as humble, helpful, and articulate will get you far as an Editorial Assistant.

Most of all, devote yourself to helping your boss, the senior editor or editor in chief to whom you are assigned, to be as successful as possible. Demonstrating that you are a team player and have outstanding "people" skills is necessary to help you gain the positive relationships and word-of-mouth recommendations that may be even more pivotal to your current and long-term success in a career in the editorial side of book publishing.

Salaries

Starting salaries range from $17,000 to $45,000, depending on the size of the publishing company and its revenue, the type of publishing company (trade versus scholarly or academic), and where the company is located. Salaries are generally higher in New York City, its surrounding areas, and other major urban settings, such as Chicago.

Employment Prospects

Because this is a relatively low-paying entry-level job, there is a lot of turnover. Most Editorial Assistants are either promoted or leave after a couple of years, so there is a constant need for new hires. It will be easier to find a full-time position if you live near or relocate to New York City, the hub of book publishing, or other urban areas with book publishing companies, such as Boston, Chicago, or Los Angeles.

Advancement Prospects

Chances of advancing to the next level of assistant or associate editor are good as long as you prove yourself and there is the budget or the job category available at a particular company for you to move up.

Education and Training

A bachelor's degree is expected for the Editorial Assistant position, especially with a major New York publishing company. Majors could range from English literature to journalism, particularly if you plan to pursue a career acquiring novels, but any major is fine as long as you have the excellent spelling, grammar, and writing skills expected of an Editorial Assistant pursuing a career in publishing. You may find that another major or minor, such as sociology, psychology, biology, or a foreign language, could give you an advantage if there is an opening working for an editor or publisher whose department or company specializes in that subject matter.

Postgraduate certificate programs in publishing and even a master's degrees in book publishing, are available at a few selected colleges and universities. (Check Appendixes I and II for details)

College internships provide valuable book publishing training that could be helpful in landing a postcollege full-time Editorial Assistant position. (For more information on available book publishing internships, see Appendix IV.)

Experience, Skills, and Personality Traits

Editorial Assistants should have basic office or secretarial skills and related experience, such as proper phone etiquette, familiarity with scheduling or confirming appointments, and the editing skills of proofreading, evaluating manuscripts, and obtaining advance endorsements on new books. An Editorial Assistant should have a pleasant personality, high energy, an ability to handle a lot of details and activities at once, patience, and the ability to get along with people. With the increase of electronic transmission of manuscripts and editing with software programs, such as Microsoft Word, excellent computer skills are a necessity for today's Editorial Assistant.

Unions and Associations

The Technical, Office and Professional Union, Local 2110 of the United Auto Workers (www.2110uaw.org), represents Editorial Assistants at several of the major book publishing companies. There are numerous associations that Editorial Assistants may find valuable for networking, information, and job leads. The Women's National Book Association, with chapters in New York City and other major cities, holds monthly panel discussions (www.wnba-books.org). The Association of American Publishers (www.publishers.org) provides career information. The Association for Women in Communications (www.wom-com.org) with chapters in 10 cities including New York City, maintains a job listing service.

Tips for Entry

1. Get a college internship at a publishing company, especially if it will provide opportunities to move up at that company.
2. Take a postgraduate training program in book publishing, such as the Columbia Publishing Course, the certificate program in book publishing or Summer Publishing Institute at New York University, the summer Publishing Institute at the University of Denver, or a similar program. (See Appendixes I and II for listings.)
3. Read *Publishers Weekly* (www.publishersweekly.com) and www.publishersmarketplace.com on a regular basis, especially the classified ads or job announcements.
4. Attend writer or publishing conferences, particularly if speakers include editors at publishing companies who might discuss specific job openings.
5. Network with those in the book publishing industry through local chapters of national associations, such as Women's National Book Association (www.wnba-books.org).
6. Research what companies you want to work at by visiting their Web site, reading articles about that company, or talking with current or past employees. Contact the human resources department for information on any current job openings for Editorial Assistants.
7. Register with an employment agency for the publishing industry, such as Lynne Palmer in New York City. Meet with a recruiter and get your résumé on file.
8. Check out www.bookjobs.com, a site for entry-level publishing jobs in all categories, as well as www.craigslist.org, www.mediabistro.com, or jobs posted through your network or in the jobs section of www.linkedin.com.

COPY EDITOR

CAREER PROFILE

Duties: Edits manuscripts for spelling and grammatical errors and for consistency; marks nonfiction book manuscripts for heads

Alternate Title(s): In-house Copy Editor; Freelance Copy Editor

Salary Range: Varies widely; $25,000 to $65,000 at major publishing companies; $15 to $30 per hour for freelancers

Employment Prospects: Fair for staff jobs; good for freelance opportunities

Advancement Prospects: Poor

Best Geographical Location(s): In-house jobs, if working at the company is required, are mostly found in major publishing centers, such as New York City, Boston, Chicago, or Los Angeles; freelance Copy Editors can work from anywhere as long as they have access to mail delivery and/or the Internet for electronic transfer of files

Prerequisites:

Education and Training—A bachelor's degree with a major, minor, or extensive courses taken in English is expected; a graduate degree in English, publishing, or communications is recommended; working for publishing companies as an editorial assistant, assistant editor, associate editor, or editor will provide useful training

Experience—Reading and editing copy, including articles for the school newspapers at the high school,

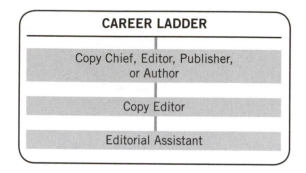

CAREER LADDER

Copy Chief, Editor, Publisher, or Author

Copy Editor

Editorial Assistant

college, or graduate school level, will be useful experience; at least one to three years of experience working at a publishing company as an editorial assistant, assistant editor, associate editor, or editor is expected

Special Skills and Personality Traits—Attention to detail; superior knowledge of correct English, including spelling and grammar; if editing is done on a computer, knowledge of word-processing software, such as Microsoft Word; able to meet deadlines; able to work with a team that will include the editor and author, as well as the production department; able to communicate in writing what needs to be addressed by the editor or the author; able to understand and follow publishing company's house editing style; freelance Copy Editors must be able to get and retain client publishers

Position Description

The Copy Editor is the essential link between the author, the editor, and the proofreader. He or she reviews a manuscript after the author and editor have signed off on it for such basic writing concerns as proper spelling, grammar, and word usage as well as more stylistic issues, such as consistency in novels (if the hero was riding in a red car at the beginning of the book, is the car still red in the last chapter?) and style issues in nonfiction (if the production department has created a design for the interior of the book, the copy editor may mark up heads [A head, B head, C head, etc.] to match that design).

A Copy Editor, depending on the size of the publishing company, may be spending his or her days actually

copyediting and proofreading a manuscript or may be supervising an in-house or freelance staff who do the actual editing, looking over their work, and making sure each project stays on or close to its schedule for completion. Copy Editors need to be highly organized in tracking multiple projects simultaneously. Another task for the Copy Editor may be the development and ongoing maintenance of an in-house style guide. An in-house Copy Editor will be spending time interacting with a book's editor to know when manuscripts are expected from authors so he or she is able to allot time to copyediting that project, or to assign it to an available staff or freelance Copy Editor.

Depending upon how large a publishing company is, the Copy Editor may also function as a proofreader, although, if possible, it is ideal for these functions to be handled by two separate individuals. The Copy Editor will ask questions (called author queries) if something is unclear in a manuscript. The author will be asked to deal with these issues and possibly do some rewriting before the manuscript is then returned to the editor, who will then pass it along to the production department who will send it to the printer.

Salaries

Salaries for Copy Editors vary widely. If someone is an in-house Copy Editor, working for a major publishing company and on salary with benefits, the salary may range from $25,000 to $65,000 or more and vary, depending upon the company's revenues, as well as its location, with companies based in metropolitan areas like New York City or Los Angeles paying more than smaller companies located in suburban or rural communities.

For the freelance Copy Editor, pay is often based on a per-hour rate, $15 to $30 per hour. Some Copy Editors receive steady work from the same publishing companies or authors or years; others may be continually finding new clients on a book-by-book basis.

Employment Prospects

For staff jobs, employment prospects are only fair, since cutbacks have led to more and more Copy Editor positions being phased out in favor of freelance Copy Editors. For freelance Copy Editors, the employment possibilities are good, since practically every manuscript needs a Copy Editor before it is considered consistent and accurate enough to go to the printer.

Advancement Prospects

Although a Copy Editor could use his or her skills to move to another job category in book publishing, such as editor or author, it is hard to advance as a Copy Editor, since there is little notice associated with this job (compared with that given to the editor, who is often credited by an author as pivotal to a book's success). Still, advancement is possible if a Copy Editor develops a reputation for meeting deadlines; being easy to work with; picking up every single typo, grammar problem, or consistency error; and being associated with books that are well-received, especially if their editing is commended.

Education and Training

A bachelor's degree with a major, minor, or extensive courses in English and writing expected. For specialized copyediting, such as for novels, textbooks, or specialized subjects such as history or cooking, additional education in that area may be useful. A graduate degree in writing, publishing, communications, or English literature is recommended. Copyediting is a skill learned through on-the-job training, so the more copyediting experience the better, especially done under an outstanding Copy Editor acting as your mentor. Depending what style manual a publishing company uses, such as *The Chicago Manual of Style,* a Copy Editor would be expected to have a thorough working knowledge of that manual as well as being up-to-date on any grammatical or stylistic changes to the manual once there is a new edition available.

Experience, Skills, and Personality Traits

Copyedit anything and everything, from school newspapers or literary journals to local newspapers. Get as much copyediting experience as you can, working for a newspaper, magazine, or book publisher and obtain recommendation letters from satisfied employers/customers (clients).

A Copy Editor needs to be able to give advice on how to improve a manuscript by looking at the bigger picture, taking care of inconsistencies and reorganizing the book so it is better. He or she also needs an eye for details and an excellent command of the English language, including spelling, punctuation, grammar, and proper tenses. The ability to be consistent is important, and a drive for perfection is a trait that will get you far in the demanding, precision-based career of a Copy Editor.

Since so much copyediting is done electronically today, a Copy Editor is expected to know standard software programs, such as Microsoft Word or QuarkXPress, and how to edit with that program, as well as transmit the edited manuscript over the Internet.

Copy Editors often create a style sheet for each manuscript; he or she must adhere to that sheet. Another necessary skill is being able to communicate what needs to be questioned, or changed, with the author, editor, proofreader, or other staff working on the project.

Unions and Associations

Membership is such associations as the New York City–based Editorial Freelancers Association (www.the-efa.org) or the American Copy Editors Society (www.copydesk.org) may prove helpful for networking and for its job board.

Tips for Entry

1. Become a master editor and wordsmith. Excel in grammar and sentence structure.
2. Take courses in editing and copyediting, and let your professor know that you want freelance or staff opportunities.

3. Join the Editorial Freelancers Association (www. the-efa.org), with more than 900 members, and network. Make sure your biography is included in their online and print directory.

4. Go to writer and publishing conferences or the annual BookExpo, and hand out your business cards. Let everyone know you are a Copy Editor. Include the names, phone numbers, and e-mail addresses of satisfied customers who will sing your praises.

5. Develop expertise as a Copy Editor so publishers or authors with books in that genre (such as mysteries or romance novels) or category (such as self-help or textbooks) will approach you.

6. Do a direct mailing to writing or publishing associations, and attend networking parties or panel discussions with time for networking. Let others know you are looking for a job as a Copy Editor or for freelance clients.

7. Referrals are key in getting freelance projects. Tell everyone who is satisfied with your work to recommend you to authors, literary agents, and publishing personnel. If allowed, have those on publishing lists on the Internet send a post about you with contact information for follow-up.

8. Look at job openings that are posted at www. craigslist.org, www.mediabistro.com, www.book-jobs.com, or through your professional network or in the jobs section of social media sites especially www.linkedin.com.

PROOFREADER

CAREER PROFILE

Duties: Reads over the final manuscript, after the editor and copyeditor have finished editing; checks for typos, inconsistencies, and misspellings

Alternate Title(s): Lite Copy Editor

Salary Range: $.75 to $2 per page, depending on type of materials; $25 to $40/hour.

Employment Prospects: Poor for full time; Good for freelance work

Advancement Prospects: Poor

Best Geographical Location(s): With the Internet and overnight mail service, proofreaders can now be located anywhere, although making the contacts to get the assignments may be easier if working or living in a major publishing city, such as New York

Prerequisites:

Education and Training—A bachelor's degree is expected, including majoring in English with courses in grammar, along with additional on-the-job training in the grammar, editing, writing, and style requirements for proofreading a book manuscript

Experience—Working at a publishing company or being mentored on a freelance basis by a seasoned and well-respected proofreader is a way of learning the necessary techniques and skills

Special Skills and Personality Traits—Patience; an eye for details; consistency; able to deal effectively with book authors, literary agents, and editors; able to meet deadlines; conscientious

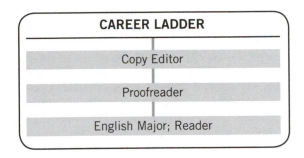

CAREER LADDER

Copy Editor

Proofreader

English Major; Reader

Position Description

The Proofreader is the last person to see the manuscript after the editor, copy editor, and book author have made all their changes. There are several stages in the process from manuscript to published book that might rely on a proofreader. The most common employment for a Proofreader is after the manuscript has been finalized and after it has printed, reviewing the typeset version. The Proofreader is to assure that the printer will get letter-perfect copy, whether the notations are made on the hard copy or electronically with tracked changes.

Proofreaders are also necessary for making sure there are no typos, spelling errors, or grammatical mistakes in the front or back cover copy, as well as the spine or any press releases or catalog copy.

Sometimes the role or job of a Proofreader is confused with that of the copy editor. The copy editor is looking for stylistic and content issues that the proofreader rarely gets into although there may be some light editing done by some Proofreaders.

The copy editor may create a master style sheet for the proofreader to follow; if the copyeditor does not provide such a sheet, the proofreader should create one or ask the author or editor to supply one. Having a style sheet will help maintain the consistency of a manuscript in terms of grammar and spelling.

Salaries

This is usually a freelance job that is paid for an a per page basis, from $.75 to $2 a page. Some proofreaders charge by the hour ($25 to $40 per hour). Rates may vary if material is excessively complex, demanding, or even hard to read, or if the project is done in a huge rush. Some larger companies, however, may employ one full-time, salaried Proofreader.

Employment Prospects

Most Proofreaders are hired on a freelance basis. Therefore, full-time employment prospects are poor. Part-time or freelance employment opportunities, however, are good. Proofreaders may be employed by printers, publishing companies, or individual authors.

Advancement Prospects

Getting known as an excellent Proofreader often leads to multiple jobs from the same publishing company or author. There is little room for advancement, however, since a Proofreader does the same task but on different projects. If you aspire to becoming a copy editor, point out what style changes you would implement if you were employed to do so.

Education and Training

Proofreaders are expected to have a college degree and excellent writing skills, including grammar and spelling. A thorough knowledge and mastery of the most recent edition of the style guide that a publishing company is following, such as *The Chicago Manual of Style*, is expected. Working for a publishing company or any kind of publication where proofreading symbols and skills are taught is useful background. Being on staff as a proofreader, even at a law firm, will provide excellent training for proofreading books.

Experience, Skills, and Personality Traits

Proofreaders need to be consistent and reliable. They need to be able to meet deadlines and work with a range of personalities and levels at the company, from the copy editor to the editor to the author. The head copy editor may hire freelance Proofreaders, so being able to work well in a team situation is also important. Perfectionism is a good trait in a Proofreader, who needs to have a very trained eye and a consistent ability to find and correct any errors in a manuscript. Confirming the spelling of proper names may require doing some research or flagging the manuscript (pointing out the word or item in question) for the author or editor to follow up on.

Unions and Associations

Since so much of proofreading is done through freelancing, as well as word-of-mouth recommendations, it may be helpful to join an association of editors and proofreaders, such as the Editorial Freelancers Association (EFA) (www.

the-efa.org). A directory of members is available at the Web site, as well as an e-mail discussion list. EFA also maintains a job alert for its members, regularly sending information via e-mail about available jobs.

Tips for Entry

1. Work for a publishing company in any capacity, and let it be known that you want to do proofreading.
2. Take a course in editing or proofreading and tell the teacher, especially if he or she works in publishing, that you are open to freelance work as a Proofreader.
3. Join publishing associations, such as the Women's National Book Association (www.wnba-books. org), and let the members know that you are available for proofreading.
4. If you have friends or coworkers who are writers, offer to proofread a sample of their writing gratis to start getting work samples of your proofreading skills.
5. Go to writer conferences or publishing trade shows where book editors may congregate, and hand out your business card, letting everyone know that you are available as a Proofreader.
6. Check *Publishers Weekly*, the *New York Times*, and such job sites as www.mediabistro.com, www.monster.com, www.bookjobs.com, www. craigslist.org, and www.hotjobs.com for job openings.
7. Go to the Web sites for the publishing company you want to work for and see if they list job openings right at their site. (If you need help finding contact information for publishing companies, consult the most recent edition of the *Literary Marketplace*, updated annually.)

INDEXER

CAREER PROFILE

Duties: Creates the index for a nonfiction popular book or textbook, which enables the reader to locate specific names, topics, or references

Alternate Title(s): In-house Indexer; Freelance Indexer

Salary Range: Usually done on a freelance basis, indexing fees vary, based on the length and complexity of the index that is being prepared, but usually run around $1,000 for the standard 225-page nonfiction book (may be more for a complex encyclopedia and less for a shorter book); Indexers may also charge per page, per entry, or by the hour, ($20 to $25/hour) with experienced Indexers earning higher fees than new Indexers

Employment Prospects: Fair

Advancement Prospects: Fair

Best Geographical Location(s): Most Indexers work on a freelance basis, as long as there is access to client publishers or authors to get the work, creating an index can be carried out anywhere, since projects are distributed electronically, by delivery services, or through the regular mail

Prerequisites:

Education and Training—A bachelor's degree is expected; some background in English or library science is helpful; a graduate degree in research or library science is recommended; credit or noncredit courses in how to create an index are helpful; on-the-job index or editing training

Experience—On-the-job training at a trade publishing company in the editorial or indexing department or for a textbook or for a reference book publisher

Special Skills and Personality Traits—Logical and creative thinkers able to see relationships between subjects and have a sense of order about what topics should go where and what concepts someone might want to explore; understanding of what to list and how to list it; able to use indexing software; attention to detail; able to perform repetitive task of reading and rereading the book while writing the index to search for connections, names, places, and topics

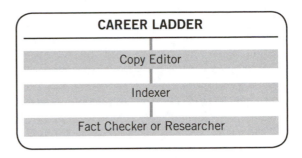

CAREER LADDER

Copy Editor

Indexer

Fact Checker or Researcher

Position Description

Most nonfiction books and all textbooks require an index, a section in the back of the book where names, places, topics, and subjects are categorized for ease in locating them within the text. For research purposes, librarians and students especially like an index so they can quickly locate a concept or a piece of information without having to skim through the entire book.

Indexing is both an art and a skill. One can teach someone the fundamentals of indexing, such as how to arrange items alphabetically as well as the style or punctuation for an index, but learning what to include and what to leave out is the art of indexing.

Some publishing companies even have their own guide to indexing that they distribute to Indexers, in addition to specific instructions as to style considerations for that company or for a particular book.

Throughout the writing and editing stages of preparing a new book, an author or an editor may take notes about what they would like to have in an index. But the index is usually not prepared by the Indexer until the book is already typeset and in the final stages of preparation for publication, when page proofs are available with page numbers that can be cited in the indexing. A draft of the Index may be shared with the book's editor and author to assess if there are any terms of concepts that are missing that should be added before the Index is finalized. The Indexer, however, is the one who is ultimately responsible for the headings and subheadings, the terms that are written in the index, the placement of those terms, as well as its accuracy.

Salaries

Salaries vary widely, with per-page rates from $3 to $12, and per-project rates average $1,000 for a typical, 225-page trade nonfiction book. Rates are generally higher for a more complex textbook and lower for a simpler, shorter nonfiction book. Fees may also be computed by the hour ($20 to $25 per hour).

Employment Prospects

Since Indexers usually work on a freelance basis, employment is difficult to obtain initially, but once a publisher works with someone and likes his or her work, they will often use the same person again and again. Certain types of books, such as textbooks or directories, depend on an excellent index; targeting educational or reference book publishers for job opportunities might be a way to increase the likelihood of employment.

Advancement Prospects

Advancement as an Indexer may mean supervising several Indexers or possibly starting an indexing service that works with client publishers and coordinates the Indexers that are hired. Besides that type of advancement possibility, which requires entrepreneurial and management skills, in addition to completing indexes, Indexers might expand their services to include more editing, copyediting, or proofreading.

Education and Training

A bachelor's degree is expected. A major in library science, English literature, or publishing will be helpful. If you plan to specialize in creating the index for a certain kind of book, such as a science or psychology textbook, having courses, a major, or a master's degree in that field is recommended.

Training in the proper way to create an index is mandatory, whether it is learned on the job, by attending courses, or by reading about indexing and teaching yourself.

Experience, Skills, and Personality Traits

Get experience editing and indexing by working for a trade book or educational book publishing company. A paid or unpaid internship in the copy department of a major publishing company or assisting an Indexer will also be beneficial.

An Indexer needs to have a logical mind but also be able to think like the typical reader of the book he or she is indexing. What would someone be most likely to want to find in this book? What topics? Names? Titles? Subjects? How should that material be categorized?

Indexers need to have excellent spelling, punctuation, and grammatical skills, as well as be able to follow the style sheet that an editor or publishing company provides. If the editor or author used a computer program that marked words or phrases for use in the index, the Indexer needs to know how to access that informa-

tion and to decide if he or she will use it in the final index.

An Indexer needs to be patient, thorough, and persistent in reading and rereading a manuscript until the index is complete. He or she needs to be somewhat of a perfectionist, as he or she must check and recheck the index for errors. The Indexer is often brought in at the very end of the production process, when the final manuscript has been approved and typeset so the page numbers can be inserted in the Index. The ability to work under intense deadline pressure is another necessary personality trait.

Unions and Associations

There are more than 1,100 members in the American Society of Indexers (www.asindexing.org). The association offers educational programs as well as networking through its annual meeting. Indexers also belong to the Editorial Freelancers Association (www.the-efa.org), which has monthly meetings in New York City, where it is headquartered.

Tips for Entry

1. Get a paid or unpaid job or internship working for an editor or an Indexer, helping to put an index together, and learn the trade.
2. Take a course on indexing and ask your teacher to recommend you to editors, authors, publishers, or book packagers who need an Indexer.
3. Approach publishing companies that publish nonfiction books with indexes, or book packagers that package nonfiction books, especially educational or reference book publishers or packagers, and find out who hires their Indexers. Follow up with a résumé, a cover letter and, if appropriate, a sample of your work. If you need help finding publishers, consult the most recent *Literary Marketplace.* You can also search online at the Web site for the Association of American Publishers (www. publishers.org). Their Web site has a list of the more than 300 member publishing companies with hyperlinks to their sites. Many of those companies list contact information or even a hyperlink to the human resources department.
4. Go to the Web site for the Association of American University Presses (aaupnet.org), or contact the association for a list of member publishers. These educational publishers are likely to need the services of Indexers.
5. Since in the United States the author is responsible for providing his or her book's index (or the publisher will hire an Indexer and charge the

fee against the author's future royalty earnings), consider approaching a nonfiction or text book author directly. Offer to provide an index to get a work sample. If the publisher accepts the index, your fee would be paid for by the publisher (as an advance against the author's royalties) or by the author.

6. Network at writer and publisher trade shows, conferences, and monthly meetings, and bring along your business cards announcing your availability as an Indexer. (See the listings for such regional and national associations and trade shows in the Appendixes V and VI).

7. Attend the annual meeting of the American Society of Indexers (www.asindexing.org), held in a different city each year. Also consider joining and becoming active in one of the local chapters of the association, networking with other members and attending educational workshops.

BOOK PACKAGER

CAREER PROFILE

Duties: Puts together a complete project, including author, editor, and any other necessary elements, such as photo research or permissions, and then finds a company who will publish it (or is approached by a publisher who asks the packager to complete a project for that company)

Alternate Title(s): Book Producer; Development Consultant

Salary Range: Varies widely from a per-project basis to getting an advance and royalties that may have to be split with the author and/or the author's literary agent; fees may range from $20,000 with some complex educational projects going as high as six figures for one or more packages

Employment Prospects: Fair

Advancement Prospects: Fair

Best Geographical Location(s): May be done from anywhere in the world, but working near or in the major publishing centers, such as New York City, makes it easier to have access to the publishing companies that will be pitched the Book Packager's projects

Prerequisites:

Education and Training—A bachelor's degree is expected; an advanced degree is recommended, especially if a Book Packager plans to specialize in that field, such as in early education textbook projects; any on-the-job training in any aspect of book publishing is useful, especially working in the editorial or production department; working as an intern or paid assistant for a smaller or independent publishing company, where you may do multiple jobs that are performed by different individuals at a larger house, may be especially useful

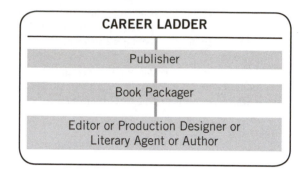

CAREER LADDER

Publisher

Book Packager

Editor or Production Designer or Literary Agent or Author

Experience—Production and editing experience at a book publishing company or even in newspaper or magazine publishing is useful; working in any office situations will be helpful to learn about how to be a team player, as well as how to either delegate effectively or take orders; most Book Packagers have spent two to 10 years working in various editorial or production jobs at book publishing companies, developing the skills and contacts to enable them to go out on their own

Special Skills and Personality Traits—Able to envision the finished book; visionaries although publishers may come to them with an idea that they ask the Book Packager to package for them, often it is the Book Packager that has to come up with the concept, from start to finish; creative and able to conceive of projects that in-house editors have not devised themselves; attention to detail; ability to start a project and stay with it for months or years; love of books and research; people person; ability to delegate and multitask

Position Description

As publishing companies have trimmed their in-house staffs to keep their overhead lower and as smaller, independent publishing companies have sprung up that lack all the staff that is required to produce a book from start to finish, the Book Packager has emerged as a powerful and unique job category. For the book publisher, using a Book Packager can be a win-win situation. The publisher, who has a way to print and distribute the finished book product, eliminates devoting all the in-house

resources to nurturing authors or production teams for months or years until the final product is ready. Instead the Book Packager takes on all those functions, acting almost like a minipublishing company, but the Book Packager stops short of printing, distributing, or selling the books that he or she makes happen, at the wholesale or retail level.

Book Packagers are especially useful for a series of books, since he or she gets all the personnel needed in place for the first book, and the same personnel can be reused for additional volumes. For example, an educational publisher might go to a Book Packager and ask him or her to create a series for grades one through six, with finding an author right through to hiring the indexer for the finished work. The publisher may be involved in certain decisions related to the project, as well as giving the final go-ahead to the manuscript and approving the design for the series. But it is the Book Packager who hires (or fires) those working on the package. The publisher generally takes care of the publicity for the series, as well as the sales and marketing.

The Book Packager may work for just one publisher for several years if the project is complex and lucrative enough. Alternatively, a Book Packager may have numerous smaller projects in development with different publishers. Only one or two aspects of the publishing process may be packaged through the Book Packager, such as finding the author and the illustrator for a children's book; producing the book may then be done in-house (or the Book Packager may get the book all the way to the printer but not take care of delivery of the finished books).

Salaries
Salaries vary widely, depending on the project, the publisher that hired the Book Packager, and whether the fee is for a one-book project or a series. Fees can range from $20,000 to six figures, with major New York City trade or educational publishers paying more than medium and small companies. Out of that fee, the Book Packager often has to hire all the creative, editorial, and production personnel necessary to complete the book or series, with some projects even requiring the delivery of bound books to the warehouse.

Employment Prospects
Employment prospects are fair for this very specialized aspect of the publishing industry. It is difficult to sell a manuscript to a book publisher; it is that much more challenging to sell a concept or a series of books to a publisher and ask for thousands or even hundreds of thousands of dollars to then create those books.

Advancement Prospects
If a Book Packager gets a reputation for creating books or series in a cost-effective way, and those projects are well-reviewed and financially successful, there may develop a great demand for his or her services. It is hard for a Book Packager to advance in the business without numerous major, successful projects associated with his or her book packaging company.

Education and Training
A bachelor's degree is expected, with a major, minor, or courses in business, English literature, publishing, graphic design, or marketing. A graduate degree in publishing or in the area that the Book Packager plans to specialize in, such as history or education, is recommended. Since the Book Packager is competing with all the salaried, staff positions for a particular project, the more prestigious credentials and specialized skills related to the proposed book, the better.

On-the-job training, as an intern or paid assistant, in any and all aspects of the book publishing industry will be useful to the Book Packager. He or she needs to know as much as possible about every part of the business.

Experience, Skills, and Personality Traits
Work in book publishing as an acquisitions editor or editor or in the production department so you understand the way a book evolves from the author's manuscript to published product.

Book Packagers need to be excellent managers, since they work with so many people, from the author and his or her literary agent to freelance or staff editors, copy editors, indexers, researchers, permissions editors to members of the production team, from the production editor and illustrator to the printer.

Knowing how, as well as what, to delegate, is essential, as is having superior project and time management skills. Since the Book Packager is usually responsible for hiring and managing a staff, as well as paying for all the services that the project requires, he or she should have excellent accounting skills and the ability to keep track of expenses. Expertise in using accounting or finance software or the ability to delegate those tasks to a financial manager is also expected. Being able to get estimates and prices for the various services or products that are needed is also necessary.

Excellent communication skills are also essential, since the Book Packager needs to generate work over the phone and through e-mails, in-person meetings, or networking at trade shows or publishing parties.

Being a hard worker and detail-oriented are other personality traits of the Book Packager. Creativity is essential, since he or she needs to be one step ahead of the industry in order to sell ideas to publishing companies before they come up with them on their own in-house. Book Packagers have to be exceedingly well-organized, as well as able to follow through on ideas and projects and pleasant to work with.

Unions and Associations

Founded in 1980, the American Book Producers Association (www.abpaonline.org) is a networking and educational membership association. Every fall they offer an all-day educational seminar that is a guide to book packaging.

Tips for Entry

1. Join the American Book Producers Association (www.abpaonline.org), and network with members. Offer yourself as an unpaid or paid intern to one of the member Book Packagers to learn the business.
2. Find an author with an amazing idea and develop a book package to approach literary agents or publishers about pursuing.
3. Attend BookExpo, the annual trade show for the book publishing industry held in May or June each year, and network with Book Packagers.
4. Check out the announcements at www.media bistro.com for Book Packagers looking for assistants or interns.
5. Network at publishing industry association monthly meetings and panels, such as those held by the Women's National Book Association (www.wnba-books.org), and let everyone know you want to be a Book Packager.
6. Contact publishers listed in *Literary Marketplace* or at the Web site for the Association of American Publishers (www.publishers.org), and pitch your skills as a Book Packager to the person in charge of book development (such as the senior editor, editor, or editor in chief). Be prepared to present specific projects that are targeted to that company, as well as an itemized budget about what the project will cost and information about why they should hire you to package it for them.

AUTHOR

NOVELIST

CAREER PROFILE

Duties: Writes the manuscript for a novel or fictitious book; carries out any research that may be necessary as background for writing the work

Alternate Title(s): Author; Book Author; Fiction Author; Mystery Writer; Romance Writer

Salary Range: $0 to millions of dollars

Employment Prospects: Fair

Advancement Prospects: Poor

Best Geographical Location(s): A novelist can create his or her novel from anywhere in the world

Prerequisites:

Education and Training—A high school diploma is expected; a bachelor's or graduate degree is recommended. Courses in English literature may be especially helpful; training in the basics of writing and specialized educational training may also be useful, such as a master's in criminal justice or an M.D. degree, if a novelist plans to specialize in a type of fiction; reading a lot of books and practicing one's writing provide excellent training for a future novelist; on-the-job training may also be helpful as background for the setting of novels—for example,

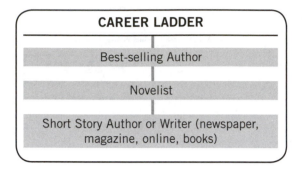

CAREER LADDER

Best-selling Author

Novelist

Short Story Author or Writer (newspaper, magazine, online, books)

working at a hospital for writing novels with a medical setting

Experience—There is no substitute for actually writing fiction, whether short stories or novels; from writing and rewriting the novelist will gain valuable practical experience

Special Skills and Personality Traits—Curious mind; ability to create plots and memorable characters; excellent writing skills; hardworking; disciplined; goal oriented; patient; able take criticism; not afraid of a highly competitive and crowded profession

Position Description

Novelists are very highly regarded in the book publishing business, and becoming a Novelist is a goal of practically every fiction author. Being able to support oneself from the advances or royalties for your novels may take many years to achieve, if at all, but it may be possible to write and sell novels as a secondary income if your writing is outstanding enough and you are able to find a publisher for your work, although some are even earning money by self-publishing.

Many Novelists have another career in addition to writing books—lawyer Louie Nizer wrote legal novels, Robin Cook is a doctor who also writes medical thrillers, and John Grisham is a lawyer. Elmore Leonard, who finally "broke out" after he had published numerous novels, worked in advertising. Tom Clancy was an insurance agent until his novels produced enough income that he could write full time. Mary Higgins Clark began as a magazine writer, but by the fifth novel she was able to devote herself to just writing fiction.

It is often many years, and books, until a Novelist becomes an "overnight" success. In an interview with the coauthor Jan Yager, best-selling suspense Novelist Harlan Coben, whose books include *Tell No One*, shared about his writing career, noting that he wrote his first novel while still in college, but it was never published. Nor was his second novel. After graduating college, instead of going to law school, he took a job in the family travel business. Coben kept that job, and kept writing, for the next eight years, through book after book, until his writing career was successful enough that he became a self-supporting author.

Coben sold his first novel for $2,000 after sending a query to someone he saw mentioned in a *Publishers Weekly* job column; he recognized her name from his alma mater, Amherst College. He wrote her a letter and mentioned that he had a novel, but that it was commercial and he knew that the company she worked for published a different kind of fiction. But he asked her if she could recommend someone at another publishing company who might read his novel.

It turned out that her company was trying to publish more commercial fiction, so she bought his first and then his second novel, printing around 4,000 copies of each book. Coben kept writing novels and getting published as his sales and popularity increased. "Each one sold progressively better," Coben notes, as he built his career to his current *New York Times* best-seller status.

"The best experience I know is to keep writing," says Coben. After his first two novels, he decided he really wanted to write suspense. He wanted to write a novel that someone would take on vacation and enjoy reading so much that you "did not want to leave the hotel, you want to read the book."

Another way that aspiring Novelists support themselves along the road to fame and fortune is to teach writing at the college and graduate school level. Once successful, Novelists may be honored by "writer-in-residence" positions, which usually require teaching fewer courses, sometimes just one seminar a week, and possibly working with selected individual students.

Novelists are usually divided into two broad categories: those who write for adults and those who write for children or young adults. (See the separate profile for Children's Book/Young Adult [YA] Author). However, there are Novelists who are crossing over into both categories. Carl Hiaasen, who is known for his adult thrillers, now has a book out for young adults, *Hoot* (and he is also a newspaper reporter for the *Miami Herald*).

Within the broad category of adult novels, there are numerous classifications that publishers use to acquire books and bookstores use to shelve and sell the novels, including literary fiction, mystery, suspense, romance, and historical fiction. Within each of those categories, there are even more distinctions, such as the classic "whodunit" mystery and the detective novel.

Although all Novelists have the same basic skills—excellent writing ability, including the ability to create original and memorable plots and characters—each type of fiction has its own traditions and requirements. Literary fiction is harder to define and categorize; there is regional fiction, such as the so-called southern Novelists, as well as those who write historical novels or psychological fiction.

Novelists who write a certain type of fiction may want to join associations for that type of novel, such as the Authors Guild (www.authorsguild.org) for literary fiction, the Romance Writers of America (www.rwa.org) for romance novels, and the Mystery Writers of America (www.mwa.org) for mysteries, suspense, and thrillers. Regional and national conferences are offered each year, as well as awards to apply for, opportunities to network with editors and publishers looking for new talent, and lectures by published, successful novelists. (Check out the listings in Appendix III under "Associations.") Also writers are often very generous to other writers, especially aspiring Novelists, whether they meet them through associations, by attending conferences, or by receiving an e-mail or letter. As long as an aspiring Novelist is polite and succinct, many accomplished Novelists are open to providing encouragement or even suggestions. But do not take it personally if a Novelist turns down your request to read your manuscript either for an advance blurb (endorsement) or to recommend you to an agent or publisher. Writers have to preserve their time for writing and making their own deadlines; it is okay to ask for a reading, but you should take any "no's" that you get graciously and without hostility.

For every fiction book author whose name is a household word, there is the struggling book author who may have published one, two, or more books, perhaps even to some excellent reviews and modest sales, but who cannot make a living at his or her writing. They continue to write in addition to their "day job," holding out hope that a book will take off and become a runaway best-seller.

In the last decade, with the introduction of word processing programs that enable book authors to typeset their manuscript, not just write it, there has been an increase in self-published authors. Instead of selling the manuscript to a small or university press or a major publishing conglomerate, the author acts as both author and publisher. There are estimates of anywhere from 4,000 to 50,000 self-publishers in the United States today.

But most self-published books have a hard time getting distributed in large enough quantities to justify the time, money, and effort that goes into the book. With the increasingly vast numbers of self-published books, it has gotten harder and harder for a self-published book to get noticed by critics or offered for sale in chain or independent bookstores. (Selling online, however, is an option that has definitely leveled the playing field for self-published book authors. As long as the author/publisher can drive buyers to the online bookstores or to their own Web sites for sale, distribution is at least possible.) Still, there are self-publishing success stories: M. J. Rose self-published her novel, *Lip Service;* it was picked up by a major book club, and she went on to sell the novel to top New York publisher and to obtain a New York literary agent, who then sold several additional novels.

An analysis of the biggest best sellers in 2007, however, found that six major publishing houses—Simon & Schuster, Hachette, HarperCollins and Holtzbrinck,

Random House, Penguin USA—accounted for 87.5 percent of the best sellers on the list.

Novelists need to keep up with what else is being published so that he or she will not "reinvent the wheel" or be considered derivative rather than fresh and new. It is also important to make the first novel that is published the best that it can be, because there is a tradition in publishing of celebrating "first Novelists." There is also a saying that it is easier to get a first novel published than it is to publish the second one. The reality behind that statement is that as hard as it is to get that first opportunity, if the review attention to the novel or the sales are insignificant, it will be that much harder to convince the first publisher or a new one to take a second chance. Although fiction tends to be more review-driven than nonfiction (which is author-driven, meaning that an author's promotional efforts can have more of an impact on the sales of a nonfiction book, because it often is topic-based), Novelists should find out what they can do to help with the promotion of their novels to increase visibility and sales.

Salaries

It may be harder to get a novel published than a nonfiction book, and the initial advance may be miniscule until a novelist has a proven track record and devoted fan base, but it is also true that the earning potential for novels is generally bigger than for the typical nonfiction book. If a novel takes off, it can sell in the millions of copies, and there is a likelihood that it may also be sold to a movie producer. Although only a small percentage of novels actually become movies, the option money for a movie sale may be formidable for best-selling novels.

Novelists may get little or no advance from a smaller publishing company, or they might receive the multimillion dollar contracts and royalties in the millions similar to such household names as Stephen King, James Patterson, and Jackie Collins. The range of money that a Novelist could expect to earn varies widely, from no advance to a six-figure advance for an especially high-concept novel or an author who already has name recognition in another field. If a Novelist develops a steady audience, his or her advance and royalties might increase with each subsequent novel; if the audience fails to grow, especially if the advance is not earned out by sales, it may prove harder to find a publisher at all.

Employment Prospects

It is hard to break in as a Novelist, because there are so many more writers creating the novels than there are slots for publishing their books. It is also extremely difficult to develop a new Novelist into a revered author with a fan base, so publishers have to be very cautious about acquiring and publishing unknown Novelists. For that reason, Novelists who also have a name in another field may have an advantage over complete unknowns. Television producer Stephen J. Cannell, for example, started writing novels a few years ago and has become a best-selling author. Because of all the small or independent press and self-publishing options today, prospects for getting a novel published are fair. Of the estimated 300,000 new books published in 2008, 47,541 were fiction, according to Bowker.com; the remainder were nonfiction and juvenile titles. Competition to get a novel published is exceptionally fierce.

Advancement Prospects

Excellent reviews and impressive sales figures are hard for new Novelists to obtain, so advancement prospects are poor. Advancement will depend on growing an audience, and selling enough copies to either be able to pay to self-publish the second book or earn out the advance from a publishing company, who may then be open to a second contract and publication.

Education and Training

A high school diploma is expected. Although a bachelor's or graduate school degree is not required for a Novelist, but since the chances of making a living at writing fiction are so slim, it is beneficial to have a solid education as something to fall back on in case becoming a best-selling Novelist takes longer than planned. The knowledge and writing experience that is gained during school may help the Novelist, since writing usually improves with practice. There are some very successful Novelists without a college degree, however; Margaret (Meg) Chittenden is an award-winning author of 30 novels, including *More than You Know,* in her 32-year writing career. She did not go to college, because, as Chittenden notes, she "came from a long line of coal miners in the north of England," and they "couldn't afford college."

Attend writer conferences and take degree or nondegree courses in literature or creative writing as well as in the areas that apply to the kind of novels you want to write, such as forensic science or criminology, if you wish to become a mystery writer, or history, if you wish to write historical fiction.

Experience, Skills, and Personality Traits

Working for a Novelist, literary agent, or publishing company may be a useful way to get your foot in the door, since you might have an appropriate opportunity to let them read your work in progress. For many Novelists, just getting their work read in the first place may be the biggest hurdle to overcome. For others, learning what advice to take, and what to reject, can be the turning point in her or his career. Meg Chittenden, for example, notes: "When I first started writing, I was put off by people telling me 'Write what you know.' I learned that I could find out anything through research." Based on her experience and her success as a novelist, Chittenden, who is also author of the nonfiction book *How to Write Your Novel,* now offers this advice to beginning writers: "I tell them, 'Know what you write.'"

Novelists need tenacity and the ability to withstand criticism. They have to be able to keep writing despite rejection, the financial pressure of probably having to earn a living from a full-time or part-time job while continuing to write, and even getting published without adequate monetary compensation. Being observant, thick-skinned, and sensitive are other personality traits that Novelists often possess.

Unions and Associations

Membership in a union or association is not required but might be useful in terms of networking, training, and becoming savvy about contracts, publishers who are looking for new novelists, and conferences to attend. The National Writers Union (www.nwu.org) has Novelist members, although it tends to cater to nonfiction writers, especially those writing articles for newspapers or magazines. The Authors Guild (www.authorsguild.org) has thousands of Novelist members, as does the Mystery Writers of America (www.mwa.org) and other writer associations listed in Appendix III.

Tips for Entry

1. Study fiction in college or graduate school and write a novel as part of your degree. Your writing teacher or adviser may have a relationship with book editors who are receptive to considering the superior work of their students.
2. Attend writing and publishing conferences, and go especially to sessions with buying-book editors who will tell you what they are looking for. Consider approaching the editors and finding out if they are open to submissions from new authors.
3. Find a literary agent who will read your novel, believe in it, and then sell your novel for you.
4. Sell the movie rights to a major studio, director, or actor or actress to your unpublished manuscript, and book editors may knock on your door for the novel.
5. Get advance endorsements for your novel from best-selling authors who are willing to stake their reputation on your talents as they declare that your novel is amazing and worth reading (and publishing).
6. Attend writing conferences and workshops during the year and over the summer and network with the faculty and other students. Ask if they will read your finished novel and, if they are enthused about it, recommend it to a literary agent, manager, or publisher.
7. Write an amazing novel that everyone raves about and get it to a literary agent or publisher.
8. Read *Writer's Digest, Publishers Weekly,* and other publications for Novelists or about the publishing industry. Contact those agents or editors who seem like a good fit with your novel's theme, style, or setting.
9. Like Harlan Coben, network with alumni from your college, graduate school, or high school who work in the publishing industry. Ask them to read your novel and, if they like it, to share contacts with you for you to pursue as a possible literary agent or publisher.
10. Go to Publishers Marketplace (www.publishersmarketplace.com) and see if there are any publishers or literary agents listed for you to approach who might read your novel and buy it or represent you.
11. Buy a copy of the *Literary Marketplace (LMP),* or use the one at your local or college library. Contact literary agents or publishers listed in the *LMP* and ask if they would read your novel.
12. Learn how to write a compelling cover letter synopsizing your novel so that agents, publishers, or movie producers ask you for your manuscript for consideration.
13. Go to the annual BookExpo, held in May or June in a major urban area, such as Chicago, New York City, Los Angeles, or Washington, D.C., and go from booth to booth, networking with all the exhibitors and looking for a company that would be a good fit for your novel.
14. Get the *International Literary Marketplace* and try to get published in another country if you are unable to get published in the United States. Once you are published, especially if your work is well received, it may be easier to find a publisher (or literary agent) in the United States.

NONFICTION BOOK AUTHOR

Duties: Writes books for adults that are based on facts

Alternate Title(s): Author; Book Author; Biographer; Historian; Business Book Author; Reference Book Author; Cookbook Author

Salary Range: $0 to millions of dollars, with most nonfiction books getting advances in the $2,000 to $20,000 range, depending upon the size and type of the publisher (trade or popular/commercial versus university press) and the projected size of the book's readership (although advances for celebrities or best-selling authors can be in the six figures)

Employment Prospects: Fair

Advancement Prospects: Fair

Best Geographical Location(s): Anywhere, since research can be conducted online and writing can be completed in any location and submitted by mail or electronically

Prerequisites:

Education and Training—A high school diploma is expected; a bachelor's or graduate degree is recommended, especially if a nonfiction author plans to specialize in a type of writing, such as history, science, art history, or biography; during college and graduate school, certain required tasks, such as learning how to conduct research and write term papers, provide useful training; learning how to conduct interviews will help the nonfiction author

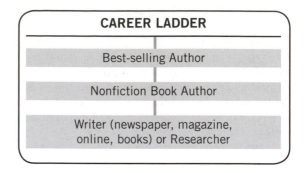

CAREER LADDER

Best-selling Author

Nonfiction Book Author

Writer (newspaper, magazine, online, books) or Researcher

with his or her research skills; writing and rewriting are excellent training, as is editing or writing for a school or college newspaper or, after graduation, at a newspaper or for a magazine

Experience—Writing newspaper, magazine, or online articles; working for a book author; any job that lends itself to exploration in a comprehensive way so that it could become the basis of a book; being a business leader or consultant

Special Skills and Personality Traits—Attention to detail; curious mind; excellent research skills; ability to stick with a major task for months or years at a time; self-starter; organized; willingness to promote one's published books

Special Requirements—Not necessary for the nonfiction writer, but if there are licenses or certification within a field that the author is writing about, it is helpful for the author to have those credentials

Position Description

One of the most prestigious and essential jobs in book publishing is that of a published book author. Nonfiction Book Authors provide factual information to readers, along with history, biography, and opinion. There are no age requirements or age limitations to becoming a published Nonfiction Book Author. Not only do Nonfiction Book Authors continue producing book after book way into their seventies, eighties, and older, but first-time book authors are discovered at any age as well.

The chances of getting published, and being successful, are much better for Nonfiction Book Authors than for novelists. Of the approximately 100,000+ new titles that are published in the United States annually, the majority are nonfiction (factual books, including textbooks) compared to just 5,000 that are fiction.

Authors who write nonfiction books for the general public are writing books that are called "trade" books. Those who write books for schools or colleges are textbook authors. Other Nonfiction Book Authors write books that are more scholarly and fall into the academic or professional category of nonfiction books. These books might be published by university presses, such as Yale University Press, instead of commercial trade publishers, such as Random House or Doubleday.

Nonfiction Book Authors need to write well and, in most cases, must be able to do primary and secondary research. Some types of nonfiction, however, such as the autobiography, memoir, or personal essay, may be based on someone's day-to-day activities.

Nonfiction Book Authors often write books in addition to having another job, such as lawyer, teacher, consultant, speaker, entrepreneur, business executive, nurse, or police chief. Your goal may be to become a full-time Nonfiction Book Author or just to publish a book every now and then while keeping your full-time job. There is also a lot of controversy over whether an expert, celebrity, or business leader who hires an author to ghostwrite or coauthor a book with him or her should be considered a book author. There is so much prestige attached to writing the book oneself that celebrity authors will often emphasize that they did, indeed, write the book, even if they had the assistance of a coauthor.

Book authors need to know what else is being written and read in their field, whether it is career advice, artist biographies, or Civil War history. Some Nonfiction Book Authors will be notable in their respective fields first and then they will author a book as part of a natural progression in their career. For others, being a Nonfiction Book Author is their career, and they may change topics that they write about, spending additional years gaining the necessary knowledge to write a new book, as well as possibly coauthoring with established experts.

Nonfiction Book Authors usually need to continue their education long after they graduate from college (although attending school, obtaining a degree, or having an advanced degree is certainly not necessary to be a successful or respected book author). Even if a Nonfiction Book Author has a Ph.D. or an M.D., additional self-learning or formal training related to the subject of his or her book may be necessary.

Those Nonfiction Book Authors who write trade books for the general public, especially if published by one of the major publishers, may have different financial and sales expectations related to their books, with the hope of selling at least 10,000 to 25,000 books. Those goals may be unrealistic, however, even though some Nonfiction Book Authors sell hundreds of thousands or millions of copies. Those who write for university presses or professional imprints, by contrast, may be pleased to sell just a few thousand copies of a book, since the audience is seen as smaller and the prestige of being published may be more important than the financial renumeration. (In the latter case, a majority of the authors are professors at colleges and universities in addition to being book authors.)

It is useful to understand the concept of the "frontlist," "midlist," and "backlist" book. A front-list book is a book that is considered to be a major offering by that publishing company for that season. (Most publishing companies divide their new offerings into just two seasons, fall and spring, although some also have a summer season, and a few also publish books for the winter season.) Only a few books out of dozens or hundreds will be considered front list book for that publishing company. Being a front-list title means being at the front of the catalog and also given the best treatment, including advertising dollars and extra attention by the publicity and sales staff. Books that are not expected to sell that well are considered midlist titles. Any book that has been published and available for a while, for around three months, is then considered a backlist book. Backlist titles no longer generate publicity for being new, so the book's topic or subject matter or the author's expertise will be reasons why a book will continue to get attention.

A willingness to travel to meet in person with the editor and publicity department of the publishing company may be advantageous.

Salaries

Nonfiction Book Authors may earn from nothing (except for free copies of the book), if it is for a scholarly house that does not offer an advance, to typical advances of $2,000 to $20,000 from major houses for new or non–best-selling authors. Best-selling Nonfiction Authors, such as psychologist Dr. Phil McGraw and consultant Dr. Stephen Covey (*The 7 Habits of Highly Effective People*) earn millions of dollars. In general, unless a book is a best-seller, Nonfiction Book Authors have to earn money from other sources or jobs to supplement their book advances and royalties.

Employment Prospects

There are more employment possibilities for Nonfiction Book Authors than for novelists, since the greatest number of books that are published are nonfiction, and there is a continual need for new or updated information. However, the chances of getting published as a Nonfiction Book Author are just fair since competition is so stiff. If you take the time to develop your writing skills and your knowledge of a specific topic, setting you apart from the competition the possibility of getting published will be improved.

Advancement Prospects

Meeting deadlines, being praised for excellent research and writing skills, and getting noteworthy reviews will help a Nonfiction Book Author get additional book projects. However, advancement will be largely based on how many copies of a title is sold; also noteworthy is whether the author receives awards, achieves foreign sales, and becomes esteemed in his or her field. Nonfiction Authors also need to keep in mind the various publishing options for their work, from the major New York houses to the medium-sized or smaller publishing company, the university press, and even the option to self-publish.

Education and Training

From the earliest school years, learning the proper research techniques for writing a term paper will help the Nonfiction Book Author. A bachelor's or graduate degree is helpful but not required. If a Nonfiction book author plans to specialize in a certain field, an advanced degree in that field will be useful.

Working as the paid or unpaid research assistant to a book author or even a professor will be excellent training for nonfiction book authorship.

Taking a course in how to write a nonfiction book in an adult learning program may also prove useful.

Special Requirements

Although it is not necessary for a Nonfiction Book Author to have a license or certification, it may be helpful to have those credentials if they pertain to the subject that you are writing about. For example, if you are writing a book on hospitals for a general audience, because this is a specialized area, it might be expected that such a book have a nonfiction writer who is an M.D. or for an M.D. to team up with a general nonfiction writer. Whether there are licenses, certifications, or other special requirements for a nonfiction writer will vary by subject matter and discipline, with requirements for those writing medical or health nonfiction being different than for someone writing nonfiction about more nonspecialist topics, such as writing essays, biography, or general commentary.

Experience, Skills, and Personality Traits

Learning how to write newspaper, magazine, or online articles will be useful as experience for writing a nonfiction book. Nonfiction Book Authors need to have excellent research and writing skills as well as a curious mind and an eye for detail. They are driven to find out information and to present it in a clear and well-written format. Patience and organization are essential while researching and writing a book-length project. Being able to delay gratification is also crucial, since a book may take anywhere from a year to 10 years to research, write, and publish. Being able to take rejection is important, since the road to publication can be long and arduous. Knowing which suggestions to accept from editors or literary agents and which to reject can make or break a book project. Being able to work well with other people is also essential, since the

book author, even if he or she researches and writes alone, will have to interact with an editor and the production, sales, and publicity teams at the publishing company, as well as with the public and the media when the book is published.

Unions and Associations

Union membership is not necessary, but there is one union, the National Writers Union (www.nwu.org), which has book author members. There are numerous associations for Nonfiction Book Authors, including the Authors Guild (www.authorsguild.org) and the National Association of Science Writers (www.nasw.org) for science writers. See Appendix III for list of writer associations.

Tips for Entry

1. Work at a publishing company or literary agency in any capacity while you continue researching your nonfiction book. When you are far enough along with the book, show it to someone there who could recommend it for representation (if shown to a literary agent) or sale (if shown to someone at the publishing company).

2. Attend writer conferences and go to the panels on book authorship. Speak to the panelists if they are acquisitions editors at publishing companies and see if they would be interested in the topic of your book. (See listing's in Appendix VI for writer conferences, such as the annual American Society of Journalists and Authors conference [www.asja.org], held in New York City on a Saturday each spring which usually has at least one panel on getting a book published.)

3. Work for a published Nonfiction Book Author as a research assistant. Prove yourself, and you may even be asked to help coauthor a book. If you have a book of your own, your boss might read it and, if he or she likes it, might help you to sell it.

4. Take a course or seminar in how to write a book and get it published. (See listings in Appendix II for available courses.)

5. Work with a writing or book publishing coach who could help you develop a strategy for completing your first nonfiction book.

6. Read *Publishers Weekly* to see who is looking for what kinds of books and also to stay up on the competition in your field.

7. Teach a course related to your research at a local college or university, an adult learning school, such as the Learning Annex (www.learning

annex.com), or the noncredit programs, such as those offered by New School University (www.newschool.edu), and an editor may find you.

8. Attend the annual BookExpo held each May or June in a major city in the United States and meet with exhibitors and attendees, seeking out opportunities to sell your nonfiction book project.

9. Learn how to write a book proposal, and use your proposal to find a literary agent who will sell your book to a publishing company for you.

10. Get known as an expert on the topic that you would like to write about. Then go on a local or network television or radio show based on your area of expertise, and literary agents and publishers may call you and ask if you want to write a book.

11. Contact the local newspaper, especially if its articles are picked up by the national syndicates, and see if they want to assign a reporter to write about you and your area of expertise.

12. Write an op-ed piece or a newspaper or magazine article about the topic of your book, and editors and literary agents may find you. You can also use that article in your submission packet, along with your book proposal, to try to interest a literary agent or publisher.

13. If you exhaust all other options, explore self-publishing as way to get into print. (See the Bibliography, for useful books to read and Web sites to visit to get you started if you wish to pursue the self-publishing route.)

CHILDREN'S AND YOUNG ADULT BOOK AUTHOR

CAREER PROFILE

Duties: Writes the text that becomes a book for infants, juveniles, or young adults; may also illustrate the book

Alternate Title(s): Picture Book Author; Teen Writer; YA Author

Salary Range: $0 to millions of dollars, with most earning from $1,000 to $3,000 per book ($10,000 to $20,000 a year)

Employment Prospects: Fair

Advancement Prospects: Fair

Best Geographical Location(s): Anywhere, since work is sent in electronically or through the mail; should be willing to travel to the publishing company for meetings if necessary

Prerequisites:

Education and Training—A high school diploma is expected; a bachelor's degree or graduate as well as an advanced degree in writing, education, or a specialization, if books rely on an advanced body of knowledge, are recommended; courses in children's literature, education, child psychology, and any topic that is the subject of a nonfiction children's book is useful; working as a paid or unpaid apprentice to a Children's or Young Adult Book Author could be useful

CAREER LADDER

```
Best-selling Author
        |
Children's or Young Adult Book Author
        |
Novelist, Nonfiction Book Author,
Teacher, or Children's Librarian
```

Experience—Teaching or working with children or teens as a librarian or educator could be useful as a way of knowing more about the target reader

Special Skills and Personality Traits—Excellent writing skills and the ability to tell a story or, in a nonfiction book, to convey information to a younger audience, from picture books for the youngest children through school-age and teenage readers

Special Requirements—Not required, but for authors of nonfiction books, licensure or certification may be necessary to establish the writer as an expert in the field (or a writer could partner with an expert and coauthor a book)

Position Description

Book Authors who write for children are usually categorized by the age group of the audience that they are writing for, such as "read-to" books intended to be read to an infant or toddler by a parent or teacher; picture books, which have just a few words on the page as well as illustrations; early-reader books, with more words; and young adult books, typically appealing to middle school or high school students.

The most impressive recent example of the sales potential of even one best-selling children's book is, of course, the first novel by J. K. Rowling, *Harry Potter and the Sorcerer's Stone,* and the additional books in the series that have followed. British author J. K. Rowling is now one of the richest women in the United Kingdom, with earnings upward of $70 million in just one year. You have an example in the book publishing industry

of the kind of blockbuster usually associated with the movie industry.

But the fact remains that getting established as a Children's or YA Book Author is still very difficult. Competition is extremely keen, and publishers tend to use the same Authors over and over again once they have a good working relationship and they feel they can trust an author to consistently produce the age-level and quality book that they need.

Also the Children's Book Author has a much harder time selling directly to the end user. For children's books, especially, the buyer is the parent, teacher, or children's librarian—not the infant, toddler, or child who will be having the story read to him or her. Fans will outgrow the work of a Children's or YA Book Author, so he or she has to continually cultivate new readers. By contrast, if you write for adults, you can grow your fan base directly, through newsletters, bookstore presentations, and advertisements or talk shows viewed by potential readers.

Children's Book Authors sometimes also illustrate their own books, such as Maurice Sendak and the late Shel Silverstein. However, the two skills are often seen as very distinct, and children's book publishers may prefer to get only the story from the Children's or YA Book Author and then hire the illustrator on their own. Trying to sell a package, with illustrations by the author or by another illustrator, may actually be harder than trying to sell just a story.

Of course, there are also books that cross over into a variety of age groups—books that appeal to youngsters and adults alike, such as all of the *Harry Potter* novels, which have been read and loved by adults around the world, *Red Badge of Courage* and *Tom Sawyer*, or *To Kill a Mockingbird*.

There are also examples of nonfiction authors and novelists for adults also writing for children and teens, such as mystery author Carl Hiaasen, who wrote the YA novel *Hoot*.

In the last decade, with the introduction of word processing programs that enable Book Authors to typeset their manuscript, not just write it, there has been an increase in self-published authors. But many self-published books, especially fiction works lacking an author with a track record of sales, have a hard time getting distributed in large enough quantities to justify the time, money, and effort that goes into producing the book.

Katie Davis is a Children's Book Author and illustrator who has seven published books. Davis shares her career path from college to the publication of her first children's book: "I graduated with a bachelor of science from Boston University. I've always been creative but never thought I could earn my living as an artist. I could write, though, so after graduating I went into public relations and advertising. After getting fired six or seven times, I figured I should be working for myself. I'd been writing and illustrating picture books—really bad ones—for decades. Then, in 1996, I attended the Society of Children's Book Writers and Illustrators conference. I met people in the business, and I learned what I needed to know to write really good books and get them published. *Who Hops?* came out just before my 40th birthday."

For Davis, like so many novelists, the road to publication took many years of learning what works and does not work by trial and error.

Salaries

The advance against royalties for a typical children's book, unless the author is a celebrity or a best-selling author, may range from no money upfront to several thousand dollars per book plus royalties. Children's Book Authors may also be asked to write books on a work-for-hire basis, whereby they get a flat fee of several hundred to several thousand dollars per book, but they do not share in any future royalties based on the sales performance of the book. If a Children's Book Author is also the illustrator of the book, she or he would get an additional fee for the artwork. Children's or YA Book Authors may get a larger advance for a book. Advances and royalties are negotiable. If an author uses a literary agent, 10 to 15 percent of the monies due are paid to the agent on a commission basis. Other sources of income for a Children's Book Author are foreign sales, although it is often hard to sell children's books in other countries, because of cultural differences and stylistic preferences for artwork. (Even though the artwork is separate from the text, if a foreign publisher wants to buy a children's book without the art, they would then have to commission a local artist to do new art, which is a labor-intensive and lengthy process.) Children's Book Authors often speak at libraries or at schools. Some do it just for the opportunity to grow their reputation and fan base as well as to have the chance to sell copies of their books. Others ask for a fee, which is usually from $100 to $500 (but, of course, celebrity Children's Book Authors may get even higher fees).

Most Children's Book Authors have other jobs, such as working as a librarian, teacher, or editor at a children's book publisher and write books as a second job for extra income. Those who write full time need to be prolific, writing and selling multiple books a year in order to earn a living wage.

Employment Prospects

Becoming a Children's Book or YA Author is especially difficult. Employment prospects will be increased if you have an exceptionally fresh and unique concept, outstanding writing, and expertise in the field you are writing about, if it is a nonfiction book. A reputation for writing adult books, or celebrity status, may make booksellers, librarians, or parents more likely to give your first children's book a chance. However, there is a need for new children's book authors of fiction; as hard as it is to break in, it is not impossible.

Advancement Prospects

Writing a blockbuster best-selling book with terrific sales is the best way to advance. Winning awards and getting rave reviews will also help. It will be very difficult to advance after the first book or two is published without something very distinctive about the books that would motivate publishers to buy another. In the children's and YA book area, being prolific is important; writing 50 to 100 books or more is the kind of lifetime output that is expected. Exploring every publicity option that a publisher offers to you and even hiring a freelance book publicist are ways to advance your career.

Education and Training

A high school diploma is required. A bachelor's or advanced degree in English, psychology, early childhood education, writing, or a specific field of study, if you wish to write nonfiction, is recommended. A graduate degree in English literature or writing is recommended for novelists, while nonfiction authors might pursue a master's in his or her subject of choice.

Special Requirements

Although it is not necessary for a Children's or YA Book Author to hold a license or have certification, it may be helpful to have those credentials if they pertain to the subject about when you are writing. For example, if you are writing a book on rocks for a general audience, because this is a specialized area, it might be expected that the book be written by someone with a degree in geology or for a general writer to team up with an expert who might coauthor the book or provide a technical review of the manuscript. Whether there are licenses, certifications, or other special requirements for a Children's or YA Book Author will depend on subject matter, with requirements for those writing medical or health nonfiction being different than for writers of nonfiction about nonspecialist topics, such as biographies or general commentary. However, even for those topics not requiring a degree, there is the expectation that the writer will do whatever research is required to present the information based on up-to-date and reliable data.

Experience, Skills, and Personality Traits

Working with children will definitely be useful for the Children's Book Author, especially with the target age group, such as infants, toddlers, or elementary school, middle school, or high school students. Whether you work as a paid teacher, librarian, or school counselor or as a volunteer in an after-school program, understanding the way children talk, interact, and develop interests will be useful training for the Children's or YA Book Author. Read widely in children's literature, from classics, such as *Alice in Wonderland* or works by Hans Christian Andersen, to more contemporary best sellers, including *Goodnight Moon, Where the Wild Things Are, If You Give a Mouse a Cookie,* and *Olivia.* Read the literature in the age group that you wish to write for, from "read-to" books to YA novels, such as Louis Sachar's *Holes.*

Children's Book Authors need to be able to tell a story without being preachy. They need to create memorable characters, dialogue, and plots that children or teens will remember and care about. In the last decade, young adult literature has taken on very timely topics, such as suicide and betrayal of friendship. But topics have to be handled in a certain way and in language that fits the profile of the young adult reader/book.

A Children's or YA Book Author should be able to identify with and remember what it was like to be a child or a young adult. He or she should have a curiosity about the world, excellent writing skills, good research skills a vivid imagination, and the ability to create unique, noteworthy, and exciting stories or well-researched nonfiction books that are topical and interesting.

Since building a career as a Children's or YA Book Author may depend on building an audience through library, school, or bookstore readings and appearances, an outgoing personality and a love of travel will also help you to advance.

Unions and Associations

The leading international association for Children's Book Authors is the Society of Children's Book Writers and Illustrators (www.scbwi.org), which was founded in 1971 and has more than 19,000 members in 70 regions. Librarians, educators, publishers, editors, illustrators, and agents are also members of the society. There is an annual educational conference, and the Golden Kite Award is presented each year for the best fiction and nonfiction books.

Tips for Entry

1. Join the Society of Children's Book Writers and Illustrators (www.scbwi.org) and attend local and national conferences.
2. Find a literary agent who wants to represent you and your writing to publishers.
3. Read *School Library Journal* and keep up with the trends in children's literature.
4. Work as a paid or unpaid intern at a children's book publisher. When it is appropriate, let it be known that you also write children's books.
5. Meet children's book illustrators and let them know that you have manuscripts available for submission and/or illustrating.

6. Read books on children's book writing and publishing, such as the *Complete Idiot's Guide to Publishing Children's Books,* the *Writer's Digest Children's Writer's & Illustrator's Market* (updated annually), or *The Essential Guide to Children's Books and Their Creators,* among other titles.

7. Attend children's book or writer conferences and introduce yourself to the children's book editors who are on panels. Find out about the kind of material they are looking for and how to go about submitting material to those editors.

PRODUCTION

MANAGING EDITOR

Duties: Coordinates all the books being published by overseeing each project from idea to finished book including its editing and production; may manage the budget as well as coordinate the staff of in-house or freelance editors, copy editors, proofreaders, graphic designers, and production editors

Alternate Title(s): Editorial Manager; Managing Director

Salary Range: $35,000 to $75,000

Employment Prospects: Fair

Advancement Prospects: Fair

Best Geographical Location(s): Wherever there is enough publishing activity to sustain a full-time position, although there will be more potential employers in such major book publishing hubs as New York City, Washington, D.C., Boston, and Chicago

Prerequisites:

Education and Training—A bachelor's degree is expected with a major in English, writing, journalism, or a related field; a graduate degree in publishing or writing is useful; on-the-job training at a publishing company working in various departments, especially editorial or production, for several years is required

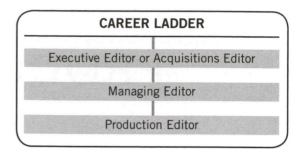

CAREER LADDER

Executive Editor or Acquisitions Editor

Managing Editor

Production Editor

Experience—A minimum of three to five years' experience at a book publishing company with a firsthand mastery of book production as well as copyediting and proofreading, supervising staff, as well as experience scheduling multiple titles as well as managing a budget

Special Skills and Personality Traits—Superb organizational and time management skills; excellent negotiation, leadership, and communication skills; computer skills including desktop publishing or producing a book manuscript electronically; attention to detail; able to handle multiple tasks simultaneously; patient but firm

Position Description

The Managing Editor takes charge of every phase of the creation of the book, from idea to finished book. Depending upon the size of the publishing company, and the way that the job functions are organized, the Managing Editor will supervise a staff of in-house or freelance copy editors and proofreaders, editors, and graphic designers. The Managing Editor is responsible for scheduling each phase of the book production process as well as managing a budget. Another task that the Managing Editor may be asked to handle is deciding on training that the various staff members need as well as planning those seminars and working with the human resources department or an outside speaker bureau to hire the consultants or trainers to offer those training programs, such as time management or training on the latest computer software.

As Andrea Rotondo, Managing Editor at New York–based Schirmer Trade Books & Omnibus Press notes:

"My title is managing editor, but at a larger company, I'd be called editor in chief or acquisitions editor. I'm part of a small-to-midsize publishing company that also does music publishing and song rights. I handle around 15 to 20 titles a year, doing everything from brainstorming the direction of the catalog to acquiring and editing new books. I also prepare materials that will be helpful to the sales and marketing departments."

Salaries

Salaries range from $35,000 to $75,000 depending upon the size and location of the company.

Employment Prospects

Employment prospects are only fair because some companies have absorbed this job category into other job functions such as the production editor or the editor performing some or all of the Managing Editor's functions.

Advancement Prospects

Since this job category is often eliminated at some publishing companies, advancement prospects are only fair. In order to advance, it may be necessary to relocate to another company that produces more titles and has greater revenue. The experience gained as a Managing Editor may offer training for consideration for the highly competitive jobs of editor in chief, publisher, or publishing company president.

Education and Training

A bachelor's degree in writing, English, journalism, or a related field is expected; graduate courses or an advanced degree in publishing is useful. On-the-job training working at a book publishing company in various capacities in the editing and production departments will provide excellent preparation.

Experience, Skills, and Personality Traits

A minimum of three to five years working at a publishing company is expected for the demanding job of Managing Editor. A Managing Editor should have experience editing books as well as working in the production department. The ability to set and balance a budget as well as schedule multiple titles from inception to finished book, being able to manage a staff, both in-house and freelance, as well as supervise or actually do the copyediting and proofreading of a manuscript are all skills that the Managing Editor may need. Excellent computer skills, including the knowledge of electronic editing and book manuscript production are also necessary. A Managing Editor should be a good negotiator, as well as highly organized, detail-oriented, and able to get along with people.

Unions and Associations

Belonging to various publishing and production associations may be useful for educational, networking, and job-search benefits, such as Partnership in Print (www.wip.org), the Women's National Book Association (www.wnba-books.org), or Bookbuilders of Boston (www.bbboston.org).

Tips for Entry

1. Get several years' on-the-job experience at a book publishing company, working in the production and editorial departments. Knowing every phase of putting a book together—from idea to finished book—will help you work your way up from assistant production editor to production editor to Managing Editor.

2. Join an association, such as Bookbuilders of Boston (www.bbboston.org), and visit its job bank frequently for available jobs. Network with other members and participate in their educational workshops.

3. Regularly visit the Web sites of major publishing companies and check their online job listings or contact the human resources department with your resume and salary history.

4. Look for job postings at www.publishers marketplace.com and www.monster.com as well as the print and online version of *Publishers Weekly* (www.publishersweekly.com). Follow the directions for applying, whether online, by fax, or by mail.

5. Network with editors through publishing associations, such as the Women's National Book Association (www.wnba-books.org), its regional chapters, such as the New York City chapter (www.wnbc-nyc.org), or the Women's Media Group (www.womensmediagroup.org). Let everyone know that you are interested in a Managing Editor position if one becomes available at their company.

PRODUCTION EDITOR

Duties: Handles directly or delegates all editorial work from manuscript through bound book to in-house or freelance copy editors, proofreaders, and indexers

Alternate Title(s): Production Manager; Production Director

Salary Range: $50,000 to $100,000

Employment Prospects: Good

Advancement Prospects: Fair

Best Geographical Location(s): Wherever there is enough publishing activity to sustain a full-time position, although there will be more potential employers in such major book publishing locations as New York City, Washington, D.C., and Chicago

Prerequisites:

Education and Training—A bachelor's degree is expected; graduate degree in business, publishing, or an area related to the type of publishing company, if it specializes in a subject area, such as music or education, is useful; on-the-job training in all the tasks that are required of this position, from editing (line editing and copyediting) and proofreading to indexing

Experience—Five years or more in the production department at a book publishing company; if the position is with a specific type of book publish-

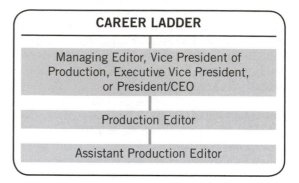

CAREER LADDER

Managing Editor, Vice President of Production, Executive Vice President, or President/CEO

Production Editor

Assistant Production Editor

ing, such as a children's book publisher or a textbook company, production department experience at a similar type of publisher may also be required; working in any job in a managerial or supervisory capacity in which multiple tasks and functions have to be scheduled and monitored will also be helpful

Special Skills and Personality Traits—Highly organized; able to take a project from manuscript to bound book; copyediting and proofreading skills; able to delegate to other in-house or freelance copy editors or proofreaders and schedule and supervise their work; excellent management skills; able to work under deadline pressure; energetic; exemplary communication and interpersonal skills

Position Description

This detail-oriented position requires the ability to follow a book from manuscript to bound book, coordinating the copyediting and proofreading of the book, as well as maintaining schedules and entering corrections from a multiplicity of sources, including the editor, author, copy editor, and proofreader. Some Production Editors do the copyediting or proofreading themselves; others have assistants in-house who perform those tasks or assign some or all of the manuscripts to freelance editors, who have to be hired, supervised, and their work coordinated.

Production Editor is a highly demanding job, especially if there are a variety of nonfiction and fiction titles each season, rather than one type of book. The Production Editor coordinates additional tasks related to each book, such as creating the index and copyediting or proofreading jacket copy. Each publishing

company may define the job requirements of the Production Editor slightly differently, but the common denominator is that he or she is responsible for all the production editorial work from manuscript through bound book, including checking galleys, proofs, and blues at all stages.

Salaries

This is a key operations job with a salary range from $50,000 to $100,000, depending upon the company's revenues.

Employment Prospects

Prospects are good for this job, since it is a key operations position at a publishing company. For this top spot, someone will have worked his or her way up the ranks in the production department, starting as an assistant or associate. Since fewer pursue the production tract in publishing, compared to editorial, publicity, or sales, someone specializing in production has good employment opportunities.

Advancement Prospects

These positions are lucrative and sought after, so it will be harder to advance past this level, since it is the top production post. Advancement would be to a management position, such as vice president of production, executive vice president, or president/CEO, rather than an operations/production job.

Education and Training

A bachelor's degree is expected with a major or minor in publishing, business, or marketing. A graduate degree in English literature, publishing, or business may be useful. On-the-job book publishing and production training is required. Working part-time or as an intern in the production department of a publishing company will provide vital skills.

Experience, Skills, and Personality Traits

For this top job, individuals are expected to have worked five to 10 years climbing the ladder in the production department of a publishing company, from assistant production manager or editor to associate up to Production Editor or director. This experience can be gained at the same company or different companies. A Production Editor needs experience managing a staff and supervising all phases of book production, from manuscript to bound book, including the text and the cover. A Production Editor should be a detail-oriented person who is highly organized. The position requires someone who is able to communicate and coordinate activities in a wide range of departments and possesses excellent computer skills.

Exemplary management skills are also necessary, as the Production Editor must delegate, supervise, and schedule the work that is assigned to others, in-house or on a freelance basis. Since book publishing is so deadline- and schedule-oriented, the Production Editor has to be comfortable with setting and meeting realistic deadlines. Since this is also often a job with seasonal fluctuations, with heavier and lighter work periods, flexibility and the ability to work long hours at times is important. A love of books and putting a book together is key. Being detail-oriented is essential, since every single part of the book is important, from copyediting the manuscript to proofreading the text on the back jacket.

Unions and Associations

Specialized associations, such as Partnership in Print in Production (www.wip.org), are useful for networking and skill-building. More general associations for those working in publishing, such as the Women's National Book Association (www.wnba-books.org), are useful for networking and educational seminars.

Tips for Entry

1. Work your way up in the production department from an entry-level position as an assistant production editor or associate production editor. Every job in production prepares you for this top job.
2. Look for jobs posted at www.mediabistro.com and www.monster.com. Follow the directions for applying, whether online, by fax, or by mail.
3. Check the Web sites of publishing companies to check their online job listings or contact the human resources department with your résumé and salary history.
4. Contact the publishing executive recruiting companies, such as Lynne Palmer Executive Recruitment, JanPlace Media Search, or Bert Davis Associates. Let them know you are looking for a job as a Production Editor. Check their available listings and ask to be considered for openings.
5. Join an association such as the Bookbinders' Guild of New York (www.bookbindersguild.org) or Bookbuilders of Boston (www.bbboston.org) which have job banks that list available production positions at a range of levels—from assistant and associate to Production Editor or coordinator.

ART DIRECTOR

Duties: Designs or supervises design of book's interior and cover; supervises designers and illustrators; may also create logos and produce catalogs, brochures, or other sales and promotional materials

Alternate Title(s): Art Director/Designer; Creative Director

Salary Range: $40,000 to $90,000

Employment Prospects: Good

Advancement Prospects: Fair

Best Geographical Location(s): In or near cities with book publishing activity, such as New York City, Boston, and Chicago

Prerequisites:

Education and Training—A bachelor's degree with a major or minor in art or equivalent from an art school is expected; a graduate degree in art or publishing is recommended; on-the-job training in a variety of studio and corporate situations, working as part of a design team

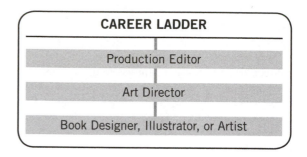

CAREER LADDER

Production Editor

Art Director

Book Designer, Illustrator, or Artist

Experience—Three to five years' working in the design department of a publishing company in a supervisory capacity

Special Skills and Personality Traits—Able to design; supervisory skills; proficient in computer technology, including the design programs QuarkXPress, Photoshop, InDesign and Illustrator; knowledge of book production; a team player; able to meet deadlines; excellent organizational skills; able to multitask and work in a fast-paced work environment; creative; a sharp eye for excellent design

Position Description

The Art Director is in charge of all the staff and free-lance designers and illustrators who create the look of a book's inside, front, back, and spine. If a publishing company is planning to do a series of books, the Art Director may create the design for the entire series so the books have a similar look, including the graphics, the text, and the colors or images.

The Art Director is the top position in the art department of the publishing company. He or she will have worked his or her way up the ladder, working as a staff or freelance book designer or illustrator, then as the assistant to the Art Director or as an associate or assistant art director. As someone arrives at the top position of Art Director, he or she may be doing more supervising of the creative works of the staff or freelance book designers or illustrators than creating the actual designs. But the Art Director will have creative input as well as final approval of a cover or an interior design of a book. He or she will then show it to the editor and editorial department, who will sometimes share it with the author, for approval, as well as with the marketing, sales, and publicity departments.

At some publishing companies, the Art Director, working with the marketing manager, sales manager, and book publicist, may also be responsible for designing the company's logo as well as for producing brochures, catalogs, and other sales and promotional materials.

Salaries

Salaries range from $40,000 to $90,000, depending upon several factors, such as where the company is located (rural, suburban, or urban area), the size of the art department, and the company's revenues.

Employment Prospects

Since every publishing company needs staff or free-lance help with both the artistic and editorial aspects of creating a new book, employment prospects are good for this position. Being artistic and creative in designing images and text is a talent that is unique and vital to the success of the look of a particular book, a series of books, and a publishing company's ability to stay competitive.

Advancement Prospects

To advance to the next level, the Art Director has to become known for his or her distinctive covers and designs. If books that the Art Director designed or supervised win awards, this will help the Art Director to advance. Keep a portfolio of front and back covers that you have designed or supervised, as well as samples of exemplary interiors of books. Make sure authors, editors, and sales and marketing departments who are pleased with your work write recommendation letters, as well as verbally share their positive attitude toward your work and your department's accomplishments, praising the books or promotional materials you designed.

Education and Training

A bachelor's degree or its equivalent from an art school is expected. An advanced degree in art or publishing is recommended. On-the-job training in a variety of art studio and book publishing situations is useful background for this job.

Experience, Skills, and Personality Traits

An Art Director should have three to five years of experience working in the art department of a book publishing company as an assistant to the Art Director or as a book designer or illustrator. Even if the Art Director job is a supervisory one, he or she would be expected to be experienced using such computer programs for design as QuarkXPress, Photoshop, and Illustrator. The Art Director is expected to stay current with trends in design in book publishing, especially as it relates to different types of books, such as children's books, adult fiction, adult nonfiction, or specialty or novelty gift books.

Since the Art Director may have to hire and supervise freelancers, as well as staff artists and book designers, he or she should have excellent managerial skills. The ability to negotiate contracts is important, as is the ability to delegate, meet deadlines, and collaborate with various departments in the publishing company. Being a team player is essential, as is being creative and having a sharp eye for design and a knowledge of book production.

The Art Director is a creative person who functions well in a fast-paced corporate environment. Communication skills—both written and verbal—need to be exemplary.

Unions and Associations

Membership in various associations may be useful for networking and educational seminars. Art Directors can join the Center for Book Arts (www.centerforbookarts.org), the American Institute of Graphic Arts (www.aiga.org), the Bookbinders' Guild of New York (www.bbgny.org), and the Graphic Artists Guild (www.gag.org).

Tips for Entry

1. Get a job in the art department at a book publishing company, preferably starting as a book designer or assistant to the Art Director. Work your way up the ladder.
2. Take noncredit or graduate courses in publishing and focus on courses that deal with production and graphic design. Network with the faculty and let them know that you are looking for a job. Show them your portfolio of original cover and interior book designs.
3. If you know any editors or authors who have books in development, offer to produce a cover on speculation. If they like it, they could pay you, but even more importantly they could agree to use your cover or interior design for the book and let others know about your work.
4. Join an association for art directors and book illustrators and designers and network. Attend monthly meetings; if there is an annual meeting, attend the educational seminars. Bring lots of business cards as well as samples of your cover and interior design.
5. Let the recruiting companies for the book industry, such as Bert Davis and Lynne Palmer, know about you and your experience in the art department at various publishing companies. Let them know that your ultimate goal is to become an Art Director, and have then keep you in mind if an opening becomes available.
6. Check the Web sites of publishing companies, and see if their job listings include positions for Art Director.
7. Send a cover letter and work samples to production editors listed in the most recent *Literary Marketplace*, and let them know your job history and availability.
8. Check listings for Art Director at such sites as publishersmarketplace.com, www.mediabistro.com, www.monster.com, and www.hotjobs.com.
9. Book publishing companies are not the only place that an Art Director can gain experience. Take a job at a design studio or company that has mainly book publishers as clients so you can build your portfolio and contacts. Also consider working for a book packager. (To see a list of book packagers, go to the American Book Producers Association [www.abpaonline.org]).

BOOK DESIGNER

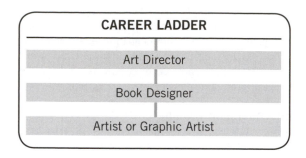

Position Description

The Book Designer is responsible for designing the book jackets or covers and the interior of each book. He or she, in discussions with the editor as well as the art director, may also decide if a book should have illustrations or photographs; he or she would then supply those original artworks or supervise other staff designers or freelancers who provide those materials. If the Book Designer also has duties for the advertising or marketing departments, he or she may also be responsible for designing brochures, ads for magazines or newspapers, and the look of the seasonal catalog, although inputting the actual data may be delegated to a design or administrative assistant. The Book Designer may also work on the creation of bookmarks and brochures for specific books, as well as prepare files for the printer.

Salaries

Salaries for Book Designers range from $30,000 to $50,000+, depending upon how senior the position is, as well as the company's revenue and location. Companies based in major cities generally pay more than those in suburban or rural locations.

Employment Prospects

This is an essential job for getting a book from manuscript to bound book. However, as more and more companies outsource all but the very basic editorial or administrative functions, finding a full-time staff position as a Book Designer may be more difficult than working as a freelancer or affiliating with a design company that services several industries, including book publishing. Creating a portfolio of your original book jacket and book designs is helpful for getting the next job.

Advancement Prospects

Advancement usually means taking on more managerial and administrative functions and doing less of the actual design work yourself. However, some Book Designers whose work is so original and creative and whose titles are singled out for their interior or cover design become in great demand as word-of-mouth spreads their reputation throughout the publishing company where they work or throughout the industry, if they are freelancers. Winning awards from prestigious design associations, publishing associations, or industry-sponsored competitions for cover design helps advancement prospects.

Education and Training

The Book Designer is expected to have a bachelor's degree in art or an equivalent degree from an art school. Advanced courses or an advanced degree in design, art, or publishing are recommended. Additional courses focused on book design are useful, especially if training was more general, rather than in the specifics of book design. Training on the computer design software that is standard in the book business, such as QuarkXPress, Photoshop, Illustrator, InDesign, and Acrobat, is also necessary. If a Macintosh computer system is being used, the Designer must be able to work on one.

Experience, Skills, and Personality Traits

Book Designers have three to five years of experience working in the design department of a book publisher designing covers, jackets, and the interior of books. If a job will also include designing brochures and ads for the marketing department, the Book Designer will be expected to have experience creating and executing those materials as well.

In addition to excellent computer and design skills, Book Designers need superb communication skills—on the phone, in writing, and in person. A Book Designer must be a team player, as he or she interfaces with a variety of departments at the publishing company, from the production department to editorial, sales, and promotion staff. He or she should be detail-oriented and able to multitask and work under pressure. Even though some artists may prefer to create in solitude, a staff position will require a lot of people-contact, as well as frequent meetings and discussions with other staff or freelance illustrators or designers.

Unions and Associations

Membership in at least one of the design-related associations with members from the book industry is useful for networking, educational, and job search reasons. For example, the Graphic Artists Guild (www.gag.org) offers a jobline as well as a Handbook of Price & Ethical Guidelines and copyright information. Chapters in Boston, Chicago, San Francisco, New York, Philadelphia, Portland, and other cities meet at their national convention. Other associations include the Chicago Book Clinic (www.chicagobookclinic.org), Bookbuilders West (www.bookbuilders.org), the Bookbinders' Guild of New York (www.bookbindersguild.org), and Bookbuilders of Boston (www.bbboston.org). Membership in more general publishing associations, such as Women's National Book Association (www.wnba-books.org) or the regional bookseller associations, such as the New England Booksellers Association (www.newenglandbooks.org) will provide access to editors, publishers, agents, and authors who might be a source of jobs or referrals.

Tips for Entry

1. Create a portfolio of sample book jackets, interior design of books, and seasonal catalogs to have something to show on job interviews or to send if applying for a job online.

2. Work in the art or design department at a book publishing company in any capacity, from intern or assistant to junior designer. Work your way up the ladder within that company.

3. Join an association for Book Designers, illustrators, or graphic artists with networking and educational opportunities as well as a source of available job listings.

4. Search the online job listings at such Web sites for media professionals as www.mediabistro.com and www.monster.com.

5. Use the current *Literary Marketplace* and contact the human resources department or art director at companies that are listed that are a good fit with your creativity and design philosophies. Send a cover letter and one or two samples of your cover art and inside design, along with a business card, and see if you can get an interview or be considered for upcoming jobs.

6. Go to the Web sites for companies that you would like to work at, from major New York City publishing giants to medium-sized companies, in New York City or elsewhere, and see if they have job listings posted right at their site. Many companies do post job openings, such as Random House (www.randomhouse.com/careers), which also has a lot of useful information at its site, including "Tips from the Pros" and "About Random House," with sections geared to college students, MBAs, and for those interested in positions at their warehouse and fulfillment center in Westminister, Maryland.

MARKETING AND SALES

MARKETING AND ADVERTISING DIRECTOR

Position Description

Whatever the budget for promoting a book, a well-conceived and well-executed advertising and marketing plan is often key to a book's success. If no one knows about a book, no matter how excellent it might be, it will be hard to get the sales that both the author and publisher need to earn an income or to stay in business. There are, of course, lots of stories about books that had no promotional budget that go on to become block-busters, but, in general, careful planning and budgeting is the key to getting the media attention and public awareness for a book that often leads to sales.

In general, "advertising" means getting attention for a book by paying for a display ad that runs in newspapers or magazines or a commercial that is broadcast on network, local, or cable television or on the radio, Internet, or even at the movie theaters. "Marketing" is

the overall campaign that includes advertising as well as publicity, such as interviews with the author of the book that appear in magazines, in newspapers, on television, on the radio, or on the Internet. Whether or not a book will have an expensive and glitzy book launch, such as a party at a New York City restaurant, or be entered in book contests, such as the National Book Awards, are some of the determinations that the Marketing and Advertising Director will make directly or through his or her team.

The Marketing and Advertising Director also sets the marketing strategy for his or her imprint at the company, or division, or, at a smaller or medium-sized house, for the entire company. Leslie Banks is the Marketing Director for Chicago-based Dearborn Trade, a medium-sized publishing company focusing on business titles. Banks graduated from a small liberal arts college in Michigan, where she was a double major in English and German. After graduation, she attended the acclaimed Publishing Institute of the University of Denver, studying all aspects of the book publishing industry. As Banks explains: "When I got back from the program, I started working as a sales clerk at Borders Books in Novi, Michigan, while I looked for a job in the publishing field. I figured that working in a bookstore for the time being was a related experience."

Banks's first job in book publishing was as an editorial assistant at Gale Research, now called the Gale Group, in the international companies division: "A friend and former college roommate was working at Gale and called to tell me that there were editorial openings in her division, and I sent in my résumé," Banks explains; networking, plus graduate training and related work experience, helped her to land that first job.

She then began working at Dearborn Trade as a book publicist. Her basic tasks included developing publicity campaign plans for each book; developing special media lists for each book; creating press materials and kits; booking radio, TV, and print interviews for the author; working with authors to develop creative media angles; conducting media follow-up via phone, e-mail, and fax; researching publications, Web sites, and media outlets for books and authors; and writing promotional copy for the company Web site.

After 13 months Banks was promoted to marketing and publicity manager with four direct reports: two publicists, one publicity assistant, and one marketing coordinator. She handled trade shows, managed the publicity budget, and wrote ad copy. Six months later she moved into her current job of Marketing Director. As part of the management team, she contributes to developing the three-year plans for Dearborn Trade and managing the marketing budget. "I really like what I am doing," says Banks. "In my current role as Marketing Director, I am involved in so many pieces of the business, and it's challenging. I am always learning something new."

Salaries

Salaries vary, depending on the company's revenues, the type of publishing, the number of titles, and whether it is based in an urban, suburban, or rural setting. On average, Marketing and Advertising Directors earn from $60,000 to $90,000.

Employment Prospects

The plans and strategies devised and executed by the Marketing and Advertising Director are crucial to the success of a publishing company. Employment prospects, therefore, are good. Some companies may combine the job of marketing with sales; the title is Vice President of Sales & Marketing.

Advancement Prospects

Well-reviewed books that sell well and excellent and continual media coverage for her or his company's titles help advancement possibilities. Getting known as a team player as well as a creative person with an excellent business sense are other traits that will help you to advance. Advancement may require getting the same job at a larger company where there will be more titles, more employees reporting to the Marketing and Advertising Director, bigger budgets as well as a larger salary for this position. If you wish to remain at the same company, it may be necessary to take on additional job functions, such as handling foreign sales, or becoming a group publisher or publisher.

Education and Training

A bachelor's degree is required. A range of majors will be useful, including communications, public relations, business, publishing, or English literature, plus additional courses in advertising and marketing. A master's degree in publishing, communications, or business is recommended.

On-the-job training in a range of book publishing jobs will also be useful background for this position. Leslie Banks, for example, worked in a bookstore, was an author's assistant, and worked at several publishing companies in a variety of editorial and publicity jobs before moving up from book publicist to Marketing Director at Dearborn Trade.

Experience, Skills, and Personality Traits

Five to 10 years of book publishing experience is expected for this senior-level position. Experience should include working as a book publicist and marketing manager at a publishing company or for a publicity company, public relations agency, or marketing firm with book publisher or author clients.

The Marketing Director needs a multiplicity of skills—from being able to create a budget and strategy for promoting specific titles to devising the advertising and marketing campaigns that will be implemented for certain front-list books deemed to be the biggest sellers. Staffing the trade show, overseeing the theme for the show, and planning special events are other job-related tasks. The Marketing Director may be delegating a lot of the day-to-day publicity or advertising tasks to in-house or freelance publicists or copywriters. But he or she is still overseeing their efforts as well as managing the marketing team.

Overseeing the biannual or tri-annual seasonal catalogue may also be one of the responsibilities of the Marketing Director, in addition to participating in the semiannual sales conferences, on site or at another location.

Tips for Entry

1. Work in any advertising or marketing positions, paid or internship, in book publishing, as a copywriter, as a marketing assistant, or as a publicist so that you acquire the necessary skills.
2. Work your way up from book publicist or advertising assistant to Marketing and Advertising Director.
3. Be exposed to as many aspects of the book publishing business as possible so you know how distribution works, as well the possible editorial, production, and publicity challenges.
4. Network with advertising and marketing executives at book publishing conferences and trade shows, such as the annual BookExpo held each May or June.
5. Check www.publishermarketplace.com, www.mediabistro.com, www.indeed.com, www.hotjobs.com, and www.monster.com for available jobs.
6. Let the leading executive recruiters in the book publishing industry, such as Lynne Palmer and Bert Davis, know that you are available for this position. Get them your current résumé, and keep them updated as you acquire more experience. Try to have a face-to-face informational interview so they get to know you besides just having your résumé. It may help to remind them to call you if a job becomes available.

BOOK PUBLICIST

CAREER PROFILE

Duties: Pitches authors to television, radio, and print for interviews that could help sell the authors' books; sends books out for review; coordinates an author tour for selected front-list authors

Alternate Title(s): Publicist

Salary Range: $25,000 to $89,500, depending on the company's revenue and size and whether the Book Publicist is in-house (staff) or freelance ($2,000 to $5,000/month with a three-month minimum commitment); Book Publicists with their own agency can earn as high as six figures

Employment Prospects: Good

Advancement Prospects: Fair

Best Geographical Location(s): For staff positions, wherever there are publishing companies requiring a full-time Book Publicist, especially New York City, but also in Boston, Chicago, and Los Angeles; freelancers may live anywhere, as long as they have access to a phone, fax machine, and the Internet, and as long as they can easily travel to meet with authors, publishers, and producers when necessary

Prerequisites:

Education and Training—A bachelor's degree is required; a major or minor in promotion, marketing, English literature, or business is helpful; a master's in business, publishing, or English would also be useful; noncredit graduate courses in book promotion; working at a television or radio station

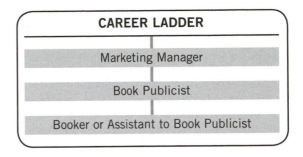

or for a newspaper, magazine, or syndicate is useful training, since the book publicist will have an on-the-job perspective when she or he tries to book authors for media or print interviews

Experience—"Selling" someone for any reason is helpful, even if it is working on a campaign at school to help get a favorite candidate elected; writing experience is important, since Book Publicists have to write press releases, create publicity campaigns, and write author biographies ("bios")

Special Skills and Personality Traits—Excellent written and verbal communication skills; persistence; detail-oriented; determined, without being overly aggressive; a fast reader; able to summarize books in just one paragraph or even one sentence; a people person; good time management skills; able to develop and manage a schedule; able to meet deadlines; able to withstand pressure and an uneven work flow

Position Description

Once the editor and author have signed off on a book and it is at the printer—six months to a year before publication—the work of the Book Publicist begins. It is his or her responsibility to make sure galleys of the book are sent out for prepublication reviews to *Publishers Weekly, Library Journal, Booklist, Kirkus Reviews,* and other magazines that will be read by the publishing industry (including booksellers, wholesalers, and distributors). Galleys are usually sent four months before the book is published to selected magazines that often have a 4–8 month lead time for book review consideration. Publicists also send out the printed book at publication time for review consideration by newspapers,

weekly magazines, and syndicates, to television and radio shows for possible author interviews.

Competition is stiff for interviews on major morning talk shows, such as the *Today Show, CBS Early Show,* and *Good Morning, America,* but getting an interview on one of those shows, especially on publication day or during that week, is often considered the sign that a major book promotion campaign is off to the right start and that the book will hopefully continue the momentum through other interviews on local shows or in second-tier markets.

Most importantly, a Book Publicist needs to have excellent relationships with producers who book the authors on their shows and reviewers who consider the books for reviews. Also important to the Book Publicist are the newspaper and magazine feature reporters or editors who may write or assign an article about their author and his or her new book, which could also help launch a new title, such as a major feature in the *New York Times, USA Today,* or *Parade.*

The Book Publicist has a very challenging job for many reasons. He or she may have a large load of new titles to handle each and every month, yet only one or two of those titles will get major publicity attention. Every author may want major attention, but not every author or every book gets it. Furthermore, a Publicist may decide that an author will actually do a disservice to his or her book by appearing on television and instead should have a radio tour or just do local book events at bookstores.

The Book Publicist should share accurate enthusiasm about new books. To artificially hype everything as a "must read" will eventually backfire, because the reviewers, writers, or producers will stop valuing that Book Publicist's word. The art is knowing which book to pitch and in what way and to what markets. Credibility is key, so the Book Publicist has to be completely versed in what is unique and memorable about an author and her or his new title. Having the right pitch and a well-written and attention-getting press release can make or break a book's initial appeal to the media.

Sometimes Book Publicists get approval from their company to give a certain amount of money to an outside Publicist on behalf of the author and his or her book. If that happens, the staff Book Publicist helps coordinate the campaign by supplying the galleys or books that the other Publicist mails out or by doing the actual mailings. The outside Publicist will do the pitches and the follow-ups, including booking the author's actual schedule.

"Touring" an author may cost as much as $25,000 today, so authors are rarely toured. Those that go might tour to as few as three cities or as many as twenty, depending on the book and the author. For authors who live nearby major cities where there are lots of national television or radio shows available, such as New York City or Los Angeles, it is possible for a Book Publicist to book an author for just the cost of a train ticket to the show or less, if the author can walk or drive to the studio. But book publishers usually decide whether they will invest the time and energy of the Book Publicist in pitching an author to major television and radio shows, a very labor-intensive and time-consuming job, based on the author's reputation and the book's projected success.

The Book Publicist has to keep up with who is hosting or producing what show and who in the print media should be sent review copies or pitched feature story ideas. They accomplish this by creating and maintaining a database of contacts as well as by reading trade publications, such as *Hollywood Reporter, Variety,* and *Publishers Weekly.* Publicists may also arrange for bookstore or library signings, so it is important to maintain contacts at independent and chain bookstores, with major library event coordinators, and with the head of the local Friends of the Library, if an author is touring to a particular city.

Salaries

Salaries range from $25,000 to $89,500, depending upon whether someone works for a publishing company or a company specializing in book promotion and if there are bonuses and profit sharing in addition to a salary. Freelance Book Publicists may work by the hour or by the day, although it is most common to charge by the month ($2,000 to $5,000, with a three-month minimum commitment). Some Book Publicists who have their own companies may earn six-figure incomes.

Employment Prospects

Prospects for entry-level book publicity jobs are good, since this is an essential job at a publishing company. There is a lot of turnover at the entry level, because the salaries tend to be low, the hours tend to be long and hard, and the work tends to be very demanding with lots of last minute concerns as well as constant phone calls to place or return.

Advancement Prospects

The head Book Publicist, or director of publicity, position is hard to achieve, as many Book Publicists vie for this senior-level position. Some advancement opportunities arise when the director of publicity advances to director of marketing. Book publicity companies may offer more senior-level jobs.

Education and Training

A bachelor's degree, with a major or minor in communications, English literature, publishing, writing, business, or marketing, is expected. A graduate degree in publishing, marketing, business, or English literature may also be helpful, in addition to noncredit graduate courses in book promotion and book publishing.

Experience, Skills, and Personality Traits

Working at a publishing company in any capacity, especially in sales, editorial, publicity, or rights, is excellent training. Having a job as an author's professional assistant and learning how to deal with calls from the media for interviews will also be helpful.

Having an internship or job at a television or cable studio, at a radio program, or for a newspaper, magazine, or syndicate will also be useful in understanding the interview process. Assisting a television or radio host or producer will give a Book Publicist an on-the-job view of the process of booking someone on a show. Journalism experience may also be helpful with crafting the sample questions that are often part of the media kit for a new book.

Unions and Associations

Having an active range of contacts in every aspect of publishing and especially with the media (television, cable, and radio) is pivotal for the Book Publicist. Book Publicists can join the New York–based Publishers Publicity Association, (www.publisherspublicity.org), which holds informative monthly luncheons, as well networking cocktail parties and workshops. Two other active groups are Book Publicists of Southern California (www.bookpublicists.org), which holds monthly dinners in Los Angeles and Northern California Book Publicity & Marketing Association (www.ncbpma.org).

Tips for Entry

1. Join book publishing publicity associations such as the Publishers Publicity Association (www.publisherspublicity.org), the Book Publicists of Southern California (www.bookpublicists.org), or the Northern California Book Publicity & Marketing Association (www.ncbpma.org). Attend their monthly networking luncheons, and find out if someone has a job opening that you could fill. As a membership benefit, the Publishers Publicity Association (www.publisherspublicity.org) has a list of available book publicity job openings listed at its Web site.

2. Work as a paid or unpaid assistant or intern in the publicity department at a publishing company and move up the ladder.

3. Work at a television or radio station or at a newspaper, magazine, or online publication so you have experience being pitched to. That will help you to be more effective when you do become a Book Publicist, and it will also expose you to Book Publicists who might offer you a job at their company.

4. Go to the annual BookExpo for those in the book industry, and network with exhibitors and attendees for job opportunities.

5. Visit www.mediabistro.com or www.publishersmarketplace.com, which often have Book Publicist jobs listed. Apply to the companies with available positions.

6. Visit the Web sites of publishing companies where you would like to work, or try to arrange an interview in person. See if there is a publicity job available or ask to have your résumé put on file for any future openings.

7. Network with other Book Publicists; they may let you know when they are leaving a job for another or there is a job opening.

8. Consider working for an independent book publicity company hired by authors or book publishers to carry out a book campaign.

9. Do the book promotion for a friend or family member's book for free. Turn it into a best-seller by getting him or her booked on major television or radio shows and having features printed in prestigious publications. Word will spread about your book publicist acumen, and publishers or book publicity companies may ask you to join their staff.

SALES MANAGER

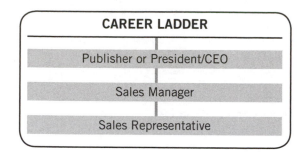
Position Description

The Sales Manager holds a crucial position; even if a publisher has the most wonderful new or backlist titles, without sales, the company will flounder and fold. The Sales Manager coordinates the sales activities of staff sales representatives or acts as a liaison with the commissioned sales representatives used by the company and devises sales strategies for key front-list books in cooperation with the marketing, advertising, publicity, and editorial departments. Depending upon the company's corporate structure, the Sales Manager may be the one who pitches new titles to the buyers at the chain bookstores as well as at the major wholesale accounts.

A key biannual work requirement, especially for most medium-sized and all major publishing houses, is the planning and coordination of the biannual sales conference. Sales representatives from all over the country, as well as such key personnel as the marketing manager and publisher, convene to discuss the upcoming list, with each book being presented by the editor or the marketing manager, one title at a time. At that meeting, the catalog for that season will be distributed, and sales strategies for each title will be discussed. Advance orders expected from the chains or wholesalers are noted, as are any major book promotion commitments from key morning or late night talk shows, bookings on syndicated radio shows, or excerpts or features in newspapers or magazines. Based on those discussions, initial print runs for the key front-list books, a list of authors who will be toured, and the allocation of any advertising dollars will be decided. The Sales Manager is expected to attend trade shows, including the national BookExpo and regional trade shows, and meet with chain bookstores (especially Borders, Waldenbooks, and Barnes & Noble) and wholesalers (such as Ingram, Baker & Taylor, and major store accounts like Costco). Managing a staff that also meets with buyers is crucial. Seeking out new special sales opportunities or supervising the special sales staff may be another job requirement.

Salaries

Salaries range from $43,000 to $130,000 or more, depending upon the size of the company, its revenue, and whether or not there are also bonuses and commissions. Salaries also depend upon how many other sales executives a publishing company employs: There may also be a national accounts manager that handles just the major chain accounts, dividing up the responsibilities of the Sales Manager.

Employment Prospects

The employment prospects for a Sales Manager, if he or she has worked his or her way up the ranks as a sales representative, are good if he or she has a proven track record of bringing in revenue to his or her employer. Numbers talk for this part of the business, as does having contacts with the key buyers in the business, relationships that could be brought to whatever job situation the Sales Manager pursues.

Advancement Prospects

Advancement prospects are only fair for this position, since this may be the highest sales position at a particular company. To advance one may have to move to another company, where the salary and size of the company may be bigger, or move to another slot at the same company, such as publisher or president/CEO. Advancement will be based on a proven sales record as well as on an excellent reputation as someone everyone likes to work with.

Education and Training

Traditionally those who reach the top in sales come from a background of business and marketing, rather than English literature (which tends to be the educational background for those who go into editorial positions); however, this is changing as more and more enter the publishing business with both an undergraduate and a graduate degree. The bachelor's degree can be in any major (including an area of interest, such as art, history, or science) and the graduate degree could be in business or marketing or publishing.

Training as a salesperson is essential for reaching this top spot, including on-the-job training as a sales representative for a publishing company. Attending seminars and courses on effective sales techniques may also be useful.

Experience, Skills, and Personality Traits

The Sales Manager job is dependent on experience and familiarity with as wide a range of roles within book publishing sales as possible—selling to independent bookstores, meeting with account managers at the chain stores, selling to wholesalers and distributors, and making special sales to corporations. The Sales Manager should also have experience attending and exhibiting in a booth at industry trade shows, including the annual BookExpo, the book industry trade show attended by 20,000 booksellers, authors, publishers, wholesalers, distributors, and the media, as well as premium trade shows, where special sales contacts and deals are made.

Unions and Associations

For networking, educational, and visibility reasons, memberships in bookseller or publishing associations, such as the Association of American Publishers (www.publishers.org), will be useful. Membership in selling associations, such as the Direct Marketing Association (www.the-dma.org), may also be beneficial for networking and skills development.

Tips for Entry

1. Get experience as a sales representative. Develop a track record of excellent sales and profits that is directly linked to your selling efforts, and you may be a prime candidate for the Sales Manager job when there is an opening.
2. Check out job listings at www.mediabistro.com and www.monster.com.
3. Go to the Web site for the company where you would like to work. Check out the jobs that are posted. If there are no current openings for Sales Manager or a related sales position, such as national accounts manager or vice president of sales, contact the human resources department and send them a résumé. Try to set up a meeting to let them know about you, even if a current job opening is not listed.
4. Attend the major trade shows for book publishing, such as BookExpo, and network by going to each publisher's booth as well as to the industry-sponsored parties and events. Bring a supply of business cards, and let people know about what you have accomplished as a salesperson. Sell yourself.
5. Read *Publishers Weekly* and attend seminars and conferences in New York City or the annual meeting of the Association of American Publishers (www.publishers.org). Keep up on industry selling

trends so that you are considered knowledgeable and a valuable asset to an employer.

6. Join the National Association of Independent Publishers Representatives (www.naipr.org), and network with other book publishing sales representatives. They may know about available full-time jobs at publishing companies that are available.

7. Become well known by all the key accounts that you sell to, such as the chain and independent booksellers, wholesalers, and special sales opportunities. Your contacts are key as is your sales track record in helping you find a job in this competitive job category.

SALES REPRESENTATIVE

Duties: Sells books to independent and chain bookstores, wholesalers, or special sales (nonbookstore) outlets, usually for a particular territory, as a staff job at a publisher or as an independent representative selling for numerous publishers

Alternate Title(s): Sales Rep; Account Manager

Salary Range: $25,000 to $75,000 depending on company size and revenues

Employment Prospects: Good

Advancement Prospects: Fair

Best Geographical Location(s): Staff positions are more likely in areas where publishing companies flourish, such as New York City, Chicago, Boston, and Los Angeles; independent Reps may live anywhere across the country

Prerequisites:

Education and Training—A bachelor's degree is expected, with a major or minor that applies to book publishing or sales, such as business, marketing, publishing, English literature, or communications; a graduate degree is not necessary for entry-level jobs, but is recommended if someone wants to go all the way up the ladder at a publishing company

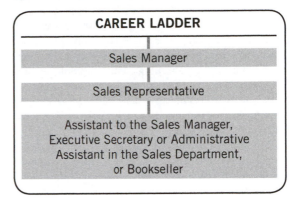

CAREER LADDER

Sales Manager

Sales Representative

Assistant to the Sales Manager, Executive Secretary or Administrative Assistant in the Sales Department, or Bookseller

Experience—Selling experience for a bookstore or a publishing company; related selling experience in any retail or wholesale situation

Special Skills and Personality Traits—Able to make a sale; good with names; pleasant; a "quick study"—able to sum up a book in just a few words and remember new products while still keeping track of older books; excellent communication and computer skills; able to read spreadsheets or use databases, such as Microsoft Excel; outgoing and friendly, without being overly aggressive; high energy; love of travel

Position Description

Sales Representatives work for a major publishing company as part of the in-house staff or as independent commissioned Reps who sell nationwide for publishers without their own sales force. One of the half-dozen largest New York City publishing companies, with upward of a thousand new titles each year and backlists of tens of thousands of titles, can certainly use the services of in-house Sales Reps who only sell their titles to bookstores or wholesalers. Medium-sized or smaller publishers, however, with anywhere from 10 to several hundred titles a year, often prefer to use commission Sales Reps who are selling their line of books as well as those of other companies.

The profit margin is very narrow in book publishing; commissioned Sales Reps are paid from a percentage off the retail list price, usually 20 to 25 percent of the cover price. With most paperback books in the less than $10 range (for mass market titles), $10 to $20 (for trade paperback), or $20 to $30 (for hardcovers)

range, it is clear that the way to get ahead financially as a commissioned Sales Rep is by having a huge volume of sales. Selling just one or two copies of thousands of books, with all the paperwork or keying in of information about those titles, will obviously be more work for less financial reward than selling thousands of copies of just a few titles and getting automatic reorders. Sales Reps are therefore under a lot of pressure to pick the books that booksellers will be able to move out of the multitude of choices among new titles and to be right in those recommendations, so that the books are sold and not returned and there are ample reorders.

Sales Representatives once spent all their time on the road traveling from bookstore to bookstore, but today a lot of selling can be done by phone, at trade shows, or through e-mail and the Internet. Still, the Sales Representative job involves more traveling than any other job in book publishing, except that of the foreign sales manager, who has to attend the Frankfurt Book Fair each October and usually at least one or two more trade shows. Commissioned Sales Representatives have to attend the biannual sales conferences of their client publishers; those meeting may be held all over the United States and even in faraway places, although with financial cutbacks, lavish sales conferences have become much less common. More and more sales conferences are being held in the conference rooms of the publishing companies. Still, a Commissioned Rep could find himself or herself going from bookstore to bookstore as well as from sales meeting to sales meeting with more time on the road than at home with family and friends.

Working for one publishing company, Sales Reps still may be based in their territory, only traveling to their employer's biannual sales conference. The United States and Canada are divided into territories; a Sales Representative will have a specific territory, which will include all the independent bookstores in that territory. Since chain bookstores usually buy at the national level, rather than by individual stores, there may be one Sales Representative whose job is selling to one specific chain, such as Barnes & Noble, Borders, or Waldenbooks. There may also be another Sales Representative who sells to the wholesalers, as a group or by territory, such as Ingram in Tennessee and Baker & Taylor in New York.

Because selling is pivotal to the economic vitality of a publishing company, having an impressive sales record can certainly help a Sales Representative advance in a publishing company. Because the Sales Representative is learning, firsthand, how the business works and developing his or her contacts with booksellers and wholesalers, learning what sells and what does not, he or she could use this job as a springboard to other aspects of the business, from marketing and promotion to publisher or president/CEO.

Salaries

There is a wide range of salaries, depending upon whether it is an in-house position, with a salary range of $25,000 to $75,000, depending on company size, revenues, and bonuses, or a commission Sales Rep position with an independent company or a publisher, with an average range of 5% to 15% on net sales (minus returns) per publisher.

Employment Prospects

There is always a need for Sales Representatives at the entry level, because every major publisher must sell their titles and there is a lot of turnover for this position. Getting a foot in the door is a lot easier than rising up the sales ranks, since advancement is so performance-oriented.

Advancement Prospects

Building a track record of sales is the best way to ensure advancement. Predicting which books are going to sell and making sure that your recommendations are the ones that break out, rather than fizzle out, is as much a matter of luck and timing as it is having enough information about each title, author, and market to make the best endorsements.

Education and Training

A bachelor's degree is expected. Any major or minor related to business or publishing will be useful, including business, marketing, publishing, English literature, or communications. If you want to work your way up the ladder at a publishing company, a graduate degree in business or publishing is recommended.

Training in any aspect of sales is useful, from selling books at a local bookstore to selling online, over the phone, or at any store. Training related to selling books in particular will be especially helpful, since the business is so complex.

Experience, Skills, and Personality Traits

The more sales and book-related experience an individual has, the better. Work for a bookstore, become an assistant to an author, or offer to sell books for a self-publisher or small press. Having Sales Representative jobs at a range of book publishers will also help you to determine what type of publishing company you want to work for, from trade to educational to textbook publishers, from a medium-sized specialty publisher to a major conglomerate that publishes a range of titles. Working as an independent Sales Representative will also provide you with valuable experience, even if you do plan to work as an in-house Rep.

Excellent communication skills and sales ability are essential. Computer skills and a love of travel are important. It is also crucial to be organized, to write up orders right away, to review new catalogues and take notes on titles in an orderly fashion, and to remember backlist titles in order to continue selling books even if they are no longer new.

Unions and Associations

The National Association of Independent Publishers Representatives (www.naipr.org) is useful for networking and finding out about job opportunities. Job opportunities are posted right at its Web site. Attending the annual BookExpo in May or June, as well as the annual regional book tradeshows held throughout the United States by the local affiliates groups of the American Wholesale Booksellers Association (www.awba.com), an association of independent booksellers, will also be helpful for networking.

Tips for Entry

1. Get experience selling so you have something to list on your résumé if there is a job opening for a Sales Representative. Experience selling books, even at a local bookstore, will be useful background, but any sales experience is beneficial.
2. Intern for a sales manager at a publishing company.
3. If you have a friend or family member who has self-published a book, offer to sell it to local bookstores and other outlets, such as gift stores. Read the book. Create selling points that will help you to effectively sell it. Write up orders for the self-publisher to fill. Learn by doing.
4. Go to a postcollege publishing program, such as the Columbia Publishing Course, the University of Denver Publishing Institute, or New York University's intensive summer program. Take all the courses related to sales (See Appendix II for listings).
5. Ask a Sales Representative at a publishing company or an independent Rep if you could tag along on a selling trip and observe everything he or she does. Ask questions without being intrusive. After you feel you have learned how the process works, ask if you could try selling even one title.
6. Check listings for Sales Representative that are posted at the Web sites for the major publishing companies. You could also contact their human resources department and send in your résumé. Let them know you are interested in a job in sales. Also check for listings at www.mediabistro.com, www.hotjobs.com, www.monster.com, or www.salesjobs.com.
7. Get your résumé to the publishing recruiting agencies, such as Bert Davis or Lynne Palmer, and tell them you are interested in a job in sales.

FOREIGN RIGHTS MANAGER

CAREER PROFILE

Duties: Arranges for foreign editions in other countries and languages of titles published in the United States, as well as buys the rights to books from other countries for distribution in the United States or translation; negotiates contracts as well as collects monies that are due; attends or exhibits at major international publishing trade shows where foreign rights are sold

Alternate Title(s): Foreign Rights Editor; Director of Foreign Rights

Salary Range: $25,000 to $75,000; varies widely, depending upon the company's size and revenue

Employment Prospects: Fair

Advancement Prospects: Fair

Best Geographical Location(s): For staff jobs, wherever there are many publishing companies, especially New York City, as well as Chicago, Boston, and Los Angeles; freelance or consultant work can be done from anywhere in the world as long as there is access to the Internet, phone, and a fax machine

Prerequisites:

Education and Training—A bachelor's degree, with a major or minor in English literature, writing, publishing, or business, is expected for staff jobs and recommended for freelancers; a master's degree in publishing or business is recommended; graduate nondegree courses or training program in publishing or a law degree is helpful, but is not required; knowledge of one or more foreign languages is useful

CAREER LADDER

Director of Foreign and Subsidiary Rights or Publisher

↑

Foreign Rights Manager

↑

Assistant to Foreign Rights Manager at a Publishing Company, or Working for a Foreign Rights Agency or Scout

Experience—Selling and buying at any level including working in a store; negotiating contracts; attending or exhibiting at book fairs or trade shows; two to four years' experience assisting a foreign rights manager

Special Skills and Personality Traits—Able to work well with people; attention to detail; comfortable communicating across cultures; excellent English and communication skills; knowledge of other languages, especially Spanish, French, German, Chinese, or Japanese is helpful; willingness to travel internationally one or more times a year and for one to two weeks at a time; patience; persistence; good memory; able to work well with numerous departments domestically and internationally

Position Description

The primary duty of the Foreign Rights Manager is to sell books to multiple foreign publishers, negotiating the contracts, collecting the advance payment that is due, and receiving the foreign edition and distributing it to the author directly or to the author's agent. The job involves traveling to foreign countries, especially Germany for the Frankfurt Book Fair in October and England for the London Book Fair in March or April, and interacting with literary agents, authors, and editors throughout the parent company in the United States, as well as those affiliated with the companies and countries that buy or sell titles in their territory. If all those tasks sound exciting and interesting, becoming a

Foreign Rights Manager may be just the right niche for you in book publishing.

The Foreign Rights Manager directly, or through his or her assistant, corresponds with foreign agents and publishers from all over the world. Meetings are arranged at international book fairs, such as the renowned Frankfurt Book Fair, or at the headquarters of the publishing company when literary agents or publishers from other countries travel to the United States for meetings.

The Foreign Rights Manager has a direct impact on facilitating the publication of new books. These include the translated edition of a book that his or her publisher is about to publish in the United States, or she or he may be acquiring the U.S. rights to a book that was first published in another country or language, such as when Scholastic bought the U.S. rights to J. K. Rowling's first Harry Potter novel, already under contract for publication in the United Kingdom by Bloomsbury Press. Foreign Rights Managers make books happen and bring in revenue that directly impacts their company's bottom line.

However, not all books will be available to the Foreign Rights Manager for sale on behalf of his or her publishing company since many authors keep the foreign rights for their literary agent to negotiate on their behalf. In that case, it is the literary agency who handles foreign rights through its domestic Foreign Rights Manager, if there is one, and its network of foreign agents with whom it is affiliated (and with whom it splits the advance due on a foreign sale, usually 10 to 15 percent to each agent, for a total of 20 to 25 percent commission). Authors who do not have a literary agent may still elect to keep the foreign rights and to hire an independent Foreign Rights Manager to sell their titles. Independent Foreign Rights Managers usually charge a flat fee to represent a title at the major book fairs, usually around $90 to $225 per title; some also get a standard agent's fee (10 percent to 15 percent of the advance) for negotiating any deals that ensue. Others turn the inquiries over to the author or publishing company, and the author, agent, or publisher negotiate the deal directly or through another agent or lawyer.

The amount of money that a Foreign Rights Manager brings in for his or her publishing company per title can range from as little as a few hundred dollars to six-figure advances for international best-sellers, although the average foreign advance is probably closer to $1,000 to $3,000 for non–best-selling titles. Some titles may sell in just a few countries, others may not "travel" at all beyond the United States, and then there are others that become mega hits—such as Jostein Gaarder's book, *Sophie's World.* It was originally published by Aschehoug Publishers in Norway, then published by Farrar, Straus and Giroux in the United Sates in September 1994; by 1997 its translation rights had been sold to 41 publishing companies around the world and it had been translated into 36 languages.

The Foreign Rights Manager usually has a product in hand that has already been tested, since it has at least gone through the publishing house's various departments to get approval and acceptance. There may be useful advance blurbs or endorsements for the finished manuscript if a Foreign Rights Manager wants to sell it from the final manuscript rather than wait for galleys or the finished book. The benefit of selling early is that the more foreign sales attached to a specific nonfiction book or novel at the time the book is being submitted for review or publicity commitments by magazines, newspapers, syndicates, television, or radio, the better its potential domestic sales. In addition to adding revenue to a book's value, foreign sales indicate interest and enthusiasm about a forthcoming book.

Major publishers will often have a Foreign Rights Manager who handles foreign rights for the entire company. He or she may also have at least one assistant. Together they submit books to interested publishers as well as attend the major trade shows for selling foreign rights: the Frankfurt Book Fair (www.frankfurt-book-fair.com), which takes place annually in Frankfurt, Germany in October; the London Book Fair (www.lbf-virtual.com), which takes place in March or April each year in London, England; and the BookExpo (www.bookexpo.com), which is an annual trade show of booksellers throughout the United States in late May or early June that has also become an international rights fair (www.bookexpoamerica.com).

Offers occur for major book publishers through the advance catalogue that announces the forthcoming books and reviews in such major prepublication trade publications as *Publishers Weekly, Kirkus Reviews, Booklist,* and *Library Journal,* as well as such international publications as the *New York Times,* the *Washington Post,* the *Los Angeles Times,* and the *Chicago Tribune.*

The ability to read and negotiate contracts is essential, as is knowing what concerns and clauses are especially important in foreign rights, such as how big an advance will be paid on signing the contract, how much time from signing the contract until publication of the book is allowed (usually 18 months), whether the royalties will be computed on the number of books printed or those sold (in countries lacking a consistent retail list price, it is usually based on the number of books printed, since the books could be sold at a variety of prices), how many copies of the foreign publisher's edition will be sent to the author and/or his or her agent or publisher (usually four to six), as well as how long the foreign publisher will have the rights (usually five to seven years).

There is a lot of detail work involved in selling foreign rights, but there is also the excitement of dealing with agents, publishers, and authors internationally as well as the necessary travel to foreign trade shows. Foreign Rights Managers, even if they use coagents in every country or territory, need to keep up with the trends in major foreign markets throughout the world in order to craft their pitches for particular titles or authors.

Of course, they can be the middle person between a foreign publisher requesting a title and its submission and acceptance by a coagent and foreign publisher. But it is also very gratifying to be able to make direct submissions of titles, based on prior knowledge of a publishing company or a territory, and have those submissions lead to sales and foreign editions.

In addition to foreign translated editions, there are also foreign sales to territories where the title will still be in English but will be sold in a foreign territory, such as books that are published in English and sold to India, Australia, or New Zealand. Books sold to the United Kingdom may alter the writing: The *z* and the *s* are usually substituted in the two languages, and there may also be terms that do not "travel well," as they say in the business. But this is obviously a very different process than is selling the translation rights to a title, which then has to be translated into a new language and often requires a new cover as well. Foreign Rights Managers want to work with well-regarded agents and publishers to assure that their author's work will be translated as faithfully and accurately as possible. It is especially important to request that no changes are made in the book's title without permission and that no cuts are made in content without prior agreement.

Command of one or more foreign languages will, of course, be useful. However, the expectation is that the Foreign Rights Manager in another country, such as Japan, is able to communicate with the U.S. Foreign Rights Manager in English, rather than the U.S. Foreign Rights Manager who is selling a book to Japan being able to read or speak Japanese.

The Foreign Rights Manager develops the annual or semiannual rights catalog, which is used to notify agents and publishers about available titles. It is usually updated for each season, fall or spring, but especially for the fall season, still the major selling season in publishing, with an emphasis on new titles available in time for the annual October Frankfurt Book Fair.

At some publishing companies, the job of Foreign Rights Manager also encompasses that of subsidiary rights manager. This may be due to cost-cutting concerns—having one person do both jobs—or it may be due to the reality that since so many authors have their agents handle foreign rights for them, there are not that many titles that a publishing company's Foreign Rights Manager would have to work with.

The other places where a Foreign Rights Manager might find work is at a literary agency, where she or he might specialize in foreign rights submissions and handling relations with the agency's coagents around the world, or as a foreign rights consultant, who takes books for authors or publishers on a fee-per-book, plus commission, basis to the international shows.

The best way to learn how to become a Foreign Rights Manager is to be the assistant to a Foreign Rights Manager and receive on-the-job training. A paid position is, of course, best but, if necessary, become a Foreign Rights Manager's unpaid assistant or intern. If you are not offered a paid trip to the key international book fairs, offer to pay your own way as long as you can go along and see, firsthand, what it is like to be in charge of a booth for a company and/or have appointments in the rights center with publishers and agents from around the world.

Salaries

Except for the few Foreign Rights Managers who are consultants and may earn a fee per book plus commission for representation at an international book fair, most Foreign Rights Manager jobs are staff jobs at publishing companies on straight salary. Salaries vary widely, depending on the size of the publishing company, its revenues, and the size of its foreign rights department, from approximately $25,000 to $75,000. Some companies may also give bonus and profit sharing. Some positions also include subsidiary rights manager as a secondary job function, and this may also impact on the salary.

Employment Prospects

Employment prospects are fair where the job is just for foreign rights; prospects improve if the job is combined with the subsidiary rights manager position, because so many authors do not allow their publishers to keep their foreign rights but instead have their literary agents negotiate those deals for them directly or through their foreign coagents. Subsidiary rights include selling postpublication rights to magazines, newspapers, and book clubs, as well as possible reprints to paperback houses. Subsidiary rights are almost always controlled by the publishing company, even if the author has a literary agent.

Advancement Prospects

Prospects are poor if the position is just for foreign rights. The advancement prospects improve if it is combined with subsidiary rights duties. Advancement for a Foreign Rights Manager will also depend on how successful he or she is at selling rights and getting impressive advances for his or her publishing company's (or literary agency's) titles. Having and maintaining a network of agents and foreign publishers who respect and like to work with the Foreign Rights Manager will also help someone in this position to be invaluable to his or her current or future employer.

Education and Training

Having a bachelor's degree is expected; someone who wants to become a Foreign Rights Manager could have a wide range of majors or minors, including English literature, business, writing, a foreign language, international affairs. A graduate degree in a foreign language, business, publishing, or even a law degree, would be helpful. Noncredit courses or programs in publishing may also be useful.

On-the-job training is pivotal for this position, whether in a paid capacity as an assistant or as an unpaid intern. Foreign Rights Manager skills are passed on from one Manager to another, as well as by doing the work and asking lots of questions of agents, lawyers, publishers, and others who have done this work before.

Experience, Skills, and Personality Traits

Attending international book fairs or at least going to the national bookselling trade show in the United States, BookExpo, and meeting with agents and publishers who have traveled there from around the world is necessary to build up the contacts that someone is this position needs. Foreign Rights Managers must be aware of trends in international publishing, as well as any domestic and international current events that are impacting on publishing purchases. Foreign Rights Managers need to be able to negotiate a book contract, to delegate, to follow-up after trade shows, and to follow through on submissions. He or she needs to be detail-oriented and comfortable making direct submissions to foreign publishers, which might lead to deals and picking the right international agents to work with for his or her particular type of books. Patience and persistence are other important traits.

Foreign Rights Managers need to be team players. They must be able to interact well with the legal department as well as with agents and publishers from around the world. Being sensitive to the differences in business etiquette internationally, understanding other cultures, and knowing what holidays and vacation periods affect other Foreign Rights Managers, publishers, or agents are also helpful. A good Foreign Rights Manager is a people person who likes to deal with individuals from around the world.

Unions and Associations

Membership in publishing associations may be helpful to develop and maintain as many relationships as possible and to thus increase the likelihood of selling (or buying) titles for foreign editions, such as the Association of American Publishers (www.publishers.org), Women's National Book Association (www.wnba-books.org), and Women's Media Group (www.womensmediagroup.org).

Tips for Entry

1. Attend international and national book publishing trade shows, such as the Frankfurt Book Fair, the London Book Fair, and Book Expo, and let everyone know that you are interested in a job in foreign rights.

2. Look for foreign rights positions at www.mediabistro.com, or get your résumé to the book publishing executive recruiters, such as Bert Davis, Lynne Palmer, and JanPlace Media Search, and let them know you are interested in foreign rights.

3. Work at a literary agency, and carve out a niche as the exclusive Foreign Rights Manager by doing so many deals and developing so many contacts and international relationships that you are invaluable in bringing in revenue from that source.

4. Take any courses in foreign rights that are given, and see if your classmates or instructors know of any openings in this specialized job category.

5. If you are already an editor or a subsidiary rights manager, ask if you could add foreign rights to your job duties. (If you are at a major publishing company where those three jobs are handled by three different people, consider switching to a smaller publishing company where you might be able to do all three.)

6. Offer to be an unpaid intern for a publisher if you are allowed to be trained by the Foreign Rights Manager.

7. Get a job as the assistant to a Foreign Rights Manager, directly or by working your way up from executive secretary or administrative assistant in the editorial or subsidiary rights department.

8. Read the special issues of *Publishers Weekly* right before and after the Frankfurt Book Fair, London Book Fair, and BookExpo, absorbing information about what the trends are in foreign rights publishing.

9. Use the *International Literary Marketplace*, published by InfoToday, and contact foreign publishers in the United Kingdom and other countries. Ask to work in those companies to

gain overseas experience before or in addition to working at a company in the United States.

10. Apply to work at U.S. companies by looking in the *Literary Marketplace* for publishers who might be currently hiring or expanding their foreign rights department.

11. Work for an independent Foreign Rights Manager or for one of the companies that offers cooperative exhibits at foreign trade shows for U.S. publishers, such as the Combined Book Exhibit. Offer to help staff the booth at one of the foreign trade shows so that you can learn more about foreign rights and begin making valuable contacts with literary agents, forcign publishers, and Foreign Rights Managers.

SUBSIDIARY RIGHTS MANAGER

Duties: Handles sales of books before and after publication to such subsidiary nonbookstore sources of revenue including book clubs, newspaper, magazine, or syndicate serialization, and reprint rights to paperback publishers

Alternate Title(s): Director of Subsidiary Rights; Director of Subsidiary and Foreign Rights; Subsidiary and Foreign Rights Manager

Salary Range: Varies widely, from $25,000 to $75,000

Employment Prospects: Good

Advancement Prospects: Fair

Best Geographical Location(s): New York City, Chicago, Boston, or Los Angeles; could also be done on a freelance or consulting basis from anywhere in the world as long as someone has access to a phone, fax machine, and the Internet

Prerequisites:

Education and Training—A bachelor's degree, with a major or minor in English literature, business, or marketing is expected; a graduate degree in publishing, marketing, or sales is recommended; on-the-job training in subsidiary rights at a publishing company or literary agency

CAREER LADDER

```
┌─────────────────────────────────────────┐
│  Director of Subsidiary and Foreign Rights │
│            or Publisher                    │
├─────────────────────────────────────────┤
│       Subsidiary Rights Manager            │
├─────────────────────────────────────────┤
│    Assistant to Subsidiary Rights Manager  │
└─────────────────────────────────────────┘
```

Experience—Working at a literary agency or publishing company; experience at any company in sales; working at a publication in the rights department; working at a newspaper or magazine and buying excerpts from publishers

Special Skills and Personality Traits—Organized; attention to detail; able to follow-up on deals, large and small; nice telephone manner; excellent people skills; able to coordinate schedules and demands of various departments, including editorial, production, sales, and marketing

Position Description

The Subsidiary Rights Manager sells rights to the titles that her or his publishing company is planning to publish (first serial rights, if it's before publication), as well as those to current and backlist titles (second serial rights, if its after publication). This position is a key job at a publishing company, because it may bring in additional or subsidiary income beyond the highly volatile and unpredictable bookstore sales and therefore it helps a publishing company to become or remain profitable. This includes selling first serial rights for a new novel that is excerpted in a major women's magazine, a post-publication sale to a newspaper syndicate, and sales to book clubs, film rights (if not kept by author), plus advances if sold to a paperback publisher for reprinting.

The Subsidiary Rights Manager has to be a consummate people person and deal maker. She or he needs to see where there could be a sale of a new or backlist title, as well as respond quickly to offers that are made by others. It is a faster-paced part of publishing than

that of acquisitions editor, with even greater flexibility and sources of deals and revenue than the foreign rights manager's job, but it is usually consists of domestic (U.S.-based) outlets and sales. The Subsidiary Rights Manager has to work hard to keep up with the editors who will be buying first serial excerpts of new titles from him or her, such as permission editors at major magazines, newspapers, newspaper syndicates, and online publications, as well as the acquisition editors at book clubs. He or she also has to be responsive to second serial inquiries from newspapers or magazines, as well as from authors or publishers who are seeking reprint rights for trade book or textbooks in preparation. (This last job function, however, may be handled by a permissions editor.) The Subsidiary Rights Manager usually coordinates her or his efforts with the acquisitions editor or editor for a new book, receiving the final manuscript from the editor or galleys from the book publicist that she or he will submit for consideration by the book clubs and print publications.

Priscilla Treadwell is the director of subsidiary and foreign rights for Bloomberg Press. Treadwell bachelor's degree and a master's came to her job at Bloomberg after earlier careers as a musician and an English and vocal music teacher. Bloomberg was a new press, and Treadwell, who "learned on the job," credits her quick rise to her current position to having "good mentors who were throwing me things." Their support combined with corporate Bloomberg's entrepreneurial culture helped her achieve a certain level of expertise in subsidiary and foreign rights within a couple of years. She emphasizes how important communication skills are for the Subsidiary Rights Manager: "You have to be articulate in writing as well as verbally." But Treadwell, who has been at Bloomberg Press for seven years, also travels often to nearby New York City, and to the international fairs, for the face-to-face meetings she says are essential for building strong business relationships.

Salaries

Salaries vary widely, from $25,000 to $75,000, depending upon the size of the company and whether the company also offers a bonus or company profit sharing.

Employment Prospects

Employment prospects are good, since most major and medium-sized publishing companies consider this an essential full-time position.

Advancement Prospects

Since this is such a specialized and favored position in publishing, advancement is fair. Few who attain these jobs leave before either retiring or moving to another comparable or higher position at another company. Advancement often means moving out of this particular job function, since Subsidiary Rights Manager is usually the highest job in its category.

Education and Training

A bachelor's degree, with a major or minor in English literature, marketing, or business, is expected. A master's degree in a related field, such as marketing, business, or publishing, is recommended, especially if you want to work your way up the ladder at a publishing company.

On-the-job training, in a paid or unpaid internship capacity, including selling or buying rights in any part of the publishing industry, would be helpful.

Experience, Skills, and Personality Traits

Selling or buying rights at a literary agency or in any branch of publishing, including newspapers or magazines, is useful experience. On-the-job training at a publishing company in editorial, sales, marketing, or the subsidiary rights department is also helpful.

The Subsidiary Rights Manager has to have an eye for selling as well as the abilities to pitch books well and successfully target the right newspaper, magazine, or syndicate for excerpting. He or she also has to have an excellent sense of timing; submitting manuscripts too soon to certain possible reprint houses, if reviews or advance buzz has not yet built up, can lead to a rejection that might have been a purchase at another time. Conversely, a very low offer that is accepted early on might have meant a much bigger advance if the rights were offered at a later date.

Taking courses in how to pitch products and in selling, including how to close the deal, may be helpful as well. Since Subsidiary Rights Managers often have to negotiate the contract, learning how to read a contract and do contract negotiations are other helpful skills.

Subsidiary Rights Managers have to be firm but pleasant, organized, able to delegate effectively, and excellent at follow-up and follow through. They have to be well-read and able to network in a wide range of circles, from the editors at paperback houses who might buy the reprint rights to hardcover titles to the managing editors at magazines who might buy first serial excerpts to new titles.

Unions and Associations

Being active in the publishing associations for publishers and editors, such as the Association of American Publishers (www.publishers.org), the Women's National Book Association (www.wnba-books.org), and Women's Media Group (www.womensmediagroup.org), may be useful for networking, but membership is not a requirement. The Women's National Book Association's New York City chapter posts job openings and positions wanted notices in their online and print newsletters.

Tips for Entry

1. Take any job in book publishing, including editorial assistant or publicity assistant, and apply as soon as there is an opening in the subsidiary rights department.
2. Ask if you could be the paid or unpaid assistant or intern to the director of subsidiary rights.
3. Attend degree or nondegree programs in publishing and take any courses in subsidiary rights. Ask your instructor, who usually works in the industry, to keep you in mind for possible job openings.

4. Attend the BookExpo, the national trade show for booksellers and the book business, and network among exhibitors and attendees.

5. Get a job at a newspaper, magazine, or syndicate buying rights to books so you become known to book editors, publishers, and Subsidiary Rights Managers. Let them know that you would like to switch over to the book publishing side.

6. Work at a literary agency or book club buying or selling rights to gain experience in the subsidiary rights area.

7. Register with publishing executive search firms, such as Bert Davis, and let them know that you are interested in a subsidiary rights job.

8. Check the publishing job offerings listed at www.mediabistro.com, www.publishersmarketplace.com, or the site created by the Association of American Publishers for entry-level jobs at www.bookjobs.com.

9. Go to the Web site for the publishing company you are interested in working at or contact the human resources department through its listing in the *Literary Marketplace*. Apply for any available jobs in subsidiary rights.

MANAGEMENT

PRESIDENT

CAREER PROFILE

Duties: Oversees the entire publishing company, from deciding which books to publish or promote to who gets hired to the vision for the company's list and future

Alternate Title(s): Publisher; Executive Editor; Founder; Publishing Director; Owner; CEO

Salary Range: Varies widely, depending on the company's revenue and if there are bonuses, as well as type of company (major corporation, medium-sized house, university press, or self-publisher); from $0 to $2 million or more, with a median salary of $135,000 (for companies with $1 million to $10 million in revenues) to $480,000 (more than $500 million in revenues) plus bonus at some companies

Employment Prospects: Good

Advancement Prospects: Fair

Best Geographical Location(s): Wherever there is book publishing activity, especially in New York City and the surrounding areas (Westchester County, Long Island, and Connecticut), as well as other hubs of publishing activity, such as Chicago, Boston, and Los Angeles

Prerequisites:

Education and Training—A bachelor's degree is expected; a graduate degree in business, finance, English literature, or publishing is recommended; a law degree is recommended; on-the-job training in a variety of workplace settings, including publishing companies, learning firsthand every phase of a business, from creating the product to its distribution and sales in the marketplace, will be helpful

CAREER LADDER

```
┌─────────────────────────────────────┐
│            Media Mogul               │
├─────────────────────────────────────┤
│           President/CEO              │
├─────────────────────────────────────┤
│  Executive or Senior Vice-President  │
│        or Editor in Chief            │
└─────────────────────────────────────┘
```

Experience—10 to 20 years in publishing and/or running a company or a department in a company or corporation, making decisions about key acquisition and distribution issues that impact on the company's bottom line

Special Skills and Personality Traits—Must understand every facet of publishing, from the acquisition of books from authors or literary agents to the production of those books to the publicizing and selling of the books over the Internet or to customers in bookstores; excellent leadership skills; excellent negotiator; business and financial savvy; able to hire, fire, and delegate to others; superb networking and people skills; enjoy traveling and attending regional, national, or international sales conferences, as well as book industry trade shows; excellent public speaker and skilled at handling interviews with the press; intelligent; well read; organized; able to do well under pressure; personable and well-liked

Position Description

At some companies, the President and the CEO (chief executive officer) are the same position; at other companies, there are two individuals with separate titles and functions.

The President and CEO of a publishing company will have different responsibilities and functions, depending on the size of the company and whether or not it is a trade publisher, with front-list nonfiction and fiction books, or a university press, educational publisher, or medium-sized to smaller press. Regardless of what books are published, however, President and CEO is generally the top position. At some family-owned

businesses, the President and CEO might also be the owner or founder.

Two traditional routes to President and CEO are to work your way up through the ranks of a publishing company, either from the editorial side from the position of editor in chief or through the sales or marketing side from the sales director or marketing director position.

Knowing every aspect of the book publishing business, from creating new products to selling the ones that are already published, is information that the President is expected to have. Being able to establish new sources of revenue and to find other companies or businesses that the company might want to purchase are other job functions.

Another way to become President and CEO is to buy the company. That is what Michael Laddin, President and CEO of Albany-based Whitston Publishing Company, did in 1999. Laddin, who majored in business at the State University of New York at Albany and who has an MBA from Rensselaer Polytech Institute, spent 20 years working for consulting companies and functioning as a marketing officer for several different businesses, as well as a few years as a visiting professor at a college, teaching business courses. But in 1999 Laddin had lunch with the previous co-owner of Whitston Publishing, a publishing company that had been around since the late 1960s. "She was looking to do other things and retire," says Laddin. "After carefully looking at the business, in December of 1999 I bought the business."

Laddin immediately created a board of advisers, best-selling authors and business leaders from "both inside and outside the industry" that have been "a really great resource" to Laddin's learning curve in this complex industry. He also joined the Association of American Publishers and attended their annual meeting and conference held each winter.

Salaries

The median salary for President/CEO of a company with revenues from $1 million to $10 million is $135,000 (according to the 2007 "Salary Survey" published in July 2007 by *Publishers Weekly*). As the company's revenue increases, so does the average salary for the President/CEO, to $350,000 to a high of $480,000 or more for companies with revenues of $100 million or more.

By contrast, there are an untold number of President/CEO positions at companies with revenues less than $1 million or even less than $100,000 with lower salaries in the $25,000 to $100,000 range.

Employment Prospects

This is the top spot at a company, so employment prospects are fair, since many are vying for this position. Having an excellent track record working your way up the ladder at a company or becoming known for selecting books that earn praise and sell well will help your reputation so you may be sought after for this job. Having others praise your managerial and leadership skills will also help your employment prospects. Being able to buy a company—on your own or with investors or other funding—will certainly help you gain the top spot.

Advancement Prospects

If you do not own the company, advancement from President and CEO might include starting or buying a company of your own. If you already own the company, you might see acquiring additional companies as the next step in your career. If you are President and CEO for a smaller company, you may want to advance to running a larger company with more titles and increased revenue (where your salary might rise accordingly).

Education and Training

A bachelor's degree, with a major in business, English, communications, or publishing, is expected. A graduate degree is business, publishing, English literature, or in a field that reflects the specialization of the publishing company you want to work for, such as music, art history, or the social sciences, is recommended.

Additional courses, for credit or on a nondegree basis, in all aspects of book publishing, from production sales, and promotion to Web site traffic development, will be useful. On-the-job training in any type of managerial and supervisory position, especially in the publishing industry, will be helpful.

Experience, Skills, and Personality Traits

A proven track record running a company, preferably a book publishing company, is usually necessary to get to the level of President/CEO. Ten to 20 years working in the business world in a variety of capacities is worthwhile experience for this high-level position. Having experience managing a staff, including delegating to individuals and to departments, as well as the ability to speak effectively about the company with the print and broadcast media, are experiences that the President/CEO of a publishing company needs to have.

A President/CEO of a publishing company will enjoy travel, as well as meet with and build up a wide range of contacts and business associates in every phase of the industry, from booksellers, librarians, and wholesalers to literary agents, authors, reviewers, and television and radio hosts and producers.

Business skills, from how to write an effective business letter to how to communicate over the phone, in person, and through e-mails, are necessary for this position. Excellent leadership skills are expected, as is a knowledge of finance and proficiency in negotiations.

The personality traits one would expect in a President and CEO are self-assurance, confidence, the ability to make decisions quickly and effectively, and the ability to work well in group or team situations.

Unions and Associations

Presidents and CEOs of most major publishing companies belong to the Association of American Publishers (AAP) (www.publishers.org) for networking, educational, and lobbying benefits. With offices in New York City and Washington, D.C., the AAP, with more than 300 member companies, works on behalf of intellectual property and copyright issues, as well as campaigns for increased awareness about opportunities for diversity in the industry.

Tips for Entry

1. Build a name for yourself as you work up the ranks in a publishing company that appreciates what you have to offer and that reflects your values and publishing interests. Learn as many aspects of the business as possible so you will have the best potential to lead a company to financial and critical success.

2. Network with the movers and shakers at your company as well as in the industry. Attend the BookExpo and the Frankfurt Book Fair held each year and any invitation-only book publishing conferences that enable you to become known to the top management at the publishing company that you would like to run.

3. Become known for discovering and bringing to your company unknown authors who earn millions of dollars and critical acclaim.

4. Let the major executive recruiting companies for the industry, such as Bert Davis and Lynne Palmer, know about you and your skills.

5. Search the job listings at www.mediabistro.com, www.monster.com, and www.hotjobs.com, as well as the print and online editions of *Publishers Weekly*.

6. Buy a publishing company, or start your own, and make yourself the President/CEO.

EXECUTIVE SECRETARY

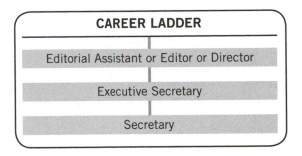

Position Description

For some, Executive Secretary is the job she or he obtains after working as a secretary for several years. Being the Executive Secretary, or assistant to the director or the CEO of the publishing company, can be a lifelong career goal. A career Executive Secretary with seniority, who becomes indispensable to her or his boss, could make as much as $50,000, plus bonuses or stock. If the director or CEO comes to rely on his or her Executive Secretary, as many do, keeping that secretary, rather than risking the break in continuity and the necessary change that goes along with hiring someone new, gives the Executive Secretary a lot of power in negotiating perks, such as additional vacation time at the holidays.

For others, however, being Executive Secretary is a way to learn how to run a company by watching and observing everything that the boss does. For these Executive Secretaries, the job is a stepping stone to someday becoming the publisher or CEO. Traditionally women worked their way up the ranks of publishing companies through secretarial jobs; men began in sales jobs, then worked their way up the ladder that way.

Whether the job is someone's end goal or a stepping-stone, there are numerous administrative tasks that must be attended to even while someone absorbs the bird's-eye view of a company that this job affords. The Executive Secretary usually answers the phone for the CEO; every call goes through him or her. She or he may be told which calls to let through, which ones to never let through, and which ones to handle on her or his own.

Maintaining the calendar for the boss is another important task, as is opening the mail and seeing that letters are sorted and answered. With the advent of e-mail, some directors ask their Executive Secretaries to go through their e-mails for them, sorting out which ones need to be answered. Others maintain several e-mail addresses so that only a small elite group has the CEO's private e-mail; all other e-mails are actually dealt with by the Executive Secretary.

Excellent written and verbal communication skills are essential, as are a lot of energy, dedication to the person who is served, as well as to the company, the ability to juggle numerous tasks at once, and a good memory. If the boss agrees, it may be possible to add on other tasks, such as reading and evaluating manuscripts, if your goal is to move up in editorial, or creating a publicity campaign, if you want to get into book publicity. Adding on more tasks, however, has to be done gradually and with your boss's full approval and blessing or you may lose the main job that you were initially hired for. Also do not be surprised if after a few years your boss, although he or she always said it was okay to move on, is annoyed when you finally do go up the ladder. He or she has probably become very dependent on you; finding a replacement will be difficult, and there will be a lot of necessary training.

Salaries

For career Executive Secretaries who stay in the position a long time, the salary may go as high as $60,000 a year, plus a bonus and stock. For entry-level positions, or those who only work for a few years, salaries may be from $25,000 to $30,000.

Employment Prospects

Employment prospects are good, since most CEOs need a competent Executive Secretary. Since so many view this position as a way to get one's foot in the door rather than as a long-term goal, there is a lot of turnover and available new jobs.

Advancement Prospects

If someone wants to make the Executive Secretary job the long-term career goal, advancement prospects are good, since a reliable Executive Secretary will be rewarded with increased pay, longer vacations, and even bonuses. Most high-level executives would prefer to have an Executive Secretary who makes a commitment to excelling in that job rather than using the job as a stepping-stone to a higher-level editorial or publicity job in the company. If that is your motive, advancement prospects are poor, since this is as high as you can go in this administrative role. Advancing to positions with greater authority and clout, such as editor or book publicist, are difficult, since those positions usually require someone who has on-the-job experience as an editorial assistant or assistant publicist in those departments rather than experience in an administrative capacity.

Education and Training

For career Executive Secretaries, a high school diploma or certificate from a business or secretarial school is required. A bachelor's degree is recommended. Pro-

ficiency in computer skills is required. For those who see this position as a stepping-stone, a bachelor's or graduate degree, with courses, a major, or a minor in book publishing, business, or English literature, will be helpful.

Experience, Skills, and Personality Traits

Working as a secretary is useful experience, even if the company is outside of book publishing. Learning how to answer the phone, screen and place calls, schedule appointments, and coordinate a demanding array of meetings, interviews, and deadlines are skills that will be widely applicable.

Unions and Associations

Any publishing, bookselling, or writing association that has networking, educational, and conference opportunities offers a chance to mingle with potential employers. See the association listings in Appendix III, and visit their Web sites to see which ones offer the best benefits.

Tips for Entry

1. Check the classified ads online at www.mediabistro.com or www.monster.com, among other job search sites, as well as in the newspapers, such as the *New York Times,* or the trade publication *Publishers Weekly* (or its online version, www.publishersweekly.com).

2. Attend a postgraduate publishing program, such as the Stanford Professional Publishing Course, New York University's intensive summer program, or the Publishing Institute at the University of Colorado. Introduce yourself to executives from publishing companies who are teaching in the program, and let them know that you are would like to start out with an Executive Secretary position.

3. Contact the human resources department at the companies you want to work at, or visit their Web sites and see if there are available jobs posted.

4. If you meet a literary agent or the publisher or CEO of a smaller publishing company and discover he or she does not have an Executive Secretary, make a good case for why hiring you would help him or her to run the company more effectively. If you are more interested in gaining experience than money, consider an unpaid internship for a certain period of time with the chance to move up to a paid position.

FINANCIAL MANAGER

CAREER PROFILE

Duties: Handles coordination of all sales from wholesalers, distributors, sales representatives, direct sales, and subsidiary and foreign sales so that semiannual royalty statements and any monies due can be issued to literary agents or authors for the book publishing company or literary agency

Alternate Title(s): Controller; Business Affairs Manager; Royalty Manager; Vice President of Finance; Vice President of Business Administration

Salary Range: $40,000 to $90,000, depending upon the company's size, revenues, and location

Employment Prospects: Good

Advancement Prospects: Fair

Best Geographical Location(s): Wherever there is a book publishing company large enough to have a full-time position, but especially in cities with lots of publishing activity, such as New York City, Boston, Chicago, or Los Angeles

Prerequisites:

Education and Training—A bachelor's degree, with a major in accounting or business, is required; a master's of business administration (MBA) is recommended; courses in publishing are also useful

Experience—Working as an accountant and in the business affairs division of a company, especially a

CAREER LADDER

```
┌─────────────────────────────────────────┐
│  CFO (Chief Financial Officer) of a       │
│  Publishing Company or Literary Agency    │
│  or Publisher                             │
└─────────────────────────────────────────┘
                    │
┌─────────────────────────────────────────┐
│  Financial Manager or Controller          │
└─────────────────────────────────────────┘
                    │
┌─────────────────────────────────────────┐
│  Accountant or Assistant to the           │
│  Financial Manager                        │
└─────────────────────────────────────────┘
```

book publisher; managing a staff, as well as managing the financial details of a multiplicity of projects and departments

Special Skills and Personality Traits—Excellent computer skills; detail-oriented; able to meet deadlines; able to work well with others, including a range of departments within the publishing company; hardworking; superb math and accounting skills

Special Requirements—Certified Public Accountant (CPA)

Position Description

A Financial Manager oversees all phases of the accounting department including accounts payable, accounts receivable, as well as preparing monthly financial reports. He or she coordinates all sales from wholesalers, distributors, sales representatives, direct sales, and subsidiary and foreign sales so that semiannual royalty statements and any monies due can be issued to literary agents or authors for the book publishing company or literary agency. Financial Managers may also advise senior management on ways to increase profits.

For a larger company, at least 10 years of experience may be required, as well as being a CPA (certified public accountant). For smaller companies, a couple of years of experience are expected; a CPA may not be required but is recommended for advancement.

Salaries

Salaries range from $40,000 to $90,000, depending upon the company's size and revenues, as well as whether it is located in a major publishing city, such as New York City, or in a rural or suburban location.

Employment Prospects

Publishing companies with 20 or more new titles a year and a growing backlist will probably need a Financial Manager, so employment prospects are good. Smaller companies may only be able to employ a Financial Manager on a part-time or freelance basis. Larger companies, publishing hundreds of titles a year, will have a full-time Financial Manager, as well as a staff reporting to him or her to help with the various responsibilities, including compiling the royalty reports.

Advancement Prospects

Since there is only one CFO (chief financial officer), usually only at the larger companies, advancement prospects for this position are only fair. It might also be necessary to advance by moving to a larger company, with a bigger salary because there are more titles and added revenue to handle. To advance at the same company, it may be necessary to become a publisher, overseeing all the operations, including acquisitions, not just the financial ones.

Education and Training

A bachelor's degree in finance or accounting and a graduate degree in accounting or business are required. On-the-job training working in the financial department of a company or for an accounting firm is expected, as is book publishing experience.

Special Requirements

Financial Managers need to have passed the CPA exam.

Experience, Skills, and Personality Traits

Three to five years of accounting and business administration experience at a company or for an accounting firm handling a multiplicity of accounts, including book publishers or literary agencies, would be expected before being able to handle this top financial position at a publishing company.

Employment at a publisher or at an accounting firm with book publisher, literary agent, or author clients, is required training for this high-level financial job.

Accounting skills are necessary, as is the ability to interact with multiple departments and individuals providing information that has to be distilled and interpreted. Excellent computer skills and the ability to personally input data or delegate to a staff of assistant financial managers and administrative assistants are necessary. For example, you may be expected to know how to use software including Microsoft Excel, Microsoft Word, and Microsoft Access. The Financial Manager has to be detail-oriented and able to meet multiple deadlines on a daily basis.

Unions and Associations

Join the associations for accountants and Financial Managers, such as the National Conference of CPA Practicioners (www.nccpap.org). Membership in publishing and media associations, such as the Women's Media Group (www.womensmediagroup.org) or the Women's National Book Association (www.wnba-books.org) could also provide useful networking opportunities for professional advancement.

Tips for Entry

1. Get the necessary undergraduate and graduate degrees in accounting or business, and take graduate credit or noncredit publishing courses or certificate programs. Network with the attendees and faculty, and let them know about your accounting and finance background.

2. Check the Web sites for the major publishing companies for available jobs. Use the *Literary Marketplace* to contact the human resources department or finance department and let them know of your availability.

3. Get your résumé to the publishing industry executive recruiting firms, such as Bert Davis and Lynne Palmer, and tell them you are qualified to be a Financial Manager.

4. Check the listings at www.mediabistro.com, www.publishersmarketplace.com, www.hotjobs.com, and www.monster.com.

5. Use the alumni directory and association of your undergraduate and graduate schools to network with graduates who work at, or own, publishing companies or literary agencies or who are authors. Ask for referrals for possible jobs in this area.

6. Join publishing associations, such as the Women's National Book Association (www.wnba-books.org) or the American Booksellers Association (www.bookweb.org), with book publisher and bookseller members throughout the United States. Check their Web sites for any job listings, or see if you can post an announcement about your availability. Attend monthly educational programs for networking as well as regional or national trade shows, such as the annual Book-Expo held in May or June each year.

DISTRIBUTION

WHOLESALER

Duties: Warehouses and sells books to customers, such as bookstores or gift stores, on behalf of the book publisher

Alternate Title(s): Wholesale Distributor

Salary Range: Varies widely, depending upon the job someone holds at the Wholesaler, from account manager or sales representative to vice president of operations, owner, vice president of national accounts, CFO (chief financial officer), or president; may range from $10,000 to $160,000

Employment Prospects: Good

Advancement Prospects: Good

Best Geographical Location(s): A wholesaler is based often in a nonurban setting such as Ingram Book Company in La Vergne, Tennessee.

Prerequisites:

Education and Training—A bachelor's degree, with a major or minor in business administration, is expected for higher-level executive jobs; a master's degree in business (MBA) is also recommended for executive positions; a minor or courses in English literature or publishing, or an advanced degree in these areas, may also be useful; for entry-level jobs, such as working in the warehouse packing orders or

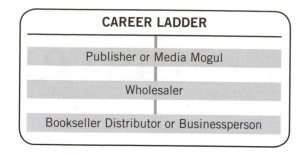

CAREER LADDER

Publisher or Media Mogul

Wholesaler

Bookseller Distributor or Businessperson

dealing with returns, a high school diploma or its equivalent is expected.

Experience—Any type of experience working in a warehouse as well as for a retail store, especially for a bookstore, will help a book Wholesaler employee gain valuable book and selling experience

Special Skills and Personality Traits—Highly organized; able to size up whether a book will be successful or not; knowledgeable about which companies will be good business risks; able to develop and operate a successful business where there is a very small profit margin; able to derive sense of success from running a successful business rather than getting the notice that usually goes to the author, publisher, or even the bookseller

Position Description

Few outside the publishing industry understand what a Wholesaler does or the part it plays in the way that books get from the publishing company to the bookseller. A Wholesaler usually has literally thousands of publishing companies as clients; the publisher sells its books, on consignment, to the Wholesaler, who warehouses the books for the publisher and then sells the books to the booksellers, librarians, or gift stores, who then sell the books to the customer (or, in the case of a library, adds them to its collection.) The reason the Wholesaler exists is that most bookstores do not have the time, money, or staff to deal with the thousands upon thousands of publishing companies from whom they may want to buy just one or two titles. Since the publishing industry is largely an "on consignment" business, meaning that booksellers are able to return the books they do not sell and get credit for those returns, it is a very complicated business to run.

Some publishing companies also rely on a distributor, and it is the distributor, who may have hundreds of publishing company clients, who acts as a go-between those clients and the Wholesaler. Some distributors, however, will only work with publishing companies that have a certain number of titles per year or sales in a certain range. (Their titles also have to be fully returnable.)

There are two major Wholesalers in the trade book industry today: Baker & Taylor, based in New Jersey, and Ingram Book Company, based in Tennessee. There are dozens of other Wholesalers, such as Brodart, Follett, Midwest Library Service, and Coutts Library Service, catering primarily to the library market. Wholesalers, besides Baker & Taylor or Ingram, become known for specializing in a certain type of book or a specific market, such as the library market.

The Wholesaler offers numerous job opportunities within the company, ranging from those who pack the books in the warehouses and ship the orders (as well as unpack the books if they are returned) to account executives, who handle specific publishers based on an alphabetical, geographical, or specialty assignment system. There are also supervisory and executive jobs available at a Wholesaler, depending on the way that the company is structured, as well as the number of employees and the layers of management considered necessary to run the business. Some Wholesalers, including Ingram Book Company, also have jobs available for webmasters, since they operate a very elaborate and extensive online ordering and information site (www.ipage.com), as well as jobs for sales representatives or publicists who help arrange the semiannual Publishers Showcase, for which publishers are invited to travel to La Vergne, Tennessee, and, for a fee, showcase their next season's titles to the Wholesaler's staff.

Salaries

Salaries vary widely, from $10,000 to $160,000 depending on the job function at the Wholesaler, from the stock clerk to the CEO, as well as the size and wealth of the company, from the small Wholesaler with several employees to a major corporation employing thousands. (See the description of each career throughout the book publishing section.)

Employment Prospects

Since so many Wholesalers are located outside of major metropolitan areas where much of the editorial functions of publishing take place, such as in New York City, Chicago, or Boston, this part of the business represents book publishing-related opportunities for those who do not want to relocate to a major urban area.

Advancement Prospects

Getting ahead as a Wholesaler will be based on proving yourself as you go up the ladder by bringing in revenue or taking on tasks that showcase your ability to develop relationships with publishers, agents, and booksellers that further your career. Since this is such a specialized part of book publishing, advancement prospects are good within the wholesale part of the industry. You can increase your chances of advancement by attending the industry events that are excellent for national and international networking and for keeping up with industry trends, such as the annual BookExpo, held in May or June, as well as the regional book trade shows held each fall by one of the nine regional bookseller associations. (See listings in Appendix III under Associations.)

Education and Training

Entry-level jobs in the warehouse packing books or processing returns usually require a high school diploma or its equivalent. If that job is just a stepping-stone to higher-level jobs at a Wholesaler, a bachelor's degree in business, with a major or minor in English literature or publishing, is expected. A graduate degree in business administration with credit or noncredit courses in book publishing is also recommended, if you plan to go all the way up the ladder.

Training in any aspect of selling, especially books, and warehousing will be beneficial.

Experience, Skills, and Personality Traits

The Wholesaler should understand as much of the book business as possible, from the roles of the author and the publishing company to those of the bookseller and the bookstore to those of the distributor and publicist. Experience in all aspects of the book business will help someone who wants to work for a Wholesaler, especially if this experience is in the job category at a publishing company or literary agency that will be comparable to the one you seek at a Wholesaler, such as financial manager, president/CEO, marketing and advertising director, or vice president of operations.

Many Wholesalers rely on print or online catalogs for selling; experience in the development and maintenance of a catalog is useful experience. Selling and having an excellent instinct about which books will sell and which ones will not will take you far in the Wholesaler business. Generating long-term business relationships with book publishers is essential, as is keeping up on book publishing trends and how they impact on the wholesale business, such as the introduction of POD (print on demand) titles.

Depending on what job you are seeking at the wholesaler company, you need to have excellent communication skills, whether talking with a customer on the phone or through e-mail, as well as superb organizational skills, since buyers may handle literally thousands of publishing company clients.

Unions and Associations

By joining the American Booksellers Association (www.bookweb.org) and the regional bookseller association where you live, you will become an active part of the publishing community, kept up-to-date by monthly newsletters and attending their yearly trade shows.

Tips for Entry

1. Attend the annual BookExpo, and network at the wholesaler exhibitor booths and at the parties

given by the Wholesalers that are open to the entire book publishing industry.

2. Read *Publishers Weekly* and become familiar with the Wholesaler community. Check the job openings listed at the back of each *Publishers Weekly* and posted at their online version (www.publishersweekly.com).

3. Research the prominent Wholesalers, such as Ingram Book Company, Baker & Taylor, Brodart, and, Follett. (Check the latest *Literary Mar-*ketplace *(LMP)* for listings. A key to the size of the company will be how many titles are warehoused, information provided by the companies in their *LMP* listing.) Contact a Wholesaler in your community or one that specializes in an aspect of book publishing that you would like to focus on. If they have a Web site, visit it, and see if they list job openings. Contact their human resources department and ask for an appointment to discuss job opportunities.

DISTRIBUTOR

Duties: Acts as the go-between with the publisher, the wholesaler, and the bookstore who gets books into the marketplace

Alternate Title(s): Sales Representative; Fulfillment Company; Sales & Distribution Service; Publisher & Distributor

Salary Range: Varies widely, depending upon the job someone holds working for the Distributor, ranging from working in the warehouse handling order fulfillment and returns to publicity, sales, marketing, finance manager, or president/CEO; may range from $40,000 to $120,000+

Employment Prospects: Poor

Advancement Prospects: Poor

Best Geographical Location(s): Wherever a major distributor is located, such as Publishers Group West in California, National Book Network in Maryland, or Consortium Book Sales & Distribution in Minnesota, with additional distributors found throughout the United States

Prerequisites:

Education and Training—A high school or bachelor's degree is useful, with courses or a major or minor in business or publishing; a graduate degree in business or publishing is beneficial for manage-

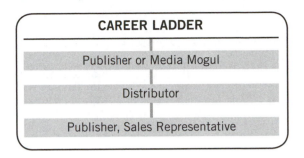

CAREER LADDER

Publisher or Media Mogul

Distributor

Publisher, Sales Representative

ment or executive jobs; any business training is valuable, especially working for a book publisher or a bookseller

Experience—Working for a wholesaler or retailer will provide valuable experience by exposing someone to the warehousing, data entry, stock management, and selling aspects of the business; part-time or summer jobs or internships in any aspect of the book business will provide useful experience

Special Skills and Personality Traits—Distributors handle hundreds of client publishers, so the ability to deal with multiple customers and thousands of products is essential; able to summarize a book in just one sentence; an excellent business sense; efficient; aware of trends in the business; bright, well-read, and worldly; enjoyment of traveling

Position Description

The Distributor has a unique role in getting books from publishers to booksellers. Most major publishing companies do not use a Distributor; they sell directly to the chain bookstores or to wholesalers or they employ a sales force. Most Distributors handle smaller or medium-sized publishing companies that do not have their own sales force or work with independent sales representatives; Publishers Group West, for example, provides marketing and distribution services to more than 160 independent publishing companies. Samuel French Trade is a specialized sales and distribution company that distributes books on theater and film. There are also a growing number of major New York publishing companies, such as Simon & Schuster and Random House, who are adding another revenue stream by acting as Distributors for independent publishing companies. In that

case, the publishing company/Distributor is located in New York City, although the publishing companies that they distribute for are based throughout the United States.

The Distributor usually helps the publishing company without its own sales force to get their books noticed by the wholesalers (who then respond to orders from the booksellers). Since the Distributor has from 50 to several hundred book publishers as clients, they sell their seasonal list to the buyer at the wholesaler, who learns about the new products or backlists being offered by the Distributor's clients through biannual catalog and face-to-face meetings or by exhibiting at the major book trade shows.

Working for a Distributor offers numerous job opportunities, such as the account managers who are assigned to a certain number of client publishing companies. Another job is that of the production manager, who may compile the semiannual catalog. For that job, it is necessary to get all the new title information from each and every publisher in addition to the supporting cover art and advance blurbs to highlight each title in the catalog. Some Distributors have a publicist on staff; others expect their client publishers to hire their own publicists. A sales manager for the Distributor may call on all the major wholesale and chain bookstore accounts Calling on the thousands of independent bookstores may be handled by independent sales representatives who work for many publishing companies as well as the Distributor. Working at the warehouse for a Distributor is another job that is available. Current and backlist titles need to be stocked, when first shipped from the printer, as well as picked and packed for each order (and put back on the shelf if it is later returned because it did not sell or was overstocked). There will also be a sales manager or director of sales who will oversee the semiannual sales conference, where each client publisher, or a representative from the Distributor, presents the key titles for the following season to the Distributor's sales force or independent sales representatives. The sales manager may also be in charge of the Distributor's booth at the annual BookExpo, including how client publishing companies will be included as well as any publicity events or selling materials that will be ready for distribution at the trade show.

The profit margin for the Distributor is quite small, since the percentage that they get from the publisher off the retail list price of the book (60 to 70 percent) to provide these services has to be shared with the wholesaler, who usually gets 50 to 55 percent. (The bookseller gets, on average, 40 percent off the retail list price.) For the 10 to 15 percent that the Distributor is left with after dealing with the wholesalers, the commissioned or staff sales representatives, who are pitching the books for the client book publishers, and the administrative staffs have to be paid. Most Distributors pass along the cost of exhibiting at the trade shows for individual client publishers to those publishers; they are invited to participate in the trade show but only if they pay for their booth and related exhibiting costs.

Distributors do not discover books, the way an editor finds an author and shepherds a book from idea to published tome, but they can help make a "sleeper hit" by aggressively marketing a publishing company's book to the wholesalers. In that way, if there is major media attention for the book or a rave review in the *New York Times* and it starts to take off, booksellers will be able to order and reorder from the stocked wholesaler.

Salaries

Distributors get a commission from the book publisher, usually 70 percent of the retail list price, but 50 to 55 percent of that is discounted (shared) with the wholesaler. Those who work for the Distributor have a wide range of salaries, from the sales representatives, who may work on a commission basis of 20 percent, to those on staff who offer publicity, account management, or other selling or administrative services. Other jobs at the Distributor include those who staff the warehouse, picking and packing books for order fulfillment, and processing returns; marketing and advertising managers; and those who work in the production department creating the twice-a-year catalog that is still the backbone of preselling in the book business. Salary may range from $40,000 to $120,000+.

Employment Prospects

Employment prospects, in general, are poor in this part of the business, as the last decade has seen many Distributors go out of business. However, there are half a dozen very successful Distributors that offer employment possibilities, and there are even a few new ones, such as the specialized Biblio Distribution, part of National Book Network.

Advancement Prospects

To get ahead working for a Distributor, sell lots of books that are not returned and find the unknown next bestseller that everyone else overlooked. In general, since this is not a growth part of the industry, advancement opportunities are poor.

Education and Training

Degree and nondegree training in business or book publishing is useful, and a bachelor's degree is expected. Working in the book business is beneficial, as is any training in selling, the backbone of the Distributor's success.

Experience, Skills, and Personality Traits

Working in the book business, especially working in a warehouse and witnessing order fulfillment as well as answering phones and taking orders, or selling product in person, are experiences that will help someone who wants to work for a Distributor. Being able to quickly summarize a book is useful, as is the ability to pick those books that are going to be successful and sell (and not get oversold or overstocked, only to be returned by the wholesaler or bookseller) are enviable skills for the Distributor employee. Having a good memory, as well as the ability to write effective catalog copy and staff a trade show booth so deals are made and books sold, are vital.

The Distributor employee needs to be persistent, pleasant, an excellent salesperson, with admirable verbal and written communication skills and the ability to deal with hundreds of client publishers and thousands of new and backlist books.

Unions and Associations

Publishing and bookseller associations, such as the Association of American Publishers (www.publishers.org) and American Booksellers Association (www.bookweb.org), are useful for networking and keeping up on business trends.

Tips for Entry

1. Attend the regional trade shows for booksellers in your area, and contact the Distributors who are exhibiting. For starters, let them know you are available if they need extra help during the upcoming busy selling season.
2. Check the Web site for the Distributor you want to work for, and see if they list available job opportunities online. Also send the human resources department your résumé, and explain why you wish to work for a Distributor and what skills you can bring to the job that the company needs.
3. Network at book publishing functions locally as well as at the annual BookExpo, held annually in May or June each year in a major U.S. city and attended by 20,000 people from the various aspects of the book publishing industry.
4. Attend seminars on the book publishing industry with speakers from major wholesalers and Distributors. Approach them and ask if there are any job opportunities at their company.
5. Bring titles or publishers to a Distributor that prove to be highly successful as an indication of your book-selling judgment.
6. Offer to provide relief for staff members at the trade shows where a Distributor is displaying new titles. This is a way to learn about the business and also to make important connections at the Distributor, as well as in the industry, by speaking with booksellers, librarians, authors, literary agents, the media, and wholesalers.

BOOKSELLER

CAREER PROFILE

Duties: Sells books to customers through brick-and-mortar bookstores or online stores

Alternate Title(s): Bookstore Salesperson; Bookstore Employee; Bookstore Manager

Salary Range: Varies widely from an hourly to annual salary, from minimum hourly wage of $6.55, up to $7.25 as of July 24, 2009. (federal minimum wage; each state may have its own minimum wage) to $25,000 a year (or more with profit sharing); store owners might earn salaries as high as six or more figures; heads of a chain or certain online bookstores might earn more than a million dollars

Employment Prospects: Good

Advancement Prospects: Fair

Best Geographical Location(s): Wherever books are sold: for brick-and-mortar stores, wherever there is a lot of customer traffic from walkers (in malls) to drivers; on the Internet, a Web site address that attracts visitors and buyers

Prerequisites:

Education and Training—A high school degree is expected for an entry-level position and a bachelor's degree is recommended; if you plan to work your way up at a bookstore or in the publishing industry, a graduate degree, especially if it provides expertise in a specialized area of books, such as history, literature, science, or travel, is recommended; on-the-job training will be helpful, including working part-time or weekends at any store during school or during summer vacations, especially in a bookstore

Experience—Sales experience of any kind is useful to a bookseller, especially selling at the retail level to customers, face-to-face as well as over the phone and over the Internet; working for a bookseller or aiming for ownership and management of the store will have different experience requirements, although some selling experience is useful no matter how high up you plan to go as a Bookseller

Special Skills and Personality Traits—Love of books; knowledge of published books; able to help customers find a specific book; research skills; able to get along with people, including other staff members, the owner of the bookstore, and customers; detail-oriented; patient

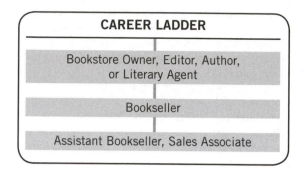

CAREER LADDER

Bookstore Owner, Editor, Author, or Literary Agent

Bookseller

Assistant Bookseller, Sales Associate

Position Description

Booksellers are those who sell books to customers, whether in person at a store, over the phone, or through the Internet for online-based stores. Today there are basically three kinds of bookstores where a Bookseller may work: for the chains, such as Barnes & Noble or Borders, with hundreds of stores throughout the United States; for one of several thousand independent bookstores, such as the Tattered Bookstore, in Denver, Colorado, which are usually just one store or several stores in a regional area owned by a private individual; or an Internet-based bookstore, such as Amazon or Barnes & Noble, which may or may not have a brick-and-mortar physical store associated with it.

For some, working in a bookstore is a temporary job, whether part time or full time, a way of learning the book business, from the very basics of selling books to customers on their way up the ladder to working as an editor in a publishing company, becoming a published author, or becoming a literary agent. For others, becoming a Bookseller is a lifelong career that is fulfilling and rewarding, whether she or he works for a chain bookstore or owns a store.

There are associations, including the American Booksellers Association (www.bookweb.org) and its regional branches, such as, the New England Booksellers Association (www.newenglandbooks.org), that offer training for new and seasoned Booksellers to help them improve their skills and profitability.

There are specialized Booksellers and bookstores, such as children's bookstores or stores that sell books on travel or in other languages. Having specialized knowledge or training will help Booksellers in specialized stores in their efforts to make recommendations to their customers for the purchases that may best suit their needs.

Salaries

There is a wide range of salaries for booksellers, from minimum wage per hour ($6.55 ($7.25 as of July 24, 2009) for federal minimum wage; each state may have its own minimum wage) to annual salaries of $20,000 and up to higher for managerial or supervisory positions. Bookstore owners may make six-figure incomes, based on the company's revenues, with the president and senior executives at some independent stores, chains, and online stores earning six figures or even millions of dollars.

Employment Prospects

Entry-level positions have good employment prospects; at the holidays or, for bookstores in resort towns during the summer vacations, there are usually excellent opportunities for part-time seasonal work (including order fulfillment for online bookstores, if you live near their warehouses). There are so many types of jobs available for Booksellers, from inventory management to sales and data entry to community resource manager, the individual who handles booking and coordinating author events. Stores also usually have managers, even several managers, depending upon the size of the store, who are in charge of all the employees at the store. There may also be a webmaster, whose job it is to maintain the Web site for the store, which offers information about upcoming author events, as well as direct sales.

Advancement Prospects

The opportunities for advancement are poor, since there are so many entry-level Booksellers and so few supervisory or managerial positions available. Having an excellent track record for sales, and having customers praise you as knowledgeable, helpful, and easy to get along with, will help a Bookseller improve his or her chances for advancement.

Education and Training

A Bookseller would be expected to have at least a high school or college diploma, and specialized advanced education would also be helpful for those who intend to sell a certain kind of book, such as history, art, children's books, or reference works.

Working at a bookstore after school, on the weekends, or during summer vacations will provide useful on-the-job training for future Booksellers. Taking a course in bookselling skills or sales could also be beneficial.

To advance to the top as a Bookseller usually means to move from direct sales to management. An advanced degree in business administration as well as excellent financial planning skills would be recommended to rise to the highest level as a Bookseller.

Experience, Skills, and Personality Traits

The more widely read a Bookseller is in both the classics and current bestsellers, the easier it is to make recommendations and advise customers, which lead to bookselling success. Any type of sales experience will help a Bookseller as he or she applies those selling and people skills to bookselling.

Today Booksellers need to know how to use a computer and software programs for database and inventory management. Some stores also expect their Booksellers to be able to research titles, so they also need to know how to access information from such industry publications as *Books-in-Print* and *Forthcoming Books-in-Print.*

Unfortunately the financial compensation to a Bookseller with college or advanced degrees may not duplicate what he or she could earn selling in other retail situations, such as department stores or specialty stores or working in sales on a commission basis. A genuine love of reading, books, and people will help the Bookseller to feel compensated in other ways.

Because customers may change their minds about what books to buy or be outspoken in their opinions about certain titles, Booksellers need patience and an open mind.

Unions and Associations

The American Booksellers Association (ABA) (www.bookweb.org) is a useful membership association for booksellers. Each year, the BookExpo, attended by more than 20,000 in the book business, is cosponsored by the American Booksellers Association and Reed Exhibition Companies. The trade show moves from city to city; it usually is held over a weekend in May or June in Chicago, Los Angeles, Washington, D.C., or New York City. There are also the ABA regional affiliates, regional bookseller associations throughout the United States. Every regional chapter has a fall trade show where the new key titles for that selling season are presented.

Tips for Entry

1. Work part time at a bookstore after school, on weekends, or during your summer vacations, and let the owner know that you want a full-time job when you graduate from school.

2. Go to the fall regional Bookseller trade show in your area or the annual BookExpo, and network with Booksellers from your area or around the country. Give them your business card and let them know you want a job as a Bookseller.

3. Go to the nearest independent or chain bookstore and ask for a job application. If a full-time job is unavailable, let them know you are available for seasonal (holiday or summertime in resort areas) part-time work if they need you.

4. Check the bookstores on the Internet, including those that also have a brick-and-mortar presence, and see if they have job openings listed at their company's store, such as Powells.com, Amazon, and Barnes & Noble.

5. Go to www.indiebound.org a program of independent bookstores throughout the United States, and check out the Web sites of member bookstores. Employment opportunities may be listed.

6. Check www.mediabistro.com or www.craigslist.org for job openings.

7. Join your regional Bookseller association. Then tell the administrator that you are looking for a job as a Bookseller.

8. Read *Publishers Weekly* and check out their want ads.

9. Find out about stores at which the owner is retiring, relocating to another state, changing careers, or liquidating. Buy the company—and you will instantly become a Bookseller.

RELATED PROFESSIONS

LITERARY AGENT

CAREER PROFILE

Duties: On a commission basis, sells books to publishers for authors; negotiates contract; collects payment of the advance money and royalties due

Alternate Title(s): Agent; Literary Representative

Salary Range: $5,000 to $250,000 (and, for a select few, millions of dollars); most agents are paid on a commission basis, 15% for domestic sales and 20% to 25% for foreign sales

Employment Prospects: Good

Advancement Prospects: Fair

Best Geographical Location(s): A majority of book publishing literary agents are based in Manhattan, although there are some prominent agents who have managed to develop thriving careers in other areas of New York State, such as Long Island, Westchester County, or upstate New York, as well as in parts of Connecticut, New Jersey, Illinois, Texas, Washington, D.C., and California

Prerequisites:

Education and Training—A bachelor's degree is expected; a graduate degree is recommended; Literary Agents are also expected to be well read in clas-

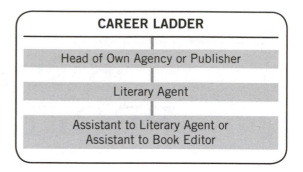

CAREER LADDER

Head of Own Agency or Publisher

Literary Agent

Assistant to Literary Agent or Assistant to Book Editor

sic and contemporary literature and to have training in basic business skills, including proper business correspondence and contract negotiations

Experience—On-the-job experience, either in a paid position or as an unpaid intern, working for a literary agent or for an acquisitions editor at a publishing company

Special Skills and Personality Traits—Able to juggle multiple projects; able to get along with people; a good listener; knowledgeable about the publishing business; responsive and pleasant; able to say "no" in a way that does not alienate people; a team player; patient; able to read quickly and retain information

Position Description

The job of a literary agent has a lot of glamour to it—meeting with authors and book publishers, the infamous business lunch, attending launch parties, the thrill of discovering an unknown writer who goes on to win the National Book Award or get $2 million for the film rights to his or her first novel. Behind all the glamour, however, is a lot of hard work, and in the early years, until an agent has found that "big" book, since most independent literary agents work on a commission basis, it can be a lean time.

There are three basic types of work situations that Literary Agents find themselves in: working for one of the large agencies, such as William Morris or ICM (International Creative Management); being an agent with a medium-sized agency of five to 15 agents; or setting up shop as a sole practitioner in a cooperative office situation or working from a home office with just one assistant. For many Literary Agents, most of the day is spent out of the office, meeting with publishers, in their offices, over lunch, or over drinks after work.

What is pivotal are the authors that a literary agent represents as well as the editors at the publishing houses who know, and trust, a particular agent.

One path to becoming a Literary Agent is to start off as a book editor. While on staff at a publishing company, you get experience reading, evaluating, editing, and taking a manuscript through all the phases of the publishing process. As you develop confidence in your editing skills as well as your selection process, you are also developing relationships at the publishing company where you work with coworkers who are also acquiring editors.

After a few years or perhaps even after a decade or longer, if you leave to set up your own literary agency or join a literary agency, you have all those relationships at your former publishing company to go to with new projects. Even though you are now on the other side of the desk, you are a familiar and trusted face.

Another road to becoming a Literary Agent is to get an entry-level job as the assistant to a Literary Agent and work your way up the ranks. Entry-level jobs are easier to come by than any other Literary Agent jobs, because the pay is so low and the work includes the very basic clerical tasks of answering the phone, scheduling appointments, and reading through manuscripts (often the so-called slush pile, the unsolicited manuscripts that some agencies are willing to wade through in the hope of finding the next overnight publishing sensation).

Book authors are sometimes demanding and sometimes unrealistic about what they may get as an advance for a book or for royalties. Without being negative or hurting a client's feelings, an agent has to convey to the client realistic business expectations. A Literary Agent also has to be able to react to a client's manuscript or idea as well as to generate ideas that attract author clients.

Three typical career paths to Literary Agent tend to be:

1. Starting out as the assistant to a Literary Agent right after obtaining a college or graduate degree in English literature, communications, or publishing (or another field) and working one's way up the ladder at the literary agency
2. Working at a publishing company, usually in the editorial department, as an editorial assistant, assistant editor, acquisitions or senior editor, or editor in chief, before joining a literary agency or starting one's own agency
3. Becoming an agent after, or in addition to, having a writing career as a published author

Becoming a successful Literary Agent depends upon having a good sense of what will make an excellent book, fiction or nonfiction, and how to cultivate a list of successful authors, as well as on having the people skills to interact well with editors and the business acumen to run a successful business (or to be a team player if working at a literary agency with multiple agents).

Contacts, or who you know, are as important in agenting as the projects that are represented. Literary Agents have to stay current on trends in the publishing industry and knowledgeable about the top editors and the publishing companies that are right for a specific property or author.

Being able to manage time is key for Literary Agents, since they have to juggle reading manuscripts and signing new authors as well as editing and submitting book proposals and meeting with editors. Keeping up on what each client is doing as well as having a list that has the right mix of authors who are complementary but not competitive with one another is also crucial. Having enough clients to be able to earn a living from the 10 to 15 percent of their earnings but not so many clients that you are no longer able to be responsive or work at your best is also key.

Many agents develop specialties that they are known for, often based on their personal and professional interests, such as sports, crime fiction, literary novels, biographies, women's issues, business books, or self-help books. Most agents also handle film rights, selling the film rights of a book to a movie studio or television company, but most do not handle screenplays; those are usually handled by an agency in the film business, often based in California.

Salaries

If you start out on your own, the first six months to a year may literally find you having trouble paying for your overhead until you make that first sale. Unless you are working for a literary agency on a salaried or hourly basis, most of the time you will get 10 or 15 percent of whatever deal you negotiate (on domestic sales) or 20 to 25 percent of foreign sales. If you sell a book for an author for $5,000 or $10,000 (the typical advance for a first-time author) or $20,000 for a midlist author, you can see how hard it is, initially, to generate enough income to constitute a living wage. Most Agents have to have a big client list, since not all their authors are selling books at the same time. Some authors need one to three years to complete the book contracts they already have, and some authors need time between projects to work on their next project until it is saleable. The key to generating an excellent income as a Literary Agent, in addition to picking authors who can command large advances and whose books earn royalties, is being able to pick authors who are prolific and reliable. Agents have to balance having a stable of prolific, successful writers that bring in income while avoiding the danger of taking on so many authors that it is impossible to keep up with all the professional and personal demands and requirements of each deal or relationship.

Attendance at industry trade shows, including the annual BookExpo each spring and at the international foreign rights shows, such as the Frankfurt Book Fair in Germany each fall and the London Book Fair each March, will help a Literary Agent with the contacts that are pivotal to the job. A Literary Agent has to be able to find new clients. Attending holiday parties for authors and speaking on panels at writer conferences may be necessary steps to finding new talent, since so many agencies do not even want unsolicited materials sent to their office.

Employment Prospects

The chance for entry-level jobs is good because the turnover is so high for clerical, beginning positions. But advancing to agent is harder, and once an agent, the standards for success are very strict: Do you generate money, and are your authors getting good buzz?

Advancement Prospects

Becoming a top Literary Agent depends as much upon the book authors the Literary Agent represents as it does on the agent. If the agent's authors are successful, the agent will be perceived as being the facilitator of that success.

Education and Training

College or graduate school education is recommended as a way of providing the literary background upon which a Literary Agent's long-term career will be based. Nondegree or degree programs in publishing may also be helpful, especially a course on being a Literary Agent, such as the one Literary Agent Peter Rubie offers each fall at New York University in Manhattan. (See Appendix II for a listing of nondegree programs and courses.) While in high school, college, or graduate school, try to work for a Literary Agent or even a book publisher.

Experience, Skills, and Personality Traits

On-the-job experience, including any internships and apprenticeships, is an excellent way to learn how to be a Literary Agent. Literary Agents need to be able to get along with people, from author clients and staff to book editors, members of the media, book reviewers, and other agents. Agents should not mind working very long hours, including reading manuscripts and meeting with book author before or after the workday since those times may be reserved for meeting with potential book buyers (the editors).

Unions and Associations

Membership in the association for Literary Agents, the Association of Authors' Representatives (www.aar-online.org), an association of more than 200 Literary Agents, is not required but is certainly recommended.

Tips for Entry

1. Get an entry-level job or a paid or unpaid internship at a literary agency and work your way up the ladder.
2. Check out the classified ads for literary agent assistants posted at www.mediabistro.com, www.publishersmarketplace.com, www.monster.com, *Publishers Weekly*, and the *New York Times*.
3. Work as an editor at a book publishing company and go to a literary agency or start your own once you feel confident in your skills as an editor and salesperson.
4. Attend any book parties that you are invited to and let people know that you are looking for a job as a Literary Agent.
5. Query Literary Agents, listed in the *Literary Market Place* and *Jeff Herman's Guide to Book Publishers, Editors, and Literary Agents* (both updated annually) and offer your services.
6. Find an amazing literary property, and if the author is not represented by a Literary Agent or under contract with a publisher, offer to represent him or her. Take the property to a Literary Agent and/or sell it to a publisher. If the book is a best seller, you will have a reputation for being able to spot an exceptional property and make a sale. You could take on other clients or use that as an example of your acumen as a Literary Agent to get a job at a literary agency.
7. Take courses on a nondegree or degree basis in how to be a Literary Agent at New York University's publishing program (www.nyu.edu), Emerson College's publishing program (www.emerson.edu), or any other school that offers a course. Ask the agent who is teaching the course if he or she would let you work as a paid or unpaid intern or assistant.
8. Become active in the online author and publisher communities such as www.authorlink.com and the author and publisher-related groups through www.linkedin.com.

TEACHER/PROFESSOR

Duties: Educates undergraduate or graduate students on a credit or noncredit basis about the book publishing business

Alternate Title(s): Full-time Professor; Adjunct Professor; Part-time Instructor

Salary Range: From $35,000 to $50,000 for full time, depending upon whether individual has a master's degree or doctorate; department heads may earn more; part-time or adjuncts may earn from $1,000 to $3,900 per three-credit course each semester

Employment Prospects: Poor for full time; fair for part time

Advancement Prospects: Poor

Best Geographical Location(s): For full-time jobs, wherever there is a publishing program offered at a university or college, such as Emerson College in Boston or New York University's program New York City; for part-time teaching, wherever there is a publishing program offered; online teaching may also open up teaching options, since only access to the Internet is required rather than being near a major publishing hub or university

Prerequisites:

    Education and Training—For full-time faculty, a bachelor's degree is required and, depending upon

what is being taught, experience in publishing as an editor, as an author, as an agent, or in the production department; a master's degree or doctorate may also be required; for part-time or adjunct teaching positions, experience in the publishing industry, especially on-the-job training and accomplishments related to the course that is being taught, may be all that is required

Experience—Teaching experience at any level, especially at the undergraduate or graduate school level; publishing experience at a publishing company

Special Skills and Personality Traits—Patience; able to communicate in writing; presentation skills; concern for others; for credit courses, ability to give exams and grade students

Position Description

A Teacher or Professor of book publishing is usually someone who has the necessary degrees to be a qualified full-time undergraduate or graduate Professor, as well as someone who has worked in publishing, either at a book publisher or literary agency, or in a related field. A full-time Teacher or Professor, teaching three to five courses, whether on the tenure track, tenured, or not, will receive an annual salary and full medical and dental benefits. An adjunct part-time Professor, who may be teaching just one three-credit course, or even a noncredit course, will earn a flat fee of $1,000 to $3,500 per course without benefits and without the guarantee for employment next semester (or even for the current semester, if too few students register for the class).

There are certainly more book publishing programs now than in past years, such as the new program at Emerson College in Boston, in addition to the graduate

programs at New York University and Columbia University in New York City, but it is still a very specialized course of study and place of employment for Teachers or Professors. Journalism or communication majors or departments are far more plentiful than book publishing programs.

For many, teaching just one or two courses, whether for credit or professional development, is a part-time job in addition to their full-time job at a publishing company or as an independent consultant or freelancer. Some schools, such as New York University, even have a union for their part-time adjunct faculty; at other schools, part-time faculty may become part of the union for the full-time faculty after they teach a certain number of semesters. They may not get benefits, but they may get certain advantages, such as the ability to apply for travel money to professional conferences, if they have taught for at least two consecutive semesters.

Salaries

Full-time Teachers and Professors, depending on whether they have a master's degree or doctorate, may earn from $35,000 to $50,000; department heads may earn more. Part-time faculty or adjuncts may earn from $1,000 to $3,900 per three-credit course each semester.

Employment Prospects

Since there are so few undergraduate or graduate programs for book publishing degrees, full-time employment opportunities are poor. There are just a handful of key schools that offer such employment, such as New York University, and competition is stiff, since there are so many Teachers who are willing to work as adjunct or part-time teachers. For part-time teaching jobs, employment prospects are fair, since, once again, this is a specialized type of teaching that is offered selectively at certain schools or learning centers.

Advancement Prospects

With so few full-time faculty positions available in book publishing programs, the prospects for advancement are poor for full time and part time Teachers/Professors. Having an excellent international reputation and experience in the book publishing field, as well as the necessary advanced degrees and students who have taken your courses and gone on to become shining stars in the book world, will certainly help your chances for advancement in academia.

Education and Training

For full-time book publishing Teachers, it is expected that someone has an undergraduate degree, a master's, and, at some colleges or to become head of the department, a doctorate. Faculty is also expected to have training in the skills of book publishing that are being taught, from writing and editing to selling, promotion, and marketing.

Experience, Skills, and Personality Traits

Working in as many aspects of book publishing as possible provides excellent experience for the future book publishing Teacher or Professor. In addition to book publishing experience at a major or medium-sized company or working for an author, teaching experience at any level, but especially the college or graduate level, will be useful. Teachers or Professors of book publishing need a thorough grasp of the skills that they are teaching, as well as the ability to communicate to others what they do and what they have observed in the business. A genuine love of learning and the ability to get along with students and other faculty members are essential personality traits.

Unions and Associations

Full-time faculty will probably be members of the union of college teachers, American Association of University Professors (www.aaup.org). Part-time faculty should make sure they are affiliated with the associations made up of those in their particular area of expertise in publishing, such as associations for book designers, editors, authors, literary agents, or publicity. (See the listings for associations in Appendix III for the appropriate associations to consider joining.)

Tips for Entry

1. Work in publishing, but also get the necessary academic credentials (undergraduate and graduate), if you want to get a full-time teaching position that requires those degrees.
2. Take courses or get an undergraduate or graduate degree in a publishing program or related field, and let your professors know that you want to teach full time as a career goal.
3. Check www.mediabistro.com and other industry online or print job listings, such as the *New York Times* or *Publishers Weekly,* as well as teaching publications, such as the *Chronicle of Higher Education* (www.chronicle.com).
4. Network with full-time and part-time faculty at such publishing programs as those of Emerson College, New York University, and Columbia University.
5. Offer to help your local college or university to start a degree or nondegree undergraduate or graduate publishing program.
6. Offer to team teach a publishing course with a colleague who is already teaching but wants to share the teaching load on a biweekly basis.

PUBLISHING ATTORNEY

Duties: Handles the legal affairs of a publishing company, literary agency, or author, including contract negotiations

Alternate Title(s): Entertainment Lawyer; Literary Lawyer; Legal Counsel; Literary Agent (with law degree)

Salary Range: Depending upon the location of the publishing company, its size, and revenues, in-house counsel's salary may range from $75,000 to $200,000 or more; if a publishing attorney is hired for a specific legal or contractual concern, payment is usually billed by the hour ($350/hour, on average)

Employment Prospects: Good

Advancement Prospects: Good

Best Geographical Location(s): For staff jobs, where major publishing companies with an in-house legal department are located, such as New York City, Boston, or Chicago; for law firms that offer legal services to book publishers, authors, or literary agents, wherever the practice is based but close enough to publishing industry clients to sustain a literary practice

Prerequisites:

Education and Training—A bachelor's degree and law degree are required; on-the-job training in liter-

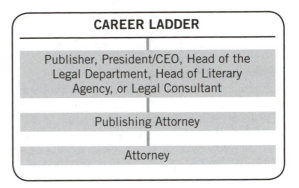

CAREER LADDER

Publisher, President/CEO, Head of the Legal Department, Head of Literary Agency, or Legal Consultant

Publishing Attorney

Attorney

ary law, including contract negotiations and issues related to copyright law, rights, and permissions

Experience—Working at a law firm, preferably specializing in copyright issues and contract negotiations, with book publishing clients, or working in the legal department of a publishing company

Special Skills and Personality Traits—Attention to detail; excellent negotiating skills; knowledge of copyright law

Special Requirements—Passing the bar exam in the state where the publishing company is based

Position Description

There are numerous legal issues that arise in the publishing business, from reading over a manuscript and determining if there is anything libelous that the publisher or author needs to worry about, especially in memoirs or biographies (known as vetting a manuscript), as well as drawing up the contract that an editor and agent have negotiated on behalf of their author. A lawyer is only brought into the actual negotiations for the book project if the author hires an agent who is also a lawyer or he or she hires a lawyer, rather than an agent, or in addition to an agent, or there are issues that need to be resolved. Publishing Attorneys may also be consulted about trademark concerns as well as copyright issues and dealing with any copyright infringement of his or her clients' intellectual property—books. This is a highly specialized aspect of law and because publishing clients, whether publishers or authors, may not be able to afford the fees that a corporate attorney could get from clients in other more lucrative industries, such as

pharmaceuticals or financial services, Publishing Attorneys tend to do it because they have a love of books as well as an affinity for publishers, authors, agents, and the literary world.

Salaries

Salaries may not be as high as doing comparable work in a non-publishing environment, except at the top law firms specializing in entertainment law, including laws concerning books or film, or as in-house counsel for a major publishing company ($75,000 to $200,000 or more annually). Pay may also be by the hour—on average, $350 per hour. To vet a manuscript, for example, which might require 10 to 20 hours, the fee may be $3,500 to $7,000 when billed at the hourly rate of $350 per hour.

Employment Prospects

Major publishing companies may have legal departments, but there are just a few houses large enough to have in-house counsel. There are more employment prospects working for a law firm that specializes in entertainment law, including book publishing, with a variety of clients, including book publishers, as well as literary agencies or authors. Publishing Attorneys also find employment as literary agents or publishers.

Advancement Prospects

This is a specialized form of law, so the advancement prospects are good if a lawyer gains a reputation in the publishing industry for his or her excellent negotiation skills and legal counsel. Some Publishing Attorneys have used their on-the-job experiences to head up literary agencies or publishing companies or to become book publishing consultants with legal expertise.

Education and Training

A bachelor's degree and a law degree are required. Continuing education courses and attendance at bar association and publishing association meetings is expected.

Experience, Skills, and Personality Traits

Working at a publishing company or literary agency, throughout college or law school in any capacity, including editorial, marketing, sales, or production, will help the Publishing Attorney understand the publishing business from every angle. Even working part time or over the summers during school at a bookstore is useful experience.

After graduation from law school, you will be expected to have experience working at law firms specializing in entertainment law, especially book publishing, or as an attorney in the legal department of a book publisher or literary agency.

Unions and Associations

Memberships in the American Bar Association (www.abanet.org), as well as in the bar association of the state in which you are practicing, are useful.

Tips for Entry

1. After law school, contact publishing companies, literary agencies, or law firms with a book publishing practice, and inquire if there are any openings.
2. Ask the associations for authors and publishers, such as the Authors Guild (www.authorsguild.org) or the Association of American Publishers (www.publishers.org), to let you know of any staff Publishing Attorney jobs that may be opening up.
3. To expand your reputation so that clients or job offers come to you, offer to write a column on legal issues for a publishing or writer newsletter for an association, such as the American Society of Journalists and Authors (www.asja.org) or the Publishers Marketing Association (www.pma-online.org). This will help get your name out as a Publishing Attorney.
4. Write a book about legal issues in book publishing to help expand your reputation.
5. Create a Web site so potential employers or clients may easily find you and your services.
6. Go to the Web sites for the major publishing companies and contact the legal department. Find out whom to give your résumé to, and ask him or her to keep you in mind for job openings.
7. Network among your college and law school alumni who are authors, publishers, or literary agents; tell them you are specializing in publishing law and looking for clients.

PERMISSIONS EDITOR

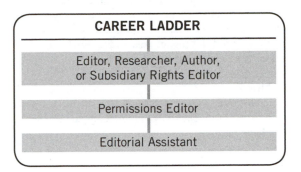

Position Description

Some projects rely on material quoted from other sources, and sometimes what is being excerpted is more than what is allowed as "fair use." The Permissions Editor will contact the copyright holder, whether it is an individual or a company, and request formal permission to use that material. Sometimes it is a permission that is given for as long as a particular copyright notice is provided; sometimes there is a fee attached. If there is a fee, the Permissions Editor will also be responsible for following up once the book is published and to get that fee to the person or company that granted the request. Some grantors also request one or more copies of the published work, and the Permissions Editor, working along with the book's editor or author, will carry out that part of the permission agreement as well.

Sometimes the permission is for original quoted material; then the Permissions Editor may be responsible for collecting the signed release forms that the author has obtained from either the named or anonymous sources for the work.

Another aspect of the Permissions Editor job may be to grant permission to those asking to reprint a line, paragraph, or longer material from the works published by his or her publishing company in another's works. The Permissions Editor will decide if it is in the best interest of his or her author or publishing company to be associated with whatever book, magazine, newspaper, online publication, or other entity that is asking for permission. (Some publishing companies now have another job category, the branding manager, who decides if a book or author that they publish should be used for other products, including stuffed animals or clothing. If permission is granted, the branding manager will decide how much money needs to be offered, as well as what period of time the permission covers and if there are also royalties due on sales.)

If the Permissions Editor grants permissions, he or she needs to make sure all the paperwork is in order on the granted request. If there is money due when the publication appears with the material that was permitted for republication, and if the grantee does not automatically send the money that is due, the Permissions Editor has to follow up and get payment.

Salaries

Salaries range from $20,000 to $40,000 for full-time staff positions, depending on the company's revenue and location.

Employment Prospects

The employment prospects for Permissions Editor are only fair, because most of the smaller publishing companies may have this job performed as one function of another job, such as subsidiary rights editor or the financial manager, if he or she also handles permissions clearance. A larger publishing company, because there may be numerous requests to excerpt or reprint their titles, may have a full-time Permissions Editor, because they are generating money for the company by granting those permissions and by following up to make sure payment is made. Except for top-selling authors, most publishers and literary agencies expect their authors to handle permissions clearances for any works they excerpt or reprint in their works on their own, with the Permissions Editor only providing the standard form that is to be used for clearance. The editor would then check that all quoted materials have been listed and that a form is signed and available for each citation requiring a permission.

Advancement Prospects

Bringing in extra revenues by clearing permissions is one way to get noticed in this obscure but fundamental publishing job. It is possible to use this job as a step toward a subsidiary rights manager or editor position, but in order to do so, the Permissions Editor has to be asking for more tasks in addition to clearing permissions. In that way, you will be acquiring the multiple skills that could make your advancement more likely. For example, ask to take on a certain number of titles so you could try to sell subsidiary rights to book clubs or magazines and newspapers. If you want to advance to assistant editor, ask if you may read over new manuscripts and provide an evaluation or ask to take on specific editorial functions while someone in editorial is on vacation (while, of course, first clearing it with the person whose job you wish to supplement).

Education and Training

A bachelor's degree in any major is expected. If you plan to work your way up the ladder in publishing, a graduate degree is recommended. You could get the degree in publishing; if you plan to focus on a certain type of publishing, such as music publishing, health books, or business books, a degree with a specialization in that area is recommended. Any on-the-job training, especially in the rights department, will be useful.

Take courses and read about fair use and copyright so that you are knowledgeable in those areas and able to recognize when a permission fee would be expected and when granting a request without a fee is acceptable.

Experience, Skills, and Personality Traits

Working in the rights department at a publishing company, newspaper, or magazine is useful background. A Permissions Editor needs to understand copyright law and the concept of copyright and permissions clearances. The concept of fair use also needs to be understood, so taking courses about this, or reading up on it, is important.

A Permissions Editor needs to have excellent clerical skills, including typing, writing business letters, and sending and responding to e-mails, as well as superb communication skills for dealing with people over the phone. She or he needs to be able to delegate effectively, as well as follow-up on requests that are made or granted.

Being detail-oriented and having a respect for and interest in copyright, copyright law, and permissions are imperative. Being able to say "no" is another crucial personality trait, since some may ask for permission when it would not be in the author or publisher's best interest to grant it (for a variety of reasons, ranging from the place where the quoted material would appear to competing project concerns). Editors also need to enforce the payment of a token or larger fee, as appropriate, when someone tries to get the material for free. (Many requesting permission are unaware that the publisher shares those permission fees, usually 50/50, with the author. It is not just the publisher who benefits from any permissions that are granted and fees that are paid.)

Since so much of being a Permissions Editor relates to being organized and knowing how and when to follow-up on requests that may have been made a year or two before, to make sure you get the required sample final book or article, as well as the fee, hone your time management skills. If necessary, take courses in organizing and time management, available through local chapters or offered by individual members of the

National Association of Professional Organizers (www.napo.net).

Unions and Associations
Membership in editorial associations, such as the Editorial Freelancers Association (www.the-efa.org), which includes researchers, indexers, writers, and editors, may provide networking opportunities that lead to freelance or full-time jobs.

Tips for Entry
1. Get any entry-level job in publishing that you can, especially at a smaller or independent publishing company, where you will perform multiple job functions. If there is a Permissions Editor, ask to be an assistant. If they do not have a Permissions Editor, ask if you could perform that function.
2. Network with authors, literary agents, and editors, and let them know that you enjoy clearing permissions for new manuscripts as well as collecting monies due for permissions that have been granted. Ask them to keep you in mind if they hear of a Permissions Editor job opening up.
3. Network at the annual book industry trade show, the BookExpo, as well as the fall regional bookseller association trade shows. Let everyone know that you are a Permissions Editor and that you are available for full-time or freelance jobs.
4. Join and participate in editorial or indexing associations that may know of job opportunities for a Permissions Editor, such as the Editorial Freelancers Association (www.the-efa.org).
5. Place an announcement in newspapers or online for social science, scientific, literary, or educational associations, such as the American Psychological Association (www.aap.org) or the National Association of Science Writers (www.nasw.org) and let their members know that you are available to clear permissions for nonfiction books or textbooks that they are working on under contract.

ASSOCIATION MANAGER

Duties: Provides services for members of the various trade associations joined by publishing companies, authors, literary agents, editors, or art directors

Alternate Title(s): Vice President; Executive Director; Director; President

Salary Range: $35,000 to $100,000+

Employment Prospects: Fair

Advancement Prospects: Fair

Best Geographical Location(s): On-site staff jobs require living near an association, with the majority based in or near New York City, Washington, D.C., Chicago, and Los Angeles; freelance or off-site jobs may be done by phone or e-mail from any location

Prerequisites:

Education and Training—A bachelor's degree is expected; a graduate degree in publishing, business administration, or marketing is recommended

Experience—Related trade association membership experience, especially in a book or literary area, is recommended; any book-related experience, including working part time or full time for a bookseller, literary agency, author, or publishing company, will

be useful background for working at a publishing association

Special Skills and Personality Traits—Basic business administration skills, including organizing educational events and conferences and annual meetings, running a membership drive, and focusing on membership retention; able to handle multiple tasks and committees; able to interact with various departments within the organization, as well as association and staff members; cares deeply about books and the publishing industry

Position Description

There are a plethora of associations servicing the various components of the book publishing industry, from the key trade association of book publishers, the Association of American Publishers (www.publishers.org), with a staff of 30 serving its more than 300 publishing company members, to the Authors Guild (www.authorsguild.org), which has 7,000 author members. All the associations require employees to staff the headquarters. Some or all of the tasks that an Association Manager may do, depending upon the size of the association and how many staff members he or she has to delegate to, include writing, editing or supervising the production of the print or online newsletter; heading the various committees that the association offers to deal with issues that are crucial to its membership; handling membership applications, renewals; and planning and carrying out the myriad of details pertaining to the monthly luncheons, dinner meetings, annual meetings, and conferences. Some of the asso-

ciation positions are volunteer or elected posts held by the association members, such as the president, but the everyday office concerns also have to be dealt with. Each association has its own formula for which jobs are paid staff and administrative and which are volunteer, elected, and held by the members themselves. (Supervising all the volunteers is another aspect of the position of Association Manager)

The paid administrative jobs may include executive secretary or administrative assistant, associate director, director, vice president, and CEO; advancement depends upon how many years someone has worked at the association, how large an organization is, and the various job categories between the entry-level position and the top post.

Katie Blough worked at the Association of American Publishers (AAP) for more than six years before pursuing a teaching career. Blough majored in political science at college and held jobs working at a survey research center and licensing images to organizations for a photo archives company before starting at the AAP. After three years in the school division, Blough switched to the trade division of the association, where, in 2000, she became vice president of the entire association. Blough initially got her job after she contacted an executive recruiting firm, a general firm based in New York City. "The first thing I love about my job," says Blough, "is that I really like the people that I work with both within AAP and at the publishing companies. The second thing I like is that I have 10 committees that I run. Each one is completely unrelated, but there is some overlap, so I get to learn so many different aspects of publishing. One committee is the industry statistics program. I collect industry statistics monthly and annually. It's a big huge project everyday. I also work with the 'Get Caught Reading' campaign, and I'm day-to-day manager of the Publishing Latino Voices Task Force. I also staff our trade executive committee, and I'm responsible for the educational seminars that we offer including the seminars at the annual meeting."

Salaries

Salaries range from $35,000 to $100,000+, depending upon the position at the company, years of service, whether the association is local, regional, or national, and whether there is a year-end bonus.

Employment Prospects

Jobs in association management are necessary to keep the industry associations running, but it is challenging to make a career out of them, since so many positions are volunteer jobs provided by members. Paid jobs are in short supply, and those who get these jobs, if they handle the demands of the jobs well, may keep their jobs for decades. It is hard to advance in an association, since some may only have a skeleton staff. Getting an entry-level job may be easier than advancing, since there is some turnover where there is less upward mobility on the horizon.

Advancement Prospects

Since so many higher-level slots are filled indefinitely, advancement prospects are fair. It is still possible to advance as an Association Manager if you prove yourself invaluable to the membership, are a team player, bring in new members, retain existing members, work hard, get known as someone whom members like to call on for assistance, and shine in your organizational skills. Being responsive to each and every request, from the staff as well as from members, in addition to performing the variety of job responsibilities that the job entails, will also help you to advance.

Education and Training

A bachelor's degree is expected, and any major could suffice. If you plan on advancing in an association or going on to head a company, an advanced degree, such as a master's in business administration (MBA), or in the field that you wish to specialize in, is recommended.

Experience, Skills, and Personality Traits

Working for any company, especially an association, as an administrative assistant or an executive secretary, is useful experience for an Association Manager. You also want to attend the annual trade show of the industry you are interested in serving, in this case the annual BookExpo, held each May or June and run by the Reed Exhibition Companies and the American Booksellers Association, as well as more specialized trade shows or conferences, such as those sponsored by the American Library Association (www.ala.org), the Association of American University Presses (aaupnet.org), or the Publishers Marketing Association (www.pma-online.org). The Publishers Marketing Association organizes a conference held several days before the annual BookExpo in the same city, covering a range of acquisitions, marketing, and sales aspects of book publishing. By attending meetings organized by Association Managers, you will become familiar with the meetings' inner workings, noting what succeeds and what could use improvement.

Those who work in the association management aspect of the book publishing industry need to be detail-oriented, well organized, and able to handle multiple tasks simultaneously. Being a people person, with excellent communication skills, whether over the phone, in person, or by e-mail, is also important, as are computer skills for data entry and contact management. Being responsive to the demands of the membership is another crucial trait, and Association Managers must work well as part of the association team. Being able to meet deadlines is also key, since there will be deadlines for monthly or annual meetings or conferences, as well as descriptive brochures and information pieces that need to be written, edited, printed, and distributed.

Unions and Associations

In addition to belonging to associations related to book publishing, such as the American Booksellers Association (www.bookweb.org) or the Association of American Publishers (www.publishers.org), associations for association professionals may also be useful, such as the Greater Washington Society for Association Executives (www.gwsae.org).

Tips for Entry

1. Research the kind of association in the book publishing industry that you want to work for by going to Web sites. See if they offer any unpaid or paid internships, and apply through the Web site, call, or make an appointment and go in for an interview. There is a selected list of associations in Appendix III. Additional listings are provided in the annual *Literary Marketplace,* as well as at such industry Web sites as www.publishersweekly.com, www.publishers.org, and www.pma-online.org.

2. Check the classified ads in local newspapers, national publications such as the *New York Times,* and trade publications, including *Publishers Weekly* or www.publishersweekly.com. Check with executive recruiting agencies, including specialized ones for the book publishing industry, such as Bert Davis and Lynne Palmer.

3. Check out the job search Web sites online, including www.bookjobs.com (a site for jobs created by the Association of American Publishers), www.publishersmarketplace.com, and www.mediabistro.com.

4. Read trade publications published by the associations for association managers, such as *Executive Update,* published monthly by the Greater Washington Society of Association Executives (www.gwsae.org). Check out the articles in the publication and follow-up with the authors if they are based at an association in the publishing industry.

APPENDIXES*

* Being listed in these appendixes does not imply that the authors or the publisher are recommending a company, product, service, union, or association, nor does omission from these lists, due to space or other considerations, imply disapproval. Throughout these appendixes, you will find street addresses for associations, organizations, or companies, Web site addresses, and other contact information. However, since this information may change at any time, including even the name of an association or company, its address, or the existence of a Web site on the Internet, neither the publisher nor the authors take any responsibility for the accuracy of any listings. The publisher and authors shall have neither liability nor responsibility to any person or entity with respect to any loss or damage caused or alleged to be caused directly or indirectly by either the professionals, associations, schools, or companies listed and/or their services to the reader(s). A special thanks to Jessica Jonas for her help in reviewing and updating the appendixes for the second edition of this book.

Any corrections to any listings in this book, or any suggestions for possible inclusion of additional listings for future editions, should be sent to the authors at their mailing address: Fred and Jan Yager, P.O. Box 8038, Stamford, CT 06905-8038 (e-mail: jyager@aol.com *or* fyager@aol.com).

APPENDIX I
UNDERGRADUATE AND GRADUATE DEGREE PROGAMS

In most cases, an undergraduate degree is required to be considered for the majority of jobs in the publishing industry, so you should consider getting a degree. But there is no "one" path to having a career in publishing, especially since there are so many diverse career options. For some jobs, a degree that offers an excellent liberal arts education may be the best route. For entry-level journalism writing jobs upon graduation, by contrast, a degree from a "j school," an undergraduate (or graduate) journalism program at a college or university, may be preferable. However, if you are going into the art department, majoring in art or design might be the right path for you. If you wish to get into the advertising or sales aspect of publishing, a business, finance, marketing, or economics major might be a consideration. If you want to go into "niche" publishing, you might also want to have a major or a minor in the area in which you wish to specialize, such as biology for medical writing, management for career books, film for newspapers about the entertainment industry, or nutrition for food publications.

Contact your high school or college guidance counselor for suggestions. Your local library may have brochures or reference books about colleges, if you want to consider the advantages of majoring in journalism or mass communications as an undergraduate, pursuing an advanced degree, or finding another educational path.

In terms of a graduate degree, if you plan to specialize in a particular type of publishing, such as a music publisher, a children's book publisher, or working at a health magazine, you might consider obtaining a master's degree in a related field, such as music, elementary education, or nutrition. If you plan to pursue sales, marketing, or executive positions in publishing, a master's in business administration (MBA) is worth considering. A master's in publishing is another option; there are several well-regarded programs, such as that of New York University, with online degrees growing more common to facilitate distance learning.

For colleges offering programs in writing in general, consult the *AWP Official Guide to Writing Programs*, published by Dustbooks and updated periodically. This guide, produced by the Association of Writers and Writing Programs (AWP), lists hundreds of institutions that offer degrees in writing.

If a college or graduate program that you are interested in is not included in the selected listings that follow, one of many excellent guides to consult and a resource for colleges and universities in general is the Princeton Review's *The Best 368 Colleges*, written by Robert Franek, Tom Meltzer, Roy Opochinski, Eric Owens, and Tara Bray, published by Random House, and updated annually. You may also find the Web site for any colleges or universities absent below by doing a search on the Internet using a search engine, such as www.google.com.

A. BOOK AND MAGAZINE PUBLISHING

Relatively few schools offer a degree with specialization in book publishing or magazine publishing (compared to the more than 100 schools with journalism—newspaper—majors or departments and the greater number that have journalism courses or communication programs). Please note, however, that some journalism schools also offer courses in magazine publishing; check out the majors and courses offered at whatever college interests you. In addition to these degree programs in book and magazine publishing, there are several nondegree, postgraduate educational programs also available. (See Appendix II.) You might also select a different major in college, such as English, math, science, business, journalism, theater, or a foreign language. Then you might get additional training in a nondegree book or magazine publishing certificate program (see Appendix II) or on-the-job training through an internship (see Appendix IV).

Some of the journalism programs, listed by state after this section, may also offer courses in book publishing. Check with a specific school that interests you to see if they offer courses in book publishing.

MASSACHUSETTS

Emerson College
Department of Writing, Literature,
　and Publishing
120 Boylston Street
Boston, MA 02116-4624
http://www.emerson.edu/writing_
　lit_publishing
Offers undergraduate degrees and
a master of arts in publishing and
writing with three areas of focus:
magazine publishing, book publishing, and electronic publishing.
(There is a separate journalism and
marketing communication major
offered through the School of Communication.)

NEW YORK

New York University
School of Continuing and
　Professional Studies
Office of Enrollment Services
145 Fourth Avenue
2nd floor
New York, NY 10003
http://www.scps.nyu.edu
Offers a bachelor of science in digital communications and media and
a master of science in publishing, a
42-credit degree, that may be completed on a full-time or part-time
basis. The three concentrations
are Media Content Development,
Media Marketing and Distribution,
and Media Profitability. The faculty
are actively involved in publishing
careers and courses are offered in
midtown Manhattan.

Pace University
Dyson College of Arts and
　Sciences
Midtown Center
551 Fifth Avenue
New York, NY 10176
http://www.pace.edu
Graduate program leading to a
master of science in publishing.
Classes are held at the Midtown
Center in Manhattan.

PENNSYLVANIA

Rosemont College
1400 Montgomery Avenue
Rosemont, PA 19010
Offers a master of arts in english and
publishing with three concentrations: Editing and Writing, Production and Design, and Marketing and
Sales

B. JOURNALISM (NEWSPAPERS AND MAGAZINES)

There are numerous ways to discover which college or university might offer the right program for you. First of all, you could ask your journalism teacher or the adviser to the school paper. You could also contact the local chapter of the Society of Professional Journalists (www.spj.org) which also has a strong commitment to advancing knowledge and training for the next gen-eration of journalists. They may have a list of schools in the state or region that you wish to be in or a list of majors or areas of study that are offered.

You could also read the biographies of journalists when they win an award, such as the Pulitzer Prize, usually featured at the end of a published newspaper or magazine article, or find out where the faculty at a journalism school went to school.

You do not have to major in journalism as an undergraduate to have a career in publishing. There are many other majors available to you that have a direct or indirect relationship to a future career in publishing, such as business; biology, chemistry, or physics (if you plan to be a science writer or editor); English literature; creative writing; history; sociol-ogy; psychology; communication—the list is almost endless. You could minor in journalism, or you could even postpone your journalism training until gradu-ate school.

The Accrediting Council on Education in Journalism and Mass Communications (ACEJMC) accredits 110 schools and departments of journalism and mass com-munications at 103 colleges and universities through-out the United States and one in Santiago, Chile. Also known as "j-schools," the list that follows is adapted and edited from the list posted by ACEJMC at its Web site (www.2.ku.edu/~acejmc). It is a place to start if you wish to study journalism in college. There are certainly countless additional colleges and universities that offer a major in journalism that are not on the list that fol-lows. If you want to attend a particular school and it is not on the list, ask your high school guidance coun-selor, go to the Web site, or call the college directly and find out more about the journalism courses, minor, or major that they might offer.

At the Web site for the magazine *Editor and Publisher*, www.editorandpublisher.com, there is a selected list of more than 35 journalism schools, including the famed Graduate School of Journalism at Columbia University and the undergraduate programs at the University of Missouri's School of Journalism, University of South-ern California's Annenberg School of Communications; Northwestern University's Medill School of Journalism, and Syracuse University's Newhouse School of Public Communications, among others.

You are encouraged to contact any school directly if you have an interest in considering earning a degree there to find out what they offer and what they emphasize. Every school has a different emphasis; indeed, some schools combine print journalism with broadcast journalism, some offer courses in magazines as well as newspapers, and others offer majors or classes in public relations, advertising, and marketing.

The listings that follow, arranged alphabetically by state, offer a degree in journalism (and/or mass communications). Schools offering a master's degree in either field are indicated with an asterisk (*).

ACCREDITED PROGRAMS

ALABAMA

Auburn University
Department of Communication and
  Journalism
Auburn, AL 36849-5206
http://www.auburn.edu

University of Alabama*
College of Communication and
  Information Sciences
Box 870172
Tuscaloosa, AL 35487-0172
http://www.ccom.ua.edu

ALASKA

**University of Alaska—
  Anchorage**
Department of Journalism and
  Public Communications
3211 Providence Drive
Anchorage, AK 99508
http://jpc.uaa.alaska.edu

**University of Alaska—
  Fairbanks**
Department of Journalism
P.O. Box 756120
101 Bunnell Building
Fairbanks, AK 99775-6120
http://www.uaf.edu/journal

ARIZONA

Arizona State University*
Walter Cronkite School of
  Journalism and Mass
  Communication
411 North Central Avenue
Phoenix, AZ 85004
http://cronkite.asu.edu

University of Arizona
Department of Journalism
Marshall Building
Room 334A
Tucson, AZ 85721
http://journalism.arizona.edu

ARKANSAS

Arkansas State University
College of Communications
P.O. Box 540
State University, AR 72467-0540
http://communications.astate.edu

**University of Arkansas—
  Fayetteville***
Walter J. Lemke Department of
  Journalism
Kimpel 116
Fayetteville, AR 72701-1201
http://www.uark.edu/depts/
  jourinfo/public_html

**University of Arkansas—Little
  Rock**
Journalism Program
2801 South University Avenue
Little Rock, AR 72204
http://ualr.edu/masscomm

CALIFORNIA

**California State University—
  Chico**
Department of Journalism
207 Tehama Hall
Chico, CA 95929-0600
http://www.csuchico.edu/jour

**California State University—
  Fullerton**
Department of Communications
800 North State College Boulevard
Fullerton, CA 92834-6846
http://communications.fullerton.edu

**California State University—
  Northridge***
Department of Journalism
Manzanita Hall 210
18111 Nordhoff Street
Northridge, CA 91330-8311
http://www.jour.csun.edu

San Francisco State University
Department of Journalism
1600 Holloway Avenue
San Francisco, CA 94132
http://www.journalism.sfsu.edu

San Jose State University*
School of Journalism and Mass
  Communications
1 Washington Square
San Jose, CA 95192-0055
http://www.jmc.sjsu.edu

**University of California—
  Berkeley***
Graduate School of Journalism
121 North Gate Hall #5860
Berkeley, CA 94720-5860
http://journalism.berkeley.edu

**University of Southern
  California***
Annenberg School for
  Communication
3502 Watt Way, ASC 325
Los Angeles, CA 90089-0281
http://ascweb.usc.edu/home.php

COLORADO

Colorado State University*
Department of Journalism and
  Technical Communication

Fort Collins, CO 80523
http://www.colostate.edu/depts/tj

**University of Colorado—
Boulder***
School of Journalism and Mass
Communication
478 UCB
Boulder, CO 80309-0478
http://www.colorado.edu/journalism

CONNECTICUT

**Southern Connecticut State
University**
Journalism Department
Morrill Hall 202
501 Crescent Street
New Haven, CT 06515

http://www.southernct.edu/
journalism

University of Connecticut
Department of Journalism
337 Mansfield Road, U-1129
Storrs, CT 06269-1129
http://www.journalism.uconn.edu

DISTRICT OF COLUMBIA

American University*
440 Massachusetts Avenue, NW
School of Communication
Washington, DC 20016-8017
http://www.soc.american.edu

Howard University
School of Communication
525 Bryant St. NW
Department of Journalism
Washington, DC 20059
http://www.howard.edu/school
communications

FLORIDA

Florida A&M University
School of Journalism and Graphic
Communication
Tallahassee, FL 32307
http://www.famu.edu

**Florida International
University**
School of Journalism and Mass
Communication
3000 NE 151st Street
North Miami, FL 33181
http://jmc.fiu.edu/sjmc

University of Florida
College of Journalism and
Communications
Weimer Hall, P.O. Box 118400
Gainesville, FL 32611-8400
http://www.jou.ufl.edu

University of Miami*
School of Communication
5100 Brunson Drive
Coral Gables, FL 33124-2030
http://com.miami.edu

University of South Florida
School of Mass Communications
4202 East Fowler Avenue CIS 1040
Tampa, FL 33620
http://masscom.usf.edu

GEORGIA

University of Georgia*
Henry W. Grady College
of Journalism and Mass
Communication
120 Hooper Street
Athens, GA 30602-3018
http://www.grady.uga.edu/jour

HAWAII

University of Hawaii—Manoa
Department of Communication
2550 Campus Road
Crawford Hall 320
Honolulu, HI 96822-2217
http://www.communications.
hawaii.edu

ILLINOIS

Eastern Illinois University
Department of Journalism
600 Lincoln Avenue

Charleston, IL 61920-3099
http://www.eiu.edu/~journal

Northwestern University*
Medill School of Journalism
Fisk Hall
1845 Sheridan Road
Evanston, IL 60208-2101
http://www.medill.northwestern.edu

**Southern Illinois University—
Carbondale***
School of Journalism
1100 Lincoln Drive
Mail Code 6601
Carbondale, IL 62901-6601
http://www.siu.edu/departments/
journal

**University of Illinois at
Urbana-Champaign***
College of Communications
810 South Wright Street
Urbana, IL 61801
http://www.comm.uiuc.edu

INDIANA

Ball State University*
Department of Journalism
Muncie, IN 47306-0485
http://www.bsu.edu/journalism

**Indiana University—
Bloomington***
School of Journalism
940 East Seventh Street
Bloomington, IN 47405-7108
http://www.journalism.indiana.edu

IOWA

Drake University*
School of Journalism and Mass
Communication
2507 University Avenue
Des Moines, IA 50311
http://www.drake.edu/journalism

Iowa State University of Science and Technology*
Greenlee School of Journalism and Communication
Ames, IA 50011-0001
http://www.jlmc.iastate.edu

University of Iowa*
School of Journalism and Mass Communication
Iowa City, IA 52242-2004
http://www.uiowa.edu/~journal

KANSAS

Kansas State University*
A.Q. Miller School of Journalism and Mass Communications
Manhattan, KS 66506-1501
http://www.jmc.ksu.edu

University of Kansas*
William Allen White School of Journalism and Mass Communications
1435 Jayhawk Boulevard
Lawrence, KS 66045-7575
http://www.journalism.ku.edu

KENTUCKY

Murray State University*
Department of Journalism and Mass Communications
114 Wilson Hall
Murray, KY 42071-3311
http://www.murraystate.edu

University of Kentucky
School of Journalism and Telecommunications
Lexington, KY 40506-0042
http://www.uky.edu/
comminfostudies/jat

Western Kentucky University
School of Journalism and Broadcasting
1906 College Heights Boulevard
Bowling Green, KY 42101-3576
http://www.wku.edu

LOUISIANA

Grambling State University*
Department of Mass Communication
403 Main Street
Grambling, LA 71245
http://www.gram.edu

Louisiana State University*
Manship School of Mass Communication
Baton Rouge, LA 70803
http://www.manship.lsu.edu

Nicholls State University
Department of Mass Communication
P.O. Box 2031
Thibodaux, LA 70310
http://www.nicholls.edu/maco

Northwestern State University
Department of Journalism
P.O. Box 5273
Natchitoches, LA 71497
http://www.nsula.edu/journalism

Southern University*
Department of Mass Communications
Baton Rouge, LA 70813
http://www.subr.edu

University of Louisiana—Lafayette*
Department of Communication
P.O. Box 43650
Lafayette, LA 70504-3650
http://comm.louisiana.edu

University of Louisiana—Monroe*
Department of Mass Communications
401 Bayou Drive
Monroe, LA 71209-0322
http://www.ulm.edu/masscomm

MARYLAND

University of Maryland*
Philip Merrill College of Journalism

College Park, MD 20742-7111
http://www.journalism.umd.edu

MICHIGAN

Central Michigan University
Department of Journalism
Mount Pleasant, MI 48859
http://journalism.cmich.edu

Michigan State University*
School of Journalism
East Lansing, MI 48824-1212
http://www.jrn.msu.edu

MINNESOTA

St. Cloud State University*
Department of Mass Communications
720 4th Avenue South
St. Cloud, MN 56301-4498
http://www.stcloudstate.edu/
masscommunications

University of Minnesota*
School of Journalism and Mass Communication
206 Church Street S.E.
Minneapolis, MN 55455-0418
http://www.sjmc.umn.edu

MISSISSIPPI

Jackson State University
Department of Mass Communications
P.O. Box 17199
Jackson, MS 39217
http://www.jsums.edu/jsuoaa

University of Mississippi
Department of Journalism
Box 1848, 105 Farley Hall
University, MS 38677-1848
http://www.olemiss.edu/depts/
journalism

University of Southern Mississippi*
School of Mass Communication and Journalism
118 College Drive #5121
Hattiesburg, MS 39406-0001
http://www.usm.edu/mcj

MISSOURI

University of Missouri— Columbia*
School of Journalism
120 Neff Hall
Columbia, MO 65211-1200
http://www.journalism.missouri.edu

MONTANA

University of Montana*
School of Journalism
Missoula, MT 59812
http://www.umt.edu/journalism

NEBRASKA

University of Nebraska— Lincoln*
College of Journalism and Mass Communications
147 Andersen Hall
Lincoln, NE 68588-0443
http://www.unl.edu/journalism

NEVADA

University of Nevada—Reno*
Donald W. Reynolds School of Journalism and Center for Advanced Media Studies
Mail Stop 310
Reno, NV 89557-0040
http://journalism.unr.edu

NEW MEXICO

New Mexico State University
Department of Journalism and Mass Communications
MSC 3J, P.O. Box 30001
Las Cruces, NM 88003-8001
http://www.nmsu.edu/~journali

University of New Mexico*
Department of Communication and Journalism
Albuquerque, NM 87131-1171
http://www.unm.edu/~cjdept

NEW YORK

Columbia University*
Graduate School of Journalism
2950 Broadway
New York, NY 10027
http://www.jrn.columbia.edu

New York University*
Department of Journalism
20 Cooper Square
New York, NY 10003
http://journalism.nyu.edu

Syracuse University*
Newhouse School of Public Communications
215 University Place
Syracuse, NY 13244
http://newhouse.syr.edu

NORTH CAROLINA

University of North Carolina— Chapel Hill*
School of Journalism and Mass Communication
CB 3365
Chapel Hill, NC 27599-3365
http://www.jomc.unc.edu

OHIO

Bowling Green State University
Department of Journalism
Bowling Green, OH 43403
http://www.bgsu.edu/departments/journalism

Kent State University*
School of Journalism and Mass Communication
130 Taylor Hall
Kent, OH 44242
http://www.jmc.kent.edu

Ohio University*
E.W. Scripps School of Journalism
Park Place & Court Street
Athens, OH 45701
http://www.scrippsjschool.org

OKLAHOMA

Oklahoma State University*
School of Journalism and Broadcasting
Stillwater, OK 74078-0195
http://journalism.okstate.edu

University of Oklahoma*
Gaylord College of Journalism and Mass Communication
395 W. Lindsey
Norman, OK 73019
http://www.ou.edu/gaylord/home.html

OREGON

University of Oregon*
School of Journalism and Communication
1275 University of Oregon
Eugene, OR 97403-1275
http://www.jcomm.uoregon.edu

PENNSYLVANIA

Pennsylvania State University*
College of Communications
201 Carnegie Building
University Park, PA 16802
http://www.psu.edu/dept/comm

Temple University*
Department of Journalism, Public Relations and Advertising
2020 North 13th Street
Philadelphia, PA 19122-6080
http://www.temple.edu/journalism

SOUTH CAROLINA

University of South Carolina*
School of Journalism and Mass Communications
Columbia, SC 29208
http://www.jour.sc.edu

Winthrop University
Department of Mass Communication
219 Johnson Hall
Rock Hill, SC 29733-0001
http://www.winthrop.edu/masscomm

SOUTH DAKOTA

South Dakota State University
Department of Journalism and Mass Communication
P.O. Box 2235

Brookings, SD 57007
http://www3.sdstate.edu

University of South Dakota*
Department of Contemporary
   Media and Journalism
414 East Clark Street
Vermillion, SD 57069-2390
http://www.usd.edu/cmj

TENNESSEE

**East Tennessee State
   University***
Department of Communication
Box 70267
Johnson City, TN 37614-1709
http://www.etsu.edu/cas/comm/
   index.isp.

**Middle Tennessee State
   University***
College of Mass Communication
School of Journalism
1301 East Main Street
Murfreesboro, TN 37132
http://www.mtsu.edu/~jour

University of Memphis*
Department of Journalism
3711 Veterans Building
Memphis, TN 38152
http://umdrive.memphis.edu/
   g-journalism

University of Tennessee*
College of Communication and
   Information
302 Communications Building
1345 Circle Park Drive
Knoxville, TN 37996-0341
http://www.cci.utk.edu

**University of Tennessee—
   Chattanooga**
Department of Communication
311 Frist Hall
613 McCallie Avenue
Chattanooga, TN 37403-2598
http://www.utc.edu/Academic/
   Communication

**University of Tennessee—
   Martin**
Department of Communications
Martin, TN 38238-5099
http://www.utm.edu/departments/
   chfa/comm

TEXAS

Abilene Christian University*
Department of Journalism and
   Mass Communication
Box 27892
ACU Station
Abilene, TX 79699
http://www.acu.edu/academics/cas/
   jmc/index.html

Baylor University*
Department of Journalism
One Bear Place #97353
Waco, TX 76798-7353
http://www.baylor.edu/journalism

Texas A&M University*
Department of Journalism
4234 TAMU
College Station, TX 77843-4111
http://comm.tamu.edu

Texas Christian University*
Department of Journalism
TCU Box 298060
Fort Worth, TX 76129
http://www.journalism.tcu.edu

Texas Tech University*
College of Mass Communications
Box 43082
Lubbock, TX 79409-3082
http://www.depts.ttu.edu/
   masscom

University of North Texas*
Department of Journalism and
   Mayborn Graduate Institute of
   Journalism
P.O. Box 311460
Denton, TX 76203-1460
http://www.jour.unt.edu

University of Texas*
School of Journalism
1 University Station A1000
Austin, TX 78712
http://journalism.utexas.edu

UTAH

Brigham Young University
Department of Communications
Room E509, Harris Fine Arts Center
Provo, UT 84602-6404
http://www.byu.edu/webhapp/
   home/index.jsp

University of Utah*
Department of Communication
255 South Central Campus Drive,
   Room 2400
Salt Lake City, UT 84112
http://www.hum.utah.edu/
   communication

VIRGINIA

Hampton University
Department of Mass Media Arts
546 East Queen Street
Hampton, VA 23668
http://www.hamptonu.edu/shsjc/
   index/htm

Norfolk State University*
Department of Mass Communications and Journalism
700 Park Avenue
Norfolk, VA 23504
http://www.nsu.edu/mcjr

Washington and Lee University
Department of Journalism and
   Mass Communications
Lexington, VA 24450
http://journalism.wlu.edu

WASHINGTON

University of Washington*
Department of Communication
Box 353740
Seattle, WA 98195-3740
http://www.com.washington.edu/
   program/index.html

WEST VIRGINIA

Marshall University*
W. Page Pitt School of
    Journalism and Mass
    Communications
One John Marshall Drive
Huntington, WV 25755-2622
http://www.marshall.edu/sojmc

West Virginia University*
Perley Isaac Reed School of
    Journalism
P.O. Box 6010
Morgantown, WV 26506-6010
http://journalism.wvu.edu

WISCONSIN

Marquette University*
College of Communication
Johnson Hall
P.O. Box 1881
Milwaukee, WI 53201-1881
http://www.marquette.edu/
    comm

**University of Wisconsin—
    Eau Claire**
Department of Communication
    and Journalism
Eau Claire, WI 54702-4004
http://www.uwec.edu/
    commjour

**University of Wisconsin—
    Oshkosh**
Department of Journalism
800 Algoma Boulevard
Oshkosh, WI 54901-8696
http://www.uwosh.edu/journalism

**University of Wisconsin—River
    Falls**
Department of Journalism
410 South Third Street
River Falls, WI 54022
http://www.uwrf.edu/
    journalism/welcome.html

INTERNATIONAL

**Pontificia Universidad Católica
    de Chile***
School of Journalism
Alameda 340
Santiago, Chile
http://puc.cl

APPENDIX II
NONDEGREE PUBLISHING PROGRAMS AND COURSES

A. BOOK AND MAGAZINE PUBLISHING

CALIFORNIA

Stanford Professional Publishing Course
Stanford Alumni Association
Bowman Alumni House
Palo Alto, CA 94305-4005
http://publishingcourses.stanford.edu
Annual Book/Magazine Course for nine days in the summer (mid-July). There is a two-and-a-half day course that precedes the main course recommended for international students. Residing in the residence hall on campus is also suggested because of the program's long hours. The program is aimed at midcareer publishing progressions. Early registration and scholarship deadlines are in March and April.

COLORADO

The Publishing Institute
University of Denver
2000 East Asbury Avenue
Denver, CO 80208
http://www.du.edu/pi
A four-week graduate level summer publishing course with workshops in editing and marketing, with special session field trips. Application includes college transcripts, résumé, a personal statement, at least two letters of recommendation, and a nonrefundable $50 application fee; the deadline is April 1.

ILLINOIS

Chicago Writers and Editors Conference
http://www.magazinewriters.com
Held for three days in July since 1992, this conference is only open to 60 registrants, who get to meet editors from the top magazines and listen to them talk about what they are looking for from freelance writers. In 2008, it was held in October in Kohler, Wisconsin.

NEW YORK

Association of American Publishers
71 Fifth Avenue, 2nd floor
New York, NY 10003
http://www.publishers.org
Offers an intensive introduction to publishing course each year, usually in September or October, at its New York City office. Top publishing professionals are present from all aspects of the business, from finances and acquisitions to distribution, sales, and publicity. Other programs offered by the AAP include "Finance for Editors."

Columbia Publishing Course
Columbia University
Graduate School of Journalism
New York, NY 10027
http://www.journalism.columbia.edu
Formerly known as the Radcliffe Publishing Program and once based at Radcliffe College in Cambridge, Massachusetts, 100 students take this thorough publishing program from late June until the beginning of August. The nondegree program has a book and magazine program and is often the first step toward getting a job in publishing for its students, usually recent college graduates.

Center for Publishing
New York University
145 Fourth Avenue, 2nd floor
New York, NY 10003
http://www.scps.nyu.edu
Offers an intensive six-week Summer Publishing Institute. During the fall and spring semesters, it also offers courses toward its certificate programs, with concentrations in book, magazine, or electronic publishing and requiring five courses. One-day seminars are also offered on various aspects of the publishing business.

Publishing Certificate Program
City University of New York
Division of Humanities NAC 5/225
138th Street & Convent Avenue
New York, NY 10031
http://www.ccny.cuny.edu/
    publishing_certificate/aboutus.
    html
Started in 1997 by novelist Walter Mosley, the program offers nondegree courses for those seeking to enter the publishing business. Internships are also set up with major publishing companies in New York City.

Publishing for the Real World
Pratt Institute
144 West 14th Street
New York, NY 10011
http://prostudies.pratt.edu
Noncredit certificate program started in fall 2003 geared to those working in the business who want additional training.

B. NEWSPAPER WRITING AND EDITING

The Poynter Institute
801 Third Street South
St. Petersburg, FL 33701
http://www.poynter.org
Founded in 1975 by Nelson Poynter, the publisher of the *St. Petersburg* *Times,* the institute is committed to training future journalists and teachers of journalism, as well as to offering opportunities for skills advancement to current journalists. Seminars are offered in design and graphics; writing and editing; television, radio, online journalism; and photojournalism.

C. WRITING (NONFICTION OR FICTION)

Check with your local college or graduate schools for available nondegree writing programs. *Poets & Writers* is a monthly magazine that contains numerous display ads about the extensive nondegree writing programs offered by colleges and institutions. Consult the latest *Literary Marketplace,* updated annually, for noncredit writing programs as well.

An excellent resource for writing programs is the Association of Writers and Writing Programs (AWP) (www.awpwriter.org), which maintains an online directory of writers' conferences. *The AWP Official Guide to Writing Programs,* updated periodically and published in cooperation with Dustbooks, is a thorough resource for more than 300 writing programs throughout the United States, Canada, and the United Kingdom, as well as more than 200 writers' conferences, writing colonies, and writing centers.

ILLINOIS

Medical Writing and Editing Certificate
Graham School of General Studies
University of Chicago
1427 East 60th Street
Chicago, IL 60637
http://grahamschool.uchicago.edu
Taught by senior-level medical educators, writers, editors, and physicians, course topics include advanced medical editing, pharmaceutical writing, transferring medical data to the Web, and reporting about health care and science.

MASSACHUSETTS

Harvard Summer Writing Program
Harvard University
Division of Continuing Education
51 Brattle Street, Department S760
Cambridge, MA 02138-3722
http://www.summer.dce.harvard.edu

An eight-week program beginning at the end of June that covers a wide range of writing concentrations and areas, including editing and publishing; writing children's literature, fiction, poetry, and humor; desktop publishing; principles of editing; writing grant proposals; and autobiography.

NEW YORK

Institute for Retired Professionals
New School University
66 West 12th Street
New York, NY 10011
http://www.nsu.newschool.edu/irp
With students ranging in age from 52 to 91, the IRP offers study groups in a wide range of areas, including a writers' workshop and memoir writing.

Summer Writers' Conference
Hofstra University

University College for Continuing Education
UCCE, 250 Hofstra University
Hempstead, NY 11549-2500
http://www.hofstra.edu
Annual July writers' workshops, including guest speakers. Also sponsors an annual children's literature conference. Also offers noncredit certificate in writing.

The New School
New School University
66 West 12th Street
New York, NY 10011
http://www.newschool.edu
The instructors in the writing program are all published authors. It offers a wide range of courses, from "Tools of Effective Writing" and "Introduction to Creative Nonfiction" to "Writing from Personal Experience" and "Breaking into Women's Magazines."

APPENDIX III
UNIONS AND ASSOCIATIONS

A. UNIONS

Local 2110, Technical, Office and Professional Union
113 University Place, 5th Floor
New York, NY 10003
http://www.2110uaw.org
At major publishers, editors, senior editors, book publicists, administrative assistants, and copy editors may belong to Local 2110 of the Technical, Office and Professional Union.

National Writers Union (NWU)
113 University Place,
6th floor
New York, NY 10003
http://www.nwu.org/nwu
Affiliated with the AFL-CIO, the NWU is an association whose union members are mainly freelance writers writing for newspapers, magazines, and online, as well as books. There are local affiliates throughout the United States as well; contract advice, a job hotline, health insurance, press passes, networking, and grievance resolution are some of the benefits of membership.

Newspaper Guild International
501 Third Street NW, 6th floor
Washington, D.C. 20001-2797
http://www.newsguild.org
Begun in 1933, the Newspaper Guild is part of the AFL-CIO, and its members are also part of the Communication Workers of America. The Newspaper Guild sets minimum wages for reporters. It maintains a list of weekly and semiweekly newspapers, magazines, wire services, and news services that have union contracts.

Writers Guild of America, East (WGAE)
555 West 57th Street
New York, NY 10019
http://www.wgaeast.org
See listing below for Writers Guild of America, West. (Both branches offer similar services, but membership in each one is determined by where a member resides.)

Writers Guild of America, West (WGAW)
7000 West Third Street
Los Angeles, CA 90048
http://www.wga.org
Labor union for writers working in television, film, and radio. For requirements for membership, visit the Web site. Whether someone is a member of WGAE or WGA is based on where in the United States the writer resides, with almost three times as many members belonging to WGA as to WGAE. Also at the Web site are the up-to-date minimums for various types of writing, such as a treatment for a movie or a full-length screenplay for a television pilot, for those who qualify as members of the union.

B. ASSOCIATIONS

ADVERTISING

American Advertising Federation (AAF)
1101 Vermont Avenue NW,
Suite 500
Washington, D.C. 20005
http://www.aaf.org
Membership association for those in advertising; an online job bank with current job openings is maintained at the association's Web site.

AUTHORS/WRITERS/JOURNALISTS

American Medical Writers Association (AMWA)
40 West Gude Drive, Suite 101
Rockville, MD 20850-1192
http://www.amwa.org
Membership association, founded in 1940, with more than 4,000 medical writers. It provides educational programs as well as networking opportunities and offers a job market at its Web site for members, including full-time and freelance writing opportunities.

American Society of Journalists and Authors (ASJA)
1501 Broadway, Suite 302
New York, NY 10036
http://www.asja.org
Membership association founded in 1948, under the name the Society

of Magazine Writers, the ASJA now has more than 1,000 professional writers, mostly of nonfiction, with magazine and book credits as well as online and newspaper experience. In addition to the annual all-day writers' conference (see separate listing under Conferences Appendix VI), the ASJA sponsors monthly educational seminars or dinners, as well as publishes a directory of members, for networking and also for sale to those who hire writers. There is an online version of the directory and a writer referral service.

Asian-American Journalists Association (AAJA)

1182 Market Street, Suite 320
San Francisco, CA 94102
http://www.aaja.org
Founded more than 25 years ago, this membership association has more than 2000 members in 20 chapters throughout the United States and Asia. It offers educational programs, such as a three-day business reporting workshop, as well as an executive leadership program and fellowships for on-the-job training opportunities.

Association for Women in Communications (AWC)

3337 Duke Street
Alexandria, VA 22314
http://www.womcom.org
Educational, advocacy, and networking association, established in 1909 as a society for female journalism students. There are now more than 100 student chapters as well as dozens of regional chapters, with their own activities, benefits, and Web sites, such as job postings for staff and freelance work. The New York Women in Communications, Inc. (www.nywici.org) organized a 75th anniversary conference in April 2004 with notable female guest speakers in communications.

Association of Writers and Writing Programs (AWP)

George Mason University
Carty House, MSN 1E3
Fairfax, VA 22030
http://www.awpwriter.org
Membership association for writers and institutions, providing information about writing programs as well as educational materials on teaching writing. It also maintains a directory of annual writers' conferences, colonies, and writing centers.

Authors Guild

31 East 32nd Street, 7th floor
New York, NY 10016-7923
http://www.authorsguild.org
Established in 1912, this association of book authors and freelance writers of fiction and nonfiction sponsors a Web site, www.backinprint.com, at which authors who have the rights back to their out-of-print titles from commercial publishers may put the book back in print and start selling it again through this program. It provides contract advice for books, periodicals, and electronic rights, as well as copyright information. Annual dues are on a sliding scale based on income earned.

Cat Writers Association (CWA)

http://www.catwriters.org
A membership association ($20 a year) of writers about cats with more than 200 members in 36 states and internationally. It provides a membership directory at the Web site, as well as articles and links and an annual conference.

Dog Writers Association of America (DWAA)

173 Union Road
Coatesville, PA 19320
http://www.dwaa.org
Membership association ($40 a year), founded in 1935, of writers about dogs with more than 500 members. It holds an annual meet-

ing and produces a monthly newsletter.

Education Writers Association

2122 P Street NW, Suite 201
Washington, D.C. 20037
http://www.ewa.org
National educational and networking association for those who write about the education field. More than 1000 members.

International Association of Business Communicators (IABC)

One Hallidie Plaza, Suite 600
San Francisco, CA 94102
http://www.iabc.com
Professional network of more than 15,000 business communication professionals in more than 70 countries.

Investigative Reporters & Editors (IRE)

University of Missouri—Columbia
School of Journalism
138 Neff Annex
Columbia, MO 65211
http://www.ire.org
Founded in 1975, the IRE membership is comprised of newspaper journalists and journalism professors. It provides a job center, as well as information on issues related to investigative journalism.

Mystery Writers of America (MWA)

1140 Broadway, Suite 1507
New York, NY 10001
http://www.mysterywriters.org
International association of mystery writers and nonfiction crime writers, as well as agents and editors who deal with mysteries. It publishes an annual membership directory and sponsors the prestigious Edgar Awards, presented each May. There is a newsletter, and members can purchase labels to mail promotional materials to librarians or booksellers specializing in mysteries.

National Association of Black Journalists (NABJ)

8701-A Adelphi Road
Adelphi, MD 20783-1716
http://www.nabj.org
Membership association for black journalists, with networking and educational activities, including coordinating paid summer internships for those college students selected to work at cooperating publishers, newspapers, television, and radio stations.

National Association of Hispanic Journalists (NAHJ)

1000 National Press Building
529 14th Street NW
Washington, D.C. 20045-2001
http://www.nahj.org
Membership association, founded in 1984, with approximately 2,300 Hispanic journalists that provides a job bank and career resources, as well as networking and educational opportunities.

National Association of Science Writers (NASW)

P.O. Box 890
Hedgesville, WV 25427
http://www.nasw.org
Membership association, founded in 1934, of more than 2,400 science writers publishing in newspapers, in magazines, online, and books. It includes staff science writers and editors, as well as freelance writers and some academics.

National Federation of Press Women (NFPW)

P.O. Box 5556
Arlington, VA 22205
http://www.nfpw.org
Membership association open to men as well as women. Membership consists mainly of staff and freelance journalists, students, and magazine and book authors. It holds an annual contest for the best writing and the communicator of achievement; winners

are announced at the annual national educational conference. It also has a First Amendment Network, which alerts subscribers to pertinent legislative and executive-branch matters.

National Press Club (NPC)

529 14th Street NW, 13th Floor
Washington, D.C. 20045
http://npc.press.org
Membership association of more than 4,000 newspaper journalists founded in 1908. Weekly luncheon meetings are offered at the D.C. headquarters, as well as networking opportunities, educational workshops, and facilities for holding meetings and press conferences.

Native American Journalists Association (NAJA)

University of Oklahoma
Gaylord College
395 West Lindsey Street
norman, OK 73019-4201
http://www.naja.com
Membership association for journalists who are Native Americans, with several types of membership classifications available, from corporate and tribal media to associate, individual, and student. There are job listings at their Web site, as well as media resources. There are more than 600 individual and agency members.

Online News Association (ONA)

P.O. Box 20221
New York, NY 10101-2022
http://www.journalists.org
Journalism association for those who write or edit online. It offers Online Journalism Awards. The awards are in the categories of Independent or Affiliated Web sites. For more information, go to: www.journalists.org/awards/enter/index.html.

PEN American Center

588 Broadway, Suite 303

New York, NY 10012-3225
http://www.pen.org
Fiction and nonfiction book authors, poets, and playwrights are members of this association devoted to the rights of authors. It publishes an annual guide to prizes and grants.

Romance Writers of America (RWA)

16000 Stuebner Airline Road, Suite 140
Spring, TX 77379
http://www.rwanational.org
International association of published romance writers. There is an annual conference, as well as a cooperative catalog published quarterly for booksellers and librarians announcing new titles.

Society of American Travel Writers

7044 South 13th Street
Oak Creek, WI 53154
http://www.satw.org
Professional association comprised of writers, editors, photographers, journalists, and others who provide travel information through newspapers, magazines, travel guides, and radio and television programs. It holds an annual convention and offers a travel writing course and sponsors several awards.

Society of Children's Book Writers and Illustrators (SCBWI)

8271 Beverly Boulevard
Los Angeles, CA 90048
http://wwww.scbwi.org
Membership organization, founded in 1968, with more than 19,000 children's book authors and illustrators who belong to the national group as well as to local affiliates or chapters. It sponsors an annual educational and networking conference. Local chapters have networking events, as well as workshops and feedback groups for sharing work.

Society of Professional Journalists (SPJ)

3909 North Meridian Street
Indianapolis, IN 46208
http://www.spj.org
Founded in 1909, SPJ has 266 local chapters, with 12 regions having annual conferences. SPJ is a membership association of staff and freelance journalists and students in high school and college journalism programs. Its missions include: diversity ethics, FOI (Freedom of Information), international journalism education, professional development, and Project Watchdog. Membership categories for dues assessment include professional, retired, associate, and college/postgrad.

Washington Independent Writers (WIW)

1001 Connecticut Avenue NW
Suite 701
Washington, D.C. 20036
http://www.washwriter.org
A membership organization of more than 2,000 freelance writers; it offers educational and networking opportunities and publishes a membership directory for sale to nonmembers, as well as a monthly publication, the *Independent Writer*.

BOOK PACKAGERS

American Book Producers Association (ABPA)

611 Broadway, Suite 611
New York, NY 10012
http://www.abpaonline.org
Membership association of more than 60 book packagers and book producers in the United States and Canada founded in 1980. Each year an educational all-day seminar is held, providing an overview of the role of the book packager compared to a book publisher. There are monthly luncheons from September through June in New York

City. The membership directory is posted at the association's Web site.

BOOK PUBLISHERS

National

Association of American Publishers (AAP)

New York office:
71 Fifth Avenue, 2nd floor
New York, NY 10003
Washington, D.C., office:
50 F Street NW, 4th Floor
Washington, D.C. 20001
http://www.publishers.org
A trade association of book publishers, with more than 300 member publishers. There is an annual meeting each year (usually held in February or March) for general trade publishers. There is also a professional and scholarly division of the AAP (PSP), which has its own annual meeting in Washington, D.C., and its own Web site: www.pspcentral.org. AAP maintains an extensive Web site of information on book publishing.

Association of American University Presses (AAUP)

71 West 23rd Street, Suite 901
New York, NY 10010
http://www.aaupnet.org
Founded in 1937, a membership association of nonprofit scholarly publishers. The AAUP has 125 university press members. After September 11, the AAUP compiled a list entitled "Books for Understanding," which covered books on terrorism, Afghanistan, race relations, and affirmative action. For more information, go to www.aaupnet.org/booksforunderstanding.html.

Association of Canadian Publishers

174 Spadina Avenue, Suite 306
Toronto, ON M5T 2C2
Canada
http://www.publishers.ca

Membership association of Canadian publishing companies.

Independent Bank Publishers Marketing Association (IBPA)

627 Aviation Way
Manhattan Beach, CA 90266
http://www.ibpa-online.org
A membership association of more than 4,000 independent and smaller publishers, including self-publishers, offering cooperative marketing opportunities to bookstores and libraries, as well as representation in a cooperative booth at the major international, national, and regional book publishing trade shows. It sponsors Publishers University for several days before the annual BookExpo trade show as well as the competitive Benjamin Franklin Awards for the best book in numerous distinct categories.

National Association of Independent Publishers (NAIP)

P.O. Box 430
Highland City, FL 33846-0430
http://www.loc.gov/loc/cfbook/coborg/nai.html
Membership association of 600 small press and independent publishers, founded in 1979, by Betty Wright of Rainbow Books, and now run by Betsy Lampe, Wright's daughter. Membership includes a subscription to the electronic publication, *Publisher's Report*. There is also a membership category that includes membership in the Florida Publishers Association (www.flbookpub.org).

Small Publisher, Artists and Writers Network (SPAWN)

323 East Matilija Street, Suite 110
Ojai, CA 93023
http://www.spawn.org
Membership association for those involved in book publishing, including authors, publishers, edi-

tors, printers, illustrators, publicists, and others.

Small Publishers Association of North America (SPAN)

1618 West Colorado Avenue
Colorado Springs, CO 80904
http://www.spannet.org
A membership association of small press publishers and self-published authors. It sponsors an annual educational program as well as a monthly newsletter.

Women's National Book Association (WNBA)

P.O. Box 237 FDR Station
New York, NY 10150-0231
http://www.wnba-books.org
Founded in 1917, the WNBA is a nonprofit professional association whose more than 800 members include those who work in the book industry as editors, book authors, booksellers, and reviewers. There are local chapters in Boston; Dallas; Detroit; Los Angeles; Nashville; San Francisco; and Washington, D.C.

Regional

Arizona Book Publishing Association

6340 South Rural Road, #118-152
Tempe, AZ 85283
http://www.azbookpub.com

Association of Authors and Publishers

8919 Friendship Road
Houston, TX 77080
http://www.authorsandpublishers.org

Bay Area Independent Publishers Association

P.O. Box E
Corte Madera, CA 94976
http://www.baipa.net

Book Publishers Northwest

P.O. Box 9535

Seattle, WA 98019
http://bookpublishersnw.blogspot.com

Carolina Association of Publishers

c/o Three Pyramics Publishing
201 Kenwood Meadows Drive
Raleigh, NC 27603-8314
http://www.three-pyramids.com/cap/cap.htm

Colorado Independent Publishers Association

P.O. Box 101975
Denver, CO 80250-1975
http://www.cipabooks.com

Connecticut Authors and Publishers Association

P.O. Box 715
Avon, CT 06001-0715
http://www.aboutcapa.com

Florida Publishers Association Inc.

P.O. Box 430
Highland City, FL 33846-0430
http://www.flbookpub.org

Greater New York Independent Publishers Association

c/o Small Press Center
20 West 44th Street
New York, NY 10036
http://www.smallpress.org/gnyipa/default.asp

Hawaii Book Publishers Association

P.O. Box 235736
Honolulu, HI 96823
http://www.hawaiibooks.org

Independent Publishers of New England

P.O. Box 473
Bennington, VT 05201
http://www.ipne.org

MidAtlantic Book Publishers Association

6400 Baltimore National Pike #194

Baltimore, MD 21228
http://www.midatlanticbookpublishers.com

Midwest Independent Publishers Association

P.O. Box 581432
Minneapolis, MN 55458-581432
http://www.mipa.org

Minnesota Book Publishers Roundtable

111 Third Avenue South, Suite 290
Minneapolis, MN 55401
http://www.publishersroundtable.org

Multicultural Publishing and Educational Consortium

177 South Kihei Road
P.O. Box 2128
Kihei, Maui, HI 96753
http://www.mpec.org

New Alternatives for Publishers, Retailers and Artists

P.O. Box 9
6 Eastsound Square
Eastsound, WA 98245

New Mexico Book Association

826 Camino del Monte Rey
Santa Fe, NM 87505
http://www.nmbook.org

Northern California Publishers and Authors

3104 O Street #270
Sacramento, CA 95816
http://www.norcalpa.org/index.php

Northwest Association of Book Publishers

P.O. Box 3786
Wilsonville, OR 97070-3786
http://www.nwabp.org

Publishers Association of the South

15 Northwest 15th Street
Gainesville, FL 32611
http://www.pubsouth.org

Publishers and Writers of San Diego
c/o Bob Goodman
13146 Kellam Court #133
San Diego, CA 92130-2572
http://www.publisherswriters.org

St. Louis Publishers Association
P.O. Box 410182
Creve Coeur, MO 63141
http://www.stlouispublishers.org

Upper Peninsula Publishers and Authors Association
9001 North Pheasant Ridge
Saline, MI 49176
http://www.uppaa.org

Women's National Book Association (WNBA)/New York City Chapter
P.O. Box 237, FDR Station
New York, NY 10150
http://www.wnba-nyc.org
Local chapter of the Women's National Book Association with annual dues and its own newsletter, the *New York Bookwoman,* and an annual directory of members. Members include staff and freelance book editors, publishers, book authors, and book publicists. Monthly educational meetings are offered, as are networking get-togethers throughout Manhattan, Queens, Brooklyn, and New Jersey.

Canada

Independent Publishers Association Canada
P.O. Box 1414
Calgary, Alberta T2P 2L6
http://www.kristalverson.com/ipac/index.html

Organization of Book Publishers of Ontario
20 Maud Street, Suite 401
Toronto, ON M5V 2M5
http://ontariobooks.ca

United Kingdom

Institute of Publishing (IP)
Hamilton Court
Gogmore Lane
Chertsey KT16 9AP
United Kingdom
http://www.instpublishing.org.uk
Educational and networking membership association that covers newspapers, magazines, Web sites, newsletters, and books.

Society of Editors and Proofreaders (SFEP)
Erico House
93-99 Upper Richmond Road
London SW15 2TG
United Kingdom
http://www.sfep.org.uk
Networking and educational association, which can also be a source of part-time, freelance, or full-time work for editors or proofreaders on projects.

Women in Publishing (WIP)
Clevedon Hall, Victoria Road
Clevedon BS21 7HH
United Kingdom
http://www.wipub.org.uk
Networking and educational association for women working in book publishing.

BOOKSELLERS

National

American Booksellers Association (ABA)
200 White Plains Road, Suite 600
Tarrytown, NY 10591
http://www.bookweb.org
The leading national trade association of independent booksellers. Membership is $350 annually for bookstores and those in the industry; there is a $200 auxiliary membership. It offers discounts on shipping as well as the very popular and successful Web-based program for encouraging increased book sales (www.book

sense.com). The American Booksellers Association is the leading force behind the annual BookExpo held each May or June for several days for networking and announcing the new titles for the next fall season.

Association of Booksellers for Children (ABC)
6538 Collins Avenue #168
Miami Beach, FL 33141
http://www.abfc.com
Membership association of booksellers of children's books, as well as of children's book authors and publishers. It publishes the *Building Blocks* newsletter and an annual membership directory, and it also arranges special events related to children's bookselling at the annual BookExpo book publishing trade show each spring.

Independent Mystery Booksellers Association (IMBA)
http://www.mysterybooksellers.com
A membership association of independent bookstores that sell mysteries and thrillers. A membership directory is posted at www.mysterybooksellers.com/membersh.html.

Regional

There are 10 regional bookseller associations, listed below. The range of activities offered by these associations include an annual trade show each fall, a holiday catalog, a list of best-selling titles, a newsletter, a membership directory, regional book awards, mailing list rental, a Web site, educational seminars, and promotion programs and products. Not all associations offer each of these activities. Check with the association you are interested in to see what they offer, as well as to learn the registration and exhibiting dates for the next fall regional trade show.

Great Lakes Booksellers Association (GLBA)
208 Franklin Street
P.O. Box 901
Grand Haven, MI 49417
http://www.books-glba.org
Covers Michigan, Ohio, Indiana, and Illinois.

Mid-South Independent Booksellers Association (MSIBA)
15911 Whispering Falls Court
Houston, TX 77084-2913
http://www.msiba.org
Covers Arkansas, Kansas, Louisiana, Mississippi, Missouri, Oklahoma, Tennessee, and Texas.

Mountains and Plains Booksellers Association (MPBA)
19 Old Town Square, Suite 238
Fort Collins, CO 80524
http://www.mountainsplains.org
Covers Arizona, Colorado, Idaho, Iowa, Kansas, Montana, Nebraska, New Mexico, North Dakota, Oklahoma, South Dakota, Texas, Utah, and Wyoming.

New Atlantic Independent Booksellers Association (NAIBA)
2667 Hyacinth Street
Westbury, NY 11590
http://www.naiba.com
Trade association for booksellers in the mid-Atlantic region, including New York, New Jersey, Pennsylvania, Maryland, and Washington, D.C. It holds an annual regional trade show each fall and also provides a monthly newsletter and ongoing networking among member bookstores, librarians, publishers, sales representatives, and authors. Check the Web site for the date, fees, and filing deadlines for the next regional trade show.

New England Independent Booksellers Association (NEIBA)
297 Broadway, #212

Arlington, MA 02474
http://www.newenglandbooks.org
Covers Connecticut, Maine, Massachusetts, New Hampshire, Rhode Island, Vermont, and New York.

Northern California Independent Booksellers Association (NCIBA)
P.O. Box 29169
1007 General Kennedy Avenue
San Francisco, CA 94129-0169
http://www.nciba.com
Covers Arizona, California, and Nevada.

Pacific Northwest Booksellers Association (PNBA)
214 East 12th Avenue
Eugene, OR 97401-3245
http://www.pnba.org
Covers Alaska, Idaho, Montana, Oregon, and Washington.

Southeast Independent Booksellers Alliance (SIBA)
3806 Yale Avenue
Columbia, SC 29205
http://www.sibaweb.com
Educational and networking association for booksellers, book publishers, book authors, and anyone interested in the book business. Core membership includes bookstores in Alabama, Arkansas, Florida, Georgia, Kentucky, Louisiana, Mississippi, North Carolina, South Carolina, Tennessee, and Virginia.

Southern California Booksellers Association (SCBA)
959 East Walnut Street, Suite 220
Pasadena, CA 91106
http://www.scibabooks.org
Covers Southern California.

Upper Midwest Booksellers Association (UMBA)
3407 West 44th Street
Minneapolis, MN 55410
http://www.midwestbooksellers.org

Covers Illinois, Iowa, Kansas, Minnesota, Missouri, Nebraska, North Dakota, South Dakota, and Wisconsin.

EDITORS

American Association of Sunday and Feature Editors (AASFE)
c/o Executive Director
University of Maryland
College of Journalism
1117 Journalism Building
College Park, MD 20742-7111
http://www.aasfe.org
Nonprofit trade association, founded in 1947, of more than 120 members who are Sunday and feature newspaper editors. It provides links to member papers at the Web site, as well as links to journalism associations and organizations, syndicates, and creators.

American Society of Magazine Editors (ASME)
810 Seventh Avenue, 24th Floor
New York, NY 10019
http://www.magazine.org/Editorial/ASME
Founded in 1963, ASME is a professional membership association for magazine editors of consumer and business publications. Affiliated with the Magazine Publishers of America (MPA), ASME has more than 850 members throughout the United States. It holds monthly member lunches where magazine editors talk about their publications, as well as editorial seminars and workshops for junior-level editors.

American Society of Newspaper Editors (ASNE)
11690B Sunrise Valley Drive
Reston, VA 20191-1409
http://www.asne.org
Membership association of newspaper editors with a commitment to education and training through its job fairs, held throughout the

United States. Check the Web site for a listing of the job fairs schedule. ASNE also maintains a list of paid internships for college and graduate students.

Editorial Freelancers Association (EFA)
71 West 23rd Street, 4th Floor
New York, NY 10010
http://www.the-efa.org
National membership association of more than 900 self-employed editors, indexers, writers, and researchers. It provides an annual membership directory and job line for searching for freelance editors, and it holds monthly meetings in New York City from September through June.

Newspaper Association of America (NAA)
4401 Wilson Boulevard, Suite 900
Arlington, VA 22203
http://www.naa.org
Nonprofit association representing more than 2,000 newspapers in the United States and Canada, as well as hundreds of associate members (vendors and suppliers), students, educators, international newspapers, press associations, and foundations. Its Web site provides information on industry statistics, newspaper and vendor links, and job information.

GRAPHIC ARTS/DESIGN/ PRODUCTION

The Bookbinders' Guild of New York
http://www.bookbindersguild.org
A nonprofit association whose members are involved in making books and in the electronic media, including publishers, manufacturers, and suppliers. There is a job bank at its Web site, and it organizes the annual New York Book Show. Members from book publishing include those from production, editorial, design, and manufacturing.

Bookbuilders of Boston
49 Hawley Road
Scituate, MA 02066
http://www.bookbindersguild.org
A nonprofit organization for those in book publishing and manufacturing, it offers workshops and sponsors trips to printing plants to see firsthand the book production process. There is a job board at their Web site.

Partnership in Print Production (P3)
276 Bowery
New York, NY 10012
http://www.partnershipinprint production.org
A membership association that provides networking and educational opportunities to students and professionals in new media, publishing, and graphic arts.

Society for News Design (SND)
1130 Ten Rod Road, Suite D-202
North Kingstown, RI 02852-4177
http://www.snd.org
Membership association of more than 2,600 artists, designers, editors, publishers, photographers, students, managers, and faculty who are involved in designing magazines, Web sites, and newspapers.

ILLUSTRATORS

Association of Medical Illustrators (AMI)
P.O. Box 1897
Lawrence, KS 66044
http://www.ami.org
An international professional association that offers certification in medical illustration, as well as networking opportunities and a job hot line. There is an annual meeting and an online directory of AMI members.

Society of Illustrators
128 East 63rd Street
New York, NY 10065
http://www.societyillustrators.org

Founded in 1901, a membership association of more than 800 illustrators.

LITERARY AGENTS

Association of Authors' Representatives (AAR)
P.O. Box 237201, Ansonia Station
New York, NY 10003
http://www.aar-online.org
A membership association of independent literary and dramatic agents.

MAGAZINE PUBLISHERS

Magazine Publishers of America (MPA)
810 Seventh Avenue, 24th Floor
New York, NY 10019
http://www.magazine.org
Established in 1919, MPA represents consumer magazines. It offers a career center with job listings, job fairs, and monthly educational programs.

PHOTOGRAPHERS

American Society of Media Photographers
150 North Second Street
Philadelphia, PA 19106
http://www.asmp.org
Membership association for photographers and photo editors who publish their work in various media outlets, including magazines, newspapers, and online.

International Freelance Photographers Organization
P.O. Box 777
Lewisville, NC 27023-0777
http://www.aipress.com
Membership association for photographers and photo editors. Publishes *Today's Photographer* magazine.

National Press Photographers Association
3200 Croasdaile Drive, Suite 306
Durham, NC 27705

http://www.nppa.org
National membership association of professional news photographers and photojournalists; it also publishes *News Photographer* magazine.

Photographic Society of America (PSA)

3000 United Founders Boulevard, Suite 103
Oklahoma City, OK 73112-3940
http://www.psa-photo.org
Membership association offering educational programs and networking opportunities for photographers and photo editors. It offers certified credentials, including the CPP (certified professional photographer), CPPS (specialist or artist), and CEI (certified electronic imager).

PUBLICISTS

Book Publicists of Southern California

6464 Sunset Boulevard, Suite 755
Hollywood, CA 90028
http://www.bookpublicists.org
Founded by book publicist Irwin Zucker, a membership organization of more than 1,200 book publicists and book authors. Members receive a bimonthly newsletter, *Know Thy*

Shelf. There are bimonthly educational dinner meetings in Los Angeles, as well as annual awards for the best media campaign for a book.

Northern California Book Publicity & Marketing Association (NCBPMA)

P.O. Box 597
San Francisco, CA 94104-0597
http://www.ncbpma.com
Membership association of book publicists in the Northern California area; offers monthly meetings with guest speakers from the media; sponsors a get together at the annual BookExpo (BEA) for book publicists, local and national media, and booksellers.

Publishers Publicity Association (PPA)

http://www.publisherspublicity.org
Networking and educational association with annual membership dues. Members are publicists at the leading publishing companies, as well as at smaller presses, freelance publicists, and book authors. Contact information changes each year with new association administrators. There is a monthly e-mail newsletter and, from

September through June, monthly luncheons in Manhattan with educational panels addressing issues and concerns for book publicists. Topics cover broadcast and print media, including television, cable, radio, online, magazines, and newspapers, and related issues, such as how to pitch the media, how to create a press kit, how to deal with book authors, and interview tips and techniques.

SALES AND MARKETING

American Marketing Association (AMA)

311 South Wacker Drive, Suite 5800
Chicago, IL 60606
http://www.marketingpower.com
An association of 38,000 members in marketing. It provides networking, educational programs, and job listings.

Fulfillment Management

60 East 42nd Street, Suite 1166
New York, NY 10165
http://www.fmanational.org
Educational membership association for those involved in fulfillment, including circulation directors and managers, advertising, and sales representatives and directors.

APPENDIX IV
INTERNSHIPS

NEWSPAPERS

There is a heritage to internships in the publishing field, with on-the-job training seen as more pivotal to educational and professional growth than classroom experiences. Some schools will help students secure internships, throughout the school year or over the summer, or even as part of a co-op college program, whereby for one or two semesters in lieu of classes that semester is a full-time internship as the sole educational experience.

For those who wish to go into journalism, an internship is more than a nice way to spend the summer or to make a few extra dollars; most entry-level reporting jobs require that recent college graduates have one or more internship experiences.

Some newspapers fill the internship slots for the following summer as early as January or February, although some may still be hiring by April or May. Contact your local newspaper or the newspaper where you would like to intern, and find out what their deadlines and application procedures are. You may also want to consider a part-time internship during your fall or spring college semester.

The Web sites for the major newspaper chains may have listings for available and forthcoming internships at their local newspapers. For example, check out the Web sites for the following national newspapers, wire services, syndicates, chains, and major local newspapers, and go to the job postings and search for internships: www.careers.ap.org/index.html; www.usatoday.com, www.gannett.com, and www.newsday.com.

The American Society of Newspaper Editors maintains a listing of paid internships at its Web site: www.asne.org; Internships are also listed at www.journalismjobs.com.

The National Association of Black Journalists (www.nabj.org) has paid summer internships for selected college students. In 2003, 14 students were selected among the 50 applicants for paid summer internships at cooperating newspapers and television and radio stations including the Associated Press, *Seattle Times,* and *Atlanta Journal Constitution.* Check the NABJ Web site for application procedures and deadlines.

MAGAZINES AND BOOKS

Summer internships may be available at publishing companies or magazines of all sizes, from the smallest publishing company with a staff of just one or two to the largest New York City–based publishing corporation, such as the Hearst Corporation or Penguin Putnam, with thousands of employees. Check the Web sites for a publishing company or magazine, and see if there is a listing for summer or year-round internships. For example, at the Web site for Random House, www.randomhouse.com, there are separate sections for college students, MBAs, and those applying to their Westminister, Maryland, warehouse for summer intern positions.

Some associations, such as the Women's Media Group, an association of women in publishing and the media including books, magazines, book promotion, TV, and film, have developed an internship program whereby selected applicants are placed at the publishing companies of those members who are able to enlist the cooperation of their employers. For more information, go to the association's Web site: www.womensmediagroup.org.

Also check the internship listings at www.mediabistro.com, www.hotjobs.com, www.publishersmarketplace.com, www.monster.com, and www.bookjobs.com.

APPENDIX V
SELECTED COMPANIES, AGENCIES, AND FELLOWSHIPS

A. COMPANIES

NEWSPAPERS

Chicago Tribune
435 North Michigan Avenue
Chicago, IL 60611
http://www.chicagotribune.com

Dallas Morning News
508 Young Street
Dallas, TX 75202
http://www.dallasnews.com

Los Angeles Times
202 West First Street
Los Angeles, CA 90012
http://www.latimes.com

New York Times
620 Eighth Avenue
New York, NY 10018
http://www.nytimes.com

USA Today
7950 Jones Branch Drive
McLean, VA 22108
http://www.usatoday.com

Wall Street Journal
200 Liberty Street
New York, NY 10281
http://online.wsj.com/public/us
http://www.dowjones.com

Washington Post
1150 15th Street, NW
Washington, D.C. 20071
http://www.washingtonpost.com

SYNDICATES AND NEWS SERVICES

Associated Press
450 West 33rd Street
New York, NY 10001
http://www.ap.org
A not-for-profit news-gathering cooperative with more than 1,700 U.S. daily newspapers sharing ownership. Founded in 1848, it has 243 bureaus and thousands of reporters worldwide.

Bloomberg Business News
499 Park Avenue
New York, NY 10022
http://www.bloomberg.com

Copley News Service
123 Camino De La Reina
Suite S205
San Diego, CA 92108
http://www.copleynews.com

Reuters America
3 Times Square
New York, NY 10036
http://www.reuters.com

Scripps-Howard News Service
1090 Vermont Avenue, NW, Suite 1000
Washington, D.C. 20005
http://www.shns.com

BLOGS

Boing Boing
http://www.boingboing.net

Daily Kos
http://www.dailykos.com

Gawker
http://www.gawker.com

Hot Air
hotair.com

The Huffington Post
http://huffingtonpost.com

Official Google Blog
http://googleblog.blogspot.com

Red State
redstate.com

Workette
workette.com

NEWSPAPER CHAINS

Here are the Web sites for major newspaper chains. At those sites you will find a list of the local newspapers that are part of each chain, usually accompanied by links to those newspapers' Web sites.

Cox Enterprises Inc.
6205 Peachtree Dunwoody Road
Atlanta, GA 30328
http://www.coxenterprises.com

Gannett Co. Inc.
7950 Jones Branch Drive
McLean, VA 22107
http://www.gannett.com

The McClatchy Company
2100 Q Street
Sacramento, CA 95816-6899
http://www.mcclatchy.com

MAGAZINES

Bonnier Corporation
460 North Orlando Avenue, Suite
    200
Winter Park, FL 32789
http//www.bonniercorp.com
Publishes *Parenting, Field and
    Stream, Popular Science,* and
    several lifestyle and sports
    publications.

Condé Nast Publications
4 Times Square
New York, NY 10036
http://www.condenast.com
Publisher of *Self, Glamour, Vanity
Fair,* the *New Yorker,* and other publications.

Hachette Filipacchi Media U.S.
1633 Broadway
New York, NY 10019
http://www.hfmus.com
Publisher of *Car and Driver,
    Elle, Women's Day,* and other
    consumer and special interest
    magazines.

Hearst Corporation
300 West 57th Street
New York, NY 10019
http://www.hearst.com
Publishers of *O, The Oprah Magazine,
Seventeen, Popular Mechanics,* and
numerous other major titles.

Meredith
Headquarters
1716 Locust Street
Des Moines, IA 50309-3023
http://www.meredith.com
Publishes *Ladies' Home Journal, Parents, Better Homes and Gardens,* and
other home and family magazines.

Rodale Press, Inc.
33 East Minor Street

Emmaus, PA 18098
http://www.rodale.com
Publisher of magazines in the health
field, including *Prevention, Runner's
World,* and *Men's Health.*

Time Inc.
Time-Life Building
1271 Avenue of the Americas
New York, NY 10020
http://www.timewarner.com
Publisher of major magazines including *People, Time, Sports Illustrated,
Fortune, Entertainment Weekly,* and
others.

BOOK PUBLISHERS

Hachette Book Group
Corporate Headquarters
3 Center Plaza
Boston, MA 02108
http://www.hachettebookgroupusa.
    com
Hachette Book Group includes Mys-
terious Press; Little, Brown and Company; and Warner Books.

HarperCollins Publishers
10 East 53rd Street
New York, NY 10022
Publishes adult fiction and non-
fiction as well as children's books,
under various imprints including
William Morrow, HarperTorch, and
Harper Perennials.

The Penguin Group
375 Hudson Street
New York, NY 10014
http://www.penguinputnam.com
Publishes children's book and books
for adults, nonfiction and fiction,
under its various imprints including Riverhead Books, Penguin, and
Jeremy P. Tarcher.

Random House, Inc.
1745 Broadway
New York, NY 10019
http://www.randomhouse.com
Owned by the Bertelsmann group,
Random House encompasses more

than 100 publishing houses worldwide, including Ballantine, Bantam
Dell, Doubleday, Knopf, and many
others.

Simon & Schuster, Inc.
1230 Avenue of the Americas
New York, NY 10020
http://www.simonsays.com
Trade book publisher whose imprints
include Fireside Books, Touchstone,
Scribner, and Macmillan.

Sourcebooks, Inc.
1935 Brookdale Road
Suite 139
Naperville, IL 60563
http://www.sourcebooks.com

**Sterling Publishing Company,
    Inc.**
387 Park Avenue South
New York, NY 10016
http://www.sterlingpub.com

Wiley
111 River Street
Hoboken, NJ 07030-5774
http://www.wiley.com

Workman Publishing Company
225 Varick Street
New York, NY 10014-4381
http://www.workman.com

BOOK PUBLISHING
DIRECTORIES

Dustbooks
P.O. Box 100
Paradise, CA 95967
http://www.dustbooks.com
Publishing company and resource
for small presses started in 1964.
Publishers of the *International
Directory of Little Magazines &
Small Presses,* the *Directory of
Poetry Publishers,* the *AWP Official Guide to Writing Programs,*
the *Directory of Small Press/Maga-
zines Editors & Publishers,* and the
monthly *Small Press Review,* among
other titles.

Information Today, Inc.
143 Old Marlton Pike
Medford, NJ 08055
http://www.literarymarketplace.com
Publisher of the annually updated
Literary Marketplace (LMP) as well
as the *International Literary Marketplace (ILMP)*.

R.R. Bowker
630 Central Avenue
New Providence, NJ 07974

http://www.bowker.com
Publishes *Books in Print,* updated
throughout the year, as well as
annually, and available in print and
online versions.

WHOLESALERS

Baker and Taylor, Inc.
2550 West Tyvola Road, Suite 300
Charlotte, NC 28217
http://www.btol.com

Follett Corporation
2233 West Street
River Grove, IL 60171
http://www.follett.com

Ingram Book Company, Inc.
One Ingram Boulevard
La Vergne, TN 37086
http://www.ingrambook.com

B. AGENCIES

AUTHOR SPEAKER BUREAUS OR SERVICES

Authors Unlimited
31 East 32nd Street, Suite 300
New York, NY 10016
http://www.authorsunlimited.com
A lecture bureau representing 400
authors founded in 1990 by Arlynn
Greenbaum, who had worked at
several major book publishers in
the publicity department. Authors
Unlimited arranges paid speaking
engagements for authors, with companies and organizations worldwide.

Fass Speakers Bureau
26 West 17th Street
Suite 802
New York, NY 10011
http://www.fasspr.com

International Speakers Bureau
1401 Elm Street, 41st Floor
Dallas, TX 75202
http://www.internationalspeakers
   bureau.com

Leading Authorities
1220 L Street NW, Suite 850
Washington, DC 20005
http://www.leadingauthorities.com
A lecture bureau and video production company that connects
recognized authorities and speakers with speaking opportunities at
business and professional association meetings.

Royce Carlton
866 United Nations Plaza
New York, NY 10017
http://www.roycecarlton.com

Simon & Schuster Speakers Bureau
437 Fifth Avenue, 7th floor
New York, NY 10016
http://www.simonsays.com/
   speakersbureau/speaker_
   bureau_home.cfm

LITERARY AGENTS
There are, of course, exceptions, but
most literary agents will not accept
any unsolicited ideas, proposals, or
manuscripts from potential clients.
The standard advice is to send a
query e-mail or letter and wait to be
asked to submit an outline and/or a
sample chapter and an author biography. If submitting through regular mail, a self-addressed, stamped
envelope is expected to be enclosed.
If possible, a referral from another
client of the agent, especially a bestselling author, or from an editor or
anyone else whose literary opinion
the agent would respect, should
precede your initial contact. (For
extensive listings of available literary agents, consult these books
in the bibliography: *Jeff Herman's
Guide to Book Publishers, Editors
and Literary Agents; The Writer's
Market,* edited by Kathyrn Struckel

Brogan and Robert Lee Brewer; and
The Literary Marketplace [LMP].)

Brandt & Hochman Literary Agents, Inc.
1501 Broadway
New York, NY 10036

Michael Larsen/Elizabeth Pomada
1029 Jones Street
San Francisco, CA 94109
http://www.larsen-pomada.com

International Creative Management (ICM)
825 Eighth Avenue
New York, NY 10019
http://www.icmtalent.com

William Morris Endeavor
1325 Avenue of the Americas
New York, NY 10019
http://www.wma.com

Writers House, Inc.
21 West 26th Street
New York, NY 10010
http;//www.writershouse.com

PROMOTION

Jane Wesman Public Relations, Inc.
Jane Wesman, President
322 Eighth Avenue, #1702
New York, NY 10001
http://www.wesmanpr.com

McCall Public Relations
17675 SW Farmington Road, Suite 510
Aloha, OR 97007
E-mail: Joanne@joannemccall.com
http://www.joannemccall.com

Molstad Marketing/PR Consulting
687 Wildwood Lane
Stillwater, MN 55082
E-mail: Dendoor@aol.com

Phenix & Phenix
2100 Kramer Lane, Suite 300
Austin, TX 78758
http://www.bookpros.com

Planned Television Arts
1110 Second Avenue
New York, NY 10022
http://www.plannedtelevisionarts.com

Promising Promotion
P.O. Box 5428
Novato, CA 94948

http://www.promisingpromotion.com

Promotion in Motion
6464 Sunset Boulevard, Suite 755
Hollywood, CA 90028
http://www.promotioninmotion.net

SEARCH FIRMS FOR JOBS IN BOOKS AND MAGAZINES

Bert Davis Executive Search
425 Madison Avenue, 14th Floor
New York, NY 10017
http://www.bertdavis.com
A 30-year-old executive search firm for the book and magazine publishing industries.

JanPlace Media Search, Inc.
470 Park Avenue South
2nd Floor, South Tower
New York, NY 10016
http://www.janplace.com
Established in 2000, this is a search firm for jobs in all areas of book

publishing for those with a minimum of two years experience and up.

Lynne Palmer Executive Recruitment, Inc.
295 Madison Avenue, Suite 1002
New York, NY 10017
http://www.lynnepalmerinc.com
Executive recruiting company established in 1964 that covers the publishing and new media industries, as well as corporate communications and public relations.

Ribolow Associates, Inc.
19 West 44th Street, Suite 507
New York, NY 10036
http://www.ribolow.com
Executive recruiting firm for jobs in book publishing (as well as advertising, marketing, public relations, and new media).

C. FELLOWSHIPS

The December issue of the magazine *Editor and Publisher* (www.editorandpublisher.com) has listings of awards and fellowships available to journalists. It publishes that information in book form in the *Editor and Publisher Journalism Awards and Fellowships Directory*.

The current edition of *Literary Marketplace (LMP)*, updated annually and published by Information Today,

has an extensive section on fellowships and competitions available to authors and those in the book industry.

At www.journalismjobs.com, there is a fellowship listings page that has hot links to more than 30 fellowships for journalists: www.journalismjobs.com/Fellowship_Listings.cfm

Here is a sample of available fellowships:

Agent Fellowship
P.O. Box 775
Jerusalem 91007 Israel
http://www.jerusalembookfair.com
Offers young agents an opportunity to attend the Jerusalem International Book Fair, which is held every other year in Jerusalem, Israel. The company of the selected agents pay for the trip to Israel; JIBF covers accommodations for seven days, including all Book Fair events. Agent fellows work out of the Jerusalem Rights Center at

JIBF and meet with publishers, editors, and authors.

Alicia Patterson Foundation
1025 F Street N.W.
Suite 700
Washington, D.C. 20004
http://www.aliciapatterson.org
A 12-month fellowship awarded to five to seven full-time journalists and providing $35,000 for the year to carry out a journalism project. It is a full-time fellowship,

and most journalists will have to get a leave of absence from their job to complete the work, although freelance writing in addition to the fellowship project is a possibility. There are application requirements, including an overview of the proposed project with a budget, work samples, and four letters of recommendation, all of which must be postmarked by October 1st. (Check that the deadline is current.)

Council for Advancement and Support of Education (CASE)

http://www.case.org

More than 200 short-term fellowships are offered for journalists in 24 different fellowship programs at 22 colleges and universities.

Investigative Reporting Fellowships

University of California at Berkeley
Berkeley, CA 94720
http://www.journalism.berkeley.edu
A year-long, $45,000 fellowship program to support investigative journalism. Preference given to graduates of Berkeley's master of journalism program. Check the Web site for application information.

Jerusalem Editorial Fellowship Program

P.O. Box 775
Jerusalem 91007 Israel
http://www.jerusalembookfair.com
Young editors compete to go to the Jerusalem International Book Fair, held every other year in Jerusalem, Israel. The editorial fellow's company pays for the trip to Israel; JIBF provides free accommodations for seven days, as well as admission to the JIBF.

Nieman Foundation

One Francis Avenue
Cambridge, MA 02138
http://www.nieman.harvard.edu
An educational fellowship to study at Harvard University provided annually to 24 working journalists: 12 from the United States and 12 from other countries.

United States–Japan Foundation Media Fellows Program

Japan Society
333 East 47th Street
New York, NY 10017
http://www.japansociety.org
A fellowship is granted to midcareer working journalists for two- to three-month residencies in Japan. Salary is not provided, but round-trip airfare, a Japan domestic travel grant, and a stipend for interpreter expenses and some other costs are granted. Check the Web site for current nominations and application deadlines.

APPENDIX VI
TRADE SHOWS AND CONFERENCES

A. BOOK PUBLISHING TRADE SHOWS AND CONFERENCES

At the trade shows and conferences that are listed below, publishers (as well as multimedia producers of audio books and specialty or novelty products, such as gift books or calendars), exhibit. Attendees include booksellers, librarians, publishers, literary agents, packagers, printers, authors, freelance writers, motion picture and television producers, book reviewers, wholesalers, and distributors. Each show has a different emphasis reflected by the show's sponsoring association or location. Some shows are also open to the public for one day or more, but most are professional industry shows for the "trade only." The key emphasis of the book publishing industry trade shows is the buying and selling of rights as well as selling new titles to booksellers and librarians; networking and learning about industry and international book publishing trends are other benefits of attending or exhibiting.

NATIONAL AND INTERNATIONAL BOOK INDUSTRY TRADE SHOWS

American Library Association
http://www.ala.org
This library association of more than 65,000 members sponsors an annual conference, usually held in June, and a midwinter meeting, usually in January. Publishers, wholesalers, distributors, and multimedia companies exhibit; librarians, booksellers, authors, journalists, and others in the book industry attend. Extensive educational workshops and seminars for librarians are offered. At their Web site is a list of the cities and dates for the upcoming conferences and meetings for the next decade.

Beijing International Book Fair
http://www.bibf.net
International book trade show started in 1986 in Beijing, China.

Bologna Children's Book Fair
http://www.bfservizi.it/pages/en/index.html
This annual four-day book fair takes place in Bologna, Italy, in April, and it is the premier trade show for the children's book industry, including trade and educational publishers, foreign rights managers, literary agents, authors, and illustrators.

BookExpo
http://www.bookexpoamerica.com
BookExpo is the leading national trade show for independent booksellers and publishers to present the titles for the next fall season. Held in May or June each year in a different major city, including Chicago, Los Angeles, New York City, and Washington, D.C., major New York publishers, as well as medium-sized and smaller presses from around the country, foreign publishers, wholesalers, distributors, and producers of such ancillary book products as gift books, audio books, and calendars, exhibit. Booksellers have educational programs and networking events to attend, as well as meetings with authors and publishers, mainly publicists and sales representatives, as they walk from booth to booth. BookExpo is organized by Reed Exhibitions in cooperation with the American Booksellers Association (www.aba.org), which started the show. Other attendees include librarians, journalists, motion picture and television production companies, printers, authors, literary agents, and book reviewers. It is open to industry professionals only.

Frankfurt Book Fair
http://www.book-fair.com
Held each October for five days in Frankfurt, Germany, this is the largest and most notable book fair and trade show in the world. Since the first Frankfurt Book Fair in 1949, when 205 German publishers got together to exhibit, this annual event now attracts more than 299,000 members of the publishing industry from around the world, including foreign rights managers, publishers, literary agents, sales representatives, wholesalers, distributors, and journalists, with more than 6,400 exhibitors from more than 110 countries. Each year there is a guest of honor, which focuses on the publishing activities of one country. Educational seminars are offered, geared especially to helping foreign rights managers and acquisitions editors gain insights into the international publishing trends that could help them in their ability to do

their job and advance their careers. The Frankfurt Book Fair now also offers, for a fee, the ability to be part of the Frankfurt Book Fair online catalog, which is kept up throughout the year.

For those American publishers who are unable to exhibit in person, there are a number of opportunities to pay to have individual books placed in cooperative exhibits, such as the Publishers Marketing Association exhibit, available to member publishers and authors (www.pma-online.org), or the Combined Book Exhibit (www.combinedbook.com).

Guadalajara International Book Fair

http://www.fil.com.mx

This annual book fair, held over nine days from late November to early December, in Guadalajara, Mexico, is the world's biggest Spanish-language book event. In addition to publishing industry professionals buying and selling foreign rights and translation rights, the show is also open to the general public, and there are activities and events for children and teenagers. (There are three days that are exclusively for the trade.) More than 15,000 book industry professionals, including publishers and literary agents, from 35 countries, were in attendance at the 2002 fair, as were more than 420,000 from the general public.

Jerusalem International Book Fair (JIBF)

http://www.jerusalembookfair.com

Started in 1963, the Jerusalem International Book Fair takes place every other year in Jerusalem, Israel, in late spring/early summer. Book trade professionals from around the world gather; the 2001 JIBF had more than 750 publishers from 58 countries exhibiting. Visitors include publishers, librarians, booksellers, editors, writers, literary agents, journalists,

and media representatives. There is a highly regarded Agent Fellowship and Jerusalem Editorial Fellowship Program, which allows young agents and editors to attend the fair as guests of JIBF. The fellows' publishing companies sponsor the trip to Israel; JIBF pays for their accommodations for seven nights, as well as their admissions to all Book Fair events.

Liber

http://www.liber.ifema.es

A four-day annual international book fair held in Spain in early October open only to the trade. Exhibitors, about 800 from 20 countries, include publishers, literary agents, service providers, graphic arts companies, and professional associations. Attendees include booksellers, publishers, authors, distributors, librarians, teachers, and graphic arts publishing professionals. The location of the show alternates between the cities of Madrid and Barcelona.

London Book Fair

http://www.londonbookfair.co.uk

Held each year in London, England, the London Book Fair has grown in size and importance as a spring international rights fair attracting book industry exhibitors and visitors from around the world. Although British publishers still represent the largest portion of exhibitors, publishers from other countries, including the United States, take individual booths or exhibit in groups. Foreign rights managers and literary agents also take tables at the International Rights Centre to arrange meetings with publishers and other agents to sell foreign rights to their new and backlist titles and to buy rights. There is also an extensive educational program for book industry professionals, as well as seminars on writing and getting published, geared to the general public.

Moscow International Book Fair

http://mibf.ru/english

Since 1977, an annual publishing industry trade show in Moscow, Russia, for five days in early September.

Salon du Livre Paris

http://www.salondulivreparis.com

Organized by the Reed Exhibition Companies, this six-day book fair is held in Paris each year during the week following the London Book Fair. Open to the public, there is also a day just for the trade.

Small Press Book Fair

20 West 44th Street
New York, NY 10036

http://www.nycip.org

Since 1988, an annual public book fair, organized by the Center for Independent Publishing (Small Press Center) and held during December. Independent and small presses exhibit and the public has an opportunity to look over their lines of books, meet their authors, and buy books.

Tokyo International Book Fair

http://www.reedexpo.co.jp/tibf/english

Held each year, this trade show also attracts foreign managers and literary agents from around the world to sell rights, especially to Japan, Korea, China, and Taiwan.

REGIONAL BOOK INDUSTRY TRADE SHOWS

Every fall, each regional bookselling trade association organizes a regional trade show. Publishers, wholesalers, distributors, and specialty companies exhibit, displaying the new titles for that fall season, including books and products that they hope will be holiday purchases. Listed below are the regional bookselling associations and their Web sites, where there is information about joining the association, as well as exhibiting at or attending the trade show. Visitors include booksellers, librarians, journalists, book reviewers, television and radio producers and hosts, and magazine and newspaper feature writers. Although much more low-key than the national BookExpo, with fewer attendees or exhibitors, this is still a useful way for authors, publishers, booksellers, wholesalers, and distributors to network and get exposure for their new and backlist titles. Book and author events, including author signings, usually showcasing regional authors, are also organized for each trade show. (More information on each of the regional bookselling associations is included in those listings in Appendix III [Unions and Associations].

Great Lakes Booksellers Association (GLBA)
http://www.books-glba.org

Mid-South Independent Booksellers Association (MSIBA)
http://www.msiba.org

Mountain and Plains Booksellers Association (MPBA)
http://www.mountainplains.org

New Atlantic Independent Booksellers Association (NAIBA)
http://www.naiba.com

New England Independent Booksellers Association (NEIBA)
http://www.newenglandbooks.org

Northern California Independent Booksellers Association (NCIBA)
http://www.nciba.com

Pacific Northwest Booksellers Association (PNBA)
http://www.pnba.org

Southeast Booksellers Association (SEBA)
http://www.sebaweb.org

Southern California Booksellers Association (SCBA)
http://www.scba.bookpage.com

Upper Midwest Booksellers Association (UMBA)
http://www.abookaday.com

B. WRITING CONFERENCES

American Society of Journalists and Authors (ASJA)
http://www.asja.org
Held each spring, the ASJA annual Saturday writing conference has become a tradition in New York City, attracting aspiring and seasoned authors from throughout the United States and internationally. From early in the morning until early that evening, several panels are offered in each time slot, with panelists from the writing and publishing community, including magazine and book editors and authors. On Sunday, intensive longer workshops are offered on selected topics, which change from year to year. There is always a well-known writer as a keynote speaker at the gala luncheon. Over the years, keynote speakers have included the late Isaac Asimov, the late Alex Haley, Mary Higgins Clark, Dominick Dunne, and Pete Hamill.

Big Apple Writing Workshops
Box 810
Grace Station
New York, NY 10028
http://www.iwwg.org
Workshop in Manhattan offered by the International Women's Writing Guild, which provides opportunities for authors to meet successful published writers as well as to meet agents.

Philadelphia Writers' Conference
P.O. Box 717
Elkins Park, PA 19027-0171
http://www.pwcwriters.org
Founded in 1949, this nonprofit organization's conference lasts for three days, usually in early June. Attracting 150 to 200 attendees, the workshop sessions and seminars cover a wide range of writing specialties, from travel writing to op-ed columns, as well as magazines, poetry, memoirs, nonfiction books,

and writing for children. Literary agents and editors interact with the attendees.

Maui Writers Conference
P.O. Box 1118
Maui, HI 96753
http://www.mauiwriters.com
Intensive workshops and networking opportunities for nonfiction and fiction book authors as well as screenwriters are held each year over Labor Day weekend.

National Black Writers' Conference
Medgar Evers College
1650 Bedford Avenue
Brooklyn, NY 11225
http://www.mec.cuny.edu/nbwc
Begun in 1986, this four-day conference gathers together students, critics, faculty, book reviewers, and the general public to discuss issues related to black writers and writing.

APPENDIX VII
BASIC PROOFREADING SYMBOLS AND SAMPLE PROOFREAD PARAGRAPH

Delete	⌐	Close up space	⌒
Paragraph	¶	Spell out	sp
Insert period	⊙	Insert apostrophe	v̇
Insert space	#	Insert quotation marks	ᵛᵛ v̈
Insert comma	⋀	Insert hyphen	=
Transpose	∼	Lowercase	lc
Stet leave as is	…	Capital letters	≡

SAMPLE PROOFREAD PARAGRAPH

cap even though there is fierce competition for jobs in the publishing industry, there is a constant need for new talent and advancement opportunities abroad. Whether you choose *abound / to* working in newspapers, magazines books or a combination of all three branches of the publishing industry, these are creative, fast-paced, and ever changing businesses. Even if you work in the US the Internet gives you access to people around the world with online translation services even enabling instant translation of e-mails that need to be translate The internet has made certain aspects of the publishing industry easier, such as selling foreign rights as well as archiving previously published material for continual reference.

GLOSSARY

GENERAL TERMS

advertising   When a publisher, author, or advertising department pays for placing copy about an author, a piece of writing, or a book. Advertising is divided into classified ads, which are smaller and are usually just words, and display ads, which are larger and include photographs or illustrations. Advertising costs may be determined on the basis of the size of the ad, the number of words, the frequency that it is run (with discounts for multiple republishing of the same ad), the publication's circulation, and its placement in a publication, with some positions being more expensive than others (front or back of the publication, right or left side), as well as whether the ad is in black and white or color.

advertorial   When a magazine or newspaper hires a writer to research and write a story that is sponsored by an advertiser; advertisers are contacted to take out ad space within the article.

blogger   Someone who writes a daily, weekly, or occasional blog on the Internet, usually about a subject about which the blogger feels passionate or on which he or she has expertise. Most blogs also invite readers to share their opinions with the posted blogs.

Chicago Manual of Style   Published by the University of Chicago Press and updated periodically; a guide to the preferred way of writing, editing, and styling text.

coauthor   When two authors share a byline and write together, whether it is for a newspaper story, magazine article, or book. The way coauthors work together is highly individual, with some coauthors writing "as one voice" and others writing "in tandem" (one writer's point of view followed by the other's, and each writer is identified separately). Sometimes an expert or someone who is not a professional writer may collaborate with a professional writer, with the expert contributing the content and the writer putting it into the words that will be published, even though it is presented as a coauthorship.

copyright   Legal ownership of writing, whether it is written for a newspaper, magazine, online writing, or book. Forms are available through the Library of Congress to register any kind of writing. Books are copywritten after publication, with a sample of the book or the entire book provided to the Library of Congress. Formally copyrighting the material gives documentation in case there is any question about authorship.

deadline   A fixed date when a newspaper story, magazine article, online article, or book is due to be delivered to the editor. Deadlines may range from later that day or the next day for a daily newspaper to a few weeks for a magazine to a year or longer for a book. Whether a story is "hot" and timely, or "seasonal," may be a factor when setting the deadline.

editor   Someone who goes over the writer's copy and makes suggestions as to content and style. Editors may also decide which stories (for magazines or newspapers) or which books (for publishing companies) they want to assign to (or accept from) writers or acquire for their publication or company to publish.

endorsements   See **blurbs** (under Book Publishing).

fair use   A minimal amount of writing originally published elsewhere that is allowed to be reprinted in a newspaper or magazine article, book, or Web site for critical or educational purposes, as long as attribution to the original author and source of publication is provided, without written permission or a fee. Fair use is a very controversial concept and term, and there is, unfortunately, no universally accepted definition. When in doubt, consult a publishing consultant or attorney, the publisher, or the permissions department of the newspaper, magazine, or book publisher if you are unsure whether something you wish to quote requires special permission or payment of a fee or whether it is in the category of fair use.

freelance writer   A writer who is on assignment for a newspaper, book, magazine, or online publication on a per-project basis rather than on salary as a staff member.

ghost   When a nonwriter teams up with a writer, but the published writing, whether it is a newspaper or magazine article or book, is presented as the work of only one person, usually the nonwriter. In that case, the actual writer is a ghost. Some ghosts are paid extremely well, and part of that payment is that they are expected to keep the writing arrangement confidential. If a ghost is allowed to have his or her name on the shared project, the writer is no longer considered a ghost but is instead a coauthor.

literary agent Someone who represents an author on a commission basis to publishers for the sale of a literary property, usually a book, although some agents will also represent magazine writers, especially if they also write books and if they sell to the major magazines that pay $1 or $2 per word for a 1,000 to 3,000 word article.

literary lawyer Attorney specializing in literary issues, including copyright and contract negotiation.

movie tie-in When a book publisher ties in the publication of a novel or nonfiction book or releases a published book linked to the release of a movie based on that nonfiction book or novel.

option A payment by a director, producer, or studio for a screenplay, book, or a literary work (newspaper or magazine article) that gives that person the right to try to find independent funding sources or a studio to back making the movie. If the funding sources are not available or if the talent that the producer hoped to obtain cannot commit to the project, the option may expire, and there are no further financial or creative obligations to the writer. Options are usually for anywhere from six months to 18 months; some options have provisions for an additional payment if the option is renewed. The option may be part of an agreement that also covers the payment and terms for sale of the screenplay or property if a movie does commence production, or it can be a completely separate agreement with a second agreement drawn up once the project is "greenlighted," or definitely moving forward.

permission Those quoted by name in a book are usually required to sign a written permission release for publication of their name and quoted material. A permission is also something that is requested from a publisher, author, or whoever is the copyright owner to quote from a published work, whether a newspaper or magazine article, a Web site, or a published book, if the quoted material is more than what is considered fair use.

pitch A succinct synopsis of the key concept, plot, and characters behind a screenplay or film project that a screenwriter or literary agent verbally shares with a director or producer in person or over the phone, with the hope that the listener will want to read the screenplay with an eye toward purchasing the property and making the movie. Pitches may also be sent in writing by e-mail, fax, or regular mail. It could also be used in connection with pitching a newspaper or magazine story or article idea although when the pitch is followed up in writing, it is usually referred to as a query.

plagiarism The passing off of words or ideas as original when they are really the work of another writer.

producer The person who makes a movie happen by finding a property (novel, play article, nonfiction book) that he or she wants to see developed into a screenplay, hiring a screenwriter to write an original screenplay, or purchasing a completed screenplay (spec screenplay). It is the producer who raises the money and coordinates all the talent and personnel who make a movie. (See *Career Opportunities in the Film Industry* by Fred and Jan Yager for a detailed description of the movie producer.)

publicity When print or broadcast media writes about an author or the author appears on a talk show to discuss his or her writing. Although the media may receive a free review copy of a book or an advance copy of a newspaper story or magazine article, there is no money given to the media to secure the promotion.

published author Anyone who writes and whose writing is published in any format.

seasonal A topic or issue that has a specific time of year that it needs to be covered by a publication, such as holiday stories in December, election stories in November, and vacation stories in early spring and over the summer. Newspapers have calendars for deadlines for seasonal stories, and magazines, working three or four (or more) months ahead of the issue, may also have seasonal deadlines for Mother's Day, Father's Day, or back-to-school issues. Book publishers may also publish seasonal books, such as books on romance during February, books on weight loss during January, and books on tax-related issues during February or March.

staff writer A writer for a newspaper, magazine, or online publication who is on salary and is a part of the publication's staff. Each publication has its own policy as to whether what the staff writer creates for the publication or Web site is owned by her or his employer or, after publication, by the staff writer.

story editor Someone who looks for material that a company might want to develop into a movie, whether it is in the form of an original screenplay, a book, a play, or a true-life story written up in a newspaper or magazine article.

JOURNALISM/NEWSPAPERS

above the fold   Those stories that appear above the fold in the newspaper are the big stories designed to attract the most attention and readers.

AP style sheet   The way of writing copy that is approved by the Associated Press and that Associated Press reporters and editors are expected to follow.

banner headline   The headline that goes across the top of the front page.

byline   (See definition under Magazine Publishing.)

front page   The first page of the newspaper.

J school   A college or graduate school with a journalism program that grants degrees in journalism. Just a few of the many famous J schools include the Columbia School of Journalism, Northwestern University's Medill School of Journalism, the University of Missouri–Columbia, and Syracuse University's Newhouse School.

kill   See **spiking a story** (below) or **kill a story** under Magazine Publishing.

morgue   Where previously published newspapers or articles are stored; also called archives.

putting the paper to bed   The copy is done, and the paper is turned over to the pressman for printing.

reporter   The person who gets the news and writes up the story for a newspaper or wire service.

sources   Someone you go to for information. Each paper has its own policy about how many anonymous sources (versus named sources) are allowed in any one story.

spiking a story   When you kill a story and stop it from running. At newspapers, a story is usually spiked because there is something wrong with it: not enough attribution to sources, or the information is bogus or incomplete.

stringer   Someone who does not work directly for the newspaper but that gets paid by the paper when they call in a story that the paper does not have. A lot of the stringers are students who are going to school and do stories about what is going on at the school. Payment is usually by the word or by the inch.

tabloid   Smaller-size paper and usually has one story on the front and pictures. Examples are the *New York Post* and the *New York Daily News.*

wire service   A newsgathering operation that used to be by teletype but now is by satellite data transmission, as well as through the Internet. The only not-for-profit wire service is the Associated Press. The other major wire services are Dow Jones, Reuters, Bloomberg, and United Press International.

MAGAZINE PUBLISHING

byline   Credit by name for the author of an article.

CPM   How much it costs per thousand to get to 1,000 readers of the magazine.

dingbat   Design element that may be used at the end of an article to indicate the completion of the copy.

fact checker   Someone whose job it is to verify quotes from named experts in magazine articles. Fact checkers usually work in the magazine's research department.

first North American serial rights   Freelance writers usually want to only sell first North American serial rights to an article on assignment, which means that after the article is first published by the magazine that assigned it, the author then has ongoing rights and may resell it to other publications. Usually first North American serial rights grant the initial publisher at least six months when the article is exclusive with that publication. This is a dramatically different arrangement than when an assignment is a work for hire and the publisher retains the copyright to the article as well as all rights.

kill a story   Magazines often kill a story because the assigned story, once it is completed and submitted, cannot fit into a specific issue. Sometimes this is because the "mix" of the issue does not allow for that story, since it would be viewed as too similar to another story that is going to run, or the completed story has a theme or emphasis that does not seem suited to the magazine's target audience. If the writer has successfully completed the assignment and the magazine has to kill the story, the magazine should pay the entire fee due to the author and allow the writer to sell the assignment to another publication. A kill fee (usually only 25 percent of the total fee) should only be paid, rather than the full fee, if the reason the article is being killed is because the publication believes that the author failed to successfully fulfill the agreed-upon assignment.

kill fee   A fee, usually 25 percent of the agreed upon fee for a magazine assignment, that is paid to an author if an assigned article is unacceptable.

pass-along copies (pass-along readership)   Number of readers estimated for a magazine besides the original buyer or subscriber (such as copies passed along within a household or to friends outside the household).

pull-quote   When a phrase or words are taken from an article and inserted in another part of the article for emphasis or for design reasons so that the article is not just a big block of type.

BOOK PUBLISHING

advance   An amount of money that is paid in advance to a book author before publication of the book that is usually then held against sales earnings of the book after publication. See also **royalties.**

author   Anyone who writes, but this term is usually applied to those who write books.

backlist   A term to denote that a book is no longer a new (just published) book and that it has been available for more than three months.

best seller   A book with sales that puts it at the very top of the list, in theory, compared to all other books. There are several key best-seller lists, such as the ones maintained by *Publishers Weekly,* the *New York Times, USA Today,* the *Los Angeles Times,* and Booksense, a list of titles recommended by independent bookstores who participate in the Booksense marketing initiative. How many copies are required to be part of those top 10 books—10 fiction and 10 nonfiction—may depend on how many copies the book right above a particular rank of the list is selling. The list is also divided into hardcover and paperback (trade paper or mass market). Being on the best-seller list is prestigious, and it often leads to even more sales.

blurb   Advance quotes requested by authors or editors for the back cover, front cover, or inside front pages of a book endorsing the book. Most often blurbs from recognizable names are sought, especially best-selling authors or corporate leaders.

bookseller   Someone who sells books through a bookstore, whether the store is a physical brick-and-mortar store or an online store.

copy editor   This is the person responsible for consistency in a book's manuscript in terms of proper spelling, grammar, word usage, and style. Some copy editors also proofread the manuscript; at other houses, there are two different people performing these functions.

e-book   A book that is available electronically. It can be read on a computer screen or printed out and read on paper.

electronic book   See **e-book.**

flat fee   A sum paid to a book author for writing a book, rather than an advance against possible royalties. If a book author accepts a flat-fee arrangement, usually the author does not get compensated after publication based on how many copies the book sells.

Since there will not be any future compensation, the author should keep that in mind when accepting a flat-fee agreement. Some projects are based on a flat fee, rather than on an advance and royalty arrangement, because it is a "work for hire."

foreign rights   Permission to publish a book first published in the United States, sold to publishers in other countries for publication. The book could be translated, then published in that country in another language, or it could be sold in other countries in other editions in the English language.

front list   A new book that is being published and is considered a key title by the publisher so it is placed at the front of the list and/or catalog.

galleys   Since there are publications, such as the trade journal *Publishers Weekly,* that require books three to four months in advance of publication for review consideration, a final version of the manuscript is necessary. The galley is the typeset manuscript bound in soft covers that is the final but not the absolutely definitive manuscript of the finished book. In addition to sending the galley to newspapers, magazines, or trade publications that require a final typeset manuscript in advance of publication for review consideration, galleys are used for generating interest among movie producers, foreign publishers, and television and radio shows for possible interviews.

midlist book   A term used to describe books that are about to be published but are not considered front-list titles or books that have already been published but whose sales have not been substantial enough to consider it a best-seller or a blockbuster.

over the transom   A phrase for unsolicited manuscripts that are sent to a literary agent, newspaper, magazine, or book editor without having been requested by the agent or editor. Because of time and legal concerns, few agents or editors are willing to read manuscripts that are sent over the transom. Another expression for "over the transom" is *slush pile.*

PE (printer errors)   Errors made by the printer in typesetting the manuscript rather than by the author or copy editor. Publishers are usually not charged for printer errors, because it is the printer's fault.

POD   Print on demand. It is a printing technology that allows just one book to be printed at a time rather than printing dozens, hundreds, or thousands of books at once through what is known as a traditional short-run procedure. As long as the printing quality of a POD book is equal or even better than a short-run version, it should not be held against the publisher or the author if the book is printed on demand. There are some differences in the provisions for distributing POD books, however. POD books are often sold on a nonreturnable basis; books that are printed as a short run are often sold on a returnable, commission basis.

prepublication reviews Publications, especially such key trade publications as *Library Journal, Publishers Weekly, Booklist,* and *Kirkus,* that require galleys of a book three to four months prior to publication if they are to review the title. These publications are read by booksellers and librarians who will use the reviews to determine if they want to order and sell the title, or add the book to their library's collection.

proofreader The person who checks for typos or grammatical errors in a manuscript before it goes to the printer and after it returns from the printer.

publication date A date, usually six weeks after the books have shipped from the printer to the stores for sale, when a book is officially published.

remainder If a book stops selling in the bookstores and the publisher wants to put the book out of print, it may first remainder the copies that are still available. The book is sold to a remainder house for as little as $1 a book, and it is then sold as a bargain book at a price that is dramatically lower than the initial retail or list price.

royalties When an author's book advance is earned out by sales and foreign or subsidiary rights income, the author will begin to earn royalties for that book as long as it remains in print. Each book contract has a stipulation as to what the royalties will be for that book, in general, 7.5 percent of the retail list price for paperbacks and 10 percent of the retail list price for hardcovers. (Some publishers use the net price to determine royalties rather than retail list price.) There are so many variations on these standards, however, that authors should read up on this issue, use a competent literary agent to negotiate for them, or consult the contract departments or experts at any of the writing associations that they belong to. Some publishers also do not pay royalties but instead have a contractual agreement with the author on a flat-fee basis.

slush pile See **over the transom.**

special sales Book sales beyond the traditional bookstores, such as through corporations or specialty catalogs.

BIBLIOGRAPHY

A. GENERAL WRITING AND PUBLISHING

BOOKS

Atchity, Ken, Andrea McKeown, Julie Mooney, and Margaret O'Connor. *How to Publish Your Novel: A Complete Guide to Making the Right Publisher Say Yes.* New York: Square One Publishers, 2005.

Bacon's New York Publicity Outlets Directory. Chicago: Bacon's Foundation, Inc., 2009.

Barzun, Jacques. *On Writing, Editing, and Publishing.* Chicago: University of Chicago Press, 1971.

Blanco, Jodee. *The Complete Guide to Book Publicity.* 2nd ed. New York: Allworth Press, 2004.

Brewer, Robert. *2009 Writer's Market.* 87th ed. Cincinnati, Ohio: Writer's Digest Books, 2008.

Cameron, Julia. *The Artist's Way: A Spiritual Path to Higher Creativity.* New York: Jeremy P. Tarcher/Putnam, 1992.

Crawford, Ted and Kay Murray. *The Writer's Legal Guide: An Authors Guild Desk Reference.* 3rd ed. New York: Allworth Press, 2002.

Feierman, Joanne. *Action Grammar.* New York: Simon & Schuster, Inc., Fireside, 1995.

Jacobs, Hayes B. *Writing and Selling Non-Fiction.* Cincinnati, Ohio: Writer's Digest Books, 1979.

King, Stephen. *On Writing: A Memoir of the Craft.* New York: Simon & Schuster, 2001.

Pausch, Randy, and Jeffrey Zaslow. *The Last Lecture.* New York: Hyperion, 2008.

Strunk, William, Jr., and E. B. White. *The Elements of Style.* 4th ed. New York: Pearson, 2000.

University of Chicago Press Staff. *The Chicago Manual of Style.* 15th ed. Chicago: University of Chicago Press, 2003.

Welty, Eudora. *On Writing.* New York: Random House, 2001.

Yager, Jan. *Effective Business and Nonfiction Writing.* 2nd ed. Stamford, Conn.: Hannacroix Creek Books, 2001.

Zaslow, Jeffrey. *The Girls from Ames.* New York: Gotham Books, 2009.

Zinsser, Howard. *On Writing Well.* 30th Anniversary ed. New York: Collins, 2006.

WEB SITE RESOURCES FOR JOBS INDUSTRY WIDE

CareerBuilder.com
http://www.careerbuilder.com

Editor and Publisher
http://www.editorandpublisher.com

Yahoo! HotJobs
http://www.hotjobs.yahoo.com

Jobs
http://www.jobs.com

Linkedin.com
http://www.linkedin.com

Mediabistro.com
http://www.mediabistro.com

Monster
http://monster.com

New York Times
http://www.nytimes.com

Six Figure Jobs
http://www.6figurejobs.com

Wall Street Journal Executive Career Site
http://www.careerjournal.com

B. NEWSPAPERS

BOOKS

Anderson, David, and Peter Benjaminson. *Investigative Reporting.* Bloomington: Indiana University Press, 1976.

Goldstein, Norm, ed. *Associated Press Stylebook and Briefing on Media Law.* 42nd ed. New York: Basic Books, 2007.

Huang, Tom, and Steve Myers, eds. *Best Newspaper Writing 2008–2009.* Washington, D.C.: CQ Press, 2008.

Kovach, Bill, and Tom Rosensteil. *The Elements of Journalism: What Newspeople Should Know and the Public Should Expect.* Rev. ed. New York: Three Rivers Press, 2007.

Mogel, Leonard. *The Newspaper: Everything You Need to Know to Make It in the Newspaper Business.* Sewickley, Pa.: GATF Press, 2000.

Morgan, Bradley J., ed. *Newspapers Career Directory.* 4th ed. Detroit, Mich.: Visible Ink, 1993.

INDUSTRY PUBLICATIONS

American Journalism Review
University of Maryland
1117 Journalism Building
College Park, MD 20742
http://ajr.org

Columbia Journalism Review
Journalism Building
2950 Broadway
Columbia University
New York, NY 10027
http://www.cjr.org

Editor and Publisher
770 Broadway
New York, NY 10003
http://www.editorandpublisher.com

Online Journalism Review
USC Annenberg Online Journalism Review
3502 Watt Way
Los Angeles, CA 90089
http://www.ojr.org

WEB SITE RESOURCES

American Society of Newspaper Editors
http://www.asne.org
The American Society of Newspaper Editors has excellent information and links at its Web sites for job fairs and internships.

JournalismJobs.com
http://www.journalismjobs.com

Journalist USA
http://www.journalistusa.com
Fee-based subscription service, available on a monthly or annual basis, for jobs in journalism, marketing, and photography.

C. MAGAZINES

BOOKS

American Society of Magazine Editors. *The Best American Magazine Writing 2008.* New York: Columbia University Press, 2008.

Bykofsky, Sheree, Jennifer Bayse Sander, and Lynne Rominger. *Complete Idiot's Guide to Publishing Magazine Articles.* Indianapolis, Ind.: Alpha Books, 2000.

Johnson, Sammye, and Patricia Prijatel. *The Magazine: From Cover to Cover.* 2nd ed. New York: Oxford University Press, 2006.

King, Stacey. *Magazine Design That Works.* Gloucester, Mass.: Rockport Publishers, 2001.

Mandell, Judy. *Magazine Editors Talk to Writers.* New York: Wiley, 1996.

Mogel, Leonard. *The Magazine.* Englewood Cliffs, N.J.: Prentice-Hall, 1979.

Monti, Ralph. *Career Opportunities in Magazine Publishing.* Bloomfield, N.J.: Special Interest Media, 1999.

Pope, Alice, ed. 2009 *Children's Writer's & Illustrator's Market.* Cincinnati, Ohio: Writer's Digest Books, 2009.

Underdown, Harold D. *Complete Idiot's Guide to Publishing Children's Books.* Indianapolis, Ind.: Alpha Books, 2004.

INDUSTRY PUBLICATIONS

Freelance Success
32391 Dunford Street
Farmington Hills, MI 48334
http://www.freelancesuccess.com
Subscription newsletter that profiles at least one magazine market open to freelance queries and assignments, as well as gives the career highlights of a successful freelance writer offering inspiration and useful tips on how to succeed to other writers.

Travelwriter Marketletter
P.O. Box 1782
Springfield, VA 22151
http://www.travelwriterml.com
Monthly subscription publication available by mail or as an Internet version providing information on publica-

tions, especially magazines, with travel sections open to freelance contributions, as well as upcoming travel-related writer conferences, free or subsidized press trips ("junkets"), and reviews of related books.

WEB SITE RESOURCES

American Society of Journalists and Authors
http://www.asja.org

Journalism.org
http://www.journalism.org

Magazine Publishers of America
http://www.magazine.org

mediabistro
http://www.mediabistro.com

Writer's Digest
http://www.writersdigest.com

D. BOOK PUBLISHING

BOOKS

Applebaum, Judith. *How to Get Happily Published: A Complete and Candid Guide.* 5th ed. New York: Harper Perennial, 1998.

Curtis, Richard. *How to Be Your Own Literary Agent.* Rev. ed. Boston: Houghton Mifflin, 1996.

Deval, Jacqueline. *Publicize Your Book!* New York: Penguin Putnam, 2003.

Herman, Jeff. *Jeff Herman's Guide to Book Publishers, Editors, and Literary Agents 2009.* Stockbridge, Mass.: Three Dog Press, 2008.

International Literary Marketplace. Updated biannually. Medford, N.J.: Information Today, Inc.

Kirsch, Jonathan. *Kirsch's Guide to the Book Contract.* Venice, Calif.: Acrobat Books, 1994.

———. *Kirsch's Handbook for Publishing Law.* Venice, Calif.: Acrobat Books, 1994.

Kremer, John. *1,000 Ways to Market Your Books.* Fairfield, Iowa: Open Horizons, 1998.

Larsen, Michael. *How to Write a Book Proposal.* 3rd ed. Cincinnati, Ohio: Writer's Digest Books, 2004.

Lerner, Betsy. *The Forest for the Trees: An Editor's Advice to Writers.* New York: Riverhead Books, 2000.

Levinson, Jay Conrad, Rick Frishman, and Michael Larsen. *Guerrilla Marketing for Writers.* Cincinnati, Ohio: Writer's Digest Books, 2001.

Literary Marketplace. Updated annually. Medford, N.J.: Information Today, Inc.

Mandell, Judy. *Book Editors Talk to Writers.* New York: John Wiley & Sons, 1995.

Poynter, Dan. *The Self-Publishing Manual.* 14th ed. Santa Barbara, Calif.: Para Publishing, 2002.

Rabiner, Susan and Alfred Fortunato. *Thinking Like Your Editor.* New York: Norton, 2003.

Ross, Marilyn, and Tom Ross. *Jump Start Your Book Sales.* Buena Vista, Colo.: Communications Creativity, 1999.

———. *The Complete Guide to Self-Publishing.* 4th ed. Cincinnati, Ohio: Writers' Digest Books, 2002.

Silvey, Anita. *The Essential Guide to Children's Books and Their Creators.* Boston, Mass.: Mariner Books, 2002.

INDUSTRY PUBLICATIONS

Book Marketing Update
P.O. Box 205
Fairfield, IA 52556
http://www.bookmarket.com
Biweekly newsletter on publicity and special sales opportunities.

Library Journal
360 Park Avenue South
New York, NY 10010
http://www.libraryjournal.com
Leading trade publication about the library industry, published weekly, with book reviews as well as features on trends and news about libraries and librarians.

Partyline
35 Sutton Place
New York, NY 10022
http://www.partylinepublishing.com
Weekly two-page newsletter with annotated media opportunities in magazines and newspapers that would be useful for book authors or book publicists looking for opportunities for book promotion.

Publishers Weekly
360 Park Avenue South
New York, NY 10010
http://www.publishersweekly.com
Published weekly, this is the key trade publication for the book publishing industry. Reviews in *Publishers Weekly*

have a lot of prestige and potential sales benefits. Book-sellers and librarians read *Publishers Weekly,* also known as "*PW,*" as do talk show producers and movie producers to consider which authors they might want to book or which properties they might want to consider acquiring for movie rights.

Publishing Trends
232 Madison Avenue, #1400
New York, NY 10016
http://www.publishingtrends.com
Monthly newsletter about the book publishing industry available as a printed or e-mailed version sent as a PDF file. Profiles industry leaders, job changes, upcoming conferences, and trade shows, as well as publishes articles focused on one particular aspect of the industry.

School Library Journal
360 Park Avenue South
New York, NY 10010
http://www.schoollibraryjournal.com
Weekly trade publication for libraries in school, kindergarten through high school, with book reviews and feature articles.

WEB SITE RESOURCES

American Booksellers Association
http://www.bookweb.org
Web site of the American Booksellers Association (ABA), an association of thousands of independent booksellers and other industry professionals, with links to other book-related sites.

Association of American Publishers
http://www.publishers.org
Site maintained by the Association of American Publishers with extensive information on the industry, including statistics, as well as links to other book publishing resources.

Bookjobs.com
http://www.bookjobs.com
Web site developed and maintained by the Association of American Publishers (AAP) to highlight jobs in the book industry, especially entry-level positions.

Book Marketing
http://www.bookmarketing.com
Author, publisher, and special sales expert Brian Jud's Web site. Jud also publishes a free biweekly special sales newsletter. To sign up, send an e-mail to brianjud@book-marketing.com.

Book Marketing Update
http://www.bookmarket.com
John Kremer, a book promotion consultant, maintains this extensive site, with information on bookstores, ordering his *Book Marketing Update* biweekly newsletter, a "Tip of the Week," his upcoming seminars, and lots more.

Book Report Network
http://www.authorsontheweb.com
http://www.bookreporter.com
http://www.readinggroupguides.com
http://www.teenreads.com
Several sites with book reviews, book news, author interviews, and reading group guides available for downloading and use by book clubs.

Book Wire
http://www.bookwire.com
Book industry site with extensive links.

Creative Ways from Marcia Yudkin
http://www.yudkin.com
Informative Web site with links maintained by Marcia Yudkin, book marketing consultant.

Midwest Book Review
http://www.midwestbookreview.com
The Web site, which is updated monthly, has writing and publishing resources on promotion, associations, and copyright, as well as reader resources. Established in 1976, the Midwest Book Review publishes several monthly publications for community and academic library systems in California, Wisconsin, and the upper Midwest including the *Bookwatch, Small Press Bookwatch,* and *Wisconsin Bookwatch,* and also posts their reviews on the Internet through online bookstores such as www.amazon.com. Priority consideration for review is given to excellent self-published authors, small press publishers, and academic presses.

Para Publishing
http://www.parapub.com
Informative Web site by self-publishing guru Dan Poynter, as well as a place to sign up for Poynter's monthly free newsletter, *Publishing Poynters.* The newsletter has useful tips and upcoming events of interest to authors, publishers, and publicists, as well as a list of Poynter's speaking engagements for the next year. To subscribe, e-mail DanPoynter@ParaPublishing.com

Publishers Lunch
http://www.publisherslunch.com

A free daily newsletter, written by Michael Cader of Cader Books, about book publishing industry news, as well as sales of foreign and movie rights to books. It is also free to list deals.

Publishers Marketplace
http://www.publishersmarketplace.com
Online newsletter and site available on a month-to-month basis for $15 month in which publishers, literary agents, and those providing services to the book publishing industry may create a Web site to list their contact information as well as their key available properties. There is also a "deals" section, which enables someone to post a new deal, as well as view forums and other features. It also enables you to track the rankings of titles that you enter at two key online booksellers, amazon.com and bn.com; those rankings are automatically updated each day (more frequently for top sellers).

Publishing Game
http://www.publishinggame.com
Site maintained by Fern Reiss, author of *The Publishing Game: Publish a Book in 30 Days* (Peanut Butter & Jelly Press, 2003), among other titles, who also conducts seminars.

Publishers Weekly
http://www.publishersweekly.com
Site maintained by the publishers of *Publishers Weekly* with daily updates of book industry news, links to industry resources, archived reviews, and additional reviews.

Sensible Solutions for Getting Happily Published
http://www.happilypublished.com
Extensive site maintained by Judith Applebaum (author of *How to Get Happily Published*) covering finding a publisher, the self-publishing option, suggestions for increasing book sales, and suggested links.

Writing and Getting Published by Jan Yager
http://www.janyager.com/writing
Site maintained by fiction and nonfiction author, promotion and foreign-rights coach and workshop teacher, and the coauthor of this book, Jan Yager (jyager@aol.com). The site deals with writing and getting published, including free reprints of articles and book excerpts. Yager's upcoming seminars on writing, getting published, and promotion are also listed at the site. A useful article written by Yager, "My 'Road to Getting My First Book Published and Beyond' Story, in a Nutshell, in Case It's Useful to You?," is posted at http://www.hannacroixcreekbooks.com/get-published/.

ABOUT THE AUTHORS

FRED YAGER

Trained as a journalist, Fred Yager served in Vietnam, reporting on the war for *Stars and Stripes* newspaper, as well as sending stories back to the Associated Press.

After four years in the navy, Fred was hired by the Associated Press and, over the next 13 years, he worked as a reporter, founding managing editor of AP-TV, and an entertainment writer and film critic. Fred was the recipient of the Associated Press's prestigious Writer of the Year award.

After two years as a freelance writer, writing screenplays as well as magazine articles, Fred began working as a writer at CBS News and the CBS Morning Show. He then became editor of the Fox Seven O'Clock News, followed by 14 years at Merrill Lynch, first as vice president of media relations, then as the founder and director of Merrill Lynch Television.

From 2002 to 2009, Fred ran World News and Information Network, Inc., a communications company that he cofounded.

In addition to writing nonfiction books, Fred is the author of two novels coauthored with his wife, Jan Yager, *Untimely Death* and *Just Your Everyday People*; they have also coauthored numerous screenplays, including scripts based on their novels and original screenplays, such as the romantic comedy "No Time for Love." Fred is also the author of *Rex*, about a dinosaur, and *Cybersona,* a sci-fi thriller.

Fred grew up in upstate New York. A graduate of the City College of New York (CCNY), he lived in Manhattan before relocating almost two decades ago to Connecticut with his wife, Jan, and their two sons.

Beginning in 2009, he became Head of Publications and Communications for the financial services division of a major association.

JAN YAGER

The former J. L. (Janet) Barkas, Jan Yager began working in publishing immediately after graduate school in art therapy, as an editorial assistant at Macmillan Publishing Company, in the school division; six months later, she was promoted to assistant editor. Jan switched from educational publishing to trade, working for a year at Grove Press as an assistant to its founder and president, Barney Rosset; she was also director of foreign and subsidiary rights; she acquired several titles, and also dealt with permissions and publicity.

Jan continued her graduate school training, obtaining a master's in criminal justice followed by a Ph.D. in sociology from The City University of New York Graduate Center. She has taught criminology or sociology courses at the University of Connecticut and nonfiction writing at Penn State University as a visiting assistant professor.

Her published credits include 26 nonfiction and fiction titles, including *Friendshifts, When Friendship Hurts, Work Less, Do More, Effective Business and Nonfiction Writing,* and *Business Protocol*, with translation into more than 24 foreign languages.

In 1996, Jan founded Hannacroix Creek Books, Inc. (www.hannacroixcreekbooks.com), although she still continues to publish with other houses, such as Simon & Schuster, Facts On File, and Sterling Publishing Company. Beginning in June 2009, Jan started working as director of publicity and subsidiary and foreign rights for an independent publishing company based in Westport, Connecticut.

Jan has also published articles in newspapers, magazines, and online publications. Frequently interviewed by print and broadcast media, Jan has appeared on *The Oprah Winfrey Show, The Today Show, Good Morning America, The View,* and National Public Radio, among other shows. A professional speaker and trainer, Jan offers seminars, individual phone, and in-person coaching on book promotion, how to get published, and foreign rights.

Here is the contact information for Fred and Jan Yager: P.O. Box 8038, Stamford, CT 06905-8038. E-mail: fyager@aol.com or jyager@aol.com. On the Internet: www.janyager.com or www.fredandjanyager.com.